DATE DUE

THE TRADITION OF THE GOSPEL CHRISTIANS

The TRADITION *of the* GOSPEL CHRISTIANS

A Study of Their Identity and Theology during the Russian, Soviet, and Post-Soviet Periods

Andrey P. Puzynin

With a Foreword by Robert E. Warner

PICKWICK *Publications* • Eugene, Oregon

THE TRADITION OF THE GOSPEL CHRISTIANS
A Study of Their Identity and Theology during the Russian, Soviet, and Post-Soviet Periods

Pickwick Publications
An Imprint of Wipf and Stock Publishers
199 W. 8th Ave., Suite 3
Eugene, OR 97401

ISBN 13: 978-1-60608-999-6

Cataloging-in-Publication data:

Puzynin, Andrey P.

The tradition of the Gospel Christians : a study of their identity and theology during the Russian, Soviet, and post-Soviet periods / Andrey P. Puzynin ; foreword by Robert E. Warner.

xl + 314 p. ; 23 cm. — Includes bibliographical references.

ISBN 13: 978-1-60608-999-6

1. Protestant churches—Russia. 2 Russia—church history. 3. Protestant churches—Soviet Union. 4. Soviet Union—Church history. I. Warner, Robert E. II. Title

BX4849 .P89 2011

Manufactured in the U.S.A.

To O.E.B.

Often people's first reaction to hearing the suggestion that there should be more Christian scholarship is that the last thing we need is another set of partisan ideologues. Ideally, however, Christian scholarship should be of a different stripe. While the presentation of any viewpoint involves some partisanship and occasional polemic, Christian partisanship and polemic should also be tempered by Christian virtues. Christianity at its best teaches people that they stand not at the center of reality, but on the periphery along with everyone else. It teaches that we are not dependent on our own brilliance and insight, but on a revelation that appears foolish to many and whose source we are unable to comprehend. It teaches that humans are flawed and often self-deluded creatures and that Christians are not exceptions. Hence our scholarship should be marked out not only by firm defenses of the insights we believe we have seen revealed by God, but also by a willingness to be critical of ourselves and our own traditions.

—George M. Marsden, *The Outrageous Idea of Christian Scholarship*, 108–9.

Contents

Foreword

The first time I encountered Lord Radstock's "Gospel Christians" was in *Anna Karenina*. For Tolstoy this alien sect combined the salvific arrogance of those who consider themselves the only truly saved Christians with the illuminist arrogance of those who depend on the immediate promptings of the divine spirit. This leads, in the case of Anna's estranged husband, first to the folly of credulity and then to a self-justifying moral certainty, in which his refusal to grant Anna a divorce is to serve God, to take upon himself righteous superiority, and to give Anna an opportunity to improve herself. For Tolstoy, the Gospel Christians had nothing of value to offer Eastern European religion and culture.

If Tolstoy's account were sufficient, these willing victims of sectarian certainty would be unlikely to endure for more than a single generation. However, in this exceptional historical and theological study Dr. Andrei Puzynin provides a much richer and more reliable account of how the seeds of Keswick evangelicalism, noble in origin and idiosyncratic in style, took root and flourished in Russian and Ukrainian soil. The study of Radstock is followed by re-examinations of Colonel Pashkov and Prokhanov, the Communist revolution and the subsequent Union of Gospel Christians and Baptists that was utilized to create a pro-Soviet religious narrative, and the eventual emergence of perestroika, new national identities, and the collapse of the Soviet empire. In each era the Gospel Christians negotiate an identity between East and West, between primitivism and the contemporary, in a dialogical provisionality always subject to further iteration.

As the narrative unfolds, Dr. Puzynin demonstrates that the Gospel Christians became an indigenized form of the evangelical tradition, negotiating not only with longstanding idioms of Russian culture, but even with Soviet forms of communist atheism and nationalism. Puzynin develops a rich analysis of the interaction of Gospel and culture and demonstrates the distinctive cultural adaptability of global evangelicalism.

Behind the Iron Curtain the Gospel Christians endured. And this meant these Russian evangelicals were isolated from the rise of Western fundamentalism. The characteristic forms of emphatic doctrinal exclusivity and dogmatic ethical absolutism that became self-evident and intrinsic givens to Anglo-American conservative Protestants were not necessarily inherent or intrinsic to Eastern European forms of the evangelical tradition.

Puzynin is by no means uncritical of the policies and practices of the Gospel Christians, who at times have tended towards excessive and partly uncritical cultural assimilation within Russian "messianism" and later within the Soviet Union. He argues for the development of a third space, somewhere between the paradigms of Byzantine and pietistic Protestant forms of Christianity. Nonetheless, by examining the distinctive trajectories of their separate development, he demonstrates the extent to which Western fundamentalism is not the self-evident, the necessary, or the sole extrapolation of the evangelical tradition. This study therefore not only recovers a critical narrative of the Gospel Christians, but also provides a discrete yet searching critique of those, insiders as well as outsiders, who claim that all authentic evangelicals are necessarily fundamentalists.

Puzynin's work is still not done. He argues that the post-Soviet condition of Eastern Europe produces for indigenous Protestant Christians a double crisis of identity and relevance. Building on Kuhn and Küng he argues for a new paradigmatic shift in postmodernity, in which evangelical approaches to the Bible, hermeneutics, and doctrine require new configurations, in Eastern Europe as well as in the West. Following MacIntyre, Puzynin develops a tradition-based approach to theological reconstruction, in which the development of contemporary theology necessarily builds upon a critical rearticulation of the tradition's historical development. Building on Lindbeck's post-liberal reading of the world through the biblical narrative, the historiography of the Gospel Christians becomes the crucible for contemporary theological reconstruction, and for new initiatives in ecumenical dialogue and theology between Eastern European evangelicals and the majority Orthodox tradition.

Puzynin introduces himself in this exceptional study as not only a church historian of rigor and subtlety, but also a creative, contextual and hermeneutical theologian. His work has great originality and merit for insiders and outsiders alike, for students, scholars, and practitioners both within and beyond the evangelical tradition. This book deserves to be widely read, and Dr. Puzynin deserves an attentive readership. It is my sincere hope that this book heralds from Dr. Puzynin an international scholarly contribution of rare distinction and wide reaching significance.

Robert E. Warner
Professor of Religion, Culture and Society
University of Chester

Preface

An earlier version of this book was produced as a PhD dissertation for the University of Wales, Lampeter. I appreciate immensely the supervision of different parts of my work at different stages by Dr. Mark Cartledge, Professor Nigel Yates, and Professor Robert E. Warner over the course of four years. I am thankful to my examiners Dr. Derek Tidball and Dr. Frances Knight who asked rigorous questions and made the day of my *viva voce* exam both enjoyable and unforgettable.

Over the course of my studies, I received financial support from the University of Wales, Lampeter and the Oxford Center for Mission Studies. Joan Winfrey Wells of Denver Seminary and The Fund for Students from Former Soviet Countries generously covered the travel expenses that allowed my family to join me in the UK. Bob Lenehan and Dan Beck helped us financially as we were settling into the new context of rural Wales as a family. I am grateful to them for enabling us to be together as a family during the three years of research and writing.

There are a great number of people, far too many to mention, who helped me in different ways and at different stages of my research. I would like to express my appreciation to Dr. Darrell Cosden, who ignited the spark of research interest in me and provided critique and guidance as I was working on my initial research proposal. Dr. Sharyl Corrado, Vyacheslav Kharkiv, and Alexei Sinichkin did a wonderful job of supplying me with archival documents from St. Petersburg and Moscow. UWL Librarian Kathy Miles was most efficient in obtaining the necessary informational resources from both the UK and abroad. Keston Institute Librarian Malcolm Walker not only professionally guided me through the Keston archives, but also stimulated my thinking by asking relevant questions and making comments after my presentation at OCMS.

I would like to express my gratitude to Catherine Richardson and her husband Dr. James Richardson for their amazing hospitality and friendship. The fellowship with Kar Yong Lim and Evan Davies was a constant source of encouragement to my wife and me in the midst of the hurly-burly of life and in the course of academic routine.

Stephen Darlington and Ray Prigodich worked hard on editing the text of my manuscript for a British university and an American audience respectively. I am extremely thankful to them for helping me to get my ideas across. Realis Christian Center and its leader, Sergei Timchenko, supported me in the preparation of the manuscript for publication. Without the necessary leisure, it would have been impossible to bring this project to completion. I wish to offer my appreciation to the people at Wipf and Stock who brought this work to its present format. I thank Patrick Harrison and Charlie Collier for their careful editorial work and Jim Tedrick for his prompt and clear communication. I record my gratitude to Heather Carraher for typesetting the book. I also would like to thank SPCK for allowing me to quote extensively from George Lindbeck's book "The Nature of Doctrine."

My very special thanks go my wife Oksana and my sons Emmanuel and Benjamin, without whose presence, patience, and encouragement this long-term undertaking would never have been accomplished.

Introduction

"It is no secret that evangelical thought today is in crisis. The crisis has blown up from within as well as from without. Just about the time international communism collapsed at the start of the 1990s, evangelical Christianity in the West began eyeballing an intellectual challenge of a magnitude it had never before confronted."[1]

"I can only answer the question 'What am I to do?' if I can answer the prior question 'Of what story or stories do I find myself a part?'"[2]

"Two principal tasks of theology are to express the identity of a believing community and to help it deal with the social change that comes upon the community."[3]

THE SOCIO-POLITICAL AND CULTURAL BACKGROUND OF THE RESEARCH

The current research is focused on resolving the crises of identity and theology in the tradition of the Gospel Christians in post-Soviet Ukraine. In an attempt to deal with the crisis of identity, several competing proposals have been constructed in recent years to define the post-Soviet identity of Gospel Christians. The general dissatisfaction with both the theological practices of the tradition's past and the imposed Western, mainly North American, ways of theologizing has prompted both local

1. Raschke, *Next Reformation*, 11.
2. MacIntyre, *After Virtue*, 41.
3. Schreiter, *Constructing Local Theologies*, 43.

and Western theologians to inquire about the necessity of doing contextual theology. These historical and theological reactions to the two-fold crisis of identity and theology will be discussed and analyzed in the present research.

As one who is part of this tradition, I stand in a particular time and place and am influenced by current contextual experiences. These experiences have not only made the crisis obvious but have also contributed to its intensification in recent years. Inasmuch as the philosophical and theological developments of the twentieth century made it clear that no knowledge is unaffected by historical contingency or personal elements, I would like to provide a preliminary description of the hermeneutical horizon from which the current work is written. The following snapshot of the contemporary socio-political context in Ukraine represents the broadest contextual frame within which the tradition of the Gospel Christians operates.

This hermeneutical situation has been shaped by the political story of a new Eastern European nation that voted for independence in 1991 and that attracted the world's attention once again at the end of 2004.[4] The events of the Ukrainian Orange Revolution that year brought to the surface the crucial role of the geopolitical tension between Eastern Orthodox and Western civilizations in working out the theological problems set before Ukrainian evangelicals several years earlier.[5]

The nineteenth-century Russian debate between Slavophiles and Westernizers was reintroduced with fresh force after one of the global super-powers of the twentieth century ceased to exist.[6] However, at the end of the twentieth century the intensity of the debate over the national and cultural identity of what was formerly known as the Russian Empire increased to an unprecedented scale. It spilled over the pages of philosophical journals into the public sphere of daily life, birthing new communities and nation-states.

4. The terms *hermeneutical horizon* and *hermeneutical situation* are used here in their Gadamerian sense. The hermeneutical situation is the situation in which we find ourselves with regard to the tradition that we are trying to understand. The hermeneutical horizon is the range of vision that includes everything that can be seen from a particular vantage point in the present, although it cannot be formed apart from the tradition's past. Gadamer, *Truth and Method*, 301–5.

5. The definition of *civilization* is provided in the glossary.

6. Rabow-Edling, *Slavophile Thought and the Politics of Cultural Nationalism*, 73–84.

The collapse of the Soviet Union, the heir to the Empire, has brought about a shift in global geopolitics that has led to complex identity crises for individuals, groups, traditions, and nations.[7] The epicenter of the explosion that caused the ruin of the vast Empire built on atheistic values and driven by the forces of Russian messianism was located in Ukraine, the birthplace of Russian Orthodox civilization and arguably the heir of Imperial Byzantium.[8] Mikhail Gorbachev recognized the epochal importance of the approaching Ukrainian referendum when he said, "The Soviet Union without Ukraine is inconceivable."[9] The Ukrainian referendum on independence of December 1, 1991, delivered a death blow to the Soviet system and to the domineering ideology that had glued it together.[10] The downfall of the Soviet system and its ideology has led to multifaceted processes of the construction of new historical, cultural, and national identities within Ukraine as well. These have been shaped by the resurgence of the Russian Orthodox civilization at the eastern border of Ukraine[11] and the gravitational pull of Western civilization from the opposite side.[12] Different religious bodies that populated the former Soviet Union were also thrown into the identity-shaping crucible in which old beliefs and practices were tested by new experiences.[13]

The civilizational crack dividing Ukraine linguistically, religiously, and regionally, thus threatening its unity, was foreseen by political scientists not long after the collapse of the Soviet Union.[14] The culmination of the birth pangs of a Ukrainian identity was reached during the rigged presidential elections of 2004, when hundreds of thousands of people in

7. Huntington, *Clash of Civilizations*, 21.

8. For a historical analysis of the birth of the communist utopia out of the depths of Orthodox Russia, see Berdyaev, *Origin of Russian Communism*.

9. *Ukrainian Weekly*, 24 November 1991, quoted in Subtelny, *Ukraine*, 583.

10 For a brief history of the events, see Subtelny, *Ukraine*, 581–95.

11. Panarin, *Pravoslavnaia Tsivilizatsiia v Global'nom Mire*; Dugin, *Osnovy Geopolitiki*, ch. 5. Cf. Kappeler, Kohut, Sysysn, and Hagen, *Culture, Nation, and Identity*.

12. For a good example of the construction of a religious identity in post-Soviet Ukraine, see Mueller, *In the Name of God*. Also see a good survey of Ukrainian thought that is contributing to the construction of contemporary Ukrainian identity in Lindheim and Luckyj, *Towards an Intellectual History of Ukraine*, 3–52.

13. See Ramet, *Nihil Obstat*, 246–62; and Bourdeaux, *Politics of Religion in Russia and the New States of Eurasia*, 129–202. See also McNeill, *Western Saints in Holy Russia*.

14. Huntington, *Clash*, 37. Huntington's book was first published in 1996.

Kiev rejected the pro-Russian candidate, thereby giving an opportunity to the pro-Western candidate to win in the unprecedented third round.[15] The Ukrainian Orange Revolution had nearly pushed the country to the brink of civil war, and only international negotiations involving representatives of the European Union and Russia helped to avoid bloodshed, the possibility and scale of which had been foreseen nearly a decade earlier by John Mearsheimer.[16] The years since have demonstrated that the painful process of developing a national identity is far from over. A highly unstable political situation, caused by internal power struggles and the resurgent dispute between America and Russia over the anti-missile defense system in Eastern Europe, is contributing to the painful process. Any national referendum on Ukrainian membership in NATO or in the Common Economic Space (CES) with Russia, Belarus, and Kazakhstan that may take place in the future will clarify the underdetermined geopolitical orientation of the country in the multipolar and multicivilizational world.[17]

This compression of historical, ideological, and geopolitical processes constitutes the framework within which I will attempt to solve some of the key theological problems that have been besetting Ukrainian evangelicalism in the wake of the major geopolitical cataclysm of the second half of the twentieth century. It will be demonstrated later on that the geopolitical explosion—or, better, series of geopolitical upheavals of the twentieth century in Eastern Europe—has fragmentized the discourse and the historic memory of the evangelical tradition, producing the double crisis of relevance and identity.[18] In many respects the following historical and theological investigation could be compared to a rescue operation after a series of geopolitical tsunami strikes. Its first task is to clear the debris and drain the area before building an esthetically pleasant theological construct. This will be a project for the future, but in the meantime I suggest that you join me on a trip to a territory notorious for its bad roads.

15. Wilson, *Ukraine's Orange Revolution*, 153–55; Baker and Glasser, *Kremlin Rising*, 375–78.

16. Mearsheimer, "Case for a Nuclear Deterrent," 54.

17. See Korogodskii, "Kosovski Vyklyky Ukraiiny"; Whewell, "Kremlin and the World"; Fidler et al., "Ever Eastward? A Divided NATO Pauses at Russia's Red Lines."

18. Moltmann, *Crucified God*, 7.

THE PROGRAM IN CONTEXTUAL THEOLOGY: ITS RISE, FALL, AND PROMISE

The present research grew out of the development of a master of theology program in contextual theology at Donetsk Christian University in Ukraine in 2001.[19] The program was created to help both conservative Western missionaries and indigenous post-Soviet evangelicals to see the contextual nature of all theology, thereby smoothing out some of the tensions between these two groups. A major task was to bring into focus the reality that "the way a given group of Christians looks at Scripture, the world, Christian tradition, doctrine and dogma, and Christian life is profoundly influenced by the historical and cultural factors which have shaped their development as a people."[20] Even though to date the program has not yet actually been launched, the sparks of interest in doing contextual theology in post-Soviet Ukraine have not gone away. In this work, I attempt to think through critically some of the key questions that were originally suggested by the international team that designed the program.

Darrell Cosden and Donald Fairbairn articulated some of the key issues that need to be worked out by post-Soviet evangelicals in order to resolve a "crisis of the soul" regarding the "clash between a desire to be like the West and an intuitive rejection of the West's ways of thinking and expressing truth."[21] They rightly pointed out that post-Soviet evangelicals need to recognize the historical and cultural nature of both Western conservative theology, which had begun to become dominant at many post-Soviet evangelical educational institutions, and the theology of their own religious heritage.[22] They write:

> Slavic Protestants have intuitively absolutized their own unexamined expression of theology, while at the same time looking with uncritical admiration at the theological productions of a foreign culture, even as they sense these productions to be ill suited for a Slavic context. The solution, we believe, is for Post-Soviet Protestant theology to move from being a theology which

19. Cosden and Fairbairn, "Contextual Theological Education," 125–36.

20. Ibid., 125. In private correspondence Donald Fairbairn pointed out that although he had participated in discussions concerning the program, he was unaware of this article.

21. Ibid., 126.

22. Ibid., 125.

> is unconsciously influenced by its context to being a genuinely contextual theology. By the term "contextual theology," we mean a theology which self-consciously recognizes, examines, and critiques the historical and cultural factors which have influenced the expression of Christian life among a given group of people. Contextual theology does not seek to be the universal expression of Christian truth for all people in all times and places, for it insists that no theological expression of the faith can be the best expression for all people. Rather, contextual theology seeks to express the truth of Christianity in a way which is suited to the thought patterns and cultural inheritance of a particular audience.[23]

In a subsequent article Cosden, as a sympathetic outsider, elaborates on the original insights of the program, pointing out that the future of post-Soviet evangelical theology depends largely on the painful process of discovering the unique identity of post-Soviet evangelicals. He writes: "[I]f a mature post-Soviet Evangelical theology is to emerge . . . then these identity issues will need to be addressed seriously."[24] According to Cosden this identity can be obtained through critically dialoguing with different theologies across the globe, as well as with its own historico-contextual milieu. He continues: "Many weaknesses of Soviet and post-Soviet evangelical theology can be argued to have come from its failure to come to grips intellectually and existentially with the totality of contexts that have and do contribute to its life as a tradition (Russian, Soviet, Protestant and Orthodox)."[25]

That same year Donald Fairbairn produced a thoughtful book that invited Christians of different traditions to a productive dialogue with Russian Orthodoxy, as well as to a realization that every theological expression is culturally embedded and that the way forward is mutual dialogue.[26] Even though the book was originally intended for Westerners, it seems to have been accepted with interest by its Slavic audience, as well, now that it has been translated into Russian. It is difficult to draw

23. Ibid., 126–27.

24. Cosden, "Coming of Age," 323.

25. Ibid., 323–24.

26. Fairbairn, *Eastern Orthodoxy through Western Eyes*, ix–x, 159. Fairbairn confesses that it took him some time to move from a typical conservative North American evangelical theology to a realization of the contextual nature of every theological construct (159).

any firm conclusions with regard to the acceptance of any written theological work, however, inasmuch as theological education in Ukraine is still in an embryonic and rather chaotic state, mirroring the condition of the wider socio-political and educational context.[27] The development of contextual theology in Ukraine came to a halt in 2001.[28] The present work continues the discourse that was launched at that time.

THE NATURE AND LIMITATIONS OF THIS STUDY

Even though the program described above had the potential of moving a step forward in Ukrainian evangelical theology, it had an inbuilt weakness, which this research is intended to overcome. The Achilles' heel of the endeavor was its inappropriate historical perspective, inherited from the understandably meager and often questionable historiography written during the Soviet period or shortly thereafter.[29] This historical weakness was at least twofold. On the one hand, the creators of the program viewed the highly complex movement dubbed as "post-Soviet evangelicalism" rather homogenously, without taking into account the various roots representing divergent traditions out of which this religious movement arose.[30] The unfortunate effect of this historical perspective can

27. The conferences I have attended and the Christian journals published by various theological schools reflect a monologic and often sporadic approach. I have not been able to locate any research program that would facilitate continuous argumentative conversation by theological students in Ukraine. My perception of the reception of Fairbairn's book is based on conversations with a number of theological students from different parts of Ukraine.

28. Some aspects of contextual theology from a Western perspective have been taught in the MA program of Alliance Theological Seminary at its Eastern European extension site in Kiev, but no research materials have been put into the public domain in printed form.

29. Cf. Liubashchenko, "Problema Natsional'nogo Bogosloviia," 180–91. The article by Liubashchenko, a Soviet historian by education, contains a number of helpful critiques of the above-mentioned MA program. However, this unfocused work, which does not have any bibliographic references, reflects rather the sense of bewilderment and excitement over the prospect of constructing a theological map than a clear vision as to where to go. Throughout the historical part of our research the traditional claims of denominational historiography will be discussed and challenged.

30. Western evangelicalism is viewed by Cosden and Fairbairn as a rather homogenous phenomenon as well. They tend to identify Western theology with rationalistic approaches, without taking into account such diverse and marginal groups as the Pentecostals or the Brethren. Cosden and Fairbairn relied on a well-researched but dated work by Walter Sawatsky, *Soviet Evangelicals Since World War II*. Basically all

be seen in the published materials of a theological conference devoted to the phenomenon of Euro-Asian Protestantism.[31] In the concluding article of the slim conference report, the moderator acknowledged the lack of clarity concerning the nature of the phenomenon discussed during the conference, due to the multiplicity of Protestant bodies that comprise the movement.[32] On the other hand, the Eastern origin of post-Soviet Protestantism was wrongly assumed, while the Western evangelicalism was mistakenly identified as the "elder sibling" of the Eastern counterpart.[33]

It will be the burden of the historical research to demonstrate a more complex pattern of interaction and relationships between Eastern and Western evangelicalism. The unhelpful generalizations and misguided identification of the phenomenon in view will be corrected by focusing on one particular tradition known as the Gospel Christians, whose Western origins are not generally denied.[34] Thus the historical angle of the project is to analyze the dynamics of the tradition of the Gospel Christians (*Evangel'skie Khristiane*) with regard to its triple cord, which consists of (1) its identifying narrative (who do we say we are as a group?), (2) its theology (its contours and vectors), and (3) its practice of biblical interpretation.[35] It will be argued that the configuration of this triple cord has always depended on the state of the geopolitical force field between the Eastern (Orthodox and later Communist) and

---

theologians trying to construct a native evangelical theology stumble over this block of historical generalizations. Cf. Gololob, "Oshibka Rovoama, ili Sud'ba Otechestvennogo Bogoslovia," 125–40, and Penner, "Scripture, Community, and Context in God's Mission in the FSU," 10–38.

31. Cherenkov, *Fenomen Evraziiskogo Protestantizma*.

32. Reshetnikov, "K Voprosu o Phenomene Evraziiskogo Protestantizma," 97–98.

33. Cosden, "Coming of Age," 323–25.

34. Savinskii et al., *Istoriia Evangel'skikh Khristian-Baptistov v SSSR*, 95. I use the term "Gospel Christians" instead of "Evangelical Christians," because the religious group in view differentiates between the adjectives "evangelicheskie" and "evangel'skie" in Russian. The former is associated with Western evangelical bodies, while the latter signifies a belief in the restoration of primitive Gospel Christianity. See the discussion under the section "Why the Gospel Christians?" below.

35. In this research the diachronic study of the practice of biblical interpretation is undertaken to enhance the thick description of the historical tradition in view. In a future project, the practice of biblical interpretation will need to be reconstructed against the polyphonic backdrop of the diachronic dynamics studied in this work.

Western civilizations.[36] Due to the mercurial and polyphonic nature of the tradition, the scope of the research will be limited to the investigation of selected writings of its most prominent leaders, with the focus on this triple cord of the tradition. The large scope of research will not allow a detailed analysis of fluctuations in the tradition. It will be sufficient to demonstrate the changes of vectors and themes in order to interpolate as well as extrapolate its trajectories.

Scholarly historical research of the Russian-Soviet-Ukrainian evangelical traditions, so crucial for establishing the historical identity of a particular group, is still an underdeveloped field of inquiry. The lack of a proper historical perspective has been a serious impediment to theological creativity and productivity up to the present moment. In a recent book Heather J. Coleman boldly states, "There is virtually no published scholarly work on the Russian Baptists in English."[37] Walter Sawatsky was prompt to react, pointing out that Coleman has somewhat exaggerated the state of affairs.[38] However, from the point of view of a student of theology whose interest lies in articulating and constructing the contours of a tradition-continuous evangelical theology for the post-Soviet Ukrainian context, Coleman's assessment does not seem to be much overstated. There has never been any research whose focus was on a diachronic study of historical identities and theological dynamics within a tradition that was part of the Russian-Ukrainian evangelical movement.[39] From the point of view of the present research, Coleman has taken a step in the right direction by rejecting the path of what she dubs "confessional histories which tend to compartmentalize the Baptists rather than exploring them in relation to their milieu and to broader questions of Russian political, cultural and social history."[40] This move

36. I use the term geopolitical force field for the lack of a better one. The current experience in Ukraine is characterized by living in a space between two competing geopolitical powers. The forces at work are visible in social, political, linguistic, and religious stratifications and tensions in the society.

37. Coleman, *Russian Baptists and Spiritual Revolution*, 7. This statement is true not only for English but also for Russian *scholarly* work.

38. Sawatsky, Review of *Russian Baptists and Spiritual Revolution*, 61.

39. De Chalandeau produced a work of theological research entitled *The Theology of the Evangelical Christians-Baptists in the USSR*. However, this research was calibrated by the standards of a conservative school of theology that did not take into account either the historical dynamics or the role of the socio-political factors that shaped the tradition.

40. Coleman, *Russian Baptists and Spiritual Revolution*, 7–8. Coleman referred to

was correct in that it allowed the identity of the movement to be located in its socio-political context. However, from the very outset of her project Coleman fell into the pitfall created and perpetuated by many Western and Soviet historiographies that tended to identify a variety of diverse movements of Russian evangelical sectarianism in terms of a Baptist tradition.[41] Sawatsky correctly noticed this incorrect generalization, but his proposed solution reflected his Mennonite heritage and led directly into another pitfall. He suggested searching in Continental Reformed traditions for the roots of the evangelical group called the Gospel Christians, ignoring the fact that the origin of the particular tradition he referred to has distinctively Anglo-American evangelical roots.[42]

In order to work out the key theological problem of this dissertation, which is to construct the contours of a new historical identity and theological framework based on a diachronic analysis of this triple cord of the Gospel Christians, I will take a middle-distance realist position suitable for this theological goal.[43] The proposed middle-distance realist position is to focus on the hi/story[44] of the tradition taken in and influenced by its socio-political context at selected historical points, with the purpose of the constructive interpolation as well as extrapolation of its trajectory. The identity-constitutive historical narrative of the tradition will be foundational for the historical and theological modification

---

the following dissertations: Blane, *Relations between the Russian Protestant Sects and the State, 1900–1921*; Nesdoly, *Evangelical Sectarianism in Russia*; and Steeves, *Russian Baptist Union, 1917–1935*.

41. In private correspondence Dr. Coleman admitted that differentiating between different evangelical streams in Russia was not part of her research focus.

42. Sawatsky, *Religion in Eastern Europe*, 61. Sawatsky refers to the work of Kahle, *Evangelische Christen in Russland und der Sowjetunion*. It will be demonstrated later on that the "Continental roots" of the tradition were part of a new identity construction of the Gospel Christians after the Bolshevik revolution. It appears somewhat strange that Sawatsky, who seems to be familiar with Heier's *Religious Schism in the Russian Aristocracy* and the Brethren roots of the Gospel Christians, pushed the pendulum to the Continental Reformation, totally neglecting to mention in his review the Anglo-American holiness movement that birthed the tradition to which he refers.

43. Stern, *On Realism*, 113–28. Ford, "System, Story, Performance," 194–202.

44. In the Russian language the word *istoria* stands both for history and story. In order to maintain the merging of the semantic domains of the two distinct English terms, I will spell the word as hi/story, in order to emphasize the impossibility of epistemologically separating historical discovery from the constructive nature of writing a historical narrative.

necessary for suggesting a solution to the current crisis.[45] The research focus on the particular tradition of the Gospel Christians will make it possible to avoid the deficiencies of the presbyopic perspective of the current Western approaches. Cosden, as was mentioned above, tended to view the different traditions comprising the evangelical movement in Euro-Asia as a single and rather disoriented younger sibling of Western evangelicalism. This generalized historical perspective has not been and does not seem to be useful for a theological construction. The focus on a single tradition will also facilitate escaping from the grip of the myopia characteristic of confessional historiographies. Their perspective, as we shall see, portrays the phenomenon of Eastern European evangelicalism as the culmination of a complex spiritual evolution of the Eastern Slavs that took place independently of Western evangelicalism. The whole of the evangelical movement is viewed from this perspective as the eschatological restoration of primitive Apostolic Christianity, in contrast to the Byzantine form of Christianity that was introduced to Russia a millennium ago.[46] The origin, genesis, and deficiencies of this perspective will be discussed in the present research.

WHY THE GOSPEL CHRISTIANS?

There are several reasons why this particular tradition is chosen for research. They can be grouped into two categories: historical and theological. Historically, this tradition is relatively well documented from its very beginning until the present time. The arrival and ministry of Lord Radstock, the Anglican revivalist founder of the tradition, in St. Petersburg caused a significant public resonance that stirred prominent Russian thinkers such as Feodor Dostoevsky, Leo Tolstoy, and Nikolai Leskov to address this public phenomenon in their writings.[47] Because Lord Radstock was a well-known figure in the history of the British holiness revival, he is easily located on the map of Anglo-American evan-

45. Cf. Tanner, *Theories of Culture*, 169.

46. Karetnikova, *Al'manakh po Istorii Russkogo Baptizma*, 83; Savinskii, *Istoriia Evangel'skikh Khristian-Baptistov Ukrainy, Rossii, Belorussii: 1867–1917*, 8–25; Savinskii et al., *Istoriia Evangel'skikh Khristian-Baptistov v SSSR*, 92–95. Cf. Bachinin, *Evangel'skie Tsennosti v Grazhdanskom Obshchestve*, 49–74. Bachinin does not even mention the tradition of the Gospel Christians in his highly selective presentation.

47. McCarthy, "Religious Conflict and Social Order in Nineteenth-Century Russia," 207–44.

gelical theology. This provides a clear starting point for the tradition in the context of the Russian Empire, as well as establishing a relatively firm background of Western scholarship against which the flow of the historical identities, theology, and biblical interpretation of the Gospel Christians will be explored. Fortunately, the private correspondence of Colonel Pashkov, the first national leader of the emerging movement, was spared and is kept in the special archives of the University of Birmingham.[48] This correspondence has never before been analyzed for specifically theological purposes.[49] The private letters of Pashkov will not only confirm the location of the tradition on the map of Anglo-American theology, but also pinpoint it on the map of Russian religious thought.[50] The majority of key periodicals published by the group throughout the time of its existence have survived and are accessible for investigation as well. From the historiographical point of view this tradition has received a comparatively substantial amount of scholarly attention.[51] It will be argued, however, that the established scholarship influenced by Edmund Heier's monograph is deficient with regard to understanding the historical and theological trajectories of the Gospel Christians. Thus the written nature of the tradition and the significant amount of scholarly interest provide a somewhat established background for the development of the historical and theological argument.

From the theological point of view, the tradition of the Gospel Christians is attractive for research because of its undeniable contextual significance. The leaders of the Gospel Christians were chosen by the

48. In the present research all references to this collection of Pashkov Papers (*Perepiska Pashkova*) will be abbreviated as PP.

49. Cf. Muckle, *Nikolai Leskov and the "Spirit of Protestantism,"* and Dolina, "An Examination of Ukrainian Protestant/Baptist Church History with Particular Reference to its Origin and Development until 1939."

50. Traditional "maps" of Russian thought do not include or even mention this phenomenon that attracted the attention of prominent Russian thinkers of the late nineteenth century. Cf. Copleston, *History of Philosophy*, vol. 10, *Russian Philosophy*, and Zenkovsky, *History of Russian Philosophy*. This absence is due to the sentimental rather than intellectual nature of the tradition. However, the omission is striking due to the scale of the movement in Russia and its mediating position between Slavophiles and Westernizers.

51 Heier, *Religious Schism in the Russian Aristocracy*; Corrado, "Philosophy of Ministry of Colonel Vasilii Pashkov"; Nichols, "Pashkovism: Nineteenth Century Russian Piety"; and McCarthy, "Religious Conflict and Social Order in Nineteenth-Century Russia."

Soviet government to become the unifying center for a newly-established and government-controlled Protestant body during World War II—a body which was supposed to unite divergent Protestant groups.[52] Even though this political choice was conditioned by the extreme circumstances that revealed the deficiencies of Communist ideology during a time of existential crisis, the choice of the leadership was not arbitrary and was in line with the original unifying evangelical impetus of the Gospel Christians.[53] As a result of this political move, the theological tendencies of the Gospel Christians became dominant in the newly-established Protestant body. However, the newly created Union of Gospel Christians-Baptists immediately took on a Baptist identity, which was more politically correct for representing Soviet Protestantism internationally. But after several decades the ossified Union of Gospel Christians-Baptists started to fragment, following the collapse of the political system that had supported this post-World War II Soviet identity. Many fragments of the Baptist Union began to seek roots for their new identity in the tradition of the Gospel Christians, at least by appropriating its name.[54] These post-Soviet identity constructing processes make the approach of the present study not only meaningful but also possible.

THEORETICAL TOOLS PROVIDED BY HANS KÜNG AND ALASDAIR MACINTYRE

Having squeezed theology out of the realm of public discourse, Soviet "scientific materialism" dominated the sphere of public education until its sudden collapse at the turn of the second millennium. The ideological vacuum was speedily filled with sources coming from different quarters. It will take some time for contemporary Ukrainian theological students with either their dialectico-materialist Soviet or naïve realist conservative Western epistemological background to process the staggering number of theological approaches dumped upon them within a

52. Sawatsky, *Soviet Evangelicals*, 78–99.

53. Miner, *Stalin's Holy War*.

54. Reshetnikov and Sannikov, *Obzor Istorii Evangel'sko-Baptistskogo Bratstva na Ukraine*, 222. According to official government statistics, on January 1, 2008, there were 248 religious organizations in Ukraine that identified themselves as "Gospel Christians." See Author unknown, "Religiini Organizatsii v Ukraiini."

decade from different quarters and in rather concentrated doses.[55] Up until recently no suitable tools were available in Russian or Ukrainian that would be helpful for analyzing and modifying the theological tradition in an attempt to resolve the crisis in which it finds itself.[56] The recent translations of works of Hans Küng[57] and Alasdair MacIntyre[58] have provided sufficient instruments for navigating the post-modern theological debris caused by the explosion of the Enlightenment project in Euro-Asia. Even though their programs are calibrated for different theological goals and are based on different epistemologies, they offer sufficient theoretical background for approaching the problem of the present research. The reasons why these dialogue partners have been chosen will be provided as their programs are discussed.

Hans Küng: A Panoramic Cultural-Theological Map

Hans Küng has applied the theory of scientific paradigms developed by Thomas Kuhn[59] as a heuristic device for analyzing Christian history, as well as the history of world religions, and he makes a grand theological proposal towards a new post-modern paradigm in theology and global ethics.[60] Following Kuhn, he defines the term *paradigm* as "an entire constellation of beliefs, values, techniques and so on shared by the members of a given community."[61] To emphasize the distinctively hermeneutical nature of the term, Küng uses the following synonyms: "interpretive models," "explanatory models," and "models for

55. Cf. Cherenkov, *Fenomen Evraziiskogo Protestantizma,* 7–14. It should be mentioned that Ukrainian state universities are still in the process of establishing departments of theology.

56. This work is intended to be meaningful in both the Anglo-American and Ukrainian academic settings. The Russian language is still dominant in theological education in Ukraine.

57. Küng, *Great Christian Thinkers*: Gans Kiung, *Velikie Khrisitanskie Mysliteli.* See "Teologiia na Puti k novoi Paradigme" in *Velikie Khristianskie Mysliteli,* 364–401.

58. MacIntyre, *After Virtue*; a very poor Russian translation of the work is Makintair, *Posle Dobrodeteli: Issledovaniia Teorii Morali.*

59. Kuhn, *Structure of Scientific Revolutions.* The Russian translation of the book is Tomas Kun, *Struktura Nauchnykh Revolutsii.*

60. Küng, *Theology for the Third Millennium.* See Küng, *Global Responsibility,* 120–29.

61. Küng and Tracy, *Paradigm Change in Theology,* 7.

understanding."[62] Applying the theory to the grand picture of church history, Küng identifies six distinct paradigms in Christianity: (1) the Early Christian Apocalyptic Paradigm, (2) the Hellenistic Paradigm, (3) the Roman Catholic Paradigm, (4) the Protestant Paradigm, (5) the Modern Paradigm, and (6) the Postmodern Paradigm.[63] Besides these six paradigms, which he calls "macro-paradigms," Küng identifies a large number of meso- and micro-paradigms within each macro-paradigm. He does not provide any criteria for distinguishing meso- and micro-paradigms, however, and is satisfied with giving several examples from science and theology. The Copernican, Newtonian, and Einsteinian models are given as examples of macro-models in physics. Meso-models are represented by the wave theory of light, the dynamic theory of heat, and Maxwell's electro-magnetic theory. Micro-models are used for detailed scientific solutions (such as the discovery of X-rays). In theology macro-models are used for global solutions (such as the Alexandrian and Thomist models); meso-models are used for solving problems in the intermediate field (such as the doctrines of creation and grace and the understanding of sacraments); and micro-models are used for detailed solutions (such as the doctrine of original sin and the hypostatic union in Christology).[64] This distinction between different models (here going beyond Thomas Kuhn) allows him to transfer the theory of paradigms more smoothly into the complex field of Christian theology, thereby giving the theory more elasticity and explanatory power. The paradigm shifts in theology are correlated with epochal civilizational cultural shifts.[65] This historical consciousness and cultural embeddedness of paradigms provides a helpful interpretive matrix for understanding the identifying narrative of the Gospel Christians and their theology in relation to other Christian traditions in general and Russian Orthodoxy in particular.

Unlike the Kuhnian interpretation of the natural sciences, Küng perceives theological paradigms in a way similar to Imre Lakatos' *competing* research programs: historically shaped paradigms may (and do) continue to coexist in time, thus creating a potential for either dialogu-

62. Ibid.

63. Küng, *Global Responsibility*, 122.

64. Küng and Tracy, *Paradigm Change in Theology*, 9–10.

65. Ibid., 441.

ing or clashing.[66] The clash of paradigms happens when their respective representatives take their historically shaped forms of life as the exclusive embodiment of truth. The realization of the historical contingency of each paradigm is the engine of Küng's program, as it provides an opportunity for dialogue and peacemaking. Taking into account the relativistic epistemology of Kuhn's theory with its emphasis on incommensurability between paradigms, Küng grounds his distinctively liberal Christian approach in the epistemology of the Apostolic witness about the essence of Christianity which, according to Küng, is embodied in the historical person of Jesus Christ.[67] This move allows Küng to emphasize the common source of the Christian tradition: Jesus Christ of the Apostolic testimony contained in the canonical scriptures as the norm of the tradition.[68] However, Küng locates the Apostolic testimony in the empiricist framework typical of all contemporary liberal theologies that use experience as their epistemological foundation.[69] He identifies the hermeneutical horizons of his theological program by stating that "the first horizon of critical ecumenical theology is our present-day world of experience, with all its ambivalence, contingency, and changeableness,"[70] while "the second pole or the basic norm of a critical ecumenical theology is the Jewish-Christian tradition which in the final analysis is based on the Christian message, the Gospel of Jesus Christ."[71] In a subsequent book he makes it clear that the Gospel of Jesus Christ is founded on the spiritual experiences of the disciples.[72] As a result of being rooted in empiricist epistemology, he adopts the standards and criteria of the historico-critical method for analyzing both scripture and tradition.[73] An insufficiently self-critical appropriation of empiricist epistemology and a historico-critical set of criteria are probably the weakest parts of Küng's proposal, as they create an illusion of writing from outside a tradi-

66. Lakatos, "Falsification and the Methodology of Scientific Research Programs," 8–101. It should be pointed out that Hans Küng does not refer to Lakatos' proposal in his study.

67. Jeanrond, "Rationality of Faith," 105–21.

68. Küng and Tracy, *Paradigm Change in Theology*, 32.

69. Murphy, *Beyond Liberalism and Fundamentalism*, 22–28.

70. Küng, *Theology for the Third Millennium*, 166.

71. Ibid., 168.

72. Küng, *Tracing the Way*, 200.

73. LaCugna, *Theological Methodology of Hans Küng*, 173–95.

tion of inquiry and looking at the paradigms from a neutral perspective, even though he admits the historical and subjective nature of historical criticism, as well.[74] Küng recognizes that, after the collapse of logical positivism and critical rationalism in epistemology, the hermeneutical nature of all knowledge, including scientific and theological knowledge, should take into account the horizon of the knowing subject. "The past fifty years the discussion has moved from an abstract, positivistic logic and linguistic analysis through innumerable interim corrections to taking *history, the community of inquiry,* and the *human subject,* seriously again" (italics original).[75] However, this realization does not seem to be fully developed in his theological proposal. Fergus Kerr penetratingly critiques Küng for it. Discussing Küng's statement that an individual decides for himself whether or not to trust the Apostolic testimony, Kerr writes: "The self is pictured as having to confront that which surrounds it and then decide whether it is as it seems, or even whether it is there at all. A view point seems to be available from which one is able to survey the passing show and impose a pattern upon it. The individual seems to be free to put what construction he will upon the surrounding world. The supposition is always that one is able to view the world from somewhere else—as if one were God, perhaps."[76]

Even though Küng is not sufficiently critical with regard to his historico-critical criteria, his historical narrative is critically appropriated in the present research. It provides an explanatory matrix for understanding the relationships between different paradigms shaped by epochal cultural and political shifts in the world.

The epistemological shift towards trust in the Apostolic witness reconfigures the relativistic theory of Kuhn as applied to scientific communities of inquiry that do not answer questions about ultimate reality. "Vital questions about the whence and whither of the world and the human, that is, about ultimate and original meanings and standards, values and norms, thus about an ultimate and original reality as such, are questions of a believing trust—certainly not irrational, but utterly reasonable—or a trusting belief."[77] As a result of the shift in epistemology, Küng points out that different Christian historical paradigms pro-

74. Küng, *Theology for the Third Millennium*, 178.

75. Küng and Tracy, *Paradigm Change in Theology*, 6–7.

76. Kerr, *Theology after Wittgenstein*, 16.

77. Küng and Tracy, *Paradigm Change in Theology*, 31.

duced by epochal historico-political shifts belong to one and the same tradition that transmits the Apostolic testimony through ages and cultures. The transmission analysis helps to determine variables as well as cross-cultural and trans-contextual constants within the tradition (e.g., Christocentricity and the norming role of the canonical scriptures). The authoritative nature of the Apostolic testimony gives a platform for dialogue between historically- and culturally-shaped Christian paradigms. However, the historico-critical criteria adopted by Küng filter out other trans-contextual and trans-paradigmatic constants such as Patristic Trinitarian theology, which he interprets away as a cultural-political imposition of the fourth century.[78] This arbitrary imposition of criteria that make a claim for universal validity undermines the project and falls on the deaf ears of those who do not share Küng's empiricist epistemology and historico-critical criteria.[79]

Even though Küng's project is not satisfactory on the whole, his appropriation of the theory of paradigms is taken as a heuristic device for understanding the tradition of the Gospel Christians in the Russian Orthodox context. Küng discusses Russian Orthodoxy as part of the Hellenistic Paradigm.[80] The Pietistic revivalist movements are discussed as part of the Protestant Paradigm.[81] Küng's project as a whole will serve as a provisional map that anchors the tradition of the Gospel Christians in history. It will also provide an interpretive grid for understanding the shift of theological paradigms that took place in nineteenth-century Russia as a result of complex socio-political and spiritual processes. Thus Küng's construction will be used at the *macro level* which will be brought into focus when we need to shed light on the relationship between Orthodoxy and the Gospel Christians. It will also fulfill its function as a historical and theological map when the native constructions of identity are described and evaluated.

78. Küng, *Tracing the Way*, 207.

79. For a critique of Küng's historico-critical approach to the resurrection of Christ, see Higgins, *Tapestry of Christian Theology*, 135–54. Also Grenz and Olson, *Twentieth Century Theology*, 254–70.

80. Küng, *Christianity*, 257–78.

81. Ibid., 614–44.

Alasdair MacIntyre: A Tradition-Based Approach to Inquiry

Alasdair MacIntyre made a nuanced case in a series of books against the Cartesian turn to the self and universalist rationality.[82] Like Hans Küng, MacIntyre is a proponent of a post-modern program.[83] However, his focus on overcoming the disaster of the Cartesian turn in ethics is different from that of Küng, who is not sufficiently critical with respect to his own epistemology and criteria, as we have seen. Küng celebrates the empiricist platform of modernity and accepts its criteria for interpreting scripture and tradition with its many historically-shaped paradigms. MacIntyre takes a critical posture towards the Enlightenment and towards the epistemologies that grew out of it, arguing for the necessity of overcoming the Enlightenment heritage by returning to a pre-modern tradition-based rationality.[84] He demonstrates that the Enlightenment turn towards the self and universal epistemological foundations has robbed contemporary ethical discourse of the necessary context for rational moral enquiry. The Enlightenment project, as MacIntyre dubs it, has led to the repudiation of the social and historical aspects of moral inquiry. However, without the social aspect, which includes the virtues and practices of a community, and the historical aspect, which consists of the community's narrative and tradition, moral discourse about the purpose of human life lacks the necessary context and leads to emotivism.[85] MacIntyre defines emotivism as "the doctrine that all evaluative judgments and more specifically all moral judgments are nothing but expressions of preference, expressions of attitude or feeling."[86] Max Stackhouse summarizes the writings of MacIntyre by saying that "[they] are basically about the wisdom of the classical views of virtue, *telos,* and social coherence in close-knit communities in contrast to the foolishness of modernity with its accent on individualism, plural-

82. MacIntyre, *After Virtue*; *Whose justice? Which rationality?*; *Three Rival Versions of Moral Enquiry*. See a critique and MacIntyre's reply in Horton and Mendus, *After MacIntyre*.

83. Even though Küng can hardly be called a full-fledged post-modernist theologian in light of the critique above.

84. See a recent analysis of MacIntyre's approach to ethics in Keene, "Use of Narrative to Facilitate the Reading of Paul's Ethics," 76–104.

85. Murphy et al., *Virtues & Practices in the Christian Tradition*, 20, 28–29. The definition of the terms as used by MacIntyre is provided in the glossary.

86. MacIntyre, *After Virtue*, 11–12.

ism, cosmopolitanism and abstract science."[87] Even though this move towards tradition-based rationality could be viewed either as sectarian or radically relativist, Trevor Hart points out that MacIntyre is rather a realist of a kind:

> [Traditions] refer us appropriately to the world, and facilitate meaningful engagement with it in its rich diversity. Such traditions develop, MacIntyre argues, through the eruption of "epistemological crises"—crises, that is to say, concerning their reliability in performing the task. Something is encountered (some discovery, or experience, or alternative tradition) which forces a community to concede that its own tradition is in some respect inadequate or unhelpful. We might say that this constitutes a recognition of error . . . ; the desire and the ability to progress in knowing, is bound up with the conviction that there is a reality beyond ourselves.[88]

Nancey Murphy has attempted to summarize the realist epistemology of MacIntyre, having located him in the Anglo-American non-foundationalist tradition of post-modernity.[89] Murphy's reconstruction of MacIntyre's epistemology will be employed in the present study for understanding developments in the tradition of the Gospel Christians and for seeking to overcome its current epistemological crisis. Murphy demonstrates that MacIntyre's realist epistemology consists of two interconnected levels of justification, which she calls diachronic and synchronic respectively. By taking seriously the tradition-ladenness of standards of rationality and criteria, one needs to arbitrate somehow between competing traditions. There is no skyhook that would enable the evaluation of traditions from a position which is not shaped by a historical or cultural location. Murphy refers to an early article by MacIntyre on theories of science[90] in which he argued that "justification of theories in science depends on our being able to construct a historical narrative that makes the transition from the old to the new theory intelligible."[91] MacIntyre states: "When an epistemological crisis is resolved, it is by the

87. M. Stackhouse, "Alasdair MacIntyre," 203.

88. Hart, *Faith Thinking*, 68.

89. Murphy, *Anglo-American Postmodernity*, 57–62, 123–29. We will continue the discussion of foundationalism in chapter 7.

90. MacIntyre, "Epistemological Crises, Dramatic Narrative, and the Philosophy of Science," 69.

91. Murphy, *Anglo-American Postmodernity*, 57.

construction of a new narrative which enables the agent to understand *both* how he or she could intelligibly have held his or her original beliefs *and* how he or she could have been so drastically misled by them. The narrative in terms of which he or she at first understood and ordered experiences is itself made into the subject of an enlarged narrative."[92]

This internal justification in a given tradition Murphy calls the diachronic dimension of justification. Thus according to this realist epistemological account, a tradition that strives for an adequate explanation of reality should be able to resolve its own epistemological crises in an attempt to present a coherent argument and a narrative that establishes historical continuities from the old position to the new.

The diachronic aspect is organically connected to the synchronic aspect, as the tradition should be able to justify itself as a whole over against its rivals.[93] Murphy summarizes this synchronic aspect of the tradition's justification by meditating on MacIntyre's *Whose Justice? Which Rationality*. She says, "A tradition is to be called true if it has proved itself better than its live competitors in terms of its ability to overcome its own problems and even, in some cases, the problems of rivals that cannot be solved using the rivals' own resources and, furthermore, is able to explain why things must have appeared as they did to its predecessors and contemporary rivals from their more limited and defective perspectives."[94]The present research will incorporate the philosophical argumentation of MacIntyre as it is interpreted and appropriated for the Anglo-American post-modern theological program of Nancey Murphy.[95] It should be pointed out from the outset of the work that due to the large scope of the research, the synchronic justification of the tradition *will not* be discussed in this project. I will limit the discussion to the diachronic level of justification by attempting to resolve the internal problems of the tradition. The synchronic level of justification will require another full-fledged research project or series of projects.

The analysis of the tradition of the Gospel Christians will be focused on its historical narrative, its theological vectors, and its practice of biblical reading in community. It is hoped that this study will exercise the

92. MacIntyre, "Epistemological Crises," 140.

93. Murphy, *Anglo-American Postmodernity*, 58.

94. Ibid., 125.

95. We will return to Murphy's coherentist-pragmatic proposal in chapter 7 when we discuss the post-Soviet evangelical trajectory.

necessary virtues that would enable it to extrapolate and extend the tradition in the process of overcoming its present crises of self-identity and theology, which arose out of new post-Soviet experiences. MacIntyre's program will be used at the *micro level* of the present research. In saying that, I mean that the tradition of the Gospel Christians explored in the vein of MacIntyre represents one among many traditions that constitute the Protestant constellation on Küng's map.

THE AIM, GOALS, AND STRUCTURE OF THE BOOK

The principal *aim* of this project is to resolve the contemporary crises of identity and theology in the tradition of the Gospel Christians in Ukraine. The following goals are established to achieve the aim of the project:

1. To sketch the diachronic development of the tradition's identifying narrative.
2. To trace the dynamics of theological vectors in the tradition.
3. To detect and articulate the factors responsible for the narrative and theological dynamics that caused the current crisis.
4. To analyze diachronically the practice of biblical interpretation in the tradition.
5. To critically evaluate recent developments in the parent directory of Western evangelicalism in a search for tradition-continuous intellectual resources capable of resolving or relieving the crisis.
6. To suggest a reconstruction of the community's narrative by the appropriation of suitable resources from outside of the tradition.

The book consists of two parts: historical/descriptive and theological/constructive. The historical part, which covers six chapters, will address the first four goals. The constructive part, which consists of the final chapter, will address goals five and six.

This structure reflects the current state of research on the tradition. Much of it represents historical studies of different periods of Russian and Soviet sectarianism. However, due to the Western tendency to generalize phenomena and focus on a specific period, I will have to make some significant corrections to existing historical studies. The need for these corrections became obvious during my interaction with primary sources from different periods, in light of the larger focus of the current work and the differences in its research interests from those of previous studies.

A DESCRIPTION OF EACH CHAPTER AND THE FLOW OF ARGUMENT

The first chapter is devoted to Lord Radstock, the founder of the tradition. The burden of this chapter is to pinpoint the historical and theological location of Radstock. In this chapter it will be demonstrated that Radstock was a typical Victorian evangelical whose thought world and practices were shaped by the evangelical currents of the time. His premillennial holiness theology and pre-critical method of biblical interpretation were typical of Anglo-American evangelicalism during the second half of the nineteenth century. Radstock and his theology are the starting point of the tradition. Subsequent developments will be evaluated against the background of Radstock.

In the second chapter we will explore the content of the first magazine of the movement, the *Russian Workman*. We will demonstrate the coexistence of Orthodox and Protestant theological paradigms on the pages of this magazine. It will be pointed out that during this stage the Gospel Christians retained their Orthodox identity, while striving for the restoration of Apostolic piety in Russia.

In the third chapter the focus will be on Colonel Pashkov, a wealthy Russian follower of Radstock. It will be argued that Pashkov developed the ecclesiological restorationist trend.[96] Ecclesiological restorationism was also present in the Anglo-American evangelicalism of the time, but it was absent from the ministry of Radstock. Without changing Radstock's theology and practices, Pashkov envisioned a restoration of primitive Christianity in Russia prior to the return of Christ, which he expected would take place very soon. The prominence of the geopolitical attrac-

96. The definition of *spiritual* and *ecclesiological restorationism* is provided in the glossary.

tion of Western civilization and Russian messianism[97] will come into focus in the ministry of Pashkov. After Pashkov was expelled from Russia for an attempt to implement his vision, the tradition was characterized by the competition of two restorationist trends in St. Petersburg that represented respectively old Orthodox and new evangelical identities. The chapter also contains an analysis of the second period of the *Russian Workman* that reflects the short-lived trend of spiritual restorationism in the Orthodox Church.

The fourth chapter will cover the period between 1905, the year of the first Russian revolution, and 1910. This period, which was dominated by I.S. Prokhanov, reveals the national growth of the movement and its dependence on Western intellectual resources. Contrary to established Western historiography, it will be argued that Prokhanov did not break the continuity of the tradition going back to the time of Pashkov. Rather, he developed the ecclesiological restorationist tendency of the tradition to its logical end by attempting to establish a branch of the Evangelical Alliance in Russia. During this period Prokhanov presented the movement as a progressive, modern religion that would eventually replace what he considered to be a degraded Orthodox state church. Having selectively studied theology in Britain, Germany, and France, Prokhanov introduced a modernist trend into the evangelical tradition. The Romantic premillennialism of Radstock and Pashkov were exchanged for modernistic postmillennialist eschatology. Theology and biblical interpretation began to be formalized, following the trajectory represented by the proto-fundamentalist Moody Bible Institute.

The fifth chapter will discuss the development of the tradition during the period between 1910 and 1939. Prokhanov was still the dominant figure of this period. However, due to his failure to establish a branch of the Evangelical Alliance in Russia, he temporarily took on a Baptist identity in an attempt to organize a united Protestant front in Russia. The events prior to the Bolshevik revolution demonstrate the power of the Western gravitational pull on the Gospel Christians. We will demonstrate the role of geopolitical powers and Russian messianism in shaping and changing the narrative of the tradition in the aftermath of the Bolshevik revolution. These will become evident as we examine Prokhanov's attempt to start a new worldwide reformation that was intended to restore the primitivism and purity of the Apostolic church.

97. The definition of *messianism* is provided in the glossary.

This move resulted in a further change in the community's narrative. The theological practices of this period did not change much from the previous period, however. Our analysis of theology will reveal not only a dependence on Anglo-American conservative evangelicalism, but also a significant misunderstanding of Western theological discourse. The turbulent times of World War I and the subsequent revolutions and civil war did not promote the development of a written theological culture or of the intellectual virtues that would ordinarily be associated with such a culture.

In the sixth chapter we will focus on the period between 1942 and 2008. This period was characterized by the establishment during World War II of the All-Union Council of Gospel Christians-Baptists. Having been initiated by the Soviet government during a time of existential crisis, it was an official religious structure that created a new pro-Soviet narrative identity. Then, four decades later, the self-identifying story was reconstructed by Soviet and post-Soviet denominational historiographers in light of rising Orthodox cultural significance after Perestroika. It will be demonstrated that the self-identity of the tradition depended on the fluctuations in the geopolitical force field acutely experienced at the meeting point of the tectonic plates of the Western and Soviet (later Orthodox) civilizations. The inconsistencies of the tradition's narrative have brought about the current identity crisis. Its theological vectors were modified between 1942 and 1991. This period is characterized by a return to premillennial theology and a dependence on the intellectual resources of the Moody Bible Institute. Its practice of biblical interpretation did not undergo any major changes until 1991. The major shift that affected its theology and its approach to understanding scripture took place only after the collapse of the Soviet Union. The introduction of the inductive Bible study method and the translation into Russian of North American theologies brought the tradition to the theological crisis briefly mentioned by Cosden above.

The seventh chapter will discuss theological developments in the post-Soviet Ukrainian context and analyze certain trends in the Anglo-American evangelical constellation. Continuing the trajectory of dependence on Western evangelical discourse, I will suggest that the evangelical program based on holist (coherentist) realist epistemology provides the necessary intellectual resources for solving the epistemological crisis of the Gospel Christians. Utilizing its theological method, influenced by the postliberal theological program of reading the world through the lens of scripture, we will produce a reading of the changing narrative of the tradition in light of the story of scripture. The reading on the relationship between Christ and the powers, which affected the previous identity constructions of the tradition, is the theological climax of the reconstruction. As a result of this reading, we will demonstrate the usefulness of the holist (coherentist) theological framework for restoring the narrative consistency of the tradition in the post-Soviet period.

1

Lord Radstock and the St. Petersburg Revival

INTRODUCTION

The tradition of the Gospel Christian movement, nicknamed Radstockism early on by its Orthodox critics, began with the arrival in St. Petersburg of the British revivalist preacher Lord Radstock in late 1873 or early 1874.[1] It is impossible to understand the subsequent developments in this revivalist tradition without tracing the historical, social, theological, and cultural location of its founder.[2] The mapping of the historical and theological setting of the founder of the Gospel Christians will be used as the reference point for understanding the historical and theological vectors and trajectory of the tradition.

The aim of the present chapter is threefold: first, to locate Radstock historically; second, to describe his theological framework; and third, to analyze his theological approach to the interpretation of biblical texts. This threefold structure of the chapter parallels what was called in the introductory chapter the "triple cord" of the tradition. So the present chapter lays the foundation for understanding the tradition's narrative identity, its theological vectors, and its biblical interpretation.

1. Terletskii, *Sekta Pashkovtsev*, 3–27, and Butkevich, *Obzor Russkikh Sekt*, 460–72. For a discussion of Radstock's revivalism, see Corrado, *Filosofiia Sluzhenia Polkovnika Pashkova*, 173–77.

2. Cf. McClendon, *Biography as Theology*.

DEVELOPMENTS IN THE PROTESTANT PARADIGM AND FRAMEWORKS FOR UNDERSTANDING THE TRADITION INITIATED BY LORD RADSTOCK

In his impressive account of Christian developments in history, Hans Küng discusses revivalist movements as part of the Protestant Paradigm in the eighteenth and nineteenth centuries.[3] The Protestant paradigm shift in western Christianity happened in the sixteenth century, beginning with the radical turning of the Augustinian monk Martin Luther (1483–1546) to the Gospel narrative and to a reformulation of theology in terms of justification by grace through faith alone. This turn towards the Christocentric interpretation of the Bible through the Pauline lens of juridical justification by faith was the engine of the paradigmatic shift in theology, spirituality, and ecclesiology. This doctrine was "the heart and essence of Luther's theological contribution."[4] The succeeding developments within Protestantism in Continental Europe as well as in Britain and America took place within the framework of this theological paradigm shift. The traditional Orthodox apologetic literature of the late nineteenth and early twentieth centuries generally locates the tradition initiated by Radstock within this broad framework of Protestantism, alongside other Protestant bodies active in Russia.[5] This theological framing of the Protestant constellation accomplished from within the Orthodox theological community was sufficient for Orthodox scholars to deal with this spiritual phenomenon, which was generally considered to be a deviation from the truth contained in the Patristic tradition and preserved by the Orthodox Church through the chain of apostolic succession.[6]

The Protestant historiography is more finely tuned—partly due to later developments in the tradition and the expansion of its hermeneutical horizons, partly to the formation of its self-identity in contrast to other Protestant bodies, and partly to the unchecked prejudices of historians. The following historical sketch is intended to locate Radstock,

3. Küng, *Christianity*, 634.

4. Olson, *Story of Christian Theology*, 380.

5. Butkevich, *Obzor Russkikh Sekt*, 460–61.

6. Traditionally Orthodox works on sectarianism locate Radstock and the tradition he initiated among the mystical-rationalistic sects, which was the typical identification of movements derived from Western Protestantism. Cf. Anderson, *Staroobriadchestvo i Sektantstvo*, 235.

and the origin of the tradition initiated by him, more precisely within the Protestant paradigm.

The typical tendency of both Eastern and Western Protestant historiography is to locate the tradition of the Gospel Christians within the framework of the Baptist theological constellation.[7] There are several reasons for the appropriation of this interpretive grid, which is sufficiently plastic and transparent to allow for the possibility of influences from other traditions, including that of Radstock.[8] These diverse "influences," however, are eventually smoothed out in later readings of the past to conform to the Soviet Baptist outlook that was later represented as the apex of the spiritual evolution of Christianity that would presumably lead to the restoration of Apostolic Christianity.[9] Following are some of the factors that have led to the dominance of the Soviet Baptist restorationist perspective. (1) The privileged position of the German Baptists in Russia since 1879 prompted many sectarians of various sorts to associate with the legally-privileged tradition,[10] so that eventually the Baptist tradition became the dominant one in the Russian and Soviet context.[11] (2) Inasmuch as the leading representatives of the Gospel Christians, Johannes Kargel and Ivan Prokhanov, whose theology will be discussed in subsequent chapters, were associated with the Baptist movement for a number of years, it seemed natural to take their tradition as a species of the world Baptist movement. (3) The formation of the official Union of Gospel Christians-Baptists (The All-Union Council of Evangelical Christians-Baptists, AUCECB hereafter) in 1944 was the most important factor contributing to the establishment of the Soviet Baptist interpretive grid. It will be my task in the following historical chapters to demonstrate that this interpretive framework significantly oversimplifies the data, since it does not begin with the source of the tradition and filters out some of its subsequent dynamics. At this point it is sufficient to note that the Soviet Baptist historiographic framework is

7. Reshetnikov and Sannikov, *Obzor Istorii*, 16; Sawatsky, *Soviet Evangelicals*, 45; Coleman, *Russian Baptists*, 7.

8. Cf. Sawatsky, *Soviet Evangelicals*, 33–35.

9. *Bratskii Vestnik*, "Iz Istorii Russkogo Evangel'sko-Baptistskogo Dvizheniia v SSSR," 5 (1947). Cf. *Bratskii Vestnik*, "Prebyvanie Delegatsii Vsemirnogo Soiuza Baptistov v SSSR," 3–4 (1954); and Goutche, "Iz Trekh Rek—Odin Mogutchii Potok," 6–7.

10. Mel'gunov, *Tserkov' i Gosudarstvo v Rossii*, 57–59.

11. Cf. Muckle, "Afterword" in Leskov, *Schism in High Society*, 117.

anachronistic and does not give due justice to Lord Radstock, the founder of the Gospel Christians, who did not share the Baptist constellation of beliefs and practices as it is generally understood. Neither does it help us to understand the immediate centrifugal processes that fragmented the AUCECB following the collapse of the Soviet Union, revealing a clear difference in identity between the Gospel Christians and the Baptists. Thus, unlike the established historiographic studies that accept without sufficient criticism the assumptions from the Soviet period concerning the origin of the movement, the present work seeks to formulate a post-Soviet identity for movements that are associated with the tradition of the Gospel Christians. In this respect I will attempt to provide a distinctively post-Soviet particularistic approach to the tradition's historiography, in light of recent developments in Eastern Europe.

The relatively new scholarly historiographic strand represented by Edmund Heier[12] and Mark McCarthy[13] correctly frames Radstock within the milieu of the evangelicalism of Victorian England and Imperial Russia respectively. However, both Heier, and McCarthy, who intensively builds on Heier's monograph, focus only on the first ten years of the tradition. Both scholars assume an abrupt and somewhat radical modification after that period.[14] Even though they oriented themselves in a promising direction, as far as the present research is concerned, by focusing on the early stages of the development of the tradition and by taking into account the socio-political and cultural context of Russia, they accommodated their views to the general Protestant historiography on the topic mentioned above. Without challenging Baptist historiographies, Heier and McCarthy claim that there was a rupture in the tradition after Radstock and his immediate followers were banned and left the country. Thus according to this reading, Radstockism was a short-lived phenomenon that was later absorbed by the Baptist movement. It will be argued, however, in the chapter on Ivan Prokhanov that no radical rupture in the tradition did, in fact, occur and that Western scholars of Radstockism made a premature jump by exaggerating differences and downplaying continuities between different stages of the tradition.

The shortcomings of Heier's historic perspective can be understood by taking into account the time of his writing, when the Gospel

12. Heier, *Religious Schism*.

13. McCarthy, "Religious Conflict."

14. Heier, *Religious Schism*, 147. Cf. McCarthy, "Religious Conflict," 252.

Christians were welded with the Baptists by the State authorities into one distinctively Baptist religious body. In this respect Heier's hermeneutical horizon did not allow him to see the complexity of the heterogeneous Union that was separated from the rest of the world by the Iron Curtain. Unlike the recent contribution of McCarthy, who does not take into account post-Soviet evangelical developments or the fragmentation of the AUCECB as a result of the search for new religious identities, I will argue that the ecumenically-oriented ferment of Anglo-American revivalism represented by Radstock was never fully absorbed by the Baptist movement, whose theology and missionary drive were of Continental origin.

In the present research I side with Heier and McCarthy in perceiving Radstockism as an Anglo-American evangelical movement. The following sketch of historical and theological developments in the British Isles is intended to provide a preliminary framework for anchoring Radstock in the relevant historical and theological processes.[15] The movement of which Radstock was a part is inseparably connected to the development of the interdenominational evangelical movement in the British Isles and its colonies beginning in the 1730s.[16] David Bebbington identifies the key characteristics of the interdenominational evangelical movement: "*conversionism*, the belief that lives need to be changed; *activism*, the expression of the Gospel in effort; *biblicism*, a particular regard for the Bible; and what may be called *cruciocentrism*, a stress on the sacrifice of Christ on the cross. Together they form a quadrilateral of priorities that is the basis of Evangelicalism."[17]

Since Lord Radstock was part of the Evangelical Alliance, he and his ministry can be properly understood only within the historical-theological framework established by Bebbington. In reviewing evangelical developments since the eighteenth century, Stanley Grenz points out the following theological stages of the trajectory of evangelicalism beginning with Luther's paradigmatic shift: (1) Luther's doctrine of justification by grace through faith[18]; (2) Calvin's separation of justification from sanctification[19]; (3) the Puritan accent on church discipline of the

15. See the section entitled "Lord Radstock's Theology" for a more detailed analysis.

16. Bebbington, *Evangelicalism in Modern Britain*, 20–42.

17. Ibid., 3.

18. Grenz, *Renewing the Center*, 26–30.

19. Ibid., 30–33.

wayward and unregenerate and the retrieval of the Augustinian idea of the invisible church, modified by the doctrine of predestination[20]; (4) the personalization and individualization of the Puritan emphasis on assurance of salvation for the elect[21]; (5) the German Pietism of Spener and Franke with its emphasis on a subjective personal conversion experience (the new birth) and a transformed life that reflects God's will[22]; (6) the Methodist primacy of regenerative conversion over justification, with re-evaluation of assurance of salvation in light of the conversion experience[23]; and (7) the emphasis of the holiness movement on complete sanctification by faith through identification with Christ.[24] The features of evangelical theology correlated in many respects with the early Modernist and Romantic milieu of the times.[25] Hans Küng succinctly characterizes the general theological tendencies of this segment of the Protestant constellation that took its shape by the end of the nineteenth century: "[It was characterized by] ecstatic features, the overestimation of the personal experience, and the danger of emotional self-redemption. The church, preaching and sacraments were neglected all too much. A hostility to theology was said to have developed, ending up in a basic hostility to thought and a laziness in thinking."[26] Against this sketchy background of historical and theological developments we are ready to take a closer look at Lord Radstock.

THE MEMOIRS OF DAISY BEVAN (MARY WALDERGRAVE)

Granville Augustus William Waldegrave, Third Baron Radstock of Castletown in the peerage of Ireland, was born in 1833 and educated at Harrow and Balliol College, Oxford. Radstock graduated with a second in law and history in 1854, a second in natural science in 1855, and a master of arts in 1857. Radstock was the child of Vice Admiral Granville

20. Ibid., 34–38.

21. Ibid., 38.

22. Ibid., 42–43.

23. Ibid., 44–49.

24. Bebbington, *Dominance of Evangelicalism*, 194–97. Grenz does not include this point, as the radical holiness movement was strongly critiqued by what became mainline evangelicalism.

25. Ibid., 109–72; Stunt, *From Awakening to Secession*, 8–16.

26. Küng, *Christianity*, 634.

George Waldergrave and of Esther Caroline Puget, youngest daughter of John Puget, a director of the Bank of England. In 1858 Radstock married Susan Colcraft, whose father was J. H. Colcraft, M.P. for Rempstone and Dorset. During the course of their thirty-four-year marriage they had three sons and five daughters.[27] While visiting the battlefields of the Crimean War (1854–1856) soon after that war ended, Radstock caught a fever and barely escaped with his life. There in Russia he claimed later to have made his first covenant with God, vowing to serve him if he was allowed to live. He subsequently dedicated his life to evangelistic and charity work in the British Isles, various countries of Europe, and India.[28] The Archbishop of Canterbury, in a letter to Radstock's son, wrote: "For more than half a century your father has been in the forefront of work for our Master and for the advance of his Kingdom, and the whole land is under an obligation to one who has rendered such notable service to its highest and most sacred interests."[29]

His biographer, Mrs. Edward Trotter, who knew him personally and had access to his diaries and family letters, pointed out that Radstock was always in the process of developing and changing.[30] As a result of these processes, Radstock is depicted differently by different historians. Very often a historical portrait of Radstock tells more about the historiographer than about Radstock himself. The Soviet Baptist historiography identifies Radstock exclusively in sectarian terms as belonging to "the open church of the Darbyites."[31] Trotter states that in Radstock's later days many strong Protestants "actually thought that his sympathies were dangerously drawn towards the Church of Rome," due to his broad ecumenical views.[32] Because of the changing views of

27. McCarthy, "Religious Conflict," 46–47.

28. Trotter, *Undertones of the Nineteenth Century*, 9; *Lord Radstock*, 1–80; Fountain, *Lord Radstock and the Russian Awakening*, 10–20. See also Corrado, *Filosofiia*, 38–40; McCarthy, "Religious Conflict," 46–76.

29. Trotter, *Lord Radstock*, 54.

30. Ibid., 112.

31. Savinskii et al., *Istoriia Evangel'skikh Khristian-Baptistov v SSSR*, 80. Even though the authors make general reference to the biography of Radstock written by Trotter, there is no evidence that the Soviet Baptist historiographers were acquainted with the content of Trotter's well-researched written work. The oxymoronic phrase "Open Church of Darbyites," intended for the identification of Radstock with the Plymouth Brethren, reveals that the Soviet Baptist historiographers were familiar neither with Trotter's biography nor with the history of the Brethren movement in Britain.

32. Ibid., 115.

Radstock, it is important to try to locate him theologically during the period of his ministry in Russia, keeping in mind that he was steadily moving towards broader ecumenism as he was aging. Thus it is crucial to keep in mind that Radstock was on the verge of breaking with the Plymouth Brethren[33] during his time in Russia, or shortly thereafter. As Trotter writes: "He had courage to act in opposition to those ideals (i.e., the conservative ideals of his youth) such as when, severing his connection with the Plymouth Brethren, he renounced their interpretation of the then-accepted doctrine of eternal punishment. That action nearly thirty years before, must be judged in the light of that time and his own temperament."[34]

John Kent writes: "Admiral Fishbane (1811–1887) and Lord Radstock (1833–1913) were wealthy, eccentric Anglican laymen. Their Anglicanism was a matter of social class; they did exactly as they pleased ecclesiastically."[35] This assessment is correct, taking into account the shifting perspectives of Radstock throughout his life and his free association with different Christian groups without ever severing his connection with the Anglican Church.

In 1878 Radstock went to Russia with his family. The following memoirs of his daughter Mary, born in 1871, should help the reader understand the historical background of Radstock's theological convictions which he took to Russia in the 1870s. These memoirs are a valuable resource because they provide a glimpse into the exact period of time when Radstock was visiting Russia. Radstock is presented as an evangelical of the Victorian church.[36]

> My Father was the dominating and vital personality of the family, but at the time I am writing of, fear was the chief sensation with which he inspired his children. In later years this was quite different; he changed much. But then a strict evangelical of the

33. The Plymouth Brethren movement started in Dublin in 1827 as a charismatic protest movement against worldliness in churchmanship, ritual, ceremony, and organization. "The initial attraction of the movement was its repudiation of any ecclesiastical pretensions and its desire to merge sectarian distinctions in the simple gathering of all believers to Christ around the Lord's Table, its aversion to divisive theological systems, and the humility, zeal and even sanctity of its disciples." See Davies, *Worship and Theology in England*, 150–52.

34. Trotter, *Lord Radstock*, 101.

35. Kent, *Holding the Fort*, 148.

36. Chadwick, *Victorian Church*, 440–55.

70's, with Prussian ideas of discipline for all, servants, children and babies, his ringing voice was generally dreaded. Though affectionate and warm-hearted, and proud of his children, he quite failed to see them as individuals; they were just "the children" to him. I think he regarded them as a sort of platoon of recruits to be drilled and to carry out orders "at the double"—indeed we were literally drilled every morning for some time, and a floppy attitude would be corrected by a resounding slap on the back . . . I remember a terrible punishment being given [Monty, a brother of Mary] for a supposed lie. We were just on the point of walking to the station to London when we heard, "Papa is going to punish Monty." Soon our brother appeared with an enormous placard hanging round his neck with the word "Liar" printed in capital letters on it. Mercifully before we reached the station my mother persuaded my father to remove it. . . .[37] Neither questions nor remarks were encouraged. "You would not understand that, you are too young." "I cannot discuss that with you" were the sort of rejoinders that began to turn me into a shy, reserved and lonely child. I (was) dressed most severely as a little Victorian girl.[38]

I should mention that all our earlier friends, and almost our only ones, were Russians. This came from two reasons; firstly, that my father frequently visited Russia, where, in spite of his being "le lord Evangeliste" he was enormously popular; secondly, because of the curious blend of social and religious exclusiveness with which we were brought up. We were never allowed to associate with children who were not considered of our own class, nor were we permitted to know any children whose parents were not "true believers" i.e., evangelicals . . . I think this isolation had a disastrous effect on the whole family. It was far-reaching, even to the present time, and in early years produced a spirit of religious and social arrogance. These are the sort of phrases I remember "Papa, is Canon Dash a Christian?" and "Oh, they are the sort of people who keep parlour maids."[39]

Describing home Bible studies, Mary says,

Family prayers were quite a long affair and began with a hymn . . . Then generally there would come a pause till my father felt he had received guidance as to what part of the Bible to read and expound . . . I should doubt his words being at all suitable for that

37. Bevan, "Odd Memories of an Ordinary Person," 4.

38. Ibid., 12.

39. Ibid., 5.

> congregation of children and servants. I can't say these readings were Bible study, but rather mystical (of the evangelical type) interpretations of considerable length on a very short portion of scripture, and during my whole life at home I never got beyond the middle of St. Mark's Gospel with my father![40]

Subsequently Mary states that in later years her father made "very long a sweep" from "Calvinistic narrowness" to broader opinions during his life.[41] The Lord Radstock of the 1870s is presented as a Victorian evangelical of his own day.

WAS RADSTOCK A DARBYITE?

Even though Radstock was the originator of an influential evangelical tradition in Russia, his theology has never properly been studied by Russian or Ukrainian denominational scholars. In a recently published book, Professor V. A. Bachinin admits this.[42] Even though he tries to bridge the gap, he makes a mistake at the outset of his presentation by associating Radstock with John Nelson Darby, the leader of the Closed Brethren stream of the Plymouth Brethren movement. This incorrect association of Radstock is inherited from the Baptist denominational historiography, which indiscriminately associates the Plymouth Brethren movement exclusively with the name of Darby.[43] John Nelson Darby broke with the Church of Ireland and became the leader of the Closed Brethren. His interpretive methods were highly influential in the formation of the fundamentalist trajectory in Anglo-American evangelicalism.[44] Unlike the progenitor of fundamentalism, Radstock never broke with the Church of England, whereas he severed his connections with the Plymouth Brethren during or shortly after his visits to Russia. There are at least three reasons why denominational historians misplaced Radstock by associating him with "the father of dispensationalism," whose theology will be discussed briefly later on in the chapter. First, the Brethren

40. Ibid., 11.

41. Ibid., 15.

42. Bachinin, *Khristianskaia Mysl'*, 57.

43. It is a prominent tendency of denominational historiography to overemphasize or invent connections with movements or persons that deviated from the established church.

44. Marsden, *Fundamentalism and American Culture*, 46.

movement in Germany and France became associated with the name of Darby. The Brethren were generically called "Darbyites."[45] The Soviet, Russian, and Ukrainian denominational writers seem to rely on German writers, such as Waldemar Gutshe, who do not seem to have been interested in scrutinizing differences between distinct evangelical traditions in Britain.[46] Second, the theologian who most influenced the evangelical movement during the post-World War II period, Johannes Kargel, who was a Baptist until his return from the mission field in Bulgaria in 1884, adhered to Darbyite millenarian teaching, especially in his writings after the Bolshevik Revolution in 1917. Russian/Ukrainian scholarship assumes a theological continuity stretching from Radstock to Pashkov to Kargel, since Kargel explicitly referred to Pashkov as his spiritual mentor, and Radstock is assumed likewise to have been Pashkov's mentor. The conclusion is therefore made that the Darbyite dispensationalism and millenarianism of the later Kargel must have been shared by Pashkov and Radstock. While this line of thinking is logical, it is not supported by the evidence of Radstock's theology analyzed below. Thirdly, millenarian dispensationalism became the dominant theological teaching of the Gospel Christians and Baptists from the 1920s on.[47] It was D. L. Moody who popularized dispensational eschatology in the West,[48] and close connections between Soviet evangelicals and the Moody Bible Institute in the 1920s made millenarian dispensationalist teaching the evangelical orthodoxy for the generations to come. As late as 1993 this teaching appears in the statement of faith of Odessa Theological Seminary, the first evangelical seminary in Ukraine.[49] This denominational framework and the theological presuppositions of historians, as well as the lack of access to resources located outside of Russia and Ukraine, flattened out the more complex reality of the beginnings of the evangelical movement in St. Petersburg.

There is no sufficient evidence that Radstock was influenced by the dispensationalist theology of the Closed Brethren, which by the 1870s had become a separate denomination severely criticized by people such

45. Coad, *History of the Brethren Movement*, 86.

46. Gutsche, *Westliche Quellen des russischen Stundismus.*

47. Sandeen, *Roots of Fundamentalism*, 59–80.

48. Steele, *Substitute for Holiness*, 55.

49. Statement of Faith of Odessa Theological Seminary. "Istoriia Baptizma." Vyp. 1. Prilozhenie 1–4. CD ROM EAAA 2.0.

as Charles Spurgeon, with whom Radstock freely associated, among other prominent evangelicals of that time.[50] The arrival of the leader of the Open Brethren, the internationally-revered George Müller of Bristol, in St. Petersburg after Radstock's departure may indicate that Radstock associated for awhile with the Open Brethren stream.[51] The subsequent break with the Brethren and Radstock's ongoing identification with the Anglican Church do not provide any ground for associating him with the Darbyite theological trajectory.

WAS RADSTOCK A NON-DENOMINATIONAL CHRISTIAN?

Bachinin mistakenly states that there is no serious scholarly work on Radstock, but only sketchy biographical and polemical notes. The above-mentioned monograph by Edmund Heier was left unnoticed.[52] Heier's work on the teaching of Radstock and his Russian follower Colonel Pashkov, who became the leader of the evangelical movement in St. Petersburg after Radstock's departure from Russia, provides a thorough analysis of the early evangelical beginnings in the then-capital city of the Russian empire.[53] Heier's scrutinized and well-documented monograph does not seem to have exercised its full potential in either Western and Eastern European scholarship until recently, particularly with regard to understanding the trajectories of the evangelical movements in the Russian Empire.[54]

According to Heier, Radstock did not attempt to establish a different denomination or movement outside of the National Church. He writes, "This religious revival (in St. Petersburg) in its initial stage did

50. Trotter, "Events at Plymouth" and Mackintosh, "The First 50 Years." See also Spurgeon, "Plymouth Brethren."

51. Korff, *Am Zarenhof*, 37–38.

52. This overlooking is discouraging, because Heier's book was translated into Russian and published under the title *Redstokism and Pashkovshchina* (Moskva, 1998). There is no evidence that Bachinin was acquainted with Trotter's work either, as she does not mention Darby's name. Professor Bachinin seems to have copied the Soviet historiography verbatim without critically checking primary sources.

53. It is the only monograph to have been published on Radstock and Pashkov.

54. It should be mentioned that often Heier's references are incorrect. Coleman quotes Heier, but she mainly ignores his main thesis. McCarthy's thesis is largely influenced by Heier's monograph. However, McCarthy, like Heier, passes excessively generalized judgments on the evangelical trajectories by focusing on the discontinuities within the same tradition. See 251–53.

not aim to become a sect outside of the official church. It became such only when castigated by the guardians of Russian Orthodoxy, who failed to recognize its ultimate aim; namely the reformation of Russia on a religious and moral basis without adhering to any specific denomination."[55] If Soviet Baptist historiography tends to depict Radstock in rather sectarian and narrow terms, the historiographic angle represented by Heier tends to project Radstock in a highly ecumenical light. The former overemphasizes the Brethren identity of young Radstock before his arrival in Russia, while the latter seems to have read much of the broader ecumenism of the aged Radstock into his Russian ministry. Neither of these perspectives seems to do sufficient justice to the founder of the Gospel Christians and the subsequent developments within the tradition.

In his evaluation of the evangelical trajectory, Heier was heavily influenced by Nikolai Leskov's study of Lord Radstock and his teaching.[56] The influence of Leskov's views can be explained by his prophetic insight when he was writing in 1876:

> If a schism is conceived as [a] complete split from the Church [i.e., the Imperial Orthodox Church] accompanied by the professed impossibility of agreeing with it in the most essential fundamentals of faith, then this is not a schism . . . The whole of the Radstockist movement is a group of people who like to discuss the Word of God, salvation and justification. Their difference with the Church consists in a specific view of justification and the so called "cult of the dead," and in their discouragement of prayer to the saints and the Virgin Mary . . . They are still in the Church and will not be separated from it, provided the religious awakening which has seized them is not cooled by discouraging lack of sympathy for their thirst to take part in the life of the church . . . If, however, nothing is done for these modest and reasonable desires, then all this present-day religious ferment, which does not yet possess the characteristics of a formal schism . . . will have a definite outcome. If that happens, the only thing to remember is that the fault will not be Lord Radstock's and his

55. Heier, *Religious Schism*, 29. Even though Heier admits that the evangelical Christianity of Radstock was bound to clash with Orthodoxy, he does not explain why. See 54.

56. Leskov, *Schism in High Society*. The original was published in Russian under the title, *Velikosvestskii Raskol. Lord Redstok i ego Posledovateli* (St. Petersburg: V. Tushnov, 1877). See also Muckle, *Nikolai Leskov and "The Spirit of Protestantism."*

> followers' but the excessively slow satisfaction of these good and justified desires.[57]

The subsequent departure of Lord Radstock from Russia in 1878, as well as the expulsion of the leaders of the Radstockist movement, Colonel Pashkov and Count Korff, in 1884, seemed to prove the correctness of Leskov's assessment. Protestant scholarship has taken this explanation for granted, blaming the Orthodox Church for not understanding the good intentions of the Radstockists. James Muckle writes, "[T]hough Aristocratic followers of Radstock had no intention of founding a new denomination, when the movement eventually spread to the masses, officialdom took fright, seeing a threat to Orthodoxy and even to civil peace."[58]

In a recent dissertation on the evangelical revival in St. Petersburg, Mark McCarthy argues in a similar way:

> As an undenominational Christian, Radstock lent his support to anyone who promoted the evangelical cause . . . [He] was more interested in gospel truths concerning salvation than in methods of worship or ritual practice. In fact, he believed a time was coming when all churches would meld into one to advance the cause of the divine Kingdom. Later, this view would prove problematic in Russia.[59] Some scholars have emphasized that Pashkovites [the name of the movement after the departure of Radstock] broke from the Orthodox Church in 1884 only when their leaders were forced out of Russia and they were forced to close down their printing society. It is wise to remember, however, that the 1884 break was also the consequence of a spiritual evolution away from the Orthodox faith that had commenced long before 1884. By 1878 some Pashkovites already considered their gatherings to be church services.[60]

The concept of "undenominational Christianity" or "Biblical Christianity" attributed to Radstock by Western scholars and biographers should be re-evaluated and nuanced. Since Radstock was part of the evangelical party of the Church of England, his theological convic-

57. Leskov, *Schism*, 106–8.

58. Muckle, "Afterword," 117.

59. McCarthy, "Religious Conflict," 57.

60. Ibid., 131. It appears a bit strange that McCarthy does not explicitly challenge the undenominational nature of Radstock's theology, having meticulously described the Orthodox critique.

tions can be located within the theological boundaries and mentality of nineteenth-century England. Due to the fact that Radstock was not interested in theologizing or in entering into theological dialogue with others, his cluster of evangelical beliefs is best perceived in terms of an evangelical paradigm, using Küng's terminology, incommensurable with Orthodox Russia of the nineteenth century.[61] It was received as a theological and political threat to the Orthodox form of life and was resisted on Orthodox terms in all official discussions of Radstockism in Imperial Russia. Even the most sympathetic Orthodox writers such as Leskov looked down on the simplicity of Radstock's presentations, viewing him primarily as a catalytic agent for reform in Orthodoxy. Like many Orthodox intellectuals of the time, Leskov was well aware and highly critical of Radstock's reductionist theological convictions. He expresses his position explicitly: the reason why the aristocracy was fascinated by Radstock and his teaching was that there were no appropriate leaders in the Orthodox Church who could satisfy their religious hunger. So he says:

> So far they had not broken with the Church, but already certain tendencies were appearing—refusal to accept the teaching of the priests, but to "correct" them in a sectarian sense, adapting them to their taste. But again even here it was not a matter of changing doctrine, about which all these excellent people had the vaguest impressions, a fact which did them no good at all, of course. Not knowing the history of the Russian Church, on which until recently, when the work of Professor Peter Vasilievich Znamensky was published, no lively and well-written book was available, these people did not know who to blame and to whom to complain. Everything from start to finish boiled down to one point: the Russian Church was formalistic and lifeless, and they had "taken against it."[62]

Küng's notion of theological paradigms provides a better understanding of the reception of Radstock's message in an Orthodox country, since the concept of "denominations" is historically grounded in Protestantism. It is generally accepted that the phenomenon of denominationalism appeared in the eighteenth and nineteenth centuries

61. Cf. Carter, *Anglican Evangelicals*, 195–248.

62. Leskov, *Schism*, 100–101.

on the wave of the evangelical revival in the Anglo-American world.[63] The basic contention of the denominational theory of the church is that the true church is not to be identified in any exclusive sense with any one particular ecclesiastical institution.[64] But this late Protestant notion conflicted with Orthodox ecclesiology and theology, taking into account the Constantinian connection of the latter with the state.

The incommensurability of the paradigms represented by people such as Radstock on the one hand and Konstantin Pobedonostsev, the Ober-procurator of the Synod, on the other, was mutually sensed to the extent that both parties were universalizing historically contingent forms of life, theologies, and practices. Küng's theory of paradigms provides a wider explanatory framework for understanding the political nature of the clash between Radstockism and Orthodoxy in nineteenth-century Russia. The denominational theory of Protestantism, appropriated by Western historiographers, tends to view the liberal polity of Western civilization in rather neutral terms. However, Radstock's attitude had both theological and political ramifications, as will be seen in the chapter on Pashkov. On the one hand, the rejection of theology and critical thinking discussed below led Radstock to universalize his theological convictions, denying their rootedness in a historically-shaped milieu with a host of inbuilt theological and philosophical presuppositions. On the other hand, he realized that Orthodox officials not only possessed theological authority but were also undergirded by state power that used Orthodoxy as the glue for holding together the tottering Russian Empire. This understanding resulted in a non-dialogical attitude toward Russian priests and scholars. In a similar way, Orthodox theologians perceived Byzantine Christianity and its respective form of life in absolute terms. In so doing, they viewed Radstock as a bearer of the hostile Western civilization and distinctively Protestant theology that threatened the foundations of the Orthodox form of life. The growth of political instability coming from the radical left compelled the Orthodox to protect their self-identity, which included not only a theological component but also national and political components, inseparably interconnected with each other since the time of Constantine, Prince Vladimir, and Peter the Great.[65] The "biblical Christianity" of Radstock contained in itself

63. Hudson, *American Protestantism*, 34.

64. Ibid.

65. Cf. Zernov, *Russians and Their Church*, 131.

the seed of a new Russian identity as a European post-Reformed nation.[66] Even though he would not publicly admit that he considered the Orthodox Church to be "dead" and the Russian nation to be heathen, his attitude is revealed in the following statement: "We have only five little loaves of bread and two fish with which to feed the crowd: 80 million Russians surround us, but in our weakness we turn our gaze to Him who can do miracles."[67] This vision was not shared by Orthodox officialdom, according to whom Russian Orthodoxy played a highly important role, not only in spiritual matters but also in creating Russian identity and gluing Russian society together. Breyfogle writes: "Given the strong bonds between civil and religious authority in Imperial Russia, breaking from Orthodoxy was necessarily a political act as well. As Anatole Leroy-Beaulieu, French observer of Russia during the late nineteenth century, accurately noted: 'In the eyes of the government as well as of the people, the quality of the Orthodox Christians is (even now) the surest pledge of patriotism and loyalty.' In addition, the sectarians challenged the political and social foundations of the tsarist system to their very core."[68]

In this light, the Radstockist evolution of breaking with the Orthodox Church began not in 1878, but at the very moment the first Russian aristocrats accepted Radstock's message, biblical theology, and interpretive practices. It was only a matter of time, taking into account the sentimental and non-intellectual nature of Radstock's Christianity, which devalued the key tenets of Orthodoxy. As we shall see, Radstock's message was framed in a clearly evangelical hermeneutical mode, with a revivalist emphasis on the personal and affective conversion experience and a subsequent life of complete devotion to Christ in light of his imminent advent.

Thus the "non-denominational" and "sectarian" perspectives on Radstock represent two extremes that the present research attempts to

66. Bushkovitch, "What Is Russia," 154–61. See Coleman, "Most Dangerous Sect." Coleman makes explicit the political vision of the Baptist movement that had already found its new European identity. Even though Radstock and other early evangelical Christians of Russia rejected the rigid ecclesiology of the Baptists, they were united in their struggle for a post-Constantinian Russian identity. See the discussion under Pashkov. See also Geraci and Khodarkovsky, *On Religion and Empire*, 38–69, and Clowes et al., *Between Tsar and People*.

67. *Grazhdanin*, 16 (1876) 428.

68. Breyfogle, *Heretics and Colonizers*, 20.

avoid. On the one hand, Radstock cannot be simply identified with any sectarian group outside of the Church of England. On the other hand, his ecumenism and theology were shaped by the milieu of the British evangelical culture and would not transcend the boundaries of Protestant convictions. Heier commits a fallacy by projecting the broader ecumenism of the later Radstock onto the period of his visits to Russia in the 1870s.[69] Taking into account the dynamic nature of Radstock's personal and spiritual development, it is suggested that Radstock is best viewed as a Victorian evangelical who moved along an ecumenical trajectory.

LORD RADSTOCK'S THEOLOGY

An understanding of Radstock's theological positions is important, not only because he initiated the evangelical tradition in St. Petersburg, but also because his views continued to influence the evangelical Christians of Russia for many years after his departure from Russia. Madame Chertkova, a member of the St. Petersburg evangelical group, writes: "I am so sorry that all of us are so incapable of putting into words our devotion and gratitude to Lord Radstock, and of witnessing to the beautiful work the Lord honored him with for Russia! . . . Our intercourse with him lasted over thirty years and never varied in love and wise council."[70]

Theological Tendencies of the Time

Mark Noll provides another helpful description of the transformations that characterized the Protestant Paradigm to which Lord Radstock belonged.[71] During the three centuries after the Reformation there were transformations (1) from Christian faith defined as correct doctrine towards Christian faith defined as correct living; (2) from godly order as the heart of the church's concern towards godly fellowship as a principal goal; (3) from authoritative interpretation of scripture originating with ecclesiastical elites towards lay and more democratic appropriation of the Bible; (4) from obedience towards expression; (5) from music as

69. Heier, *Religious Schism*, 29.

70. Trotter, *Lord Radstock*, 63.

71. I am referring to the Post-Reformation Paradigm of Küng, *Christianity*, 614–34.

performed by well-trained specialists towards music as a shared expression of ordinary people; and (6) from preaching as learned discourses about God towards preaching as impassioned appeals for "closing with Christ."[72] The tradition that was brought to Russia in 1873–1874 was a result of these transformative processes that had been boiling for about three centuries in post-Reformation Europe.

Lord Radstock was neither a theologian nor an intellectual, nor did he want to be involved in any systematic or even written mode of theologizing of the sort that was typical of the evangelicals of the Reformation. Radstock breathed the air of Puritan-Pietist Christianity. His "religion of the heart" can be properly understood against the background of the Pietistic tradition and Romanticism, whose rationality came as a reaction against the dry rationalism of the Enlightenment and the scholastic dogmatism of the Reformed theologies.[73]

Radstock and His Theological Peers

John Kent locates Radstock in the Anglo-American revivalist tradition, alongside such people as Richard Weaver, Reginald Radcliffe, and Richard Morgan. "All these men were committed to an aggressive evangelical way of life before the Ulster Revival in 1859. American influence mattered more than Irish, for the publication of Finney's *Lectures* in England, and James Caughey's long visit in the 1840s, helped to stimulate the group's development."[74]

Reginald Radcliffe visited Russia in 1884 with the purpose of establishing a Russian branch of the Evangelical Alliance. Pashkov's correspondence contains several handwritten notes on Radcliffe's addresses.[75] Radstock also shared much in common with his American revivalist peer D. L. Moody.[76] Many similarities can be found in the respective theological stances of these two revivalist preachers. Radstock participated in at least one revivalist meeting conducted by Moody in Britain. His answers to Moody's questions, asked for the benefit of the audience,

72. Noll, *Rise of Evangelicalism*, 52.

73. Campbell, *Religion of the Heart*.

74. Kent, *Holding the Fort*, 101.

75. PP 2/2/13. See also Pavlov, "Extract from the diary," quoted in Corrado, *Filosofia*, 111.

76. Findlay, *Dwight L. Moody*, 227–61.

are published in one of Moody's books.[77] Radstock brought to Russia not only Protestant theology and forms of worship but also the evangelical sentimental hymns and music of I. D. Sankey, Moody's revivalist companion.[78] With regard to theological convictions, Radstock also shared many commonalities with George Müller, the leader of the Open Brethren, who enjoyed international fame in the evangelical circles of the time. It is said that during his first visit to England D. L. Moody wanted to meet two people: Charles Spurgeon and George Müller.[79] Müller in turn was visiting the places where Moody had preached, serving as an Apollos to the new converts of the revival.[80] Spurgeon invited Müller to preach in the Tabernacle Hall the same year. The arrival of Müller in St. Petersburg in 1883 was in line with his strategy of visiting places where revival had recently taken place.

These four revivalists—Lord Radstock and Charles Spurgeon (British evangelicals), George Müller (a German Pietist and member of the British Brethren), and D. L. Moody (an American revivalist)—were the pillars on which the tradition of the Gospel Christians was established through the ministry of Radstock.[81]

Sources for Analyzing Radstock's Theology

There are a number of printed resources containing Radstock's addresses, making possible a reconstruction of his theological views and interpretational practices.[82] Mark McCarthy has recently provided a

77. Moody, "Sovereign Grace," dialogue III.

78. McCarthy, "Religious Conflict," 71; Leskov, *Schism*, 109.

79. Moody, *Life of Dwight L. Moody*, 119.

80. Pierson, *George Müller of Bristol*, 248–49.

81. All of these four influential evangelical figures of the nineteenth century can be located under the rubric of evangelicalism. Besides holding to the same evangelical convictions, all four of them were involved in the Keswick movement. Lord Radstock and Spurgeon were preaching from the same pulpit during evangelistic meetings (PP II/1/b/8) and attended the same Keswick meetings (McCarthy, "Religious Conflict and Social Order," 271). Spurgeon's sermons were translated into Russian, and the early Radstockists were accused by the Orthodox of having been converted to "the faith of Spurgeon" (PP 2/2/405). George Müller personally visited St. Petersburg in 1882 and theologically influenced the St. Petersburg Christians. See Korff, *Am Zarenhof*, 37–38.

82. Radstock, *Notes of Addresses*. Radstock and Moody, *Gospel Dialogue between Mr. D. L. Moody and Lord Radstock*; Radstock, *Christian, Who and What is He*; Radstock, *Separated unto God and a Living Sacrifice*. Leskov included two sermons of Radstock

good description of Radstock's theology. However, because McCarthy's study has a historical focus, he describes Radstock's theological views without locating him on the theological map of evangelical developments in the nineteenth century or investigating his specific interpretive approaches.[83] As was said earlier, McCarthy was significantly influenced by Heier's assumption of the non-denominational nature of Radstock's theology. Hans Küng's paradigmatic approach is more suitable for understanding the theological trajectory of the evangelical movement in Russia, as it provides an explanation for the clash of the paradigms.[84]

The Three Frameworks of Radstock's Theology

Radstock's theological views can be located within three frameworks that appeared chronologically.[85] The oldest and broadest framework can be described as "Puritan-Pietistic," because the main theological themes of his addresses grew out of these two Protestant movements that influenced each other. The label "Puritan-Pietistic" is used here to denote the following features that grew out of the Continental and British Protestant paradigm of the preceding centuries: Biblicism, Christocentrism, salvation by grace through faith alone, an accent on personal religious experience and sincere moral conduct, active faith, and simple church services.[86] The next framework that appeared and grew out of the Pietistic-Puritan

delivered in Russia in 1874. See Leskov, *Schism*, 75–88.

83. McCarthy, "Religious Conflict," 62–76.

84. Küng does not mention in his thorough study the evangelical revival in Russia but focuses primarily on Russian Orthodoxy.

85. Noll, *Rise of Evangelicalism*, 50–65. The frameworks are derived rather arbitrarily from Noll's discussion of the antecedents of evangelicalism which he identifies as: Puritan, Continental Pietist, and High-Church Spirituality. Noll points out that the crucial spiritual emphasis of the High-Church was its stress on "primitive Christianity" (66). However, it seems more logical to consider "Primitivism" as a separate framework characteristic of the Victorian era, as suggested by Horton Davies (n. 87 below). Noll also states that the second legacy of the High-Church was establishing religious societies promoting personal piety and doing good among the people as a whole (67). This legacy was part of Radstock's ministry in Russia, because within one year after his first visit to Russia in 1873 his followers started the Society for the Encouragement of Spiritual and Moral Reading (SESMR) that was patterned after the British SPCK. The first book published by SESMR was John Bunyan's *Pilgrim's Progress*. Bunyan was an influential Puritan writer of the seventeenth century.

86. Enger, "Pietism," 539–41.

tradition in Britain in the nineteenth century can be called Primitivism, which was characterized by its charismatic nature, its revivalism in light of the impending return of Christ, its evangelical ecumenism, and its sacramentalism.[87] And finally, the most recent framework that played a prominent role in Radstock's interpretation of Biblical texts was that of Perfectionism, which grew out of the Wesleyan movement and the Anglo-American revivalist tradition.[88]

The Puritan-Pietistic Framework[89]

Heier argues that from the point of view of religious practice, Lord Radstock's religious activity could be linked with Wesley and his successors in early Methodism: "What he offered was a spiritual faith in opposition to the worldliness of the Established Church. His greatest desire was the reading and interpretation of the Gospel through which an intensification of faith was to be achieved and, as a consequence, salvation."[90]

Radstock's connection with Methodism should be limited to its broad pietistic component and to Wesleyan teaching on assurance of salvation. James Muckle is correct in saying that Radstock lacked the sophisticated theology of Wesley, which accommodated reason and tradition alongside experience and scripture as sources for Christian theologizing.[91] Radstock was more similar to Primitivist Methodists than to Wesley.[92]

Self-taught denominational Russian historian V. A. Popov suggests that the backdrop for the evangelical revival was German Pietism through the medium of the Evangelical Alliance.[93] Even though the im-

87. Davies, *Worship and Theology in England*, 139–43. Davies includes the following movements under the label of Primitivism: the Primitive Methodists (1812), the Plymouth Brethren (1827–1830), the Catholic Apostolic Church (1835), the Disciples of Christ (founded in 1833 and established in Britain in 1843), and the Salvation Army (1865–1879).

88. Warfield, *Perfectionism*.

89. This framework can be viewed as a meso-paradigm within the Protestant paradigm (Paradigm 4 of Küng). Küng, *Christianity*, 614–44.

90. Heier, *Religious Schism*, 32–33.

91. Muckle, "Afterword," 113.

92. Kent, *Holding the Fort*, 38–70.

93. Popov, "Evangel'skie Khristiane-Pashkovtsy."

pact of German Pietism on British evangelicalism through the medium of the Evangelical Alliance is not substantiated by evidence in his study, Popov's intuition is correct in principle.[94] Mark Noll has recently pointed out the mutual influence that existed between English Puritanism and German Pietism.[95] The compatibility of the two traditions can be observed in the biography of George Müller of Bristol, one of the most influential theological teachers of the Open Brethren, who visited St. Petersburg in 1882–1883 after Radstock's departure. Müller had been a student in Halle, the center of German Pietism, and his original impetus to start an orphanage in Bristol came from the example of the father of German Pietism, August Franke.[96] It seems to have been no problem for young Müller to integrate his Pietistic Lutheran heritage with the newly developing Brethren movement, inspired by Müller's brother-in-law Anthony Groves from within the Anglican Church, years before the Evangelical Alliance came into existence.[97] Radstock can safely be located within this broad Puritan-Pietistic frame of theological reference.

Biblicism

Radstock believed in the verbal inspiration of scripture, as did all evangelicals of his time. "Faith in the Bible was to the early evangelicals as fundamental as faith in God, and they made little distinction between the two."[98] Radstock states: "While many are doubting the Inspiration of Holy Scripture, multitudes in many lands have, for eighteen hundred years, found by experience that in proportion as they are obedient to the Divine Revelation, not one jot or tittle has failed of the promises of God to those who believe His Word. . . . His teachings present the most perfect ideals known to the human race, and His Spirit is the one power by which corrupt humanity can be regenerated and changed into the Divine Image from glory to glory."[99] Radstock was a person of the Book.

94. The first meeting of the Evangelical Alliance was held in London in 1846. See Fuller, *People of the Mandate*, 1–40.

95. Noll, *Rise of Evangelicalism*, 53.

96. Pierson, *George Müller of Bristol*, 15–62.

97. Müller, *Autobiography of George Müller*, 20–33. See also Dann, *Father of Faith Missions*.

98. Glover, *Evangelical Nonconformists and Higher Criticism*, 16.

99. Trotter, *Lord Radstock*, 149.

Leskov writes that following his conversion, Radstock severed all connections with "worldly" culture: "He renounced music on the grounds that 'he heard better sounds from heaven,' and he ceased to read all the worldly books since 'a man's life was insufficient even for the study of the Bible.'"[100]

Christocentrism

The resurrected Christ and a personal, affective relationship with Him is the major theme of all of Radstock's addresses. The following testimonies of Radstock's contemporaries can best be understood within this frame of reference. Baron von Hügel points out that "it was the Synoptic Jesus, His teachings, especially the Sermon on the Mount, which had saturated all the fibres of his mind and character."[101] It will be demonstrated below that Radstock interpreted all of reality from a Christocentric perspective.

Salvation by Grace through Faith

With regard to soteriology Radstock believed salvation to be free, present, eternal, and unconditional. This was his main message during the revivalist meetings.[102] Interpreting the Epistle to the Romans in the spirit of Luther with regard to free and unconditional salvation in Christ by grace and assurance of salvation in the present and the future, Radstock never developed or crystallized the doctrine. He called his audience to take their position in Christ by faith and start a life of personal relationship with God in Christ.

As was true of D. L. Moody, Radstock leaned towards the Arminian pole as far as the issue of predestination was concerned.[103] His theological position in this regard can be seen in the interplay of questions asked by Moody during one of his evangelistic meetings.

> Mr. Moody—**Is salvation within the reach of every man here tonight?**

100. Leskov, *Schism*, 18.
101. Trotter, *Lord Radstock*, 56.
102. Ibid., 232–33. McCarthy, "Religious Conflict and Social Order," 55.
103. Findlay, *Moody*, 242.

> Mr. Radstock—Jesus said, "God so loved the world that He gave his only begotten Son, that *whosoever* believeth in Him should not perish, but have everlasting life."
>
> Mr. M.—**What would you say to anyone who thinks he has no power to believe?**
>
> Mr. R.—He *has* the power to believe. Probably he is trying to believe something about himself, to feel something about himself instead of giving credit to God. He is not asked to realize this or that about himself, but to believe the faithful God.[104]

The Calvinist John Nelson Darby is said to have been "puzzled over how Moody could on the one hand accept the prophetic truths concerning God's sovereignty in history, and yet inconsistently allow room for a non-Calvinist view of human ability when it came to personal salvation."[105]

Radstock's evangelical view concerning salvation can be summarized as follows: the transcendent God loves his fallen creation. The themes of God's love and the fallen condition of individuals are dominant in Radstock's addresses.[106] Every human being can be saved by God's grace. In order to be saved a person needs to exercise his or her faith by believing the testimony of the scriptures about salvation in Jesus Christ. Everyone who believes this testimony is given the new nature (the new birth) by the gift of the Spirit, which makes possible both fellowship with God and a proper understanding of scripture. Without personal faith and regeneration a person cannot understand scripture, nor can they have fellowship with God. This regeneration constitutes a change in the existential orientation through which a person comes in contact with the ultimate personal reality of God manifested in Jesus and mediated by the Spirit. A mere intellectual assent to biblical truths must not be equated with regeneration.[107] True regeneration should have personal and experiential dimensions, accompanied by the receiving of God's power to overcome sin. Answered prayers and godly living are preferred over systematized theologizing. Regenerated people *know* that they are saved by taking God at his word. Unregenerated people are not

104. Moody, *Sovereign Grace*, 125.

105. Marsden, *Fundamentalism and American Culture*, 46.

106. Leskov, *Schism*, 18, 24.

107. Radstock, *Notes of Addresses*, 27.

sure about their salvation. God will not allow a saved person to be lost. If people sin after their conversion, they can be forgiven by Christ, who leads believers to Christian maturity and deliverance from the power of sin.[108] Regenerated people can be absolutely sure about their eternal security in Christ. "Before we are asked to go into service we are put on the platform of eternal salvation; and then we are told to press forward, and stretch forth a hand to those who are perishing in the waters, battling with the waves, but ineffectually, because they have not got their feet upon the Rock Jesus Christ."[109]

This middle way between Arminianism and Calvinism was never systematically thought through by Radstock, which was typical of the evangelicals of his time. Chadwick describes the evangelicals of that period in general as follows: "They were men of the Reformation, who preached the cross, the depravity of man, and justification by faith alone. Some of them were Calvinists and more of them were not. Most of them had little use or time for doctrines of predestination and reprobation."[110] The most important thing was the emotional plea to accept the New Testament's testimony about God's love in Christ and to live in the light of it.

Personal Religious Experience

The religious experience of regeneration was a central motif of Radstock's preaching. Sinners must appropriate by faith the unmerited salvation available in Christ. Human faith is the channel through which the Spirit of God gives new birth. "Are you forgiven? Are you born again?"[111] "You are in Christ, or you are not. You have received the Holy Ghost, or you have not."[112] "To be a Christian is not merely to think about Christ; it means to be in union with Christ."[113]

Writing about the theology of the German Pietist Philip Jacob Spener, Enger Trond states: "At the centre of Spener's theology was the experience of rebirth, the creation of the new person. This was the pas-

108. Moody, *Sovereign Grace*, 122–27.

109. Radstock, *Notes of Addresses*, 47.

110. Chadwick, *Victorian Church*, 440–41.

111. Radstock, *Notes of Addresses*, 17.

112. Ibid., 121.

113. Ibid., 45.

sion that united all Pietists. This was the experience that could empower faith. In the concept of rebirth we find the Pietists' main concern: it expresses humanity's absolute passivity in salvation, just as in natural birth; it expresses the total change, the new status as God's child; it focuses on the necessity of development and growth. With this re-born person a new reality has entered the world."[114]

Sharing the Pietistic assumptions that were amplified in the context of Romanticism, Radstock's Christianity had an experiential nature. He was not so much concerned about intellectual evidence, but would often say that answered prayers were his evidence.[115] The sentimental nature of Radstock's spirituality was well described by Leskov: "His ideas are shaky, but his spirit is splendid and by his success he excellently typifies the words of Taine, that 'people understand not ideas, but feelings.' 'In studying the feeling of Radstock, I myself sense that the man is in love with Christ,' one person who knows him well said to me, and this must be true. Radstock is in love, and this feeling is almost irresistible."[116]

In the same vein Trotter states: "He did not see the extension of divine claims to the whole of being and to a great extent refused the intellect its part in the redemption of man. In the intellect he still clung to the old traditions of Puritanism."[117]

Active Faith

In accordance with the Pietistic impetus of evangelicalism, Radstock was concerned with the practical application of his Christianity. McCarthy writes: "After Radstock's father's death in 1856, the rest of the family gradually turned from high society to the evangelical movement, donating the money to the religious outreach to the poor. Independently, Radstock's mother was very active in the slums of London where she entered brothels to rescue prostitutes and return them to 'a life of honorable work.' In London the Radstocks sponsored a home for recent immi-

114. Enger, "Pietism," 540.
115. Trotter, *Lord Radstock*, 103.
116. Leskov, *Schism*, 23.
117. Trotter, *Lord Radstock*, 100.

grants that could accommodate almost seven hundred people. In Paris they supported a home for girls."[118]

In this religious activity the works of charity were not separated from evangelism. In fact, evangelism was the first and foremost activity in which every Christian was expected to be involved. Leskov wrote that Radstock would often fill his pockets with copies of the New Testament and give them to passersby, even though he could not speak a word of Russian.[119]

Simplicity

In his description of a Radstockist meeting, Leskov does not mention the use of musical instruments. Biblical messages were the center of these religious meetings. The songs of I. D. Sankey were sung in English. As with the theology and preaching of Radstock, the songs were also emotion-oriented and sentimental.[120] His prayers were extemporaneous, which was very unusual for people of an Orthodox background. The space of the hall was "sacramentalized" by signs with biblical texts such as John 3:16, Luke 12:32, and Colossians 3:23 that were hung on the walls and which mistakenly were taken by some in the audience as "no smoking" signs!

The Primitivist Framework

In a sense the Primitivist framework grew out of Puritanism, with its call to return to the simplicity of the Apostolic era, its conversionalism, and its promotion of meditation on the work of the Holy Spirit.

The Charismatic Dimension

The ministry of Radstock was typically charismatic. From the outset of his meetings, Radstock assumed the role of a pneumatic preacher who was being led by the Spirit to reveal the true meaning of the scriptures. The stir of interest among the St. Petersburg aristocracy can partly be attributed to this charismatic stance.

118. McCarthy, "Religious Conflict," 51–52.

119. Leskov, *Schism*, 38.

120. McCarthy, "Religious Conflict," 71.

Mysticism. Trotter defines the word mysticism in terms of ". . . the inner meaning of the words of Scripture, the facts of history, the world of Nature. The mystic learns to discern between the world of sense, the shadow world, and the Reality that lies beyond, among the things 'which are not seen' where God is all and in all. . . . Hence to him the distinction of time, country, race and organization are subordinate to or absorbed in the all-embracing truth of the divine unity of the Spirit. . . ."[121]

This definition of mysticism in Platonic terminology is revealing, both for Radstock and for Trotter, his major biographer. Radstock was indeed interested in seeing and experiencing the transcendent reality of the resurrected Christ. However, his subjective mystical vision of certain aspects of this reality was ultimately reductionistic, because from the outset his framework for viewing the mystical reality of the resurrected Christ was limited by a Protestant theology that excluded and suppressed other forms of Christian spirituality. His preoccupation with the pneumatic Christ of faith and with mystical union with him, as well as his radical disinterest in the Christ of history and the ecclesial tradition, resembled in this regard more the spirituality of Docetism that had grown out of Platonic rationality than it did Chalcedonian Christology.[122]

Radstock is depicted as a typical evangelical mystic who waited on the guidance of the Holy Spirit in daily circumstances. Trotter provides many examples of this.[123] In one anecdote, Trotter tells how once in St. Petersburg, when Radstock was finishing a meeting with a certain person, he found himself constrained to stay on, even though his conversation was at an end. After about eleven minutes he felt he needed to leave at once.[124] Having gone out into the street, Radstock met a gentleman whom he would have missed had he gone out ten seconds earlier or later. Radstock's meeting with that gentleman had important ramifications for this new convert. Kent describes Radstock in the following terms: "He was a great renouncer: he associated the conversion of his sisters with giving up shooting, for instance. He solved the problem of his right to preach without ordination by asking God to give him three instances of

121. Trotter, *Lord Radstock*, 83–85.

122. Cf. Schreiter, *Constructing Local Theologies*, 21.

123. Trotter, *Lord Radstock*, 202–7.

124. Ibid., 206.

the value of his doing so within twenty-four hours; he received them in the form of unsolicited letters, and went on preaching."[125]

The Role of the Spirit in Understanding Texts. The mystical experience of the transcendent Christ in the present was much more important for Radstock than were historical questions about Christ. Radstock believed that biblical texts could be understood properly only when a person received illumination from the Holy Spirit. Thus, talking to a person who had reservations about biblical trustworthiness, Radstock stated: "I am not going to explain them [difficulties in the Bible]; for you cannot understand them; they can only be understood by a supernatural power; till you get that supernatural power, you will not understand. . . . Suppose you were an ignorant man, and had never seen a telescope; I say to you, Do you see that star? That star is a cluster of stars. No, you say, I have looked all my life, and my sight is clear, and it is one star, and you tell me wrong for my eyesight is right. I will not look through the telescope."[126]

Access to supernatural power (the telescope of the metaphor) comes by means of individual and personal prayer to God through Jesus.[127] Only after the Spirit is received can a person understand the meaning of the Bible. Without the Spirit the Bible is a dark text. Taking the Spirit as the starting point for understanding biblical texts, Radstock prefigured the Pentecostal way of theologizing.[128] Apologetics of this sort is consciously affective, personal, and fideistic. The text of the Bible is not understood by natural human reason or historical research. In order to overcome rationalist barriers to faith erected within the meta-narrative of modernist rationalist philosophies, one has to go beyond the boundaries of an impersonal and instrumental worldview by taking for granted the Christian meta-narrative, in which reality is perceived in personal terms, and establish a personal relationship with God by taking a leap of faith.

125. Kent, *Holding the Fort*, 126.

126. Radstock, *Notes of Addresses*, 113.

127. Ibid., 114.

128. See Dayton, *Theological Roots of Pentecostalism*, and Land, *Pentecostal Spirituality*.

The Ministry of Healing by Prayer. Lord Radstock's revivalist meetings were accompanied by many cases of physical healing.[129] He had taken up faith healing on the basis of the Epistle of James as early as 1873.[130] He believed in the operative healing power of the Spirit and the command to pray for the sick. He saw that sickness is connected in scripture with spiritual rather than physical causes.[131] Trotter writes: "Through a long life Lord Radstock remained steadfast to that Voice of God which he had heard, and when in 1905 a new witness from the Antipodes, in the person of Mr. J. M. Hickson, came to confirm the reality of Christ's healing power, and to declare that the gifts had never been withdrawn from the Church, he heard with gladness this new testimony and watched its development with great sympathy."[132]

One year before his first visit to Russia in 1873 Radstock witnessed a remarkable demonstration of the healing power of the Lord. His seven-year-old daughter was healed of curvature of the spine, which had produced great nervous irritation. The Radstocks asked a visiting American pastor to pray for their daughter. After a short prayer the girl jumped up and said, "Jesus has done it!"[133] Trotter, following the nature of the genre, tends to downplay the darker side of Radstock's faith healing. His daughter Mary, who was born in 1871, gives insight into it: "My father, being a faith-healer, no medicines were ever given to us on any occasion."[134] Writing of her experiences while in Russia in 1878, she continues: "Besides my illness . . . two at least of my sisters and brothers had diphtheric throats, while my mother had a bad miscarriage. No nurse and no doctor were called in. . . ."[135]

Revivalism

Revivalism was a characteristic phenomenon of the nineteenth century. The history and geography of revivalism suggest a phenomenon closely

129. Cf. Williams, "Healing and Evangelism," 271–85.
130. Kent, *Holding the Fort*, 148.
131. Trotter, *Lord Radstock*, 23.
132. Ibid., 24.
133. Ibid., *Radstock*, 167.
134. Bevan, "Odd Memories," 4.
135. Ibid.

linked to industrialization and modernization. Richard Carwardine notes the following characteristics of revivalism:

> Charismatic evangelists, mass audiences, Bible-based preaching, a gospel of repentance, the elevation of heart and experience over head and theology and the proliferation of dramatic, often physical, experiences of conversion, stress on born-again relationship with Jesus; the obligation to evangelize, faith in an inerrant Bible, strict personal discipline; social conservatism, and, very commonly, adventist, millennialist, and dispensationalist expectations founded on a conviction of God's personal intervention. On one reading revivalism has been a way of resisting modernity. Early Methodists sought in enthusiastic religion a warmth and social network, and an escape from uprootedness, market upheaval, and an emerging factory system.[136]

All the characteristics of revivalism as described by Carwardine can be found in the ministry of Lord Radstock. Even though Radstock was not a professional revivalist like Finney or Moody, "he was perfectly willing to associate with professional revivalists; he was present, naturally, at Smith's English Holiness meetings."[137] Kent notices that Radstock's connections with the Plymouth Brethren were typical for revivalists of that time:

> Like many of the lay revivalists of his time he had links with the Plymouth Brethren, whose hard core was mostly ex-Anglican, but whose ethos had developed in reaction against Anglican Tradition: the Brethren dispensed with the priesthood and cared nothing for the visible Church in the present dispensation. Anglicans, for whom the 'Church' had a personal rather than an institutional existence, found the ruthlessly negative attitude of the Brethren horrifying. In most ecclesiastical circles Brethren were feared as a solvent of loyalties as well as a source of strange doctrine; in the 1870s, however, the influence of the Brethren waned as their original creative leadership aged and was not replaced.[138]

Radstock was a revivalist in his own right. In the evangelical seaside and watering-place tradition, he had conducted personal missions

136. Carwardine, "Revivalism," 622.

137. Kent, *Holding the Fort*, 126.

138. Ibid., 126–27.

in Brighton, for example, in 1867, and in Scarborough in 1869.[139] Dr. Frederick Baedeker, who later had a long ministry in Russia, was converted during Radstock's revivalist meetings in Weston-Super-Mare in 1866.[140]

Radstock used the technique of multiple repetitions of main ideas which was common among revivalist preachers of the time. Leskov reports that during one of his short talks Radstock managed to ask nine times if a person "was with Christ or not."[141]

Adventism[142]

The dramatic events of the French Revolution in the 1790s had a special effect on the evangelical interpretation of scripture. Reading the Bible in the light of their immediate experience, the persecuted Protestants had developed an interpretive tradition that identified the Antichrist with the Papacy. However, the downfall of the Roman Catholic Church in France at the end of the eighteenth century opened up new horizons that reshaped the Protestant theological map of the nineteenth century. A seventeenth-century Cambridge Scholar, Joseph Mede, had suggested that "one day" in the book of Daniel (7:25) should be taken as meaning one year. According to Mede's interpretation, the fourth beast of Daniel 7, which was taken to signify the Papacy, should reign for 1260 years (time, times, and half a time = three and a half years = 1260 prophetic days = 1260 calendar years). The beginning of the Papacy was counted from the time when Belisarius entered Rome in 538, subjecting it to the Emperor Justinian's jurisdiction. In 1798, that is 1260 years later, Napoleonic armies entered Rome and banished Pope Pius IV.[143] Thus the French revolution opened a new vista in the interpretation of biblical prophecy in the light of contemporary historical events. The *parousia* was expected in the imminent future. The premillennial expectation shared by Radstock was based on the belief that Jesus would dramatically step

139. Ibid., 148.

140. Latimer, *Dr. Baedeker and his Apostolic Work in Russia*, 26.

141. Leskov, *Schism*, 77.

142. Sandeen, *Roots of Fundamentalism*, 47.

143. Stunt, *From Awakening to Secession*, 22; Carter, *Anglican Evangelicals*, 152–248; Binfield, "Jews in Evangelical Dissent," 225–70; Oliver, *Prophets and Millennialists*, 35–36.

into history and establish his millennial kingdom (Revelation 20). This premillennial expectation reflected a pessimistic and world-denying attitude. Adventist notes were often appropriated in Radstock's addresses: "Have you noticed that the Gospel is 'preached in all the world for a witness unto all nations?'"[144] There is no trace, however, of a developed system of Darbyan dispensationalism in his preaching.[145] According to the adventist teaching of John Nelson Darby, God had established several distinct historical time-frameworks, or dispensations, within which he reveals his particular purposes for a particular dispensation. With regard to the millennium, Darby believed that Christ would come the first time to take the church to heaven, meeting her in the air (1 Thess 4:13–17). The rapture of the church was believed to be followed by a period of tribulation (Matt 24:21), which would be ended by the visible return of Christ to the earth with the church, to establish the millennial Davidic Kingdom promised in the Old Testament. Radstock does not indicate that he believed in two comings of the Lord—the invisible (the rapture of the church) and the visible (establishing the millennial Kingdom)—as Darby taught.

The eschatological views of Radstock played a threefold role. First, as was the case with D. L. Moody, who quite possibly never became a thoroughgoing dispensationalist, the eschatological millenarian perspective in Radstock's preaching and teaching served the real purpose of his addresses, which was to bring his audience into contact with the transcendent and personal reality of the resurrected Christ. "It was a way of urging sinners to turn from their too exclusive concerns to contemplate more important matters of the spirit."[146] Second, taking into account the fine distinction made by James Patrick Callahan between "primitivist piety" and "restorationism," it can be argued that Radstock shared the primitivist pietistic position.[147] He consciously avoided the

144. Trotter, *Lord Radstock*, 248.

145. Carter, *Anglican Evangelicals*, 220–27.

146. Findlay, *Moody*, 253.

147. Callahan, *Primitivist Piety*. According to Callahan's thesis, the Brethren movement, in its origins, did not intend to restore the primitive Christian church with regard to spirituality or ecclesiology. Rather, having observed the pathetic condition of contemporary Christianity in Britain during the first half of the nineteenth century, the early Brethren started a non-denominational or better post-denominational movement that consisted of small gatherings of believers of different denominations who met for Bible reading and Christian fellowship. These gatherings were viewed as meetings of

restoration of primitive ecclesiological structures (and rituals such as baptism) which, according to the early Brethren view, had failed in other Western denominations. Thus, taking the position of "a mourner" with respect to historical Christianity, Radstock was not attempting to revive first-century Christianity, but was eagerly waiting for the glorious return of the Lord. This primitivist position of the Brethren may account for Radstock's unwillingness to establish any evangelical ecclesial structure in St. Petersburg, as well as his resistance to the discussion of any "denominational theologies." And finally, his premillennialist views may have played an important role in his handling of material possessions. Daisy Bevan is worth quoting again:

> Soon after this our house at Sheen of many happy memories was given up, also "the stripping" of our London House was nearly completed. My father's people, for two or three generations, had been collectors of furniture and pictures. . . . I believe some of it was really wonderful and all was good. But fiat went forth, and all was sold. . . . Books, of which there was also an excellent collection, had already gone away in "four wheeler" loads, in fact anything of value, including jewels, that my father had not forgotten the existence of, were turned ruthlessly into missionary donations.[148]

Two days before he died he wrote in a letter, "In common with many others, I believe the Lord's return is close at hand."[149]

Evangelical Ecumenism

Radstock was an active member of the World Evangelical Alliance, which had been established in London in 1846.[150] The unity represented by this alliance was born in the vortex of great social and religious uncertainties, the consequences of the French Revolution, the increasing influence of the humanistic philosophy of the Enlightenment, and the development of Marxist ideology. The first four decades of the nineteenth century had

true believers practicing biblical piety and awaiting the soon return of the Lord.

148. Bevan, "Odd Memories," 20.

149. Quoted in McCarthy, "Religious Conflict," 76.

150. See Wolffe, "Evangelical Alliance in the 1840s," 333–46; Kessler, *Study of the Evangelical Alliance in Great Britain*, 10–17; Rose, *History of the Ecumenical Movement*, 103; Fuller, *People of the Mandate*, 14–20.

also given rise to ecclesiastical movements that fragmented the religious map of the British Isles.[151] Out of the chaos of fragmentation, there grew a sense of the need to cooperate interdenominationally. The Alliance was formed as a confederation, with the purpose of promoting the Christian unity that already existed among "all who, loving the Lord Jesus Christ, are bound to love one another."[152] Even though evangelical unity was the proactive motif, the anti-Catholic and anti-Tractarian drives also played an important *reactive* role in the formation of this Protestant body. A preliminary meeting in Liverpool in 1845, which was intended to prepare the ground for a subsequent international meeting, was called "to associate and concentrate the strength of an enlightened Protestantism against the encroachments of Popery and Puseyism, and to promote the interests of scriptural Christianity."[153] The people who met in London agreed upon a doctrinal statement that defined basic evangelical views. Lord Radstock was a typical representative of this Protestant body.

One of Radstock's Russian followers gave the following testimony about him:

> All churches are equal to Radstock *in so far as they all similarly believe in salvation by faith* [italics mine–A. P.]. By invitation, and sometimes on his own initiative, he speaks to gatherings of all these denominations; but most of all he is in sympathy with the Plymouth Brethren, who have no ministers. He is not sympathetic to the Quakers, though sometimes he speaks in their meetings. In his view, the Quakers have "little spiritual life." He also has little sympathy for the Irvingites although he shares their view of the second coming of Christ, which he expects at any moment. He interprets the Apocalypse, as far as I can judge, by taking something from La Mother Guyon and something from Jung-Stilling, and adding something the source of which it is impossible to trace; doubtless it is home-grown.[154] If anyone tries to make him state his opinion on some teaching of whatever church, either he remains completely silent or, if the questioner is insistent, he will say briefly: "I cannot speak of that, it is not my affair, I can only explain the Word of God, using the text I find therein."[155]

151. Watts, *Dissenters*, vol. 2, 37.
152. Ewing, *Goodly Fellowship*. Quoted in Fuller, *People of the Mandate*, 18.
153. Wolffe, "Evangelical Alliance," 338.
154. Leskov, *Schism*, 51–52.
155. Ibid., 31.

However, this "non-denominational" attitude is limited only to the realm of the Protestant Paradigm, as we have mentioned earlier.

(The Lack of) Sacramentalism

Lord Radstock considered that outward confession of Christ corresponded to the baptism by water of the early Christians, by which they were separated forever from the world around them.[156] Radstock believed in two kinds of baptism: baptism in water and baptism in the Spirit. He defined them as baptism of the body and baptism of the soul respectively.[157] Baptism in water "is an acknowledgment of sinfulness and [of] a need of forgiveness." However, due to the fact that the ritual of water baptism had been practiced in all traditional Christian churches, Radstock appealed to Apostolic times and interpreted the meaning of baptism in the following way:

> Real baptism was when a soul acknowledged itself lost and ruined, and once for all gave itself right over to God, before the world, and was known by the world as belonging to Christ. You may have been baptized in whatever water ceremony you please; but what you need is that heart baptism into Christ, which will be followed by the sealing of the Holy Ghost. *Then* you know what conversion is.[158] This baptism is the baptism of the soul, which will be evidenced by an outward confession towards the world; it is the signing of the deed of partnership; the definite acceptance of the soul, from which time the whole inheritance of Christ becomes the portion of the poor sinner.[159]

The Slavic Baptist denominational writers attribute Radstock's lack of emphasis on the importance of water baptism to his association with the Plymouth Brethren. However, infant baptism was practiced in the Darbyite communities. The Müllerites (Open Brethren) were considered and called "Baptists" by the Closed Brethren, because Müller believed that the Bible taught that baptism should take place following the conversion experience, even though he did not impose his view on those who disagreed with him. Radstock's perspective cannot be attrib-

156. Trotter, *Lord Radstock*, 20; PP 2/1/b/8 a letter to Tikhonov dated 1884.

157. Radstock, *Notes of Addresses*, 58–60, 115.

158. Ibid., 59.

159. Ibid., 61.

uted to either Open or Closed Brethren views on the issue. His ambivalent attitude on the issue of baptism and other outward identity markers prolonged the process of separation of evangelical converts from the Orthodox Church. Leskov compares Radstock's view on baptism with that of some Russian sectarians such as the Molokans and Stundists, who also understood the ritual metaphorically.[160]

The Framework of Perfectionism

Being among those who initiated the Keswick meetings in the mid-1870s, prior to his longest visit to Russia in 1878, Radstock shared the perfectionist position of the early Keswick movement.[161] According to the teaching of Pearsall Smith, who brought this movement to Britain on the wave of D. L. Moody's revival and whose works had appeared in print in England seven years earlier, a believer can reach a state of perfection already in this life by an act of faith. Radstock seems to have shared this vision.[162]

According to this perfectionist view, there is a difference between knowing Christ as Savior and knowing him as Lord.[163] Radstock held the view that it is not enough to receive salvation by grace. That is only the first stage; the person who goes no further than this stage will be saved only as a log is from fire.[164] Christ needs to be experienced not only as Savior but also as Lord. The life of Christ mediated by the Spirit should take hold of believers to such a degree that they stop sinning and live lives of service in total dedication to the Lord.[165] Thus according to Radstock, there are three categories of Christians. First, there are nominal Christians—those who bear the name of Christ and give intellectual assent to Christian doctrines but do not possess saving faith. Such people

160. Leskov, *Schism*, 59–60.

161. Kent, *Holding the Fort*, 148; Pollock, *Keswick Story*, 34–35. It should be mentioned here that all the evangelicals who visited Russia between 1870 and 1880 were part of the perfectionist movement, which was spilling over from America to Britain and to Continental Europe. Besides Radstock and George Müller, Otto Stockmeyer and Dr. Baedeker were active propagandists of perfectionism. Baedeker served as the interpreter for the initiator of the perfectionist movement during his trip to Germany.

162. See Bebbington, *Evangelicalism in Modern Britain*, 151–80.

163. Radstock, *Notes of Addresses*, 8.

164. Ibid., 110.

165. Ibid., 9, 43.

are not to be considered real Christians. The second group of Christians consists of those people who have trusted the Lord for salvation but have not dedicated themselves completely to his service. Then, finally, the third group of Christians is comprised of those people who have come to know the Lord not only as their Savior, but also as the Lord of their lives, having thus broken the bonds and attractions of this world.[166]

The path from the second to the third stage goes through identifying with Christ by being united to Him: "He wants simply that you be united to Him; then you will not merely get the putting away of the sins you have committed; but the living God will put forth his power to keep, to save, to deliver. Not merely today; but to the end he will keep you, and will present you one day, as a proof of His grace and His love, faultless before the throne of God."[167]

The Orthodox Critique

In concluding this section on the theology of Radstock, I would like to provide a brief view of the Orthodox critical reception of his theology. I have chosen one of Radstock's most sympathetic critics, who attempted to produce a balanced analysis of his theology. According to Leskov's testimony, Radstock was acquainted with Russian Orthodox priests who lived in Great Britain.[168] However, Radstock neither understood nor wanted to understand Orthodox theology and liturgy. Being a strict Protestant of the Romantic era, he rejected outright the importance of Christian tradition. On his arrival in Russia, Radstock avoided any direct conversations with Orthodox theologians.[169] Prayers to the saints and the use of icons he considered to be unbiblical, and he rejected them outright. Leskov justly critiques this somewhat arrogant attitude. From the Orthodox point of view, Radstock is labeled a *textarian*, because "he has 'got stuck on' certain texts; but at least, unlike some lesser men, he takes his stand on texts of significance."[170] "It is reported that he said to

166. Ibid., 43, 88, 107.

167. Ibid., 63.

168. Leskov, *Schism*, 12–13.

169. Ibid., 53.

170. Ibid., 113.

Father Vasiliev, 'Apart from the Bible I know nothing, so I cannot enter into discussions of doctrine.'"[171]

However, the then-Orthodox Leskov could see the deviation of Radstock's theology and spirituality from that of the Orthodox Church. Leskov describes the points of this deviation by saying: "Firstly he has taught them some Protestant views about justification and some others which are simply muddled. Secondly, without actually saying so, he has conveyed the impression that the Eastern Church holds certain beliefs which are foreign to the spirit of true Christianity. He has taught them not to pray to the Virgin Mary and the saints, and he has flattered them that they are assuredly saved. . . . If they had come to love and to accept Christ, they should do good works and serve their lesser brethren."[172]

The key critique of Orthodox writers has to do with the reductionistic nature of Radstock's teaching. Radstock's disregard for Christian tradition was severely attacked: "In his splendid work Farrar quotes Basil the Great, Gregory of Nazianzus, John Chrysostom, Saint Bernard and others; but Radstock does not allow himself to succumb to this weakness. His formula is simpler: God saved the human race through Jesus Christ and now explains this to men through Radstock. For them to know any more about anyone or anything is superfluous."[173]

THEOLOGICAL HERMENEUTICS AND BIBLICAL INTERPRETATION

The clash between the Byzantine Paradigm and Pietistic Anglo-American Protestantism came first of all in the realm of biblical interpretation. Orthodox critics keenly noticed that "with some difficulty did ecstatic listeners to Radstock try to commit to memory some of the abundant number of texts quoted. . . . But as many of the texts could easily be juxtaposed with other texts from the same book, putting people who had mastered the letter but not the spirit of study into a very difficult position, these people did not know what to do with the overwhelming mass of contradictory texts."[174]

171. Ibid., 53.
172. Ibid., 64.
173. Ibid., 59.
174. Ibid., 105.

The method of biblical interpretation appropriated by Radstock was governed by the theological frameworks described above, as well as by the common method of typological interpretation that was prevalent in Victorian times. Even though Radstock would not admit that his reading was governed by any theological presuppositions, since he insisted that he was "just reading the Bible," these theological frameworks had been subconsciously formed by the culture to which Radstock belonged, as well as by his personal experiences. There was a dialectical process between reading texts and forming theological frameworks. It is impossible to say which was primary and which was secondary. However, the frameworks seem to have been forged by the theological and cultural convictions of the times. Being part of the Brethren movement for a number of years, Radstock believed that the Bible should not be interpreted, but rather simply read and obeyed. However, it can be seen from his addresses that depending on the audience and the aims of his presentation, Radstock would appropriate different theological frames to produce a relevant meaning that fitted his theological convictions. When he was addressing a group of evangelical Christians, his primitivist (e.g., evangelical ecumenism) and perfectionist frameworks would come to the foreground, whereas in his arguments against the modernist challenges to traditional Christian doctrines, a strictly literalist interpretation would be appropriated.

Callahan succinctly describes this primitivist reading of the Bible:

> The shift from post- to premillennialism was significant for evangelicals. It marked a turn toward a more thoroughly literal interpretation of prophecy and internal arguments over the interpretative methods employed. . . . By reading the Bible, not interpreting it, the Brethren thought themselves equipped to understand the belief and practices of the apostolic church. They appealed to their application of the Bible to the contemporary church in a direct manner; they claimed to read the Bible with a simple literalism; they argued that the Bible should be received and obeyed rather than interpreted; they advised others not to trust interpretative systems; and they rejected the allegorical reading of prophecy as a device of Satan to corrupt the Church . . . . The recourse to interpretation is a flight from obedience and can be credited to the program of Satan in order to distort the plain commands of the Bible, including its pre-millennialism.[175]

175. Callahan, *Piety*, 134, 150–51.

Radstock was not familiar with the methodology of critically interpreting the Bible. Leskov writes:

> He himself says that his whole education is in the Bible, but he can scarcely be considered a biblical expert though he has been studying it for many years. As regards those invaluable archaeological investigations and the philological and exegetic research which have recently enriched biblical knowledge, Radstock reveals no acquaintance with them at all. He even completely disregards learned biblical criticism more completely than the late Metropolitan of Kiev Filart Amfiteatrov, who, referring to Pavsky's *Survey of the Psalms,* waved his hand and said: "I don't want to know about that: David wrote them all!" And the good old elder went to his grave with the same attitude considering the hermeneutic and philological investigations of Gerasim Pavsky to be [the] height of audacity. Fortunately for him, his age was the age of silence, and audacity as typified by Pavsky's research troubled him very rarely, but now times have changed, and Radstock is not in a position where anything need prevent him from following biblical scholarship, but probably he holds to the rule that "a healthy mind needs no instruction."[176]

The Old Testament

Radstock would often preach on Old Testament passages, interpreting them in the light of Christ. If fact, he did not know any other way of interpreting the Old Testament. Christocentric typological interpretation was a cultural characteristic of Victorian times. George Landow writes:

> Nineteenth-century typologists were so successful that they produced a flowering of typological exegesis which had important influence on Victorian thought. . . . The notion that Christ is to be perceived as the central principle of human history always functioned as a hermeneutical principle as well, for the assumption that Christ is at the centre of all things encouraged the Bible reader to find Christ in the most unexpected places.[177]

176. Leskov, *Schism*, 39.

177. Landow, *Victorian Types*, 41. Landow gives the following definition of typology: "[It] is a Christian form of scriptural interpretation that claims to discover divinely intended anticipations of Christ and His dispensation in the laws, events, and people of the Old Testament" (3).

Thus interpreting Numbers 23, where Balaam could not curse Israel because of the promises God had given to Israel, Radstock notes that the nation of Israel behaved badly in the wilderness. His logic is as follows: God blessed Israel (the nation of Israel) because the promises were given to Israel (the ancient patriarch) in whom God had found no iniquity. Thus the future generation was "in Israel," to whom the promises had been given: "But even Israel himself needed to have a perfect mediator. This mediator is Jesus Christ. God blesses us in Christ. The Lord has given to Jesus Christ this promise, that they that receive Him shall become the sons of God, and it now depends on our believing this to be true, and receiving Christ by faith."[178]

In this example New Testament teaching on being in Christ is read into the Old Testament text, which is used as an illustration of God's dealings with Christians "in Christ."

Reading the story of Cain murdering Abel (Gen 4:8–11), Radstock takes Abel as a prototype of Christ and Cain as a prototype of his audience: "The blood of Jesus, your brother, cries from the ground to God. Your brother!—and you have murdered Him."[179] As in the example above, the New Testament narrative is read into the Old Testament story in order to produce an effect on the audience. People need to accept their guilty position before God by associating themselves with Cain. Other elements of the story in Genesis 4 are not taken into account. This technique allows Radstock to kill two birds with one stone: (1) to demonstrate the unity of the Bible, and (2) to conflate the horizon of the audience with the horizon of the transcendent Christ, of whom the Bible testifies. The members of the audience are drawn into the biblical story of salvation as extra-textual antitypes of biblical typology.

Psalm 50 is interpreted with a Christological-eschatological key. According to this reading, the Psalm tells the story of the second coming of Christ, who completes the salvation of believers.[180] The appeal is made to the new Israel, the new people of God, who are preoccupied with the ritualistic part of their religion but whose hearts are far from the Lord. The nominal Christian is taken as the antitype of the wicked in the Psalm: "What right have you to recite my laws or take my covenant on your lips? . . . When you see a thief, you join with him. . . . You

178. Trotter, *Radstock*, 221.

179. Radstock, *Notes of Addresses*, 75.

180. Ibid., 83.

speak continually against your brother and slander your mother's son." Radstock says that the thief is the devil and the brother is Christ. Jesus is again depicted as the elder brother who presents us faultless before God.[181] "These things hast thou done, and I kept silent" (Ps 50:21) is interpreted in light of the day of grace. God keeps silent because it is the day of salvation and grace. The nominal Christian is pronounced to be unsaved in light of the impending judgment, which "is only showing things in their true character."[182] "Jesus asks them to be saved, that they may have heart religion, heart binding to Him."[183] Radstock reads the punishment of verse 22 as eternal punishment, and the thank-offering is taken as acceptance of the gift of Christ.[184] The one who does not believe God's testimony about salvation in Christ is deceived by the devil and will be eternally punished if he does not repent.[185] There is no other way than to believe God's revelation in Christ and be united to him through the new covenant. The person who repents is called to high standards of holiness: "You cannot be married to Christ and live for the world."[186] The one who does not keep his or her purity is the adulterer of verse 18. The address ends with the rhetoric of condemnation: "If you never heard [the gospel of Christ] before, this testimony of God in the 50th Psalm is enough to condemn you to eternity. . . . He will come to punish with everlasting destruction from the presence of the Lord, those who obey not the gospel. You have to come to and own Christ as your Lord, whom God raised from the dead. If you do not you are lost, and condemnation may burst in a moment on your head."[187]

The text of the Old Testament is read through a preconceived theological grid. Details of the text that do not make any contribution are filtered out. Some details are read literally, others typologically. The literal and typological keys are used in accordance with the same Christocentric grid, with the purpose of helping the audience to view themselves in light of the biblical narrative and to produce a conversion experience.

181. Ibid., 86.

182. Ibid., 83.

183. Ibid., 88.

184. Ibid., 99.

185. Ibid., 97.

186. Ibid., 95.

187. Ibid., 101.

This kind of typological-literalist theological interpretation is used in all of Radstock's addresses.[188] Once speaking on Num 15:38, Radstock pointed out that "all the Children of Israel were to wear a ribbon of blue, the heavenly color, in order that they might look upon it and be holy, and that the outward recognition of God's calling was to be the cause and not the result of holiness."[189] In this case, the Pauline theology of divine calling and sanctification serves as the matrix of interpretation. The Old Testament text gives a visible illustration of the New Testament doctrine. The person who accepts Christ is a new Israelite who has taken his heavenly position in Christ by the divine calling. A righteous life should be the outcome of this new standing. The audience is immediately challenged to exercise faith in the divine reality in Christ.

The New Testament

New Testament passages are interpreted in a similar manner. Interpreting the portion of John 4 that recounts the conversation of Jesus with the Samaritan woman, Radstock focuses on the section where the woman starts to argue with Jesus concerning theological issues, and particularly regarding appropriate places of worship. The application he makes is immediate and challenging: "Many are speaking of intellectual difficulties, and inferentially blaming God for an imperfect revelation, while the great Searcher of hearts would show them that it is sin in their lives, as in the case of that poor woman, which has caused them to wander on the dark mountains, away from that Light."[190] Thus Radstock's answer to the intellectual doubts of his time is a fideistic appeal to the reality of Christ, mediated by the sacred text and available for anyone to experience through faith. The truth of the Bible, according to Radstock, is accessible at the level of personal faith, obedience, and experience, rather than at the level of rationalistic theologizing.

This reading of the Johannine text does not immediately proceed from its literary context. Instead, Radstock uses this passage, taken out of its original literary context, as an illustration relevant for the intellectual milieu of his time: theologizing, rationalistic sinners of the

188. Cf. Lennox, "Biblical Interpretation in the American Holiness Movement," 184–240.

189. Trotter, *Lord Radstock*, 157.

190. Ibid., 147–49.

Enlightenment are wandering about on dark mountains, while light is available to the one who trusts and it is close to them, just as Jesus was close to the woman. Radstock makes an immediate jump from the Christ of the text to the resurrected, transcendent Christ. The unconverted woman is taken as a prototype of the contemporary audience. The transcendent Christ is ready to reveal Himself experientially to the one who trusts in the testimony of scripture.

In his treatment of the twenty-second chapter of the book of Acts, Radstock follows the same theological approach to reading the biblical narrative. Describing the conversion of Saul, Radstock produces the following reading:

> After he had been walking in what he thought was light, but which was really the darkness of his own intelligence, his own reason, a great light shone round about him. . . . The very essence of the gospel is, that it is a light *from God*, it is a testimony *from God*, a revelation of things man does not understand by his *natural* intelligence. . . . He was a religious man of whom I am speaking, and I dare say you are all religious in your way; but I ask you, Is your light the light *from heaven?* Is it *your opinion* you are following, or is it the opinion of God? . . . Your opinions will not justify you at the tribunal of Jehovah.[191]

The conversion experience of Paul is reread in light of a pietistic understanding of conversion from nominal Christianity. Radstock makes the transposition, moving from the text to the reader and from the reader to the transcendent Christ of whom the text testifies. In so doing, he makes the Jewish horizons of the Saul of the text converge with the Christian horizons of his audience, for whom, in Radstock's understanding, Christianity had become a set of biblical doctrines. The light of Paul's vision is metaphorically read as the testimony of God, while the intellectualism of the nineteenth century is read into the circumstances of the first century. The members of the audience are imaginatively taken into the text, where they are associated with the religious Saul who does not know God. The roughness of the reading reveals a theological agenda being read into the text. The biblical text, "And the Lord said unto me, Arise, and go into Damascus, and there it shall be told thee of all things which you are appointed to do," is interpreted by Radstock in the following manner: "Here was a man under conviction,

191. Radstock, *Notes of Addresses*, 53–54.

but not yet forgiven. . . . [I]t is one thing to seek, and another to receive forgiveness; it is one thing to cry for salvation, and another thing to have salvation."[192] In order to explain to his audience how one receives forgiveness, Radstock has to transpose the words of Ananias concerning baptism into the "post-denominational" mode of the nineteenth century. Having argued that real baptism is the willingness of a person to be identified with Christ by means of testifying about him before a worldly generation, Radstock concludes: "Are you looked upon by the world as belonging to Christ? If you have not taken this standing before God, you are not in the sight of God baptized into Christ."[193] This baptism of the heart is followed by sealing with the Holy Spirit. Thus according to this reading, a person receives forgiveness and salvation when he or she accepts the testimony of the Gospel and determines to testify about it in the world, having received the Spirit, who "seals" this decision.

The theme of identification with Christ is prominent in the addresses of Radstock. The person who is united with Christ through faith and active testimony becomes part of the inheritance of Christ.[194] By exercising faith the person receives this inheritance, not only in the future but also in the present. Trotter gives a personal testimony concerning a time in her youth when she listened to a message of Radstock. She says: "The words were 'the exceeding greatness of His power to us-ward who believe, according to the working of His mighty power which He wrought in Christ when He raised Him from the dead,' and he added, 'not only the same power, *but the same measure of it.*' I cannot explain why these words opened up to me a vista which has never been closed, but so it was."[195]

For Radstock the resurrection life is not a future but a present experience of faith. The believer has only to submit herself in complete identification with the death of Christ. "We are not weak enough for God to energize us," says Radstock.[196]

The Old Testament is taken as a prototype against the background of the New Testament. And even New Testament passages are sometimes

192. Ibid., 56.

193. Ibid., 59.

194. Ibid., 61.

195. Trotter, *Lord Radstock*, 90.

196. Ibid., 91.

taken as prototypes for the contemporary situation, which is interpreted in the light of Christ.

Radstock's Attitude towards Difficult Texts

Having looked at accounts of Radstock's interpretation of various texts in the Old Testament, the Gospels, and the Epistles, it would also be worthwhile to consider his attitude towards "difficult texts." When one of his friends expressed doubt about the doctrine of the perpetual virginity of Mary, Radstock did not give any theological explanation, as he himself seemed to have been struggling with the question. Instead, he said: "Let us put Christ Himself first and questions about Him will find their right place. The Spirit is given to lead us into all truth, and truth apart from the Spirit is a dead thing."[197] What Radstock meant was that one should not allow intellectual doubts to undermine one's faith in the resurrected Christ. The Spirit is actively operating in the life of a believer as long as he or she keeps standing in faith and personal fellowship with him through prayer. Apart from this present experience of the Spirit who unites the believer with Christ, historical questions *about* him belong to the realm of death. Radstock's pneumatic attitude is significantly different from the fundamentalist literalist approach.[198] Radstock is happy to build his house on the "faith bank" of the famous Lessing's ditch, taking no time to bother about the Christ of history.

An Illustration of Radstock's Hermeneutics at Work in a Sermon

Leskov provides a typical address Radstock delivered in St. Petersburg.[199] The body of the sermon is made up of an abundant collection of Biblical "proof-texts" interpreted through the grid of the theological frameworks discussed above.

The sermon starts with the story of the Fall (Gen 3:9–10). The searching God is the subject of Radstock's attention. The theme of a "searching God" provides a bridge to a New Testament passage, John 4:24, where it is stated that God is looking for true worshippers. Against the background of these two biblical texts, in which God is taking the

197. Ibid., 102.

198. Cf. Gray, "Inspiration of the Bible," 9–44.

199. Leskov, *Schism*, 75–88.

initiative to find lost persons, Radstock asks his audience a direct question: "Where art thou? No matter that you were baptized in a Christian Church, where art thou?" The existential horizon of the audience is immediately brought forward in anticipation of conflating it with the horizon of the searching God, as revealed in the biblical story from Adam to Christ, while ignoring the horizon of Christian tradition from Christ to the present day. The remaining part of the sermon consists of insertions of various biblical passages, interpreted from an eschatological perspective, according to that mode of Protestant theology which attempts to fit the personal horizons of the audience into the Gospel story. Thus Radstock appropriates the parable about the eschatological feast during which a person who was not wearing a wedding garment was expelled by the king (Matt 22:11–14). "Do you know Christ, my Brethren, do you know him?" (Matt 7:23). The theme of the new birth appears (John 1:12–13). "But I know that many of you do not seek him. Good works, attending public worships: you are sewing aprons out of fig-leaves. . . . The bridegroom is coming. How will you appear in your rags?" The audience is being imaginatively drawn into the biblical story world, sown of texts of different genres, and is made to be associated both with Adam and with the person lacking a wedding garment. The whole point of this imaginative immersion into the biblical story is to help the audience discover the personal transcendent reality of God, which is being testified to in the text and which is available to Radstock's audience, as well. The following series of biblical texts is used to emphasize that (1) humanity is sinful and lost without the mercy of God (Gen 6:5; 1 Kgs 8:46; Job 14:4; Ps 14:2–3; Eccl 7:20; Rom 5:12); (2) prayers and good works cannot wash away sin (Isa 1:15); (3) God has taken the initiative to save the lost sinner with all her religious rituals and structures (Isa 1:11, 18; 43:1, 5, 25); and (4) this saving activity of God is found in the person of Jesus (1 John 1:4; 4:14; 5:12).

Having saturated his audience with Biblical evidence, Radstock continues his sermon by tying together the previous themes:

> Do you, every one of you, consider Him your Saviour, your Advocate, your Redeemer? (Isa 42:3). Come all. "Behold the Lamb of God." Crucified Christ! Look at him. God-man. God the Father forsook him. The salvation is not by our works or merits but by Christ alone. If our salvation could be accomplished by our deeds Christ did not have to die. Simply hurry to his call,

> bow the knee to the One who so loved you, and say to Him, "My soul doth magnify the Lord and my spirit hath rejoiced in God my Saviour." And he will array you in a wedding garment, and the angels in Heaven shall rejoice for you, and your name shall be inscribed in the Book of Life, for the Son has saved you from judgment and the slavery of sin. Your prayers, outpourings straight from the heart, shall be pure praise and thanksgiving, and thus loving Christ you will also love your brothers and will work for His glory (John 3:3, 16). Only having become new creatures in Christ, being born again our deeds will be accepted by God.

The sermon concludes with appeals to believers and to unbelievers. The appeal to believers can be summarized by the following points:

(1) Witness concerning your Lord, being assured of your salvation. Do good works, being ready for the return of the Lord (Acts 1:8; Matt 5:13–16, 45; Luke 12:32, 40; 17:1; 21:15, 17).

(2) Are you hated by the world or are you in tune with it? Be ready to be mocked for the name of Christ (Luke 14:26–27).

(3) Be a doer of the word, and not a hearer only (Jas 1:25–27; 2:26).

(4) Keep yourself unspotted by the world (Jas 1:28, 4:4).

The appeal to unbelievers:

(1) We do not preach anything new.

(2) You say that you have your established religion, that you attend the customary forms of worship—what else do you need? But the Lord reads men's hearts. To whom have you given your heart—to Him or to the world?

(3) You may die soon. Where will you spend eternity?

(4) The door is open before you. Any may enter the mansion; but when the Host closes the door, you will stand on the threshold and knock in vain. The door is Christ. Accept him before the judgment day takes you unprepared (Luke 13:24). Do it now.

CONCLUSION

The evangelical tradition that was brought into Russia by Lord Radstock in 1873–1874 had a clearly British Protestant origin. His theology and his practice of biblical interpretation can be properly understood in light of theological and socio-political developments in the British Isles since the eighteenth century. Contrary to the tendency of Radstock's biographers to present him either in a non-denominational ecumenical light or in a strictly Darbyite vein during his stay in Russia, Radstock should be seen as an Anglican evangelical of the Victorian and Romantic eras influenced by the Brethren movement. His ecumenism would not go far beyond the Protestant constellation of beliefs and practices. His non-systematic theology is naturally located within the Puritan-Pietistic, Revivalist, and Perfectionist frameworks that were characteristic of the evangelical segment of nineteenth-century Britain. Instead of looking at Radstock through the grid of "neutral biblicism" and that of the Orthodox power reaction to "Bible Christianity," it is suggested that Radstock's mission in Imperial Russia should be considered as a clash between the Byzantine and Protestant paradigms. Each of these paradigms had its own theology, hermeneutics, ecclesial practices, and geopolitical charge.

The theological hermeneutics of Radstock was of a typological, Christocentric, literalist, pneumatic, and experiential nature typical of the hermeneutics of the emerging holiness movement. The premillennialist hermeneutical key and the literal interpretation of prophecy that had come to the forefront in the nineteenth century as a result of the French revolution had been wholeheartedly and subconsciously appropriated by Radstock. Biblical texts were read through the grid of preconceived theological frameworks in order to achieve two major goals: the conversion of nominal Christians, and the edification of born-again Christians. In the process of producing the desired meaning, Radstock would not be constrained by literary or historical contexts. Typological interpretation was used with both Old and New Testament texts. Biblical personages were used as types either of the contemporary audience or of the transcendent Christ. The historical dimension of the historical Christ is suppressed, while the spiritual dimension of the transcendent Christ of faith is exalted. This exaltation of the Christ of faith moved Radstock to a *practically* docetic or monophysite form of Christology, which in turn did not allow him to appreciate other forms of Christian spirituality or the work of the Spirit outside his theological framework. His conscious reluctance to engage in theological dialogue with representatives of other Christian traditions directed the evangelical trajectory away from the National Church.

In the next chapter, the convergence of the two paradigms, as seen on the pages of the *Russian Workman* (1875–1881), will be analyzed. This periodical was published by Russian Orthodox followers of Radstock and was patterned after the *British Workman*.

2

The *Russian Workman*: 1875–1881

INTRODUCTION

The present chapter contains a theological analysis of the *Russian Workman*, the most important periodical published by the Radstockist *Society for the Encouragement of Spiritual and Moral Reading* (SESMR), which was launched in 1874 as a clone of the British *Society for Promoting Christian Knowledge* (SPCK). The *Russian Workman* likewise was patterned after the *British Workman*, which was supported in Great Britain by the Keswick movement.[1] SESMR was not the first Christian organization in Russia inspired by Western institutions. The history of the British and Foreign Bible Society in Russia can be traced to the beginning of the nineteenth century. It had a checkered life and its activity was strictly controlled by the Orthodox Synod.[2] However, the scale of influence of SESMR in Russia was unprecedented.[3] Heier states: "The Society developed an enormous propaganda machine unparalleled in the Russian Empire at the time. Indeed, the activities of the Society in the field of religion were so extensive and well organized that no other

1. McCarthy, "Religious Conflict," 97. The Keswick convention promoted the holiness teaching of the victorious Christian life based on the concept of sanctification by faith. See Barabas, *So Great Salvation*, 84–104. See also a comprehensive bibliography on the Keswick movement in Jones, *Keswick Movement*.

2. McCarthy, "Religious Conflict," 12–20; Florovskii, *Puti Russkogo Bogosloviia*, 147–51.

3. Ibid., 93–94.

movement could have measured up to its potential as a force capable of transforming Russia on a religious ethical basis."[4]

The *Russian Workman*, which received help from the London Religious Tract Society, was designed to reach out to the Russian working class.[5] The arrival of Lord Radstock in Russia brought not only certain theological ideas, but also evangelical culture and connections with Anglo-American evangelical institutions.

The aim of the present chapter is to demonstrate the presence of two theological paradigms that coexisted on the pages of the *Russian Workman* without confrontation or dialogue. The *Russian Workman* of this period is probably the major source for evaluating the theological convictions of the early followers of Radstock. This chapter contributes to scholarly discussion on the topic in two ways. First, it will be demonstrated that the publishers of the *Russian Workman* during this period were Orthodox Christians who were concerned with the evangelical renewal of Russia without attempting to dissent from the National Church. Second, it will be demonstrated that Protestant articles borrowed from Western sources promoted a distinctively Protestant evangelical theology whose seeds were preparing the ground for subsequent dissent along the primitivist-restorationist path of the holiness tradition represented by Radstock. The trajectories of these two mentalities will be examined in the next chapter on V. A. Pashkov.[6]

AN ANALYSIS

The first issue of the *Russian Workman* was printed on February 11, 1875. The chief editor of the periodical was Mariia Peuker, who joined the evangelical movement upon meeting with D. L. Moody in London.[7] She was involved with the Prison Society and with the British and Foreign Bible Society.[8] The journal was cheap and simple to understand. Its goal was stated in the preface to the first issue: "If the Lord blesses our endeavor to continue the journal in the way we have designed it, then the readers will find in it a story for entertainment, advice for right and

4. Heier, *Religious Schism*, 118.

5. Ibid., 98.

6. Cf. Florovskii, *Puti Russkogo Bogosloviia*, 395.

7. McCarthy, "Religious Conflict," 81.

8. Ibid.

honest living, as well as an example for encouragement. But first and foremost the reader will be able to see in every story and in every good thought the One who has taught people to love each other and help each other."[9]

The first Western scholarly evaluation of the *Russian Workman* was made by Edmund Heier:

> The *Russian Workman* was the most important publication of the Radstockist Society for the Encouragement of Spiritual and Ethical Reading. Although the journal was non-sectarian, non-political, and not in the least polemical, and disseminated only cheap and instructive ethical reading among the common people, Leskov dismissed it as an "unnecessary venture." What annoyed him most was that much of the material, consisting of various religious illustrations and moral stories, was taken from the Religious Tract Society in London without remolding it to suit the milieu of the common Russian people.[10]

A more detailed analysis was made by McCarthy, who supports Heier's thesis on the non-denominational nature of the journal.[11] McCarthy analyzed the historical and literary aspects of the *Russian Workman* and came to the conclusion that the journal in general was "pro-European and pro-Western."[12] Commenting on the theological stance of the journal, McCarthy repeats Heier: "[A]voiding references to confessions, it treated all issues from the perspective of 'mere Christianity.'"[13] Neither Heier nor McCarthy has taken seriously enough into account the detailed analysis of the Orthodox scholar Terletskii.[14] Terletskii detected the heterogeneous nature of the journal with regard to the theological content of the articles. According to Terletskii some of the articles have purely Protestant, anti-Orthodox content, while others were written by Orthodox writers. However, Tereletskii suspects that the Orthodox articles were printed as a smokescreen in order to spread "the Pashkovite teaching among the people."[15] Neither of these perspec-

9. *Russkii Rabochii* 1 (1875) 2.
10. Heier, *Religious Schism*, 72.
11. McCarthy, "Religious Conflict," 96–109.
12. Ibid., 103.
13. Ibid., 106.
14. Terletskii, *Sekta Pashkovtsev*, 58–63.
15. Ibid., 63.

tives does justice to the heterogeneous nature of the *Russian Workman* or to the subsequent development of the tradition. It was argued in the previous chapter that Radstock presented not neutral Biblical teaching but a specific Protestant evangelical approach to reading biblical texts and interpreting reality. Thus Heier's "instructive ethical reading" and McCarthy's "mere Christianity" do not do justice to the distinctively Protestant nature of the material included in the *Russian Workman.* Terletskii's assessment, published years after the leaders of the emerging evangelical movement challenged the Orthodox and state authorities, was viewed through the prism of the later development of the tradition. Even though my perspective is closer to Terletskii's assessment of the *Russian Workman,* I take the material included therein without Orthodox prejudices against the motives of the journal's publishers. The next chapter, on V. A. Pashkov, will confirm the assumptions concerning the sincerity of the editor of the *Russian Workman,* as well as the development of the two trajectories.

The Byzantine Paradigm

Even though the journal was modeled after the *British Workman* and used much material translated from British sources, the Orthodox component is prominent.[16] The content of the first issue of the journal is paradigmatic in this regard. The issue begins with a fictional story whose main personage is an Orthodox priest. The plot of the story is straightforward. In a Russian village a school teacher, Mr. Nikolai Matveevich Zaitsev, dies. A well-to-do elder of the village, Ivan Fedotov, invites the people who have gathered in the school hall before proceeding to the cemetery, waiting for the arrival of the priest and landlord, to drink hot tea, because it is very cold outside. Fedotov emphasizes that he does not encourage drinking vodka, as was customary to do on such occasions, because it would reflect an attitude of disrespect to the spirit of the deceased, who had propagated the virtue of temperance. The conversation at the teakettle revolves around the theme of the *spirit* of Nikolai Matveevich, which according to the word of the priest will live for a long time in the common vestry. One of the guests expresses a feeling of unease at the idea of a spirit living in the vestry. The priest, Father Alexander, who worked closely with the deceased teacher, explains what he meant

16. See Meyendorff, *Byzantine Theology.*

when he talked about the *spirit* of the teacher living among them. The main point of the priest's speech is that Zaitsev left a good heritage, having planted the seed of God's Word in the hearts of his pupils. This good seed is producing good fruit even in the present, namely a good and moral life in many of his disciples. The absence of good seed leads to a life of debauchery and drunkenness in pubs. Thus Father Alexander tells the people that he had in mind the life and teaching of Zaitsev, not his disembodied ghost. The priest argues against the spirit of Western Enlightenment and nihilism prominent in Russian universities which challenges Christian values: "Knowledge and reason do not always go hand in hand. There are many educated people in the world who manage to live without the Word of God and faith."[17] Thus he complains that it would not be easy to find a substitute for the godly and knowledgeable Zaitsev. Father Alexander makes his point clear at the end of the instruction: "Each man has two masters: the head and the heart. Both of them must be directed towards the good by a timely sowing."[18] After the priest's speech the local landlord Nikolai Dmitrievich encourages the listeners to pray that the Lord would send another teacher-sower. Thus the priest, the landlord, and the deceased teacher are depicted as godly Orthodox Christians who encourage a virtuous life of faith and sobriety. The fictional story about the death of a school teacher, the instruction of the priest, and the prayer of the landlord call the readers to think about their own life-values and the education of children.

The second article in the first issue provides a biographical sketch of the prominent Russian scholar Mikhail Lomonosov. It is pointed out that the scholar was of poor descent and was initially taught to read by his mother, who was the daughter of an Orthodox deacon; in contrast to his mother, his father was illiterate. The author of the biography emphasizes the fact that Lomonosov started his educational journey by reading scripture in a local church and that he became the best reader of the Psalter. The author points out Lomonosov's faithfulness to the Russian Empress, as well as his success and the royal recognition that came as the result of his hard and honest work. The biography of Lomonosov

17. "The seminarians were fed on a version of the Christian Religion which ignored the social and intellectual problems of the contemporary world. . . . It is not surprising that many of them lost not only their vocation but their faith after such training." See Zernov, *Russian Religious Renaissance of the Twentieth Century*, 47.

18. *Russkii Rabochii* 1 (1875) 3.

is intended to serve as a real-life example of the priest's sermon in the preceding story. The national motif in the story is prominent. The author concludes the sketch in the following way: "Lomonosov demonstrated with his life to the entire *Russian* world what a persistent will and honest work can do."[19]

The biographical sketch is followed by a fictional story about a workman named Ivan who heard a sermon in church. The sermon contained a short passage from the book of Isaiah: "Why spend money on what is not bread, and your labor on what does not satisfy?" (Isa 55:1–2). The text was interpreted in the sense that one had to quit visiting pubs and spending money on what was useless. Ivan gave up drinking vodka and with the money he saved bought Christmas gifts for children. He started reading the Gospel and building his life in accordance with its teaching. The narrative ends with a story of how Ivan helped a young woman come to God and be reconciled with her parents whom she had offended.

Taking into account the content and structure of the first issue, one can come to the conclusion that the editor of the journal was not interested in any sort of rationalistic theologizing. The journal was designed to promote traditional Russian values and a way of life that encouraged readers to take seriously matters of faith, work, and relationships with others. The major theme of the journal was the importance of the Word of God which is able to transform people's lives. The main means of transferring biblical values was the genre of narrative, which was a prominent tool for transmitting ideas in the Russian society of the time. The first issue of the journal depicts the key players of Russian society: the priest, the peasant, the landlord, the scholar, and the workman. The brief reference to the reverent attitude of the prominent scholar toward the Russian Empress, as well as the prominent role of Orthodoxy, demonstrates that the *Russian Workman* was intended as an Orthodox journal within Monarchical Russia. There is no hint in the first issue of the presence of any themes from Radstock's teaching.

The paradigmatic nature of the first issue of the journal can be confirmed by a careful reading of further issues of the journal, giving attention to the presence of the Byzantine paradigm. None of the issues of the journal contains any references to non-Orthodox missionaries or to other denominations that were operating in Russia. Russia is depicted

19. Ibid., 4. Italics added.

as an Orthodox country within which only Orthodox missionaries work, disseminating Christianity among the non-Russian ethnicities (*inorodtsy*).[20] Western missionaries are mentioned as examples of evangelistic ministry either in pagan countries or in the Protestant outskirts of Russia. In the first phase of the *Russian Workman* (1875–1881), one can clearly see the Orthodox orientation of some of the contributors. The writer of the article about the mass baptism of Russia in the days of St. Vladimir depicts the event in a very positive light, which would hardly have been possible for a Protestant writer.[21] The practice of worshipping the relics of Alexander Nevskii is mentioned without any negative comment of the sort typically found in the writings of Protestant authors of the time.[22] A short hagiography of John the Baptist concludes with a petition to John: "O you who have fulfilled your calling, great forerunner in the Kingdom of God, pray for us sinners who cannot fulfill our calling."[23] The *Russian Workman* encourages the reader to attend liturgy in an Orthodox temple.[24] "Keep strictly the Lord's Day, attend God's temple, try to pray at home with all the members of your family, and do not forget to read the scriptures."[25] It is assumed that the readers are using icons for worship at home. The author recommends using bagasse oil for icon lamps, because this particular oil does not cause fires.[26] In one of the fictional narratives a woman instructs a boy: "You should believe in Christ the Savior and participate *in all of the sacraments* of his Holy Church besides baptism, as well as *submit to her saving guidance*."[27]

The *Russian Workman* of this period contains a short excerpt from Innocent, the Metropolitan of Moscow, who gives an Orthodox account of soteriology.[28] Salvation in Christ is viewed in terms of Christ's sharing and glorification of human nature. Christ's incarnation, crucifixion,

20. Ibid., 6 (1876) 22.

21. Ibid., 7 (1875) 27.

22. Ibid., 8 (1875) 31.

23. Ibid., 8 (1878) 30.

24. Ibid., 11 (1875) 44; ibid., 12 (1875) 46–48.

25. Ibid., 2 (1876) 8.

26. Ibid., 7 (1877) 26.

27. Ibid., 2 (1876) 8 (italics added).

28. Ibid., 2 (1876) 6. On Innocent of Moscow, see Barsukov, *Mitropolit Moskovskii i Kolomenskii po ego Sochineniiam, Pis'mam i Rasskazam Sovremennikov*; Barsukova, *Prosvetitel' Sibirskikh Stran*; Korsunskii *Mitropolit Moskovskii i Kolomenskii*; and Fialkin, "Sviatitel' Innokentii Mitropolit Moskovskii i ego Missionerskaia Deiatel'nost."

and glorification opened the way for humankind to participate in this salvation. The grace of God is perceived in terms of the Holy Spirit who has been given to believers. Believers cannot walk on the path of God without the assistance of the Holy Spirit. The concept of salvation is presented as a *corporate* spiritual journey to heaven along the path made by Christ.

Nikolai Leskov produced a thorough compilation of sayings of the Church Fathers about the Bible. This compilation was published in the *Russian Workman* throughout the entire year of 1879.[29] The compilation brings the Patristic tradition into view. By bringing the Church Fathers to the Russian audience, Leskov hoped to influence people to read the Bible through the prism of the Patristic tradition.[30] Leskov was convinced that the Patristic tradition contained the spirit of true Christianity which he believed was essential for the revival of the stagnated and stifled state religion. This compilation is probably one of the most significant components of the *Russian Workman*. However, the approach of reading scripture through the Patristic tradition was never developed.

Finally, the Orthodox-national mentality of the *Russian Workman* is revealed in its coverage of events of the Turkish War: "It has been more than 400 years since the time when the Turks, the haters of the Christian faith, established their rule over our brethren (*edinoplemenniki*) and coreligionists (*edinovertsy*), the Serbians and Bulgarians. . . . In the month of June [the Christians] unanimously took up arms for the protection of their poor brethren. . . . Let us pray to God that the present fight of our brethren will end honorably for the Christians."[31] The interference of the Russian Emperor in the conflict is presented in an elevated tone.[32] Almost every issue published in 1877 contains detailed information from the battlefields, highlighting the heroic acts of the Christians against the Muslims.

Having analyzed the material with eyes open to the presence of the Orthodox paradigm, one can hardly escape the conclusion that the *Russian Workman* contained prominent Orthodox themes. The Western approach that tends to view the journal as reflecting the "mere

29. The beginning of the compilation is found in *Russkii Rabochii* 11 (1878) 44. The conclusion is found in ibid., 11 (1879) 44.

30. Sperrle, *Organic Worldview of Nikolai Leskov*, 39.

31. *Russkii Rabochii* 8 (1876) 31–32.

32. Ibid., 10 (1876) 43.

Christianity" of later evangelicalism is not supported, given the prominence of Orthodox themes. The first Russian followers of Radstock were solidly committed to their Russian Orthodox identity. They believed that Orthodox Russia needed a spiritual renewal that would be evident in the changed lives and character of the Russian people without changing their Orthodox identity, including its beliefs and rituals.[33] This pietistic tone of the journal was in many respects reminiscent of the pietistic themes of the Alexandrean epoch of the first two decades of the nineteenth century.[34]

The Protestant Paradigm

The presence of the Protestant Paradigm in the pages of the *Russian Workman* can be seen from the absence of a single instruction in the journal to read the scriptures in interaction with *church tradition.* This paradoxical absence is better explained not by reference to "mere Christianity," but by the theological uncertainty of the editor and of the Russian contributors as to *how to read the scriptures.* On the one hand, the St. Petersburg followers of Radstock continued to identify themselves with Russian Orthodoxy; but on the other hand, they did not know any other way of reading and interpreting the Bible than that of the English lord and of the British institutions with which they were in partnership. Orthodox seminaries were not much in touch with contemporary realities and did not provide any alternative way of dealing with the scriptures, which had only recently been translated into Russian.[35] As far as biblical interpretation was concerned, Radstock advocated a very simple way of reading the Bible: just *read it and obey it.*[36] However, Radstock not only advocated this approach to interacting with scripture but also provided interpretive keys, together with samples of how to read the Bible in a particular way. As was demonstrated in the previous chapter, this way of reading the Bible was shaped and formed by the Protestant Anglo-

33. Zernov, *Russian Religious Renaissance*, 35–85. The decadence of Orthodoxy was a concern of some prominent priests of the time who were later canonized. See Smirnov, *Zhizn' i Uchenie Feofana Zatvornika.*

34. Florovskii, *Puti Russkogo Bogosloviia*, 131–53.

35. The four Gospels were printed in Russian in 1860. The complete text of the New Testament in Russian came out in 1863. The entire Russian Bible was printed in 1876. See Chistovich, *Istoria Perevoda Biblii na Russkii Iazyk.*

36. Hatch, "Sola Scriptura and Novus Ordo Seclorum," 59–60.

American culture of the nineteenth century. Orthodox spirituality, theology, and forms of worship were not explicitly critiqued. However, the theological trajectory of Radstock implicitly contained a highly critical and dogmatic attitude towards Orthodoxy. In this sense, Radstock was not only fulfilling the role of a catalytic agent within the Orthodox Church, as is assumed in Protestant scholarship, but he was also playing the role of a tideway that directed the flow of the religious awakening away from Orthodoxy in the direction of the Keswickian theology of holiness, and connected with its restorationist tendencies.

Assurance of Salvation

The key theological accents of the *Russian Workman* of this period correspond to the theology of Radstock. Even though the journal does not directly identify Russian Orthodox culture with paganism, some of the articles borrowed from Protestant sources nonetheless assume that any Christian who is unable to give a positive reply to the key questions of post-Reformed theology is a pagan and an "unbeliever" under the wrath of God. These questions were about justification by faith and assurance of salvation. According to this pietistic and Methodist view, only "a born-again" person can be called a true Christian.[37] Christian identity is built on an individual, personal experience of God's grace, based on belief in justification by faith.

The first explicit reference to this way of forging Christian identity is found in the fourth issue of the *Russian Workman*.[38] The author tells a story about an aborigine who had converted to Christianity some time earlier. The aborigine meets an unbelieving European. In the flow of their conversation, the aborigine snatches a worm out of the bonfire and puts it on his chest. In response to the astonished European, the aborigine explains that what he has done signifies his own salvation from hell. He himself had been like the little worm, but God had snatched him from the fire and caused him to rest on the divine heart. At the end, the author of this story addresses the Orthodox reader: "O you reading

37. See Busch, *Karl Barth and the Pietists*, 133–237. Busch demonstrates the hermeneutical stance of pietists in their critique of Barth's theology. It is a common tendency in pietism to believe that one has the "biblical viewpoint" over against the theological interpretations of non-pietists.

38. *Russkii Rabochii* 4 (1875) 15.

these lines, do you acknowledge yourself an unworthy sinner saved by the blood of Christ? Do you tell others about Jesus? Are you sure about your salvation?"[39] This typically evangelical way of marking Christian identity is found throughout various issues of the *Russian Workman*. "Dear reader, is your name written in the book of life?"[40] "If you have not been born of God nor washed in the blood of Christ, you are still in your own sins and the wrath of God rests on you."[41] "Everyone should ask themselves: have I been born from above? Am I a new creature? Have I taken off the old man? Have I acknowledged my sins? Do I hate sin? Do I long for holiness? Do I love the Word of God? Do I pray with faith and consistency? Do I do good?"[42] A negative reply to these rhetorical questions implies that a person is not saved and can be identified with the eschatological chaff that will be burned.[43] The concepts presented in these rhetorical questions are derived from the New Testament. However, some of the key concepts such as "being born from above," "a new creature," and "taking off the old man" are open to different interpretations. The pietistic understanding of these concepts is framed in strictly individualistic and experiential terminology. This imposition on the everyday reader of a culturally-conditioned hermeneutical framework for the interpretation of biblical concepts, while evading dialogue with Orthodox theologians, was paving the way for Protestant proselytizing under the smokescreen of biblical teaching.

The most obviously Protestant content published in the *Russian Workman* was a multi-part article entitled "About Buildings."[44] This article appears in three consecutive issues. The main concern of the author is to stress the importance of building the house of one's faith on a sure foundation, which consists of justification by faith and assurance of salvation. In the article the author draws an analogy between the tradition of the Pharisees condemned by Christ in Mark 6:7–8 and extrabiblical Christian tradition.[45] He argues against the monastic tradition and against memorized prayers that, he says, cannot save one from the flood

39. Ibid.

40. Ibid., 10 (1875) 40.

41. Ibid., 5 (1877) 20.

42. Ibid., 9 (1878) 33.

43. Ibid.

44. Ibid., 8 (1879) 29; ibid., 9 (1879) 36; ibid., 10 (1879) 38–39.

45. Ibid., 9 (1879) 36.

of death. He also affirms that a believer who has received the Spirit does not sin, since he has become a new creature. "The dragonfly enjoys flying. It would never crawl like a worm."[46] Individual believers can become saints by an act of faith. The new nature imparted by the Spirit protects people from sinning. Interestingly, the article was never finished, "because of reasons beyond the control of the publisher."[47] It may well have been that it did not pass Orthodox censorship.[48]

Protestant theology is also presented through compilations of biblical verses taken out of context. For example, one compilation includes the following verses: Deut 30:19; 1 John 2:1; and Eph 2:1, 5.[49] The texts are intended to be read in the suggested sequence. This kind of intratextual reading reflects the Protestant trajectory of thinking. There are only two choices: either eternal punishment or salvation (Deut 30:19); the way of salvation is found only in Jesus Christ (1 John 2:1); salvation is received by grace through faith in Christ (Eph 2:1, 5). This kind of reading of the Bible with the accent on personal assurance of salvation had an unresolved potential for conflicting with Orthodox soteriology, with its corporate, historical, and mystical dimensions.[50]

In a sense the *Russian Workman* can be seen as promoting the reading of the Bible under the guidance of Protestant teachers in the Orthodox Church. The dogmatic attitude of the Protestants, coupled with the dogmatism of Orthodox officials, provided no foundation for productive dialogue. The fact that some Orthodox Christians totally appropriated evangelical theology and rejected Orthodoxy as a dead religion can be easily understood against this non-dialogical background.

Adventism

The millenarian motives of the *Russian Workman* are identical to those of the non-dispensational premillennialism of Radstock.[51] According to the authors of various articles, the second coming of Christ is approaching. This can be discerned from the signs of the times, namely the return

46. Ibid., 10 (1879) 38–39.

47. Ibid., 11 (1879) 44.

48. See Leskov, *Sobranie Sochinenii*, vol. 10, 457–64.

49. *Russkii Rabochii* 5 (1875) 19.

50. Starogorodskii, *Pravoslavnoe Uchenie o Spasenii.*

51. Gribben and Stunt, *Prisoners of Hope.*

of the Jews to Palestine and the worldwide preaching of the Gospel. Thus believers should be spiritually awake and ready for the return of the Lord.[52] Christ is coming back only once to receive the elect and to judge unbelievers.[53] The elect are those whose "heart is ready" (Ps 57:7), who are born of the Spirit and taught by him. The great tribulation is interpreted in terms of the final judgment (Heb 10:31). The dispensational interpretive grid of Darby does not appear on the pages of the *Russian Workman*.

BIBLICAL INTERPRETATION

The rare examples of biblical exegesis found in the *Russian Workman* are characterized by an absence of historical and grammatical analysis. The texts are read typologically through the grid of Protestant holiness theology, characterized by Romantic influences.[54] The scriptural texts are read in such a way as to be directly relevant to the spiritual formation of the readers, appealing to their emotions. The texts are used as a springboard to help readers make progress in their spiritual journey toward complete devotion to Christ.

The Old Testament

The text of Gen 32:24–32 describes an enigmatic event in the life of Jacob. This passage, which tells the story of Jacob's wrestling with a divine stranger, is interpreted by an expositor in the *Russian Workman* as follows: "The Lord was wrestling with [Jacob] to lead him to acknowledge his weakness. Notice that the text does not say that Jacob was wrestling with the stranger. It was God's work with Jacob. . . . [T]he death sentence must be written on the flesh; the power of the cross needs to be experienced and accepted before a believer starts walking joyfully before God. We can know God's power when we know our weakness."[55] This reading of the biblical text demonstrates the priority of the Keswickian theological framework. According to the Keswick teaching on holiness, the believer should experience the cross of Christ through identification with

52. *Russkii Rabochii* 3 (1879) 10 and ibid., 4 (1879) 14.

53. Ibid., 12 (1876) 46.

54. Bebbington, *Holiness in Nineteenth-Century England*, 80–83.

55. *Russkii Rabochii* 9 (1879) 35.

him in his death.[56] All hope in natural gifts and human strength should be abandoned in order for the life of the resurrection to be manifested. The life of Jacob is projected onto the life of faith of Christian believers. The dislocation of Jacob's joint is equated with the sentence of the cross on the flesh. Interpreting Ps 84:6, "As they pass through the valley of tears they make it a place of springs," the writer says: "[I]t means that the people devoted to the Lord find springs of comfort in Jesus Christ as they go on their earthy journey in the midst of many sorrows."[57]

New Testament Texts

Gospel texts are similarly read through the Keswickian theological grid. The thought and experience of the interpreter are directly read into the lips of biblical personages. The words of Simeon, "[Y]ou now dismiss your servant in peace" (Luke 2:29), are taken to mean: "Now I can die in peace and live in peace. You have loosened my bonds so that I will not be a servant of sin but will belong to Christ wholly. My eyes that have seen your salvation do not want to see the vanity of the world. You have set the captive free. You have bought me with a precious price, so that I will walk with no fear in holiness and truth before you all the days of my life."[58] Keswickian theology is put on the lips of Simeon with the sole intention of helping the reader to appropriate the same theological perspective and to adopt the attitude of Simeon as interpreted by the commentator.

An Example of Biblical Intratextuality in the Framework of Justification by Faith

The gospel narrative about the feeding of the five thousand (John 6:5–15) is read as an allegory, depicting the spiritual experience of a Christian who has been justified by faith. Even the small details of the narrative are filled with this sort of symbolic content. Jesus' instruction to the people to *sit down* is said to illustrate the fact that Jesus is a savior, and not a judge in whose presence people need to *stand*. The green grass of

56. Barabas, *So Great Salvation*, 88–93.

57. *Russkii Rabochii* 3 (1878) 12.

58. Ibid., 2 (1879) 6.

the passage is interpreted intratextually in terms of Ps 23:2, where the Lord is depicted as the Good Shepherd. In light of the imagery of that Psalm, Jesus is considered to be the Divine Shepherd who provides for his sheep. The expositor leads the reader to heed the call of Christ and come to him in order to obtain justification by faith and assurance of salvation. Only by being juridically justified by faith can a person eat Christ as *the bread of life.*[59] By the end of the exposition the reader realizes that the Gospel story is not about a miracle of the multiplication of food, but is rather about one's present fellowship with Christ. This reader-oriented theological performance weaved a world out of the biblical texts, fusing within it the horizons of the text(s) and the present concerns of the reader.

CONCLUSION

The *Russian Workman* contains two theological paradigms, which coexist side by side without entering into dialogue with one another. On the one hand the Byzantine paradigm reflects the need for believers to belong to the Orthodox Church, participating in all her rituals and accepting her guidance. On the other hand the stories and sermons taken from Western sources reveal a conservative Protestant spirituality similar to that of Radstock, in which the identity-marking elements of Orthodoxy, such as the importance of the Patristic tradition, liturgical services, prayers to the saints, and the use of icons, do not play a significant role. The non-dialogical coexistence of the paradigms and the non-intellectual nature of the journal are symptomatic of the incommensurability that became evident with the growth of the evangelical tradition in Russia.

The approaches to biblical interpretation in the *Russian Workman* are identical to those of Radstock. The biblical text is read typologically through the grid of holiness theology, ignoring historico-grammatical considerations. The interpreter is concerned exclusively with fleshing out the significance of the biblical passage in terms of people's experience of salvation in Christ and their moral transformation by the power of the Spirit. The key genre of the journal is narrative. The biblical texts interpreted in the journal are also taken primarily from the narrative parts of scripture.

59. Ibid., 7 (1878) 25–26.

The narrative of the community of the *Russian Workman* can be articulated as follows: we are Russian Orthodox Christians who believe in the importance of reading and obeying the Word of God by living a virtuous life in light of the impending return of Christ. Readers should not trust the ritual aspects of Orthodoxy without also seriously taking into account their own personal devotional and moral life. Believers should be born of the Spirit and have assurance of salvation based on justification by faith. Even though we believe in the Orthodox identity of Russia, we also believe that God is working in other lands through other Christian expressions.

In the following chapter we will explore the development of the Byzantine and Pietistic paradigms among the St. Petersburg followers of Radstock, focusing on the ministry of V. A. Pashkov.

3

V. A. Pashkov (1831–1902): A Clash of Paradigms

"The history of relations between the Eastern Orthodox and Protestant Evangelical traditions has never been written. One does not have to search very far, however, to see that their past relationships have been predominantly characterized by a long negative history of proselytism, persecution, mutual suspicion, hostility, fear and ignorance."[1]

INTRODUCTION

This chapter is focused on the biography and theology of Colonel Vasilii Aleksandrovich Pashkov, who became the leader of the evangelical movement after Radstock's departure from Russia in 1878.[2] The studies done by Edmund Heier, Sharyl Corrado, and Mark McCarthy have provided much historical material on the development of the evangelical movement in St. Petersburg. My concern is to demonstrate the evolution of the Anglo-American revivalist paradigm and its separation from the Byzantine paradigm, the presence of which has not been brought to the forefront by previous studies. I continue to argue against the commonly-held view that Radstock brought a neutral vision of the moral transformation of Russia, based on a purely biblical foundation. The separation of the revivalist paradigm from Orthodoxy is important for at least three reasons, all of which have been neglected by other scholars.

First, there was in Pashkov's vision a geopolitical dimension that was either overlooked or downplayed by previous researchers. Pashkov

1. Nassif, "Eastern Orthodoxy and Evangelicalism," 212.

2. Cf. Corrado, "Gospel in Society," 52–70.

took a pro-Western position in the contemporary arguments between Slavophiles and Westernizers (*Zapadniki*). His non-dialogical attitude towards the Orthodox Church should be attributed not only to external factors, such as the defensive power reaction of the Orthodox clergy, but also to the internal Protestant view that envisioned the Protestant paradigm to be superior to that of Orthodoxy. This attitude of superiority, as well as the theoretical basis for it, is revealed in Pashkov's correspondence with the lay Anglican scholar Alexei Vladimirov, discussed below.

Second, the evangelical movement in Russia was inspired and energized by the idea of the messianic role of the Russian nation, a belief colored by chiliastic motives prevalent in nineteenth-century Russia among both Slavophiles and Westernizers.

Third, there was a change in the community's story, which resulted in a change in its self-identification (from Russian Orthodox to Russian evangelical) and a modification therefore of its biblical interpretation and rituals. The Pashkovite period (1878–1895) reflects the coexistence of the two paradigms, but in a different configuration from that of the Radstockian period (1874–1878) described in the previous chapter.[3] Some of Radstock's followers were proselytized into the neo-Protestant version of Christianity, having abandoned their Orthodox identity, while others, mainly the female aristocrats, remained in Orthodoxy while practicing neo-Protestant spirituality.

This chapter will conclude with an analysis of the second phase of the *Russian Workman*. The aim of the analysis is to demonstrate shifts in the content of the public journal, illuminated by the private correspondence of Pashkov.

V. A. PASHKOV: A BIOGRAPHICAL SKETCH

Vasilii Alexandrovich Pashkov was born in 1831. As a child he received the best education possible, attending the prestigious Corps of Pages, and he was accepted into the Chevalier Guards (*Kavelergard*) upon graduation with the rank of cornet. By the time he retired from service, he had risen to colonel (*polkovnik*), the highest rank within the Guards.

3. I decided to conclude the period at 1895, because Pashkov's correspondence with St. Petersburg does not provide sufficient material for research after that year. Cf. Randall, "Eastern European Baptists and the Evangelical Alliance, 1846–1896," 32.

He was introduced to the highest society of St. Petersburg at an early age.[4] Colonel Pashkov was one of the wealthiest men in Russia.[5] He became a follower of Radstock during the English lord's first visit to Russia in 1873–1874. In correspondence with Fr. Ianyshev six years after his conversion, Pashkov describes his life before that experience as that of a nominal Orthodox churchgoer who "lived a sinful life trying to serve two masters."[6] It is significant that Pashkov did not have religious concerns and at first tried to avoid meeting with Radstock.[7] His conversion came as a direct result of Radstock's prayer, which deeply impressed Pashkov even though he had not been touched by or even interested in Radstock's message. After his unexpected conversion, he invested his wealth and energies in multiple charitable activities of a social and religious nature, which are well documented in the historical studies.[8] The distribution of Protestant tracts throughout the Russian Empire; preaching in the contemporary Russian language; evangelistic trips to different places in Russia; the growing influence of the movement among the masses and among different sectarians, students, and the wider Russian society—all were leading the movement towards a painful collision with the State Church that reached its climax in 1884.

Pashkov had a lasting friendship with Lord Radstock. Both held revivalist meetings in Paris in 1886, following Pashkov's expulsion from Russia two years earlier.[9] Their private correspondence lasted until Pashkov's final days.[10] Corrado calls Radstock Pashkov's mentor.[11] Some of Pashkov's contemporaries pointed out that he copied not only the homiletical illustrations of Radstock, but also some of his mannerisms.[12] This close relationship with Radstock explains why Pashkov's theology and practices were, at least initially, virtually identical to those of Radstock.

4. Corrado, *Filosofiia*, 33.

5. Heier, *Religious Schism*, 109.

6. Ianyshev and Pashkov, "Sushchnost' Ucheniia," 4.

7. Liven, *Evangel'skoe Probuzhdenie v Rossii*, 16.

8. Heier, *Religious Schism*, 197–225; Corrado, *Filosofiia*, 114–48; McCarthy, "Religious Conflict," 132–47.

9. PP II/1/c /44.

10. PP 2/20/1–9.

11. Corrado, *Filosopfiia*, 44–45.

12. Ibid.

After his unsuccessful attempt to establish a branch of the Evangelical Alliance in Russia in 1884, Pashkov moved to Great Britain. He did not sever his ties, however, with the evangelical movement in Russia, which he continued to support both spiritually and financially, as can be seen in his correspondence. Pashkov died in Paris in 1902 and was buried in Rome.[13]

PASHKOV'S CONNECTIONS WITH THE EVANGELICAL ALLIANCE AND PROTESTANT MISSIONS

Through Lord Radstock the evangelical movement in St. Petersburg was connected to the Evangelical Alliance and to the Keswick Convention. Pashkov's correspondence includes several letters that confirm his close ties with these Protestant bodies. The first letter from the German branch of the Evangelical Alliance is dated April 18, 1879.[14] Pashkov also received an official invitation to attend the seventh conference of the Evangelical Alliance in Bale, France, in September 1879.[15] Several months later one of the members of the organizing committee of the conference in Bale, Otto Stockmeyer, visited St. Petersburg and taught the St. Petersburg group.[16] Like Radstock, Müller, and Baedeker, Stockmeyer was an active participant in Keswick meetings in England.[17]

After his expulsion from Russia, Pashkov continued to work with the Evangelical Alliance. He helped to organize a collective appeal by the evangelical churches of Britain and America to the Russian Tsar Alexander III and the Synod about the persecution of evangelical sectarians in Russia.[18] In his private correspondence with representatives of the Evangelical Alliance Pashkov refers to the National Church of Russia as a "dead church," thus identifying himself with the Protestant movement.[19]

13. Corrado, *Filosofiia*, 163. The memorial gravestone (#1960) is located in the Protestant Cemetery in Rome.

14. PP 2/2/95.

15. PP 2/2/96.

16. Korff, *Am Zarenhof*, 29.

17. McCarthy, "Religious Conflict," 114.

18. PP I/8.

19. PP 2/1/f/14, dated July 31, 1884.

Pashkov was among the first Russians to support Protestant missionary institutions. He sent a check for the East London Institute for Home and Foreign Missions as early as the spring of 1880.[20] He also supported Hudson Taylor's China Inland Mission in 1882.[21] And Pashkov generously supported Protestant missionaries such as Dr. Frederick Baedeker and John Melville working in Russia,[22] This historical background is given to demonstrate Pashkov's firsthand acquaintance with the wider world of evangelical Protestantism prior to his collision with the Orthodox authorities.

PASHKOV'S STATEMENT OF FAITH

After having been publicly accused by a seminary student, Vladimir Popov, of teaching some heretical views, Pashkov produced a statement of faith in 1880.[23] After attending a Pashkovite gathering, Popov wrote an article in *Tserkovnyi Vestnik* ("The Church Herald") claiming that Pashkov taught in a Protestant spirit against the Orthodox Church. The seminarian saw the stress on justification by faith alone in Pashkov's preaching as a direct attack on Orthodoxy. He correctly deduced that Pashkov's soteriology subverted Orthodox ecclesiology, soteriology, and spirituality. The editor of *Tserkovnyi Vestnik*, Fr. Ianyshev, gave Pashkov an opportunity to defend himself against the accusations. Archpriest Ioann Ianyshev was the head of the St. Petersburg Theological Academy, the spiritual mentor of Nicholas II, and an active participant in ecumenical meetings with the Old Catholics between 1871 and 1894.[24] Pashkov's correspondence with Fr. Ianyshev, which took place in April, was published in *Tserkovnyi Vestnik* in May.[25]

In his statement of faith Pashkov pointed out that he had had no theological education and that he did not pretend to be a teacher. He claimed that he therefore did not touch on any debatable questions in

20. PP 2/12/1.

21. PP 2/2/339.

22. PP 2/2/327; 2/3/54.

23. Popov, "Voskresnyia besedy g. Pashkova," 12–13.

24. Florovsky, "Orthodox Churches and the Ecumenical Movement Prior to 1910," 207–8. Ianyshev is depicted as an ecumenically-open Orthodox priest.

25. Ianyshev and Pashkov, "Sushchnost' Ucheniya," 6–7. See also PP 2/1/f/12 and Korff, *Am Zarenhof*, 73; McCarthy, "Religious Conflict," 117–27.

his talks. In his third letter to Ianyshev, dated April 28, he pointed out that some of of Ianyshev's questions took the discussion beyond the boundaries of general Christian witness, requiring the sort of in-depth knowledge a Christian teacher would have, but which he said he lacked. He assured the Orthodox censor that his activity did not go beyond the boundaries "of a general Christian witness."[26] Pashkov's correspondence with Ianyshev is an example of evasive dialogue, since Pashkov refused to continue any correspondence on the issue.[27] It is also revealing in that Pashkov was obviously unaware of the theological and philosophical filter he had inherited from Radstock with regard to the interpretation of the Bible.

Every paragraph, and often every sentence, Pashkov wrote includes a New Testament reference typical of the conservative Protestant way of arguing by means of proof-texting.[28] The quotations are taken from different books of the New Testament. In the first part of his confession Pashkov describes his life as a worldly Christian whose heart was not with the Lord. In the second part, he discusses the center of his teaching, namely justification by grace, the unconditional love of God, and its personal appropriation by faith. In the third part, he speaks about his present ministry and various aspects of his teaching. Pashkov believes that salvation is brought about exclusively and directly by God. In his testimony, God is the one who opens his eyes to see the meaning of scripture. Pashkov describes the process of his conversion as a conscious and personal appropriation of the work of Christ. He never refers to the Patristic tradition or to the creeds of the Eastern Church. His confession is written in strictly individualistic and experiential terms, reflecting the convictions of Radstock. Pashkov's individualistic and experiential confession demonstrates that the Radstockian revival was not a revival within the Orthodox Church. Rather it was a conversion from the superficial crust of Byzantine ritualism into a distinctively Western post-Reformed mode of Christianity.[29] Neither Pashkov nor the emerging

26. Ibid.

27. PP 2/1/f/12/d.

28. Pelikan, *From Luther to Kierkegaard*, 49–75.

29. See Leskov's letter to Suvorin in Sperrle, *Organic Worldview*, 39. Leskov opposes the true Christianity of the searching spirit to Byzantinism, which is understood in terms of fixed ritual and dead dogma.

evangelical tradition of the Gospel Christians was ever acquainted with the mature teachings of Orthodoxy.[30]

A Theological Outline of the Confession

As was stated above, Pashkov's theology, his approach to Bible reading, and his homiletical style were no different from those of Radstock. Pashkov's confession lacks any trace of Orthodox theology. Rather, his nominal Orthodox experience is associated with his life before what he considered to be his true Christian conversion. His confession is firmly established on a Protestant foundation.

The Trinity: The notion of the Trinity is not developed. God the Father is presented as a judge who justifies the believer. The Son of God is presented as the Savior who brought about salvation by his death and resurrection. The Holy Spirit is the one who produces the fruit of a good life in the believer.

Bibliology: Pashkov does not mention the Bible as such. For him the Bible is the Word of God, although he never quotes from the Old Testament in his confession.

Anthropology: People are dead as a result of sin. They cannot save themselves.

Christology: Christ is identified as the Son of God, who is the only mediator between God and people. He is the only source of salvation. He and his work constitute the central message of Pashkov's preaching.

Soteriology: Complete salvation is achieved by Christ once and for all. People must accept the testimony of scripture personally and find their position in Christ. Salvation received through Christ is eternal. Believers can have total assurance that they possess eternal life. Having been saved, believers are called to live the life of the resurrected Christ. There is no place for antinomianism. True faith is revealed in good works, which are viewed as the fruit of the Holy Spirit, given by the Father to those who wholeheartedly belong to the Son of God. In order to be saved one has to appropriate the Gospel *personally*.

Ecclesiology: The church of the living God consists of its living members. That is, those who believe in Christ are redeemed by him, belong to him, and love him. These living members include those who lived in the past, those who are alive in the present, and those who are yet to be born.

30. Florovsky, "Orthodox Churches and the Ecumenical Movement," 177.

Replying to Ianyshev's question as to whether he accepts the authority of the Church (meaning the Orthodox State Church), Pashkov uses the term church in the New Testament sense (Eph 4:11–13). As far as church mysteries are concerned, Pashkov believes that they are relevant only for believers (1 Cor 11:29). He refused any further dialogue that might clarify terminology.[31]

Angelology: Pashkov believes in the existence of the devil. The goal of the evil one is to hinder people from seeing the true path of salvation in Christ by grace.

Eschatology: Pashkov makes no direct reference to eschatology in this confession. This absence is significant, as it demonstrates that personal conversion and moral transformation, in line with the Protestant understanding of salvation by faith, were the key themes of Pashkov's addresses.

It can be safely stated that Pashkov's theological reply to Ianyshev did not reflect any points of difference with the theology of Radstock discussed earlier. Like his spiritual mentor and friend, Pashkov decided to shy away from any clarification of his theological positions, hiding his convictions under the vague phrase "general Christian witness."[32]

The Paradigms Clash

On the same day, May 10, 1880, that Pashkov's confession of faith was published, the new ober-procurator of the Synod, K. P. Pobedonostsev, wrote a letter to the tsar accusing Pashkov of a distorted interpretation of scripture and of holding Protestant meetings in his mansion.[33]

> This doctrine, laid down in the one-sided and narrow way in which Mr. Pashkov repeats it, is extremely dangerous. . . . But what is even more important is the fact that although Mr. Pashkov repudiates being a sectarian, he in fact shuns and repudiates the

31. PP 2/1/f/12/d.

32. Terletskii, *Sekta Pashkovtsev*, 68–74.

33. See Zernov, *Russian Religious Renaissance of the Twentieth Century*, 64: "Pobedonostsev was a professor of law and tutor to the Emperor Alexander III (1881–94), a man with a clear mind and a genuinely religious disposition, a friend of Dostoevsky and a trusted adviser of two monarchs. In spite of his intelligence and zeal he must be numbered among those who prepared the downfall of the Empire. . . . He fought against the disintegration of the Empire by seeking to suppress any progressive movement."

> Orthodox Church. He preaches without having received the blessing of the Church (to say nothing of the permission of the civil authorities) and puts himself on a Protestant footing, ordering his prayer meetings after the Protestant fashion and carefully avoiding saying anything in reference to the Most Holy Virgin, the Mother of God, or the Saints and the Holy Images. . . . The Church alone possesses the full, clear, catholic interpretation of the whole text in the sense of catholic belief, and everyone who separates himself from the Church or sets himself up as a preacher becomes a sectarian. . . . Therefore before it is too late, it seems necessary to put a stop to Pashkov's meetings without delay . . . and to try to prevent the spreading of the new sect, toward which the Church and the State, which have been undivided in Russia, cannot remain unconcerned.[34]

Pobedonostsev compares Pashkov with what he calls "narrow-minded socialists" who had become a threat to Russia. For the ober-procurator of the Holy Synod no distinction existed between religion and politics.[35] The religious activities of Pashkov were considered as destructive as the political activities of opposition groups, including socialists and nihilists, whose ideology was also inspired by the non-Orthodox West.

Count Korff states concerning some rumors that were widespread in Russia after the assassination of Alexander II in March 1881: "They maintained we were a dangerous socialist party which hides under the mask of Christianity."[36] Pashkov and Korff represented the values of the Reformation, which contained the notion of separation between the National Church and the State, as well as the notion of religious tolerance. Even though they did not consider their views to be political in nature, they did indeed include a strong political component that had its origin in the post-Reformed West. Pashkov's convictions and activities also included yet another political dimension which was of much concern to Pobedonostsev. The successful activities of Pashkov and Korff in the Don region and southeastern Ukraine were troubling the government, because of the age-old strife of the Cossacks on behalf of Ukrainian independence. "Unable to achieve this freedom the Ukrainians sought the

34. See Pokrovskii, *Pobedonostsev i ego Korrespondenty. Pis'ma i Zapiski*, vol. 1, 331, 335–38; vol. 2, 445, 456–57. Pobedonostsev, *Pis'ma Pobedonostseva k Alexandru III*, vol. 1, 284; vol. 2, 158–60.

35. Zalystra, "Protestantism: Theology and Politics," 12.

36. Korff, *Am Zarenhof*, 46–47.

fulfillment of their dream in the spiritual sphere. According to Orthodox historians the individualistic nature of the Ukrainian Cossacks and their desire to be free from all bonds made it easy for them to adopt a teaching which would liberate them from all civil and religious authority of the Russian Empire."[37]

The anonymous writer of a letter to Pobedonostsev said: "At the present time the evangelical propaganda in Rostov is carried on by a certain Mr. Kolupaev, who is distributing religious brochures by Pashkov and Burov. Oh, woe unto you, if they succeed in converting the Cossacks. The majority of the Cossacks are already on their side."[38] Pobedonostsev was concerned in 1880 that "the heresy from the North" (that is Radstockism-Pashkovism) could join the heresy from the southwest (that is Stundism) and that this fusion could be a deadly threat to the Orthodox monopoly and the Russian Empire.[39] Thus from Pobedonostsev's point of view, Pashkov and his activities had significant potential to disrupt Orthodox influence. The Protestant ideas of Pashkov, as well as his financial ability to implement them, were not only weakening Orthodoxy but also were threatening the unity of the Empire for which Orthodoxy served as the ideological glue.[40]

The Results of the Collision

As a result of this confrontation, Pashkov was forbidden by the official *ukaz* on May 25, 1880, to continue his meetings, and he left Russia for several months. Pashkov's friend, Fedor G. Terner, wrote to him on May 29, 1880:

> I hope that this temporary break in your Christian activity can lead to success in the struggle for freedom of conscience and to a revival of faith which is being suppressed by formalism. I would just like to plead with you about only one thing. Do not attribute the sins of our local Russian Orthodox Church to the teachings of the Universal Orthodox Church. Unfortunately, historical factors nourished the spirit of formalism and the superficial approach

37. Heier, *Religious Schism*, 140.

38. Pokrovskii, *Pobedonostsev i Ego Korrespondenty*, vol. 2, 884–85.

39. Stundism is a Protestant pietistic dissent movement that started in the German colonies of southern Ukraine.

40. Florovskii, *Puti*, 402–6, 415.

> many have taken toward the affairs of faith. It will be difficult to come out of this condition, but I have hope that we will. . . . I recommend that you get acquainted with true Orthodox teaching. Read Khomyakov. You will find that true Orthodoxy contains all that you believe and love.[41]

There is no evidence that Pashkov listened to the advice of Terner. The subsequent course of events proves that Terner's concerns were valid and that Pashkov consciously broke with state-governed Orthodoxy, the formal side of which he knew very well. Later he acknowledged to Terner that he was leaving Orthodoxy, which caused Terner to end his contacts with Pashkov.[42]

One catalyst in bringing about this break was a massive amount of correspondence with sectarians living in different parts of Russia who, upon reading the published correspondence with Ianyshev in *Tserkovnyi Vestnik,* recognized the similarity of Pashkov's views to their own. Baptists, Stundists, Molokans, and others started to invite Pashkov to meet with them, to ask him doctrinal questions, and to solicit material assistance for various needs.[43] Sectarians often appealed to Pashkov for help in connection with oppression by local Orthodox priests.[44] Pashkov supported them both financially and spiritually by distributing tracts and other religious literature.[45]

CORRESPONDENCE WITH VLADIMIROV

The correspondence of Pashkov includes letters from Aleksei Vladimirov, which seem to have played an important role in Pashkov's understanding of his mission in Russia. The first letter from Vladimirov is dated May 23, 1883.[46] It is not clear from the correspondence whether Vladimirov had written to Pashkov earlier; the information provided in the available

41. PP I/3, 6.

42. McCarthy, "Religious Conflict," 230–31.

43. Letters from Ukraine, the Caucasus, Latvia, and other parts of Russia are abundant in PP. See 2/2/277: a letter from Stepan Prokhanov (Vladikavkaz); 2/21/3: a letter from Ratyshnyi (Ukraine); and 2/2/298: a letter from Latvia.

44. PP 2/21/3.

45. PP I/3, 19–20.

46. PP 2/24/5. The collection "Perepiska Pashkova" at the University of Birmingham contains five letters written by Vladimorov to Pashkov. The last letter available in the archive is dated July 24, 1883.

letters is sufficient, however, to lead to the conclusion that Pashkov was acquainted and in agreement with the radical Protestant ideas of one of the brightest Protestant thinkers in Russia, whose name and works were later lost among the annals of history. The study of Vladimirov's ideas will help us understand Pashkov's radical attitude and his courage in attempting to establish a branch of the Evangelical Alliance in Russia in the spring of 1884, as well as his correspondence with his St. Petersburg coreligionists after his expulsion from Russia. The name of Alexei Vladimirov has not been mentioned by historians, even though his insights may, in fact, have played a significant role in the development of the evangelical movement in the Russian Empire.

Not much is known about Aleksei Porfir'evich Vladimirov beyond the information he gives about himself in his letters to Pashkov. They are written from Vil'na.[47] Vladimirov informs Pashkov that he graduated from the Moscow Spiritual Academy in 1852.[48] This was at the time when Filaret Drosdov, the Metropolitan of Moscow who was in charge of the Academy, had been significantly influenced by Protestant theology.[49] It may be deduced from the correspondence that Vladimirov was married to an Englishwoman and had converted to Anglicanism.[50] He had made a decision to take his son out of the public educational system, because as a father he did not want his son to be taught "a religious lie, which is the worst of all lies," by an Orthodox priest. Vladimirov points out that Russian nihilism has roots in this religious hypocrisy that was prevalent in Orthodox education.[51] He refers to Orthodoxy as "baptized paganism" which has "monopolized Russia."[52] His key appeal to Pashkov

47. Contemporary Vilnius, the capital city of Lithuania.

48. PP 2/24/8.

49. Florovskii, *Puti*, 166–84.

50. Vladimirov does not state this explicitly. In his first letter to Pashkov he talks about a person he knows who had an academic and church education, converted to Anglicanism, married an English woman, and despised Orthodoxy for its lies. The following letters reveal that Vladimirov himself fits this description very well. He was completely disappointed with Orthodoxy, and in his second letter he quotes an English hymn (2/24/6); in his fourth letter he informs Pashkov that he had been educated in an Orthodox academy (2/24/8), thus giving hints to Pashkov about his personal experiences.

51. Cf. Berdiaev, *Istoki i Smysl Russkogo Kommunisma*, chapter 2. See also his "Nigilizm na Religioznoi Pochve," 197–204; Zernov, *The Russian Religious Renaissance*, 47.

52. PP 2/24/5.

is that the latter should use his connections in high society to lobby for a change in the law, providing for "complete religious freedom."[53] Vladimirov's concern is that Western Russia, the place where he is living, is being derussified by Polish Catholicism. The Russian government's attempts to introduce Catholic services in the Russian language has failed. Vladimirov has an idea as to how to fortify Russian influence on the Western borders, and he considers Pashkov to be a possible solution to the problem. Knowing of the immense wealth of the colonel, he suggests to Pashkov that he buy thousands of acres of land in northwest Russia and move evangelical Christians there, so that they can counteract the Catholic Polish influence. Vladimirov thinks that Russian interests can best be pursued by Russian Protestants (Molokans, Stundists, and others). "Murav'ev tried to secure Russian interests by involving Old Believers but it did not succeed."[54] Pashkov's reply to Vladimirov, written on July 3, 1883, has not been kept. One can judge from Vladimirov's next letter that Pashkov is pessimistic about a law granting *complete* freedom of conscience, as well as about his ability to change the situation.[55] Pashkov is quoted as having said that evangelical teachings are considered to represent the most vicious sectarianism.

Vladimirov's Worldview

The major importance of Vladimirov lies not in his concern for the Russification of the northwestern borders of Russia, but in his view of Protestant Christianity, which he considers to be the apex of religious evolution. He perceives Pashkov as a bearer of this messianic teaching capable of saving Russia from moral stagnation and the denationalization of its Western frontiers.[56] Pashkov in turn commends Vladimirov for being a defender of *the truth*. Vladimirov's ideas seem to have provided Pashkov with a new quasi-messianic vista, as well as a new sense

53. Ibid.

54. PP 2/24/6. On the politics of M. N. Murv'ev in Western Russia see Dolbilov, "Kul'turnaia Idioma Vozrozhdeniia Rossii," 227–68.

55. "O Darovanii Raskol'nikam Nekotorykh Prav Grazhdanskikh i po Otpravleniiu Dukhovnykh Treb." Quoted from Garadzha, *Religovedenie*, 340; Reshetnikov and Sannikov, *Obzor Istorii*, 107–8. According to the law the sectarians were given freedoms but not the freedom to propagate their ideas among the Orthodox.

56. Edmund Heier advocates a similar view in his study. See Heier, *Religious Schism*, 118.

of his role in the living out of the historical significance of Russia and of evangelical Christianity.[57] Pashkov and Korff's subsequent defiance of the secular authorities in 1884, which is described but not explained by historians, can be better understood from the viewpoint of Pashkov's acquaintance with the ideas of this Russian Anglican thinker.[58] Vladimirov writes:

> The religion determines the state. The superiority of Protestantism can be seen in such countries as Germany, Denmark, Sweden, Holland, England, Scotland, and the North American states. The difference between the influence of Catholicism and Protestantism can be seen in two neighboring countries: the United States and Mexico. Protestant North America prospers. Mexico is poor even though it has an abundance of material resources. And even within the same region the colonies of the Molokans, Dukhobors, and Stundists have a higher level of culture than the Orthodox living nearby. . . . Even when stricken and scattered in prisons and thrown onto the wild outskirts of Siberia and the Trans-Caucasus region, the Molokans and Dukhobors, these early Protestants of ours, would bring culture into the places of their exile. And in wild desert regions they created a peaceful life and enjoyed abundance. The reason for all these phenomena is clear. In its essential nature, Christianity is universal, eternal, and absolute. However, in its *manifestation* it is local, temporary, and conditional. Thus the form of Christianity in a particular location at a particular time is conditioned by certain historical factors and by appeals to the unique demands of the human spirit during that particular epoch. When these factors pass away, the local form of Christianity becomes obsolete and must be replaced by another form, conditioned by new factors and appealing to new demands of the human spirit. Thus Orthodox Christianity was the form during the first half of the Middle Ages (fifth to tenth centuries). It was largely Eastern. The Catholic faith was the form during the second half of the medieval period (tenth to fifteenth centuries), and it was largely Western. Protestantism is the form of Christianity for the most recent ages. And it is a universal form of Christianity. It frees people from ritualism and does not restrict the free investigation of the human mind. Now I will ask you, which of the loaves of bread is more nutritious—the old hardened loaf or the fresh one? Which nation will win the battle—the one that has newest weapons or the one that fights

57. Duncan, *Russian Messianism*, 6–30.

58. Corrado, *Filosofiia*, 148.

> with the old weapons of their great grandfathers? For this reason, when we labor for our heavenly fatherland, we should not forget about our earthly fatherland. In our earthly fatherland at the present time we are faced with a serious religious-political issue, the so called Russian-Polish issue. The essence of the issue is this: Will the Russian people be overcome by the Polish people, or will it be the other way around in this important part of the Russian State called Western Russia? . . . Poland is going to spread Polish Protestantism to win Russian people in Western Russia. We should cultivate Russian Protestantism in the region to win Russian people for [both] the heavenly and earthly fatherland. . . . This is worth thinking about, because only that nation which appropriates Protestantism earlier and more fully will be able to win over its rival.[59]

Having heard from Pashkov that evangelical Christianity is considered the most vicious sect, Vladimirov shares his optimistic vision for Russia, even though he is indignant toward its "baptized paganism" and its government.

> The leaders of the most enlightened nations make "freedom of conscience" the capstone of their politics. Even though the persecutors of the truth can cause much harm to individuals, they will not be able to hinder the whole work in the slightest. *When the sun is rising over a country and the light of day begins to shine all around, only a fool will attempt to preserve the darkness of the night and stop the advancing light. The One who lives in heaven will laugh at him. And the fact that the sun is rising over Russia can be observed even by a blind man. So taking as a motto the words of the prophet, "In quiet and in hope is your strength," let us exclaim, "Glory to you for having revealed to us the light."*[60]

Vladimirov's pattern of thought is shaped by Hegelian philosophy and is structurally similar to Marxist and Darwinian dialectical thinking. Like Marx, Vladimirov perceives the evolution of human societies in history and their ideological nature.[61] But unlike Marx, his thought is theistic and nationalistic. In a sense, Vladimirov's thought, with his starting point in religion rather than economics, anticipates Max Weber's critique

59. PP. 2/24/7, dated June 17, 1883.

60. PP 2/24/8, dated July 24, 1883. Italics added.

61. Ball, "History: Critique and Irony," 124–42. The first volume of Marx's *Capital* was translated into Russian in 1872. That was four years before the Synodal Bible was published in Russian.

of Marxism two decades later.[62] Protestantism is perceived as the universal synthesis of Eastern and Western forms of Christianity. However, religion is used pragmatically as an ideological weapon in the geopolitical struggle and in the upholding of national interests. According to this view, the future of Russia, as well as its identity, is Protestant, in Protestant Europe. His thought, as seen in this correspondence, has no trace of millenarian motives. Vladimirov is an ideologist and pragmatist, and this makes him different from emotion-driven romantics such as Radstock and Pashkov. Unlike the majority of the *Zapadniki* (Westernizers), who also propagated the Western path of development for Russia, Vladimirov envisions a Protestant orientation, rather than a humanistic one.[63] Vladimirov's perspective introduced Pashkov to an alternative view of the relationship between the Byzantine and Protestant paradigms. Even though Vladimirov does not use the actual term "paradigm," the concept is present in his reasoning. In his view there are three paradigms, which he locates sequentially. Eastern Orthodox Christianity is perceived as the most archaic paradigm, destined to die out. The Protestant paradigm proclaimed by Pashkov represents the latest and most universal form of Christianity, and it is seen as being able to overpower the Western Catholic paradigm so prevalent in Western Russia at that time. The basic storyline presented in Vladimirov's thought is no different from that of Radstock and Baedeker, who perceived the whole of Russia as a land to be conquered and enlightened with evangelical teaching.[64] Orthodox critics were partly right in calling the evangelicals a socialist movement.[65] The similarities between socialists and evangelicals went deeper than mere resemblances in certain activities among the masses. The modernist structure of thought that radically denied the past, as well as the ideological struggle for the new Russia as part of Western civilization, were common to both movements. The pro-Western Russian intelligentsia targeted the Russian autocracy as the enemy, believing that Russia "would be able to achieve socialist order before the rest of Europe."[66] The

62. Lowith, *Max Weber and Karl Marx*, 120–26.

63. Hudspith, *Dostoevsky and the Idea of Russianness*; Berdyaev, *Russian Idea*; Riasanovsky, *Russia and the West in the Teaching of the Slavophiles*; Devlin, *Slavophiles and Commissars*.

64. PP 2/3/18, dated November 7, 1882.

65. Korff, *Am Zarenhof*, 46–47; Heier, *Religious Schism*, 131.

66. Zernov, *Russian Religious Renaissance*, 5.

evangelicals did not challenge the monarchical order of Russia, but targeted the State Church instead. Both movements were trying to undermine the fusion of "autocracy and Orthodoxy" established by Peter the Great, in order to make Russia a progressive part of Western civilization. It will be demonstrated below that Pashkov believed that "Russia would be the first country in Europe where the Church of true believers would be united into one, to convince the World that Jesus Christ was sent by God." These movements should be considered as parallel streams in the process of the geopolitical reorientation of Russia at the turn of the nineteenth century. This philosophical understanding was a key component in the multilayered hermeneutical filter that influenced Pashkov's approach to biblical interpretation.

Vladimirov Tackles the Critique of Bogdanovich[67]

In the spring of 1883 the prefect of St. Isaac's Cathedral, E. Bogdanovich, published open letters to Pashkov in which he accused Pashkov of disseminating Protestant teaching, which was not in accord with Orthodoxy on the following key points:[68]

1. Pashkov has not been appointed by the Church to teach. His teaching is leading people away from the Orthodox Church, with its rituals and forms of worship. Having rejected the Orthodox Church, Pashkov has cut the cord of Russian identity. Pashkov is a new religious impostor who is shattering the unity of the Church (John 17:21).[69]
2. Pashkov does not honor icons and the saints.[70]
3. Pashkov is bribing people into his sect.[71]
4. Pashkov is corrupting people by teaching that salvation is attain-

67. I have decided to incorporate the unpublished debate between Bogdanovich and Vladimirov found in Pashkov's correspondence to demonstrate that Pashkov was acquainted with evangelical apologetics. Arguably, the tract written by Vladimirov represents most likely the best theological arguments in Eastern evangelicalism.

68. PP I/4; Bogdanovich, *Otkrytye Pis'ma Starosty Isaakievskogo Sobora g. Pashkovu.*

69. Bogdanovich, *Otkrytye Pis'ma*, 3–5.

70. Ibid., 5.

71. Ibid., 7–8.

> able by faith alone, without works. This teaching may be good for a German, "who soars on the wings of his thought in the sky of abstraction," but the Russian person will take the teaching to the extreme.[72]

Bogdanovich criticizes Pashkov for reading scripture selectively and for giving undue emphasis to certain New Testament passages, thereby "stirring the water of scriptural teaching."[73] According to Bogdanovich, Pashkov's teaching can be expressed in just two words: "We [are] saved."[74] Bogdanovich emphasizes the importance of human involvement in the process of salvation in Christ. Human participation, he says, cannot be ignored (Matt 11:12; Jas 2:14, 17, 19).[75] He attacks early Keswickian teaching on perfectionism as an example of sectarian teaching. Expressing his ire in parentheses as he quotes a tract, the Orthodox priest cannot make sense of the Keswickian language:

> What Jesus did on the cross was complete (?!). The cross of Christ is the first part of God's story. The cross of Christ has solved the problem of sin. The believer should not stir up this question any more (sic!). The believer should find his place on the other side of the cross. The second part of God's story starts with the resurrection of Jesus. The cross deals with the old creation. The resurrection launches the era of the new creation. Sin, flesh, and death belong to the first part of the story. The believer belongs to the second part. Human opinions have covered up this teaching of God's Word.[76]

Bogdanovich becomes indignant over this interpretation.[77] He appeals to the history of the Church, explains that the practices of Orthodoxy do not contradict scripture, quotes Russian poetry, and appeals to Pashkov *not to destroy the unity* of the Church with Western doctrine.

Vladimirov replies to Bogdanovich to acquit Pashkov of these Orthodox accusations.[78] He uses the language and reasoning of

72. Ibid., 11–12.

73. Ibid., 12.

74. This is only two words in Russian.

75. Ibid.

76. Cf. Nee, *Normal Christian Life*, 65–75.

77. Bogdanovich, 15.

78. PP I/4, dated June 25, 1883. The theological reply of Vladimirov has never been published, even though he sent it to Pashkov. My point is that Pashkov was acquainted

Protestant theology, without attempting to counteract Bogdanovich on Orthodox terms. Thus what Bogdanovich perceives as "self-appointment," Vladimirov suggests should be seen as "appointment by God." "The prophets of old, such as Isaiah, were sent directly by God. Could not Pashkov have had the same experience?"[79] The diachronic aspect of Orthodox tradition and the Orthodox view of Church unity are simply ignored. What Bogdanovich takes as the work of the devil, Vladimirov presents as the very work of God, who destroys the false unity of the false Church. The non-use of icons is justified by a direct appeal to the New Testament times of Christ and His Apostles. Icons are taken to be a product of the paganization of Christianity. Bogdanivich appeals to Russian history and culture with its veneration of icons; Vladimirov counteracts by appealing to the civilized West and to its most advanced Protestant countries, which do not make use of icons. The issue of salvation by faith alone is also approached in a typically Protestant vein. Vladimirov appeals to the history of Western theology and argues that Pashkov is a representative of sound Christianity in the line of Augustine, Aquinas, and Jansenius, while Bogdanovich shares the heretical theological convictions of Pelagius, Duns Scotus, and Molina with regard to the question of salvation. "The one who believes in salvation by faith alone does good works as a result of his faith and gratitude, while the one who does good works in order to receive salvation has impure motives." An appeal is made to philosophy to demonstrate the complexity of the task of defining "good works." "From the practical point of view, the teaching that salvation is received through faith plus deeds causes psychological turmoil and leads to asceticism, while the truly orthodox teaching that salvation is received through faith alone brings peace, hope, and joy."[80]

At the end of his address, Vladimirov turns the tables, depicting Bogdanovich as a theologically ignorant opponent. Pashkov is depicted as the defender of the true orthodox faith, while Bogdanovich "looks like a knight who attacks [an] opponent whose hands are tied."[81]

The correspondence of A. P. Vladimirov with V. A. Pashkov demonstrates a new configuration of the two paradigms that were consciously

with Protestant theological argumentation, which helped him to carry on with his vision of transforming Russia after the model of Western liberal societies.

79. Ibid.

80. Ibid.

81. Ibid. Vladimirov was referring to Pashkov's lack of theological education.

recognized by Pashkov. Both the Protestant and Byzantine paradigms claim absolute possession of the truth, and both are culturally shaped. Vladimirov presents a view of Protestant Christianity that is grounded in the philosophy of Hegel. According to this view, Western Protestantism is the synthetic and universal religion of both East and West. Vladimirov belongs to the camp of *Zapadniki* (Westernizers). He looks to the West pragmatically and is not bound by Church tradition. His knowledge of theology is used exclusively for apologetic purposes. Bogdanovich, on the other hand, represents the Slavophile position, in which the tradition of the Eastern Church and the historical way of Russian Orthodoxy is taken as the frame of reference. The Western world is perceived as the enemy, threatening to invade and destroy ancient truth and Russian identity.[82] Each paradigm interprets scripture and Church tradition differently through their respective hermeneutical lenses. Both Vladimirov and Bogdanovich made the mistake of universalizing their particular paradigms. This universalizing of particular historical manifestations of the Christian faith prevented the possibility of dialogue for many years to come. Vladimirov's correspondence provides a good platform for understanding both Pashkov's horizons and the historical events that led to his expulsion from Russia.

EXPULSION FROM RUSSIA

Several months after his correspondence with Vladimirov, who provided a messianic vision for Protestantism in Russia, Pashkov decided to challenge the authorities once again. In the spring of 1884 Pashkov and Korff attempted to unify the scattered evangelical sects of Russia with which they had previously established relationships through their vision for creating a Russian branch of the Evangelical Alliance.[83] Representatives of different Protestant groups attended a conference, among them Molokans, Dukhobors, Stundists, Mennonites, and others. Some members of the Evangelical Alliance of Britain were invited as well. The Alliance was represented by Dr. Baedeker and Reginald Radcliff. The Mennonite historian Walter Sawatsky gives the following evaluation

82. On Slavophiles and Westernizers see Berdyaev, *Russian Idea*, 51–89; Copleston, *History Of Philosophy*, vol. 10, *Russian Philosophy*, 26–44; and Losskii, *Istoriia Russkoi Filosfii*, 10–65.

83. PP I/3, 25, 26.

of the meeting, which demonstrates a lack of awareness of the massive international evangelical program, the theological foundation behind it, and the geopolitical drive towards the Protestant West. Sawatsky states, "[A]s a result of Pashkov's irenic style, it became possible to call the first meeting of the proposed *Russian Baptist Union.*"[84] Paradoxically, the vision of a Russian branch of the Evangelical Alliance, which Pashkov and the British representatives intended to establish, was thwarted by the Baptists, who refused to take communion with those believers who had not been rebaptized.[85] Significantly, this conference was viewed as defiance of the authorities, who had prohibited it several days earlier.[86] Historians do not explain why Pashkov and Korff challenged the secular authorities, in light of the direct confrontation that had taken place four years earlier.

Pashkov's conversion to the Protestant paradigm, which construed Christian identity differently from Orthodoxy, as well as Vladimirov's understanding of historical processes provide an explanation for the decision. In an attempt to unite the true church of the born again on the graveyard of the "baptized paganism that monopolized Russia," Pashkov expected God's vindication of his disobedience towards the civil authorities. Vladimirov's powerful exposition sheds some light on the event. This course of action, however, gave Pobedonostsev a strong argument to use in convincing the new Tsar Alexander III, whom he had tutored, of the need to expel Pashkov and Korff from Russia upon their refusal to stop their preaching activity. The vision of establishing the Evangelical Alliance was never realized in Pashkov's lifetime.

THE THEOLOGICAL VISION OF PASHKOV AS REVEALED IN HIS PRIVATE CORRESPONDENCE[87]

Having severed ties with the traditional authority of the Orthodox Church, and having no desire to tread the doctrine-based route of es-

84. Sawatsky, *Soviet Evangelicals*, 35. Italics added.

85. Korff, *Am Zarenhof*, 57.

86. Corrado, *Filosofiia*, 146–48.

87. This section should be viewed as a supplement to the description above of the theology of Pashkov. The previous theological sections were intended to articulate Pashkov's public theological stance and the subsequent theological clash that resulted in his expulsion from Russia. In this section I will focus on theological themes that

tablished Protestant denominations, Pashkov had to rely on the Spirit-based approach to the reading of scripture that had been introduced by Radstock and subsequently by George Müller. This neo-Protestant approach to scripture is better understood as moving to the logical end of the Protestant trajectory of *sola scriptura*. The center of Pashkov's theological hermeneutics was his belief that the Spirit guides both individual believers and communities of believers into a correct understanding of scripture. An Orthodox critic summarized this attitude in the following way: "Take a Bible, pray to God to grant you understanding like the Apostles, open the Bible. You find the spot that Christ showed you, you read it and the light enters you. . . . You do not need to go to Church, prepare for communion, or talk to a Russian priest, nor receive any of the sacraments. You yourself are an apostle and have all the sacraments."[88]

Pashkov's approach is a typical example of reading the Bible in the vein of the pre-Pentecostal holiness tradition. Biblical texts are read selectively, without taking into account their historical or literary contexts or even grammatical considerations. Pashkov's correspondence has not been analyzed in previous studies from a theological point of view. In my analysis of the theological themes in Pashkov's correspondence, I will focus on those themes that differ somewhat from those of Radstock discussed in the previous chapter. Pashkov's interaction with the evangelical sectarians of Russia resulted in a slight modification of some Radstockian themes.

The Unity of the Church

The theme of church unity was as important for Pashkov as it was for Lord Radstock. From the Orthodox point of view, Pashkov was disrupting church unity by his activity. However, from Pashkov's viewpoint, he was trying to unite the true church, which he associated with the evangelical Christianity of Radstock. Orthodoxy as such was considered to be a deviation from biblical truth. Pashkov's vision of church unity was driven by two New Testament texts, John 17:17 and Eph 5:25–27, where we read that "Christ loved the church and gave himself up for her to make

were not articulated in public. This private correspondence will be counterbalanced by an analysis of the *Russian Workman*, which represented views of the early Pashkovites in the public domain.

88. *Grazhdanin* 8 (1874) 2. Quoted in McCarthy, "Religious Conflict," 158.

her holy, cleansing her by the washing with water *through the word*, and to present her to himself as a radiant church, without stain or wrinkle or any other blemish, but holy and blameless."[89] In Pashkov's interpretation, the unity of the church can be achieved when believers of different convictions come together to study the Bible in the spirit of mutual love. As a result of this *fellowship* and common Bible study, he believed that Christians would come to the same conclusions regarding every question, thereby putting aside all human traditions and misconceptions that are not derived from the Word of God.[90] Pashkov assumed that *the word* of which Paul was writing in the passage in Ephesians was the canonical Protestant Bible that had recently been published in Russian. As an example of "human teaching," he mentioned paedobaptism, which had become one of the stumbling blocks to unity at the meeting in April 1884.[91]

Pashkov's view was reinforced by George Müller, who visited Russia in the winter of 1882–83 and devoted a significant period of time to teaching the St. Petersburg believers.[92] Gutsche states that Müller baptized Pashkov and most likely introduced the practice of breaking bread on a weekly basis.[93] Gutshe does not refer, however, to any primary sources for his information, which is typical of the denominational historiography of the Soviet period. The Orthodox critic Terletskii says that Pashkov himself baptized Molokans in Novovasilievka as early as 1881.[94] This may mean that Pashkov himself had been baptized earlier than 1881. Possible confirmation of this suggestion can be found in a private letter Pashkov wrote to Burov from Paris in 1885 in which he states that he had been "baptized several years [*let* in Russian] earlier following a thorough study of scripture."[95] Had Pashkov been baptized by Müller in 1883, the Russian phrase *neskol'ko let* (several years) would not have been technically correct, as the word *let* (literally "summers")

89. PP II/1/b/86 (frame 297), dated May 16, 1885. The reference is made to Eph 5:25–27.

90. PP II/1/c/18; II/1/c/70.

91. PP II/1/b/86.

92. Müller, *Autobiography*, 544–47; Korff, *Am Zarenhof*, 31.

93. Waldemar Gutsche, *Westliche Quellen des russischen Stundismus*, 58–60.

94. Terletskii, *Sekta Pashkovtsev*, 98. Terletskii includes a reference to *Russkii Vestnik* 2 (1886) 860.

95. PP II/1/c/18.

is ordinarily used with reference to five or more years. Pashkov does not specify when, where, or by whom he was baptized. Most likely it happened abroad in 1880, after he was required to cease his religious activities and leave Russia for the first time. The practice of the weekly breaking of bread was well established by the 1890s.[96] The suggestion in Gutsche's report that the idea of establishing the weekly breaking of bread came from Müller during the early days of his ministry in Russia seems to be credible.[97] Taking into account the fact that Radstock did not practice either the breaking of bread or baptism while in Russia, one can see the development of new rituals that reinforced the story of the Gospel Christians and contributed to a new self-identity for some of the members of the St. Petersburg group.

Following the troublesome experience of the disrupted congress of 1884, Pashkov carried on intensive correspondence with believers of different religious convictions, insisting that Bible-believing Christians should strive for unity with each other. He believed in Russia's messianic role in the task of the fulfilling the prayer of Christ. In his letter to a Mennonite minister, I. Wieler, he writes: "We should ask the Lord that the unity of all members of his body in Russia would be revealed in visible form to outsiders, so that they will believe that Christ came from God by seeing his followers' mutual brotherly love and unity. The world still hopes that *Russia will be the first country that will fulfill this cherished wish of Christ. What kind of blessing shall we expect when this unity is accomplished?*"[98]

Writing to Mr. Tikhonov shortly after his expulsion from Russia in 1884, Pashkov says:

> To my joy I have never heard even a single debate about baptism or the Lord's Supper, even though I have seen many famous Christians. But I have seen them working together and preaching to unbelievers from the same pulpit, one after another. There was Spurgeon who is a Baptist; there was Lord Radstock who understands baptism spiritually; and there was an Anglican pastor who baptizes infants. Each of them understands the Lord's communion differently. But they were united in spirit and did one

96. Corrado, *Filosofiia*, 112.

97. Müller, *Autobiography*, 150.

98. PP II/1/b/4, November 17, 1884. Italics added. Cf. The socialist belief that Russia would become the first socialist country in Europe. See Zernov, *Religious Renaissance*, 5.

> work by preaching Christ who is God's power and God's wisdom. Praise God that the most famous of his servants are learning this lesson. They fight against the present evil. . . . They teach that we should live in holiness, peace, and love before the Lord.[99]

Pashkov put great hope in a conference that was scheduled to be held in the village of Astrakhanka in May 1885. In his letter to Wieler he mentioned that Kargel would be going to Astrakhanka as a representative of the St. Petersburg Christians and that he was praying for unity and a spirit of love.[100] At the same time, he wrote a letter to Deliakov, who practiced paedobaptism. In this letter he presented to Deliakov his vision of unity based on Ephesians 5:26–27, when believers come together in the spirit of love and check their teachings against the testimony of scripture: "Peace and love should make it easier to attain unity, even with regard to diverse opinions, so that all will say the same thing and there will not be different opinions among you."[101]

In an attempt to push the other evangelical party towards union Pashkov wrote a letter to Mikhail Ratushnyi, one of the prominent Baptist leaders. The thrust of the letter was that British Baptists were not separated from other believers. He mentions that he had been in Spurgeon's church, where "even unbaptized believers took part in communion."[102] His hopes began to collapse, however, in the summer of 1885. After receiving a letter from Deliakov, Pashkov accused him of being a stumbling block to unity.[103] He became impatient and tried to prove to Deliakov that paedobaptism does not have a scriptural foundation. "I am deeply convinced that everyone who, without bias, starts studying scripture with regard to baptism will come to one and the same conclusion."[104]

On the other hand, in a letter written to St. Petersburg in August 1885, Pashkov expressed his concern about the rigid position of the Baptists, who did not want to participate with Gospel Christians in communion because of their different understanding of baptism. "Do

99. PP II/1/b/8.
100. PP II/1/b/84.
101. PP II/1/b/86.
102. PP II/1/b/29.
103. PP II/1/ b/100.
104. Ibid.

they not understand that complete unity in understanding can be accomplished when people gather together as members of one body?"[105]

Let me summarize at this point some of Pashkov's hermeneutical assumptions. On the one hand, he believed that it would be possible to organize an all-Russian movement which would be based exclusively on the Protestant foundation of *sola scriptura, sola gratia, and sola fide.* Pashkov cut his ties with the National Church and adopted the revivalist view that the true church consists only of "born-again Christians." This ecclesiology envisioned Russia as part of Western Protestant civilization. The term "born again" was understood largely in terms of a personal conversion experience that starts with faith in the biblical testimony. He believed that scripture contains a clear answer to every disputable question of doctrine and practice. Priority was to be given not to any doctrine or regulation, but to the spirit of love and fellowship through which the Bible should be scrutinized. As a result of spiritual unity and a communal reading of the Bible, it would be possible to reach unity in matters of doctrine and practice, as well. To achieve this vision, Paskhov had to plead with the Baptists to accept other believers who did not share their rigid interpretations concerning the necessity of water baptism by immersion and the Lord's Supper. On the other hand, he pleaded with non-Baptists to reexamine their teachings on debatable points in light of scripture. The goal, however, was not conformity to a particular teaching, but the overall unity of the emerging evangelical church. During this period Pashkov believed that Russian evangelicals would not only be able to form a heterogeneous Evangelical Alliance, but eventually arrive at an all-embracing unity that would include uniformity in belief and practice. The Orthodox Church was not taken into account. Pashkov considered it to be by and large a dead church, founded on human tradition and not on the Word of God. However, continual disunity among evangelicals and the divisive spirit of the Baptists, influenced by the rigid theological position of the Hamburg School of Theology, began to shatter Pashkov's expectations.

Pashkov's most obvious dissatisfaction with the German Baptist tradition is revealed in his private correspondence with various people concerning a young missionary, a certain Mr. Gerasimenko, who was supposed to go to Hamburg Seminary. When asked to sponsor

105. PP II/1 b/119.

Gerasimenko's studies in Hamburg, Pashkov replies negatively. He suggests that Gerasimenko go instead to the East London Institute for Home and Foreign Missions. Pashkov is ready to pay all the expenses for Gerasimnko in London: "While the fee there may be high (£50), out of this school come missionaries with bigger hearts and broader opinions, which do not condition one's membership in the body of Christ on the rite of baptism. . . . I am somewhat concerned about the narrow notions of the German Baptists. Therefore I do not want to participate in sending a Russian missionary to their school."[106] In another letter to Wieler, dated October 9, 1885, Pashkov expands his idea:

> When Gerasimenko's heart warms up to people who are preparing to devote their lives to the Lord in distant pagan lands; when it extends to such a degree that he would not even dare to ask to which denomination another zealous servant of the King of Heaven happens to belong; when he would not even want to know the name of the society in which that servant had previously participated, but instead would consider his comrade who serves the same Lord to be a member of one and the same Body—only then could he go to Hamburg to learn the German orders and gain confidence in the German language.[107]

In a letter to Dr. Baedeker, dated October 31, 1885, Pashkov explains the whole situation with Gerasimenko and suggests that Wieler himself should come to Britain to see how things are done there: "I suggest that it would be much better for [Gerasimenko] to go to Mr. Grattan Guinness, where he is not likely to get such a narrow view of baptism as in Germany. . . . I will request Lord Radstock to give (Wieler) a letter of recommendation to Spurgeon. He might go to George Müller as well and give an account of the work in South Russia."[108]

Much later, in March 1887, Pashkov writes to Gerasimenko himself, who has by then spent a year and a half in London: "I do not consider it the will of God to give you money to become a student in Hamburg. It has been put in my heart to invite you to go Basel this summer. If you agree, I will write a letter to the rector."[109]

106. PP II/1/b/139, dated September 1885.
107. PP II/1/b/141.
108. PP II/1/c/4.
109. PP II/1/d/19.

Pashkov's attitude towards the Baptist tradition is telling. The denominational rigidity of the German Baptists was not acceptable from the point of view of a person whose ecclesiology and spirituality had been shaped by the mentality of British non-denominational movements such as the Open Brethren, the Evangelical Alliance, and the Keswick Convention.[110] The following history of the relationships between the Gospel Christians of St. Petersburg and the Baptists can be properly understood only against the background of the qualitative differences between these two traditions.

Unity in Diversity

It did not take Pashkov long to come to see the naïveté of his original vision of unity. As early as January 1887 Pashkov celebrated the unique evangelical movement among the Jews in Russia. In a letter he sent to Rudolf Fedorovich, most likely a Lutheran pastor, he writes: "Having gathered information about this movement among the people of Israel, I have come to the conclusion that our government has been established by God himself for the protection of the emerging community of the new Israel, so that they would not be fused with any of the existing confessions, but on the contrary would preserve their national and, at the same time, all-Christian significance."[111]

In a letter to Wieler written at about the same time, Pashkov emphasizes that the merging of this movement with any other confession "would deny the national Jewish character of the movement and its significance."[112]

A more mature confession of Pashkov appears in a letter sent to a certain Mr. Porfiri in July 1888:

> Fellowship with the brethren is necessary for edification and for expanding the heart and correcting overly-narrow notions. I was mistaken for a long time while searching for unity notionally, so to say—that is, unity not only in the same understanding of the most important foundations, but even in secondary regulations of the scriptures. I was looking for outward unity. But I

110. I use the term "non-denominational" in a restricted sense, referring to Protestant denominations.

111. PP II/1/d/2.

112. PP II/1/c/139.

> have come to understand that true unity consists exclusively in unity of spirit. This kind of unity can and often does exist among people with different understandings of different passages of the Word of God. Those who truly love the Lord and want to fulfill his will are united with Him and with each other.[113]

Bibliology and Bible Study

In Pashkov's correspondence, a high view of the Bible and its inspiration is explicitly articulated. Pashkov believes that the Word of God is not deficient in any way. "*Everything* that Jesus heard from the Father he handed over to the disciples and . . . the Holy Spirit would remind them of *everything*."[114] He specifies that the Word of God consists of both the Old and New Testaments.[115] He believes that the key to the correct understanding of the Bible comes from God's Spirit, when the Bible is searched with a prayerful spirit. "May the Lord grant [female believers] the ability to distinguish what comes from him and what comes from man."[116] This view is consistent with Müller's instructions for reading the Bible.

> Above all [the reader] should seek to have it settled in his own mind that God alone, by His Spirit, can teach him, and that therefore, as God will be asked for blessings, it becomes him to seek God's blessing previous to, and whilst reading. . . . The Holy Spirit is the *best* and *sufficient* teacher. . . . Learned *commentaries* I have found to store the *head* with many notions, and often with the truth of God; but when the Spirit teaches, through the instrumentality of prayer and meditation, the heart is affected. The former kind of knowledge generally puffs up, and is often renounced when another commentary gives a different opinion, and often is found good for nothing when it is to be carried out in practice.[117]

Pashkov echoes Müller almost verbatim in his correspondence on theological matters over the next decade. In a letter he wrote to a

113. PP II/1/d/165, frames 442 and 443.

114. PP II/1/b/66.

115. PP II/1/c/76.

116. Ibid.

117. Müller, *Autobiography*, 21–22. Italics added.

young believer, a certain Mr. Rozov, in 1888, Pashkov says: "The more I read, my dear friend, creations of the human mind, even of the mind of believing authors, the more I am convinced that only one thing is necessary, only one thing is helpful for the spiritual life, and that is the direct searching of scripture, the constant study of it so that we can directly learn from the Lord, who commands us to learn from him and not from people. A secure position for us consists in being grounded in scripture and having only one interpreter—that is, the Holy Spirit."[118]

Several years later, in 1896, having received a request from one of the ministers concerning the possibility of sponsoring his theological studies, Pashkov replies negatively, explaining his position in Müllerite terminology: "One does not need theology for successful ministry to the Lord." He refers to uneducated apostles, quoting 1 Corinthians 2:4–6, and states that the preaching of the Gospel is ministry by the power of the Holy Spirit.[119]

Having no external railing to constrain the subjective nature of interpretation, the Pashkovites were left only with the option of discussing different interpretations and evaluating them among themselves.[120] In December 1884 Pashkov wrote a letter to Kargel, in which he inquired about deviations from "the truth" which had been detected earlier among some of the St. Petersburg believers.[121] The key question was whether the troublemakers were open to being critiqued. A clear example of the validation of an interpretation is seen in Pashkov's correspondence with Kargel and with one of the aristocratic women. Pashkov perceived that an evangelical church should be established in St. Petersburg, and so he wrote to Kargel in February 1885:

> If the brethren have seen that the Orthodox Church has left the commandments of the Lord, having replaced them with human traditions, they should not be advised to approach the church they have left in those instances when they have a necessity, such as registering a newborn baby or having a wedding. On the other hand, none of these necessities can be fulfilled in a lawful manner

118. PP II/1/d/120.

119. PP II/1/e/19, dated January, 1896.

120. This method of biblical interpretation is similar to the Anabaptist approach to interpretation, with the exception that the Anabaptists interpreted the Bible through a different theological grid, which had been formed in the sixteenth century in Germany. See Murray, *Biblical Interpretation in the Anabaptist Tradition*.

121. PP II/1/b/17.

> while we are not granted the right to leave Orthodoxy and start an evangelical church. But to establish such a congregation it is necessary that the Lord would make it known to the people who would be in a position to lead it.[122]

Several months later Pashkov received a letter from one of the aristocratic women in St. Petersburg, who reported:

> The brothers said at the meeting that they wanted to leave the Orthodox Church and start an evangelical church. All the women refused, each giving their own reason. I said that it is not good, having started in the Spirit, to finish in the flesh. We should not become "another sect" or "society." I do not see from the Word of God that Christ wants to fence his pasture; but we want to fence off a piece of land in order to enjoy a cozy life by having our own ceremonies. The brothers agreed with me. Rozov said, "We should thank God because whenever we want to do our own will, He destroys our plans and reveals his will."[123]

This correspondence is important from both a historical and hermeneutical point of view. On the one hand, it shows that the majority of the St. Petersburg believers did not leave the Orthodox paradigm in order to practice the pietistic spirituality of Radstock. Pashkov's theological conversion to Protestantism was not advertised publicly. The aristocratic women still inhabited the Radstockian configuration of the paradigms and, while continuing to read the Bible in the Protestant way, had no desire to leave the "Orthodox Temple." From a hermeneutical point of view, the correspondence demonstrates that the St. Petersburg evangelicals arrived at a solution to pending problems through open discussion. The will of God for the present moment was determined by means of the most felicitous interpretations within the community.

Ecclesiology

The dominating ecclesiological concern in Pashkov's correspondence has to do with the establishment of an evangelical church in St. Petersburg. It has already been mentioned that according to Baptist writer S. Sannikov, the church in St. Petersburg began as a result of Pashkov's having been

122. PP II/1/b/36.

123. PP 2/2/26.

baptized by Müller in 1883.[124] However, Pashkov's correspondence reveals that his baptism was a private matter that had nothing to do with the establishment of an evangelical church in St. Petersburg. To be more precise, Pashkov, like Müller himself, was concerned that structuring a congregation of believers according to the pattern of existing denominations would ruin his vision for the interdenominational unity of "brethren" in the spirit of Christian love.

Pashkov forcefully rejected the idea of electing a presbyter for the congregation in St. Petersburg. His concern was that an elected pastor might crystallize a particular teaching and impose it on the congregation, turning it into yet another evangelical sect. "We should not make the mistakes that other churches have made,"[125] he wrote. Pashkov envisioned an unstructured charismatic community in which each member would operate with his or her received gift: "We shall patiently wait until the Lord himself will teach us to walk in accordance with his will and to receive from his hand the manifestations of the fruit of the Spirit in the church, which he desires to pour on all members of his Body. Remember that the perfect treasure of understanding is given to hearts united in love, and after that the Lord manifests gifts by which the different ministries of the members are distinguished from each other."[126]

The impetus for establishing a more structured congregation resulted from the separation of a growing number of St. Petersburg believers from Orthodoxy. Pashkov was one of the first followers of Radstock to become convinced that the doctrine of the Orthodox Church did not correspond with "biblical teaching," which he did not much differentiate from Radstock's interpretation of it. Most likely Pashkov wanted Kargel to lead the congregation, because upon his return from Bulgaria Kargel shared the same vision as Pashkov. However, Kargel did not have the dis-

124. Sannikov, *Dvadtsat' Vekov Khristianstva*, vol. 2, 517. Sannikov mistakenly states that the meetings before the arrival of Müller were patterned after the Darbyan fashion. However, the "Closed" Brethren associated with the name of Darby were much more structured and had more similarities with the Baptists with regard to their rigidity of doctrine. According to Spurgeon, "This party [the Müllerites] differs as much from the Darbyites as the day from the night. We do not admire their peculiarities, but they are usually a fraternal, evangelistic race, with whom communion is not difficult, for their spirit is far removed from the ferocity of Darbyism." Quoted from Spurgeon, "Mr. Grant on the 'Darby Brethren,'" n. 2.

125. PP II/1/ b/66, dated April 2, 1885.

126. Ibid.

position to become the pastor of any local congregation. His desire was to take up the ministry of an itinerant preacher.[127] The person promoted to this position was a young man by the name of I. Rozov.

Writing to Rozov in early March 1885, Pashkov said: "We do not see in the Word that presbyters were elected by the church. They were set in place by the apostles or their delegates. Therefore *the election* of anybody to this position would be a deviation from the Word."[128] A month later, in his letter to the whole community of believers in St. Petersburg, he clarified his idea and concern.

> The presbyters, according to the Word, were set in place by the apostles and by those who along with them were God's instruments for delivering the people, of whom the church was established, from Satan to God. Does this not mean that any other way of electing a presbyter is a deviation from the Lord's instruction? The purpose of the admonition is love from a pure heart. May the Lord unite you and fuse our hearts into one by his all-encompassing love. Take just this one concern about this fruit of the Holy Spirit. All the other gracious gifts of the Lord will follow.[129]

Pashkov's major concern, as seen in his correspondence, was that no one person or group of leaders fully shared his vision. In a sense, he had been the apostle to the congregation by means of his intensive preaching in Russian following the departure of Radstock, whose ministry had been limited by and large to the aristocracy who could understand English and French. The absence of the office of pastor seemed to him to facilitate the sort of charismatic community reflected in the First Epistle to the Corinthians.

However, the situation got out of control. In the summer of 1886, the St. Petersburg believers decided to elect Rozov as a presbyter. Pashkov wrote a letter in which he expressed his concerns and argued on scriptural grounds that Rozov was, in fact, ineligible to be a presbyter, given his youth and the fact that he was not married.[130] Pashkov took quite literally the text of 1 Timothy 3:2 and 6. However, the believers proceeded with their proposal and Rozov became a presbyter. In a letter to Rozov written in November 1886, Pashkov accepted this decision

127. PP 2/13/39.
128. PP II/1/b/45.
129. PP II/1/b/66.
130. PP II/1/c/101.

and gave Rozov some pastoral instructions, suggesting that he should start visiting those who had fallen away from the Lord. The themes of spiritual warfare and life in the Lord were dominant.[131] In 1888 Pashkov suggested to Rozov that the congregation should be separated from the Orthodox Church, so that the believers would not have to be dependent on that church for registering weddings and issuing birth certificates. It follows from the correspondence that as late as 1888 the believers in St. Petersburg were still not separated from Orthodoxy as a congregation. Some of the believers who had left Orthodoxy individually tried to bribe Orthodox priests to give them the needed documents when a baby was born or a wedding was planned.[132] Pashkov considered this unethical. In his view, the congregation should have tried to join some existing evangelical confession just for the purpose of dealing with such formalities in connection with the state. He looked forward to better times, however, when the St. Petersburg congregation would be independent of all ties with any confession, so as to implement his ecumenical vision.[133]

In the summer of 1888, the St. Petersburg congregation became bitterly divided over the issue of electing more new presbyters. Pashkov again pleaded with them to consider his understanding of God's Word. And he appealed to the newly-elected presbyters to step down from their positions because of the unscriptural foundation of their election.[134]

Four years later, Dr. Baedeker informed Pashkov that the St. Petersburg group was still divided over the issue of presbyters and the ritual of baptism. "I feel more than ever persuaded that the result of attempting to organize a church is simply disastrous,"[135] Dr. Baedeker wrote. The issue was not resolved even by May 1896, when the congregation was still divided, as some of the believers considered themselves to be "more biblical" than others. Pashkov exclaimed, "When will this unrighteous judgment be over? Who has set them as judges over the brethren?"[136]

131. PP II/1/c/124.

132. The evangelicals seem to have stopped attending Orthodox temples and participating in Orthodox services. Bribery was used in order to obtain official documents without participating in the rites of the Orthodox Church.

133. PP II/1/d/120.

134. PP II/1/d/158.

135. PP 2/3/173, dated February 27, 1892.

136. PP II/1/e/162.

Baptism

As has already been pointed out, Pashkov believed that the Bible teaches that the rite of baptism should be administered subsequent to one's personal conversion experience. Under the influence of the Baptists, with whom he had been in correspondence, Pashkov deviated from Radstock's interpretation of baptism. In his letter to Burov written from Paris in 1885, Pashkov commends Burov for having been baptized. It follows from this letter that even one of Pashkov's closest associates had not known about Pashkov's own baptism.[137] Pashkov informs Burov that he himself had been baptized several years earlier. However, having said this, Pashkov emphasizes that baptism does not change anything in the believer with regard to her standing before the Lord: "We become members of the Body of Christ not through baptism. The Body of Christ consists of all those who are born again, of those who had been far away but were brought near by the blood of Jesus. God forbid that a slogan be made out of baptism or that some kind of standard be established by which we will measure the members of Christ, splitting them apart."[138]

Predestination

Like Radstock, Pashkov did not develop any doctrine concerning predestination. When Gerasimenko, the student in London, asked Pashkov about the issue of election, noting that he did not agree with the teaching that some people are predestined to hell, he received a brief reply. Pashkov said that he also did not believe in predestination to eternal punishment: "God does not destine anyone to punishment but wants everyone to be saved. He took the sin of the whole world. We were born free but corrupted. We can get rid of our sin by coming to the Savior. A loving relationship with God cannot exist without freedom. We need to be free to come to God."[139]

In the spirit of Radstock, who emphasized the operating power of the Spirit in the present, Pashkov interpreted texts about election with a focus on the present life. "The Lord having foreknown us, predestined us to be like Christ—to be like him not only in the future but also in

137. PP II/1/c/18.

138. Ibid.

139. PP 2/10/4; II/1/c/52; 2/10/4; see also II/1c/122.

the present."[140] Calvinistic teaching on predestination to salvation was rejected. Not being interested in any form of theoretical theologizing, Pashkov interpreted predestination in terms of the theology of holiness that had grown out of the Wesleyan stream. Thus believers are predestined to be like Christ in the present (Romans 8:29). The whole issue of predestination is perceived in terms of the freedom of the believer to actualize God's will of complete sanctification in the present.

Perfectionism

With regard to the doctrine of predestination, the presence of the perfectionist teaching of the early Keswick meetings can be detected in a letter Pashkov wrote to Wieler in January 1887:

> Christ is striving to establish his reign in some pre-elected vessels of mercy, because it is said of him that he rules *among* his enemies, so that *these vessels* are made sharers of his victory and later of his glory. May the Lord help us, who are these pre-elected, to put the crown on the head of Christ with our own hands, freely, so that, having been delivered from our enemies, we can serve the Lord without any fear, in holiness and joy *all* the days of our life, and have an opportunity to bring others into the kingdom of God, being the lights of Christ in the world, which diffuse not their own dim light, but the light of Christ. Let the Lord fill us with his Holy Spirit, the Spirit of truth who testifies about Christ *abiding* in us. I pray to the Lord constantly for myself that I may be baptized with the Spirit and fire. I impatiently expect to be clothed with power from on high, so that my ministry can become a ministry that can indeed glorify the name of my Lord and Savior Jesus Christ.[141]

The above passage contains many allusions to Biblical texts, none of which is taken in its own context. Pashkov marked certain words, thus adding emphasis. The driving theme uniting these texts is the abiding of Christ in the believer and reception of the power of the Spirit for productive Christian ministry. The enemies Pashkov refers to are the demonic powers. Baptism with the Spirit and fire most likely refers to

140. PP II/1/c/83, dated 1886.

141. PP II/1/c/139.

complete sanctification in the vein of the early Keswick movement, with an emphasis on Christian ministry.[142]

Ethics and Sanctification

Pashkov's ethical instructions are based on the concept of the mutual abiding of the believer and Christ in each other by means of the Holy Spirit. Writing to Peter Smirnov in Sakhalin, Pashkov states: "A constant abiding of Christ in you and you in Christ is needed for you more than for anybody else. Let the Lord fill you with love in the Holy Spirit. Let him give you meekness, so that the image of Christ may be developed in you. I commit you to the Lord and to the Word of his grace. Let the Holy Spirit instruct you through his one Word with regard to all truth. . . . Let him give you the spirit of prayer, so that you may constantly come to him and draw from the spring of the never-ending love of the Father."[143]

Pashkov is concerned that some Christians were using the teaching of salvation by God's grace as a ground for immoral living.[144] Although he does not provide specific references, his pastoral admonition is based on quotations from the New Testament: (1) The grace of God is not a basis for debauchery (Jude 4); (2) the unrighteous do not inherit the kingdom of God (1 Cor 6:9–10). When quoting the Corinthians passage Pashkov rephrases the New Testament text. While the Apostle Paul originally wrote, "Do not be deceived," Pashkov brings forward the aspect of spiritual warfare: "Has the devil deceived you?" This reference gives him an opportunity to make a connection with the book of Revelation (20:10, 15), where the immoral are destined to be thrown into the lake of fire. Pashkov seems to understand this text quite literally.

In a letter written to Mariia Ivanovna in 1885, Pashkov gives an account of life in the Spirit. He meditates on the Epistle to the Romans and talks about the law of the spirit of life in Christ. "Exclusively by faith we can remain in this state of grace. When you believe, the power of the Lord operates in you. When you have a small doubt you lose this

142. Bebbington, *Evangelicalism in Modern Britain*, 158; Price and Randall, *Transforming Keswick*, 35–36.

143. PP II/1/b/53.

144. PP II/1/c/90.

power."[145] These Keswick themes would be developed later in the works of Johann Kargel.

Spiritual Warfare

Pashkov was well aware of the reality of the spiritual domain of evil. Lieven in her memoirs gives a graphic account of an exorcism accomplished by Pashkov before his expulsion from Russia.[146] Spiritual warfare is one of the most prominent themes in the letters of Pashkov. "Our fight is against the sinful spirits who had possessed us as their slaves and from whose dominion Christ delivered us."[147] According to Pashkov, a person who deliberately sins is under the influence of the devil. Pashkov usually describes in experiential terminology the reality of Christ as our deliverer from the power of sin. The forgiveness of Christ and his presence should be visible in our daily lives.[148]

A letter to believers in Vetoshkino written in 1887 provides a good illustration of Pashkov's views on this topic.

> If [the Lord] allows the Evil One to tempt us, it is for one purpose only, that we, by coming to Christ the Savior, will experience his protection and his majesty. Let the victory of Christ over evil be accomplished not in areas unknown to us, but in our own hearts, so that we would know the Savior by personal experience, and not just by hearing from others. We can serve the Lord to the extent that we give over control of our lives to the Spirit of Christ. . . . If the presence of Christ is not recognized by outsiders, then we do not bring about any good, but, even worse, we become a stumbling block to the world, despite the fact that we reject all the outward regulations [of Orthodoxy] that have no significance before God and confess our Lord by calling him Lord. Why are our peasants not attracted by the grace of Christ? None of them is affected by the testimony of believers or by reading the Word available in every house. This is very strange and sad.[149]

145. PP II/1/c/20.
146. Lieven, *Dukhovnoe Probuzhdenie v Rossii*, 19–23.
147. PP II/1/c/123.
148. PP II/1/b/82.
149. PP II/1/d/32.

Women's Ministry

In 1887 Pashkov reports in a letter his experience of listening to a woman preacher at one of the conferences. He says that at first many attendees of the conference felt uneasy listening to a female preacher. However, their opinion changed drastically by the end of the sermon. Pashkov commends women who are gifted in preaching.[150] Corrado claims that it was a common practice for women to preach during Pashkovite meetings.[151] Pashkov, like Radstock, was driven by personal experience of the Spirit. Even though, with all rigidity, he took literally the text of 1 Timothy 3, where Paul gives instructions about the qualifications of presbyters, and applied it to young Rozov, he does not seem to have struggled much with 1 Timothy 2:9–15, where the same author forbids women to teach and instructs them to be quiet in church and to be concerned instead about rearing children. Thus Pashkov's biblical hermeneutics was of a circumstantial nature and largely dependent on his personal spiritual experience.

Contextualization

Pashkov realized that the form of presentation of the Gospel message is bound to a particular culture. In a letter written to an English publisher, he complains that the illustrations given in a particular biblical tract are so tied to the English evangelical culture and to specifically English experiences that they would not be understood by Russian children, who are not at all familiar with English institutions such as Sunday schools. Pashkov gives his opinion as to the kind of presentation that would be more congruent with the Russian mentality. He says: "When [tracts] are translated literally, they quite lose their meaning. The only kind of tract that is likely to [impact] the young in my country is some interesting narrative taken from life and illustrating the power of regeneration exercised by the Spirit of God over the human soul. The translation of the leaflets is much too literal; the language is unsatisfactory to such a degree that the leaflets ought not to be circulated at all."[152]

150. PP II/1/c/70.

151. Corrado, *Filosofiia*, 55–56.

152. PP II/1/d/55. The letter was written by Pashkov in English.

Radstock's daughter Mary resonates with Pashkov's concerns: "[M]y parents sent me to take a large copy of 'The Pilgrim's Progress' to an old man whose villa garden was next to ours. It was a Russian translation and illustrated, but apparently there being no suitable Russian pictures, Chinese ones were used, and Christian was duly represented with a pig-tail! To this day, it is a mystery to me why the publishers should have thought these pictures more akin to Russia than the usual ones."[153]

Evangelism by Giving Money

There are at least two letters among Pashkov's papers that he wrote to people he did not know personally. He sent them money at their request and gave a detailed testimony concerning the love of Christ. In one letter Pashkov sends money to an unbeliever and calls on him to accept Jesus.[154] In another letter Pashkov sends his support to a person who was involved in Christian ministry. Pashkov was unsure, however, about the message the person was preaching. Thus he includes in the letter a clear presentation of the Gospel. Even though he had never met the addressee in person, Pashkov makes an appeal to this person to preach this simple message of the love and transforming grace of God.[155]

In both cases Pashkov used his financial resources to help people enter into a personal relationship with God. Pashkov did not refer to any specific Christian church, confession, or denomination. His concern was rather with having a personal relationship with God, regardless of the specific teachings of any particular denomination.

Attitude towards Orthodox Beliefs, Practices, and Believers

Pashkov heard rumors that some evangelicals were teaching that people should stop going to the Orthodox Church and worshipping icons. He said that they should not teach this:

> We should preach that everyone should be born again, that everyone should become a new creation born of God through the Word, that everyone needs Him who alone redeemed [us from] our sins with his sacrifice and in whom alone we have redemption

153. Bevan, "Odd Memories," 9.

154. PP II/1/C/78.

155. PP II/1/f/20.

> by His blood. . . . People may stop worshipping icons or going to the Orthodox Church but at the same time be far from Christ as far as their hearts are concerned. . . . If we say to anybody that the path of salvation is in leaving the Orthodox Church or in giving up the worship of icons, we lead people astray just as much as those who say that people are saved by obeying the rituals established by the church. My dear ones, is not Christ, the living Savior, the only one whom we need? Should not we point to him alone from the Word of God, saying that He is the only Savior given to us by God? [156]

Answering questions from Burov concerning the perpetual virginity of Mary and a certain icon, Pashkov replies in the manner of Radstock, who tackled the same question at about the same time. Pashkov says:

> Concerning the question as to whether the Virgin Mary had other children after the birth of the Lord, not much is said. This means that the Holy Spirit or the Wisdom of God decided it was not necessary to reveal this matter to us, having included just one word in Matthew 1:25, and having mentioned the brothers of the Lord without specifying whether they were his blood brothers or cousins. . . . As far as the picture is concerned, what you call an icon was made by an artist who was not a believer. Anyway, this matter of the icon is of no importance.[157]

In early spring 1885 Pashkov received a letter from an Orthodox priest, Father Ioann, who asked Pashkov to help him establish a printing house for the production of the kinds of materials that were published by the Society for the Encouragement of Spiritual and Moral Reading, which had functioned during the period between 1876 and 1884. In his reply Pashkov expresses his position towards toward the Orthodox priest in the following way: "I consider you as a believer in Christ who loves us lost sinners. . . ." However, Pashkov does not want to publish Orthodox literature alongside evangelical literature.

> I want to publish books that cohere with the teaching of the Word of God and not with human tradition. . . . I do not wish to assist in printing materials that fit the requirements of Orthodox spiritual censorship in all respects. . . . I cannot help you to establish a printing house that would be obligated to publish books that I would never distribute. . . . When tolerance is established in our

156. PP II/1/b/91, dated May, 1885.

157. PP II/1/c/33.

> laws, it may be possible to continue our negotiations concerning a printing house.[158]

This correspondence demonstrates that (1) Pashkov was standing upon a purely Protestant foundation, considering the canonical scriptures to be the only reliable source for faith and practice; (2) he was unconcerned about "unclear" passages of scripture and was Christocentric; (3) he argued against all discussions and disputes concerning secondary matters that might block the way to saving faith in Christ; (4) he accepted as brothers Christians of other biblical convictions, including Orthodox priests; (5) he was willing to cooperate with believers from other confessions, including Orthodox priests, as long as this cooperation was in line with his religious convictions; and (6) he had a vision of Russia as a country with freedom of conscience.

Eschatology

Pashkov's eschatological views were in line with the premillennial eschatology of Radstock and George Müller.[159] In a letter written in 1884, Pashkov revealed his expectations regarding the second coming of Christ: "This revival among the Jewish people is such a wonderful thing . . . because it points to the fact that Jesus' return *to the earth* is at hand (Rom 11:12, 15)."[160] But although Pashkov believed in the imminent return of the Lord, he was either not acquainted with or did not accept dispensationalist teaching about two distinct comings of Jesus and about the pre-tribulational rapture of the church. Writing to Wieler three years later, in 1887, he suggested: "I think that believers should become peddlers and go about with goods to different villages, so that on their way they could remind people about the coming judgment and the Savior."[161] Thus while Pashkov's eschatology can be classified as premillennial, millenarian themes were not prominent in his teaching.

158. PP II/1b/55, dated March 13, 1885.

159. Müller, *Autobiography*, 34.

160. PP II/1/b/ frame 22. Italics added.

161. PP II/1/d/6.

CONCLUSIONS REGARDING PASHKOV

The history and theology of the evangelical movement in St. Petersburg during the period between 1880 and 1895 reveals a new configuration of theological paradigms. The key leader of the movement, Colonel V. A. Pashkov, was converted into the Revivalist paradigm and envisioned Russia as becoming part of Western civilization, as can be seen in his affirmation of Vladimirov's thoughts. Unlike the Russian intelligentsia, who had a somewhat similar structure of thought, the Gospel Christians chose a religious path for Westernizing Russia, shaking the foundations of the State religion without challenging monarchical autocracy. Even though Pashkov did not challenge the State Church publicly, his private correspondence reveals his total break with Byzantine Christianity as such. However, this break was not carried out in cold, sectarian fashion, as he was ready to cooperate with individual Orthodox believers, so long as this cooperation fitted his theological convictions. The period between Pashkov's expulsion from Russia in 1884 and his death in 1902 has not previously been studied.

From a theological point of view, Pashkov's private correspondence reveals the process of the separation of the Protestant paradigm from the Orthodox paradigm on the ecclesiological level. A growing number of evangelicals came to the conclusion that the Orthodox Church had deviated from their perception of biblical truth, and that there was a need to establish an evangelical church along primitivist-restorationist lines. The majority of the aristocratic women, however, still adhered to the Radstockian configuration of the paradigms; they consciously did not want to become part of another sect by leaving the National Church, even though they believed in and practiced Radstockian spirituality. Ecclesiologically, Pashkov wanted to structure the evangelical group in St. Petersburg after the pattern of the Open Brethren. He also dreamed of wider cooperation between various denominations according to the pattern of the World Evangelical Alliance whose conference he attended in 1879. Unlike the Orthodox members of the intelligentsia, Pashkov believed that the unity of the church was attainable on the platform of evangelical Christianity, rather than on the platform of Orthodoxy.

Theologically, Pashkov was influenced by the Keswick teachers, and especially by George Müller. His theological position with regard to ecclesiology can be characterized as primitivist-restorationist, as he believed in the operation of the gifts of the Spirit, even though the group had not experienced any supernatural manifestations. The Brethren practice of "reading the Bible under the guidance of the Spirit" denied the importance of any theological tradition or of theoretical theologizing. The Bible needed to be read by faith, the illumination of the Spirit needed to be experienced, and the illumined text needed to be applied practically in one's life. Having no external criteria for validating certain readings, Pashkov and the St. Petersburg Pashkovites discussed problematic issues, seeking the guidance of the Spirit by listening to different viewpoints. Such open discussion either led to an easy preliminary solution, or else consensus was not reached for many years. Pashkov did not see much value in being grounded in any theological tradition, including those of the Reformation. He held this conviction without realizing how much theology from previous generations was being taken for granted (e,g., the Nicene Creed or the teaching of the Reformers concerning salvation by grace through faith). He sincerely believed in the necessity and sufficiency of Bible reading and of waiting for the guidance of the Spirit. This rather individualistic approach to theology and spirituality made Pashkov vulnerable to being guided by the subjective Romantic-Modernist spirit of the age, mistaking such guidance for guidance by the Spirit of God. Pashkov did not recognize the presence of the hermeneutical and cultural filters he had inherited from his Orthodox upbringing and from his relationships with Western evangelicals.

The identifying story of some members of the community changed. Pashkov no longer considered himself Orthodox. Rather, his self-identity was formed by his association with Western evangelicalism and Western civilization. In the new story, Pashkov saw a need for the spiritual transformation of Orthodox Russia, as a result of which Orthodoxy would be replaced by an evangelical form of Christianity. Conversion from one paradigm to the other was signified by the introduction of rebaptism and of weekly breaking of bread among the members of the community.

THE *RUSSIAN WORKMAN*, PHASE 2: 1883–1886

In this section we will explore the content of the *Russian Workman* during the mid-1880s. Our goal is to demonstrate that the aristocratic publishers of this journal were not following the ecclesiological restorationist agenda of V. A. Pashkov. The journal continued to be published during the first two years following Pashkov's expulsion from Russia.

A Theological Analysis of the *Russian Workman*

The *Russian Workman* continued to be published in 1883 by A. I. Peuker, the daughter of the previous editor.[162] The journal contained different genres, including homilies, hymns, biblical biographies, testimonies, and fictional spiritual narratives. The mode of theologizing was in harmony with the Patristic and pietistic conviction that theology is about spiritual transformation rather than intellectual reasoning about God. The configuration of theological paradigms during this period differed from that of the previous period. The stricter policies of Orthodox censorship implemented by Pobedonostsev, as well as internal processes within the evangelical group in St. Petersburg, produced a different blend of Orthodox and Protestant perspectives. The issues of *RW-2* became more bibliocentric and theologically homogeneous. Almost every article included footnotes with biblical references. This feature grasps one's attention when compared to the more informal outlook of *RW-1*. The journal became narrower, as well, with regard to the range of its topics. Articles of a purely educational nature are not found during this period. The scope of *RW-2* was spiritual and devotional, by and large.

The Orthodox paradigm is represented by a wide spectrum of articles written by Orthodox monastic writers of the past and present—e.g., Macarius of Egypt,[163] Ephraim the Syrian,[164] John Chrysostom,[165] Tikhon Zadonskii,[166] Eusebius the Archbishop of Mogilev,[167] and archpriest Vasilii Grechulevich[168]—as well as articles borrowed from the

162. The *Russian Workman* published between 1875–1881 will be abbreviated *RW-1*; the second period of the journal will be referred to as *RW-2*.

163. *Russkii Rabochii* 6 (1886) 2.

164. Ibid., 5 (1883) 7; ibid., 7 (1883) 7.

165. Ibid., 6 (1884) 2.

166. Ibid., 5 (1883) 4–6; ibid., 6 (1883) 5–8; ibid., 7 (1883) 7; ibid., 8 (1883) 8; ibid., 9 (1883) 6; ibid., 11 (1883) 6; ibid., 12 (1883) 7; ibid., 4 (1884) 6; ibid., 8 (1884) 2; ibid., 11 (1884) 4–5; ibid., 8 (1885) 8; ibid., 9 (1885) 4; ibid., 10 (1885) 7–8.

167. Ibid., 11 (1885) 6; ibid., 2 (1886) 6.

168. Ibid., 5 (1886) 7.

Orthodox journal *The Sunday Reading* that had been published earlier.[169] The most quoted author in *RW-2* is Tikhon Zadonskii (1724–83), who was canonized by the Orthodox Church in 1863. He had been influenced significantly by Pietist theologian Johann Arndt (1555–1621).[170] The Pietistic spirituality of Tikhon Zadonskii resonated with the heartfelt spirituality of the Radstockist movement that had also grown out of the Pietist milieu.

The Protestant authors are not named or explicitly referred to. However, the Protestant pietistic perspective can be seen in the fact that none of the issues of this period refers to the Orthodox Church, its liturgical services, its mysteries, or its traditions. All the personages of the narratives come to God personally through the testimonies of their friends, acquaintances, or relatives.[171] The readers are called to approach God personally, in order to receive the renewal of the Holy Spirit, who makes spiritual life possible.[172] The idea that without heartfelt devotion to the Lord outward religiosity has no significance runs through all the issues of this period.[173] A person receives individual and instantaneous salvation from eternal hell by means of a direct appeal to God.[174] *RW-2* contains many examples of personal conversion and reception of new life. The criteria for verifying one's spiritual state consist of the following questions: (1) Do you love the Lord with a love that turns you away from sin? (2) Do you pray by talking to God? (3) Do you read God's Word with love and consistency? (If you love reading worldly books, you do not love the Lord.[175]) Thus the practical piety rooted in personal Bible study and prayer is used as a gauge for evaluating the quality of one's Christianity.

The figure of an Orthodox priest is not found at all in *RW-2*. In contrast to the instructions concerning parenting given in *RW-1*, the only article written on this topic in 1883 does not mention the church even once.[176] Material from the Church Fathers and Orthodox writers

169. Ibid., 5 (1885) 5–6; ibid., 9 (1885) 7.

170. Smolich, *Russkoe Monashestvo 988–1917*, 1333–34.

171. *Russkii Rabochii* 1 (1883) 3, 5, 7; ibid., 3 (1883) 4–6.

172. Ibid., 1 (1883) 8.

173. Ibid., 2 (1883) 2.

174. Ibid., 5.

175. Ibid., 3.

176. Ibid., 4 (1883) 4–7.

is chosen selectively, and exclusively from a Christocentric and pietistic perspective, in order to enhance the readers' personal devotional and moral lives, regardless of their ecclesiological views. Readers who are acquainted with other writings of the selected Orthodox authors would assume that the editor is grounded in the Orthodox tradition. However, the selective ethical readings from the Fathers do not shut the door to evangelical Protestants, who would not embrace the whole of the Orthodox tradition and theology.[177]

The Protestant emphases of Radstock's teachings on salvation by faith, assurance of salvation, and living the victorious Christian life by faith must have been filtered out by Orthodox censors. Thus the perfectionism of Radstock is replaced by the Orthodox path of repentance advocated by Tikhon Zadonskii: "to come to Christ, to repent and pray and knock on the doors until the image of Christ is revealed in us."[178] Assurance of salvation is given from an eschatological perspective, with the emphasis on Christ rather than on one's personal sense of assurance: "My hope and salvation is Christ-God [*Khristos Bog*]; Christ *will* save me because I *am* a sinner; He came to save sinners."[179] Faith in Christ and good works are not separated from each other in the issues of the journal from this period.[180] A Christian can be lured by love for the world and lose the "heavenly goods promised to those who love God."[181] Without knowing the history of the *Russian Workman* and the movement behind it, one could easily take the issues of this period for Orthodox periodicals, whose main thrust was to revive the spiritual lives of lay Orthodox readers. However, because the journal did not contain references to the Orthodox Church as such, it could also be utilized effectively by evangelical sectarians who were distributing Pashkovite Protestant literature among the masses.

The absence of key Protestant themes is important, as it reveals that these specifics of Protestant teaching were not of major concern to the editor and publishers, who were constrained by Orthodox censorship on the one hand and the sectarian particularities of the Baptists on the other. The most important thing was that readers should take their Christian

177. Terletskii, *Sekta Pashkovtsev*, 33, 62, 63.

178. *Russkii Rabochii* 11 (1884) 5.

179. Ibid., 8 (1885) 8.

180. Ibid., 2 (1886) 6. Cf. Starogorodskii, *Pravoslavnoe Uchenie o Spasenii.*

181. Ibid., 10 (1885) 8.

faith and morality seriously. The Orthodox theology of the journal should not be attributed exclusively to the constraints of censorship. The fact that during this period the aristocratic women of St. Petersburg did not want to leave Orthodoxy and start a separate evangelical church with a distinctive statement of faith suggests that this theology cohered with their ecclesiological convictions. The key ecumenical intuition of Radstock that Christian unity can be achieved not on the platform of one's doctrine but on the basis of heartfelt devotion to Jesus and love towards one's neighbor was appropriated by the Orthodox followers of Radstock in St. Petersburg. The Orthodox theological creed was taken for granted; no new doctrinal theology was intended to be articulated. Personal devotion centered on the Christ of the scriptures and on love for God and others was the key driving force of the *Russian Workman* of this period.[182]

In contrast to *RW-1* the issues of this period do not include any political or nationalist components. The only reference to the Tsar is given in the prayer that was pronounced during his inauguration.[183] The motif of national Christianity, which was prominent during the previous period of the journal, is not found at all. The focus shifts from national ecclesial institutions to a private mode of Orthodox spirituality. With regard to theological dynamics, Protestant theology, which was prominent in the articles of the first period, is replaced by Orthodox theology and spirituality. If the first period of the journal could be characterized as "the Protestant reading of the Bible in the Orthodox Temple," the second period can be metaphorically viewed as "the Orthodox reading of the Bible outside of the Orthodox Temple." This Eastern form of lay evangelicalism found in *RW-2* is unique, in the sense that it was not grounded in Protestant doctrine and spirituality, at least among some serious followers of Radstock in St. Petersburg. Unlike Pashkov and Korff, who were converted to a distinctively Protestant expression of Christianity, the aristocratic women of St. Petersburg represented a genuinely non-denominational spirit and theology that transcended ecclesiological differences. There is no reason to doubt their theological convictions as represented in *RW-2*, just as there is no reason to doubt the sincerity of their generous financial support of conferences of evangelical sectarians

182. Ibid., 6 (1886) 8.

183. Ibid., 5 (1883) 8.

during this period, regardless of their theological disagreements with them.

Biblical Interpretation

Even though *RW-2* is predominantly Orthodox in its theology, the only article explicitly devoted to biblical interpretation can be classified as purely Protestant. The author of the article is not named, which gives reason to suspect that it was derived from Protestant sources. The article is entitled "How to Read the Holy Scriptures"; it encourages the reader to explore the Bible with the purpose of hearing the voice of God.[184] Unlike Orthodox writers who emphasize the importance of reading scripture in the light of Patristic tradition, the author of this article pursues an individualistic approach to scripture. "In order to understand the Bible and believe its message one should obey it. Read scripture with the unshakable intention of fulfilling its commandments and imitating the lives of its saints. The major source of doubts is not one's mind but one's will."[185] The basic assumption of this recommendation is that the message of the Bible is clear; one just needs to obey what the biblical text says. The unnamed author of the article likens the Bible to a tree. The Old Testament represents the roots, trunk, and bark, while the New Testament represents the fruit. The reader is encouraged to read the Old Testament typologically from the Christocentric perspective of the Apostles. "Let us try to understand how the Almighty was leading his people, revealing himself in the person of Jesus Christ and calling them from darkness into his wonderful light."[186] It is suggested that the model of typological interpretation found in the book of Hebrews be emulated when interpreting Old Testament texts. The key to unlocking scripture is a godly life. "The meaning of scripture is very clear to those who live in accordance with God's commandments."[187]

Biblical texts are interpreted with the single purpose of transforming the reader into the image of Christ, beginning with the present realities of the reader's horizon. Difficult passages of scripture are interpreted figuratively. Tikhon Zadonskii tackles Ps 137:8–9: "O Daughter

184. Ibid., 5 (1884) 2–4.

185. Ibid.

186. Ibid.

187. Ibid.

of Babylon, doomed to destruction, happy is he who repays you for what you have done to us—he who seizes your infants and dashes them against the rocks."[188] He takes the infants as standing for sins, which Christians should dash before they grow up and become strong.

The text of 1 Chr 16:35, in which David prays for the nation of Israel, is read by an unnamed author in the light of Jesus' prayer about the unity of believers (John 17:17; 11:52): "Save us from all evil, sin, self-will, and any kind of earth-binding chain. Gather us so that we will be one in purpose, one in deed, in complete unity of spirit and thought, so that by loving and helping one another, we may follow a single path."[189] This reading of the text can be properly understood against the background of the evangelical meetings that were taking place during this period.

Conclusion Regarding the *Russian Workman*

The issues of the *Russian Workman* published during the period between 1883 and 1886 reveal an important change in the theological outlook of the journal. It had become narrower with regard to the represented themes. The key focus of the journal was now on personal spirituality, personal faith in Christ, and personal devotion to the Lord, based on personal Bible reading. The specifically Protestant theological emphases and themes of the journal were gone.

Theologically, the journal reflected Orthodox spirituality, as it did not highlight the importance of justification by faith or discuss the difference between justification and sanctification. Christian salvation was perceived in the Orthodox fashion as a relationship with God that begins with faith in the Gospel. Assurance of salvation in the present was replaced by assurance of being saved in the future by Christ who came to save sinners. Perfectionist themes with an emphasis on the new nature are not found in the *Russian Workman* of this period, nor was the doctrine of salvation by faith alone emphasized in the Protestant fashion. The accent was rather on the equal importance of orthodoxy and orthopraxy in the Christian journey. The journal leaves the impression that the editor and its contributors were seeking the unity of Christians not on the theological or dogmatic level, but on the level of

188. Ibid., 8 (1885) 8.

189. Ibid., 4 (1886) 1–2.

practical devotion to the Lord. The conscious absence of ecclesiological and soteriological particularities of either an Orthodox or Protestant nature allowed the journal to be published and to be distributed among Christians of different convictions even after the expulsion of Pashkov and Korff from Russia.

The biblical interpretation contained in *RW-2* is defined by a high view of scripture. The Bible is a divinely inspired book that needs to be obeyed: "The teaching of the Bible is clear to those who obey it" is the motto of the article devoted to Biblical interpretation. None of the articles published in the journal makes use of historico-grammatical analysis of biblical texts. Biblical interpretation is thoroughly governed by the pre-modern theological convictions of the authors. Interpretation of Old Testament texts is characterized by Christocentrism and Christocentric typology. New Testament passages tend to be interpreted literally.

This pietistic configuration of the Radstockian tradition that draws its sources largely from Orthodox writers did not have a prominent following. It was represented by aristocratic women who did not break their ties with the Orthodox Church and yet believed that pious Christians of different traditions can experience unity built on devotion to Christ. But the central riverbed of the tradition went along the restorationist path that was led by V. A. Pashkov. In the next chapter we will explore the restorationist trajectory of that tradition, focusing on the life of its most influential leader, I. S. Prokhanov.

4

The St. Petersburg Evangelical Tradition: 1905–1910

INTRODUCTION

The Western historiography of the St. Petersburg evangelical tradition sharply distinguishes the period of Radstock and Pashkov from subsequent developments within the tradition. Under the influence of Edmund Heier's monograph, Western historians make a sharp distinction between the "non-denominational," biblical Christianity of Radstock and the Baptistic transformations of the tradition that are mainly associated with Ivan Stepanovich Prokhanov.[1] Heier claims—mistakenly, as I will show below—that Prokhanov "was opposed to the free Bible-Christianity as initiated by Radstock. Although the coming of Prokhanov provided for some the desired missing central authority and theology, it provoked in others the feeling of belonging to a sect."[2]

Unlike Heier, Orthodox critics of the evangelical tradition recognized both its Western origin and its non-denominational Protestant ethos, which was different from the narrower views of other Protestant streams. D. L. Bogoliubov emphasized the particular danger the Gospel Christians posed to the Orthodox Church, because of their tactical flexibility in cooperating with any Protestant denomination for the purpose of creating a united Protestant front in Russia.[3] However, there is no account in Orthodox religious studies that covers theological developments in the evangelical tradition.

1. Heier, *Religious Schism*, 147–48; McCarthy, "Religious Conflict," 251–54; Corrado, *Filosofiia*, 164–71.

2. Heier, *Religious Schism*, 148.

3. Bogoliubov, "Pashkovtsy, ili 'Khristiane Evangelicheskogo Ispovedania,'" 101.

Slavic evangelical historians tend to minimize the Western nature of the St. Petersburg tradition, arguing for its original para-Orthodox roots.[4] According to this view, evangelical Christianity in Russia was a direct result of the activity of the Holy Spirit on the hearts and minds of people who read the scriptures in their own language.[5] Western missionaries such as Radstock played a role as catalytic agents in this process. Evangelical theology is said to have resulted from Bible reading that was largely unaffected by the historico-cultural atmosphere of the times. The historical setting is perceived in terms of fertile ground for the growth of an indigenous movement, driven by the Spirit and accelerated by Western missionaries. Western influences became obvious only at a later stage, when the regenerated individuals were looking for a new ecclesial expression.[6] The identical conclusions of Western and Eastern evangelicals are taken as conclusive evidence that the movement had been led by the same Spirit, who works universally, re-creating the unpolluted Christianity of the Apostolic era. The theology of biblical primitivism, absolutized and removed from the historical process and cultural skin of the nineteenth century, is taken as a universal yardstick for evaluating other Christian movements that have a place in Christian history.[7] Slavic evangelical scholars do not focus on the theological dynamics of their own tradition because of their static and ahistorical view of the nature of theology. The major focus of their research is on the chronology of events, with a static description of primitivist theology or of different variations thereof.

The works of Soviet scholars of religion correctly note the Western derivation of evangelical Christianity in St. Petersburg and its constant contact with the Western world.[8] However, the key focus of Soviet scholarship is on the ideological struggle against all kinds of religion, and the dynamics of the theological identification of this theological tradition within the context of social change are not taken into view. According to this view, any religious system is built on a metaphysical illusion, which is supported by Western capitalism.[9] Having no theological acuteness,

4. Vasil'eva, "Sovremennyi Russkii Protestantism," 96–100.

5. Karetnikova, *Al'manakh Russkogo Batisma*, 3–4.

6. Reshetnikov and Sannikov, *Obzor Istorii*, 59, 71.

7. Golovashchenko, *Istoria Evangel'sko-Baptistskogo Dvizhenia v Ukraine*, 4–8.

8. Iartsev, *Sekta Evangel'skikh Khristian*, 4–6.

9. Mitrokhin, *Baptizm*, 5–9; Klibanov, *History of Religious Sectarianism*, 252.

atheistic scholars classified the St. Petersburg evangelical movement as a branch of the Baptist movement, without recognizing its origin in the British pan-evangelical milieu.[10]

In the present chapter it will be argued that there were no abrupt shifts in the heterogeneous revivalist tradition of St. Petersburg. The Protestant paradigm was not revolutionized by the socio-political changes in Russia at the beginning of the twentieth century or by the appearance of new leaders. Rather, the tradition continued to evolve and develop progressively in the direction set by Lord Radstock and V. A. Pashkov.

PIETISTIC PRIMITIVISM AND RESTORATIONISM

In the previous chapter it was demonstrated that in the mid-1880s tension existed between two distinct tendencies that had emerged in the movement. On the one hand, the aristocratic group tended to maintain the original pietism of Radstock, having no desire to abandon their Orthodox identity in order to start a new denomination in Russia.[11] On the other hand, some of Radstock's followers began the process of drifting from pietism as a religion of the heart to the ecclesiology of evangelical restorationist-primitivism, with its vision of establishing a primitive Apostolic church.[12] V. A. Pashkov and M. M. Korff were among the first to break with the official Church on the level of personal conviction. Neither of them, however, ever left Orthodoxy while in Russia, in order not to compromise the newly-begun ministry of the revivalist movement.[13] In the previous chapter these two tendencies were called pietistic primitivism and restorationism respectively.[14]

The representatives of pietistic primitivism stressed the importance of regeneration without criticizing the ritualism of the Orthodox Church. The primitivist Pashkovites did not encourage newcomers to leave the Orthodox Church, but the home meetings centered around Bible reading and the breaking of bread were considered sufficient for one's salva-

10. Klibanov, *History of Religious Sectarianism*, 286.

11. Ibid., 248.

12. *Utrenniaia Zvezda*, 35 (1910) 1. Cf. Freeman et al., *Baptist Roots*, 226–32; Blane, "Relations between the Russian Protestant Sects and the State, 1900–1921," 63.

13. Cf. *Evangel'skaia Vera* 1 (1940) 9.

14. Calahan, *Primitivist Piety*, 183–86.

tion and growth in grace.[15] At the beginning of the twentieth century the restorationist tendency began to dominate the movement, as can be seen in the first Pashkovite creed, as well as in the established practice of believer's baptism.[16] The representatives of restorationism aimed to reinstate the primitive Apostolic church, breaking ties with the official Church, which was considered to have drifted away from the simplicity of Apostolic teaching. The restorationist tendency was reinforced by constant contact with Baptist preachers visiting St. Petersburg.[17] Tension between the two tendencies had been ongoing from the time of Pashkov until the first decade of the twentieth century. The laws on religious liberty enacted in 1905 allowed the restorationists to fulfill Pashkov's dream of establishing a Gospel church in Russia, and I. S. Prokhanov became the continuator of the pan-Russian evangelical vision.[18]

The key representative of pietistic primitivism was I. V. Kargel, who worked for years with Dr. Baedeker. For a time he was referred to by Orthodox critics as a leader of the "Plymouth Brethren," thereby pointing to the origins of the movement.[19] A member of the Evangelical Church, Lieven, in her memoirs, identifies Kargel with the group of "free Christians" who followed the key principles of Radstock's teaching concerning the importance of spiritual regeneration and the secondary nature of rituals.[20] Lieven emphasizes that Kargel, like Radstock, steadily moved towards a freer position throughout the course of his life.[21] The tendency towards pietistic primitivism was not long-lived from an ecclesiological point of view, however, due to both external and internal factors. The external factors included the strong anti-sectarian activity of the Orthodox Church, which had chosen the strategy of ideological warfare against those whom she considered to be dissenters. Neither Orthodox priests nor the evangelicals were ready for productive theological dialogue, both demonstrating rather a "black-and-white," dogmatic mentality. Attacks by Orthodox missionaries as well as physical

15. Cf. Dvinskaia, "Kak Zavlekaiut Pashkovtsy Pravoslavnykh Prostetsov v Svoi Seti," 581–91.

16. *Pashkovshchina*, 1–8.

17. Plett, *Istoriia Evangel'skikh Khristian Baptistov s 1905 po 1944 God*, 25.

18. Bogoliubov, *Kto Eto –Pashkovtsy, Baptisty i Adventisty*, 30–31.

19. Kahle, *Evangel'skie Khristiane*, 73.

20. Lieven, *Dukhovnoe Probuzhdenie*, 99–104.

21. *Evangel'skaia Vera* 1 (1940) 8–10.

persecution until the time of the Bolshevik revolution by representatives of the official Church accelerated the process of separation from an Orthodox identity, severing the link between the Protestant and Byzantine paradigms.[22] The 1905 decree on religious liberty, which followed Russia's defeat in the Russian-Japanese war, was another external factor that worked against the primitivist tendency. This new law provided the freedom needed to create a new identity which was more understandable to the working class, who comprised the majority of the St. Petersburg Pashkovites.[23] The restorationist model was simpler and internally coherent, and it made clear the reasons for the low state of the official Church.

The internal factors responsible for the ecclesiological fading of the primitivist tendency were related to some of I. V. Kargel's personal traits. Kargel was not Russian, which significantly inhibited his influence among the Russians. He was a Bible teacher and not an organizer who could persuasively diffuse his vision. The second unifying conference of Russian Protestants that took place in 1907 revealed these deficiencies of Kargel. Having been elected as the chair of the conference, he allowed the leading Baptist, Dai Mazaev, to dominate the meetings and to thwart the vision of an Evangelical Alliance by pressing and imposing the Baptist agenda.[24]

The tension between pietistic primitivism and restorationism existed not only at the level of ecclesiology, but on the plane of theological emphases as well. Kargel's primitivism was eschatologically oriented towards the imminent return of Christ, and his eschatological emphasis was accompanied by an equally important emphasis on deepening the spiritual lives of believers in the vein of the Keswickian theology of sanctification.[25] Theologically, Kargel was influenced by dispensationalist writers, who largely shared this primitivist theology. In contrast, the restorationist vision of Prokhanov was oriented towards the past, towards the lost ideal of Apostolic Christianity. The ideal of lost Apostolic primitivism was in turn used as a fulcrum for social and political activ-

22. *Utreniaia Zvezda* 37 (1910) 1; ibid., 44 (1910) 1.

23. Herrlinger, "Class, Piety, and Politics," 259–61; Sawatsky, *Soviet Evangelicals*, 42.

24. Kahle, *Evangel'skie Khristiane*, 111.

25. Kargel, "Khristos Osviashchenie Nashe," 49–113.

ity. These theological differences became more obvious during the subsequent period of the tradition.[26]

Despite the differences in theological and ecclesiological accents within the movement, the leaders of the Gospel Christians were united in their commitment to the vision of founding an Evangelical Alliance, based on key evangelical values and on the common spirit of devotion to Christ. The lifelong cooperation of Prokhanov and Kargel, based on these values, is demonstrated in various evangelical periodicals. Both of these leaders participated in organizing a branch of the Evangelical Alliance in Russia and taught some of the six-week courses open to people from all Christian denominations.[27] Both of them chaired conferences of the Evangelical Christians in St. Petersburg.[28] Both of them taught at St. Petersburg Bible Institute in the 1920s.[29] And the appeal to the Christians of the world entitled "The Resurrection Call" was signed by both of them in 1928, when Prokhanov left Russia for good.[30] Thus the stratification of the tradition should be viewed within the framework of unity in diversity and of organic continuity with its origin. Prokhanov and Kargel played complementary roles in developing the outlook of the tradition for years to come. I. S. Prokhanov dominated the theological stage of evangelicalism in Russia during the first four decades of the twentieth century.

IVAN STEPANOVICH PROKHANOV (PROKHANOFF)

I. S. Prokhanov was born in 1869 to a Molokan[31] family in Vladikavkaz. The family had migrated there from Saratov Province in response to

26. See the discussion below of creeds written by Kargel and Prokhanov.

27. *Bratskii Listok* 10 (1906) 12.

28. The Archive of the Evangelical Christians-Baptists in Moscow (hereafter, Archive ECB), 11.e.8.4; 11e.26.1.

29. Karetnikova, "Ivan Veniaminovich Kargel," 686; Skopina, "Iz Biographii I. V. Kargelia i ego Docherei," 696–97.

30. *Evangel'skaia Vera* 4 (1933) 17.

31. The Molokans are a religious sect that came out of the sect known as the Dukhobors (Spirit-wrestlers). The Dukhobors are first mentioned in Russian history after the epoch of Peter the Great, which may indicate that these sects whose historic origins are unclear have Protestant roots. Many similarities, as well as some differences, have been pointed out between the Dukhobors and the Quakers. The Molokans, like the Dukhobors, rejected the ritualism and hierarchy of the Orthodox Church, taking the

Orthodox persecution.[32] In the mid-1870s his father, Stepan Antonovich Prokhanov, was converted to Baptist teaching and became a leader of the congregation in Vladikavkaz.[33] In the introductory chapter of his autobiography, Prokhanov identifies three key influences that shaped his life during his formative years. The first was his identification with the suffering, marginalized group of Molokans.[34] He links suffering for the faith with the sufferings for Christ and with the desire to obtain religious liberty. When Prokhanov mentions the classics of Russian literature, he gives special attention to Nekrasov, who emphasized in his literary work the theme of the suffering of the marginalized.[35]

The second key influence on Prokhanov was that of education, and particularly of his acquaintance with socialist theories advocating the socio-political liberation of Russia.[36] The socialist thrust had his wholehearted support. In his view, Christianity was to become the fifth essence of socialism, to make it complete.

> "If you can gain your freedom, do so" (1 Corinthians 7:21). In this statement, clear approval of a peaceful liberation movement is displayed. The Lord approves movement towards liberty. It is our duty to pray that this liberation, as the birth of a new life, may come painlessly and with a minimal number of victims. Our most important petition should be our prayer that this liberating movement may be complete, that it will result in the sort of freedom which can be given only by the Lord—that is, freedom from the power of sin and vice, freedom from all kinds of darkness and obscurity.[37]

Prokhanov emphasizes that his key disagreement with socialism is his rejection of the atheistic philosophy which is embedded in socialist thought. Having gone through a period of doubts and existential de-

---

experience of the Spirit as the starting point for their spirituality. For a more detailed discussion see Anderson, *Staroobriiadchestvo i Sektantstvo*, 371–420, and Woodcock and Avakumovic, *Doukhobors*, 18–61. A detailed analysis of Molokan history and teaching is found in Butkevich, *Obzor Russkikh Sekt*, 266–360.

32. Prokhanoff, *In the Cauldron of Russia*, 29. See Blane, "Relations between the Russian Protestant Sects and the State," 52–59.

33. PP 2/2/293; Klibanov, *History of Religious Sectarianism*, 234.

34. Prokhanoff, *In the Cauldron of Russia*, 35.

35. Ibid., 36.

36. Ibid.

37. *Bratskii Listok* 9 (1906) 1.

cisions, prompted by his acquaintance with the philosophical systems of Schopenhauer and Hartman, he found a source of optimism in the Gospel.[38] The optimism of modernity, characterized by a belief in education, progress, and the necessity of social transformation, is Prokhanov's key worldview filter.[39]

Prokhanov defines the third key influence during his formative years as "a powerful but silent appeal to the beauty of nature."[40] Romantic influences of the era, with its accent on emotion and feeling, are displayed in Prokhanov's poetry. His theology and ministry can be understood through the prism of these three influences: the liberation motif in its evangelical form, set in the Modernist and Romantic frameworks of the nineteenth century.

There are two more factors which are important for understanding Prokhanov's worldview. They are his prophetic assurance that he was fulfilling a special role in God's plan and his audacious boldness in evaluating his own abilities and achievements, while downplaying the achievements of others. During the time he was writing his autobiography, Prokhanov was convinced that he was a special instrument in the hand of God for developing the evangelical movement in Russia. He sees God's intervention in his life from early infancy, when the doctor announced his death on the tenth day after his birth.[41] Prokhanov says, "When I heard about this for the first time, I thought: Surely the power of the Omnipotent appointed me to live and solve a special problem set by him for my life."[42] His certainty that he had been given a special mission to humanity was also based on a dream, which he identified as a vision. In the dream, young Prokhanov saw Christ throwing golden coins to gathered crowds in Vladikavkaz. Prokhanov was catching the abundant flow of coins with a sack. However, at the end he found nothing in the sack. All the coins had been gathered by the people. "This dream strengthened my feeling that God's purpose for my life was that I should be a transmitter of His gifts to needy humanity."[43]

38. Prokhanoff, *In the Cauldron of Russia*, 45.
39. Ibid., 9–10.
40. Ibid., 38.
41. Ibid., 29.
42. Ibid.
43. Ibid., 40.

Attached to this belief in his special prophetic role was Prokhanov's boldness in expressing a high opinion of his own achievements and talents. Describing his school days, Prokhanov states: "A characteristic which must be set down as a simple statement of fact was my notable intellectual development and erudition. Teachers and pupils were often astonished to hear from me quotations which it was considered impossible to expect from one of the students."[44] One of the paragraphs in his autobiography has the caption, "I make a startling prophecy."[45] Prokhanov predicted in the 1890s that one day evangelical Christians would preach in Orthodox temples. These two features of Prokhanov's character hindered his ability to evaluate evenhandedly the achievements of other people and to engage in productive theological dialogue. An example of his biased attitude towards others is his statement that he was the first person to publish an evangelical periodical in Russia. He omits any mention of the impressive period of Pashkov's printing activity and missionary outreach.[46]

Connections with the Evangelical Alliance and V. A. Pashkov: Prokhanov's Theological Education

In 1894 Prokhanov appealed to the Evangelical Alliance to sponsor his periodical. His initiative was not supported, however.[47] Taking into account that Dr. Baedeker was staying in St. Petersburg during this period, it was most likely through him that contact with the Alliance had been made. In 1895 Prokhanov was appointed to hand a petition, signed by 1000 members of the Evangelical Alliance, to the new Tsar, Nicholas II. This petition was similar to the one initiated by Pashkov three years earlier.[48] However, because Prokhanov left for London in 1895, the petition was never delivered by him. The circle of Prokhanov's fellowship in London was identical to that of Pashkov. The president of the Evangelical Alliance,

44. Ibid., 39. This statement is smoothed out in the Russian edition of the book: "A characteristic feature of my life was that I started to contemplate simple facts and to note my thoughts down in the diary. As a result of it I could notice the growth in my intellectual development and erudition."

45. Ibid., 83.

46. Ibid., 67.

47. Randall, "Eastern-European Baptists and the Evangelical Alliance," 32.

48. PP 1/8.

Mr. Adams, and Dr. Baedeker dissuaded Prokhanov from studying theology at a university, citing his poor command of English. Instead they suggested that he study at Bristol Baptist College.[49] A year later, Prokhanov and Baedeker appeared together at the fiftieth anniversary meeting of the Evangelical Alliance. Baedeker introduced Prokhanov as "my young friend."[50] At this time Prokhanov decided to leave Bristol and spend several months at a Congregationalist school, Hampstead New College, in order to become better acquainted with other non-conformist denominations.[51]

Besides his two-year stay in Britain, Prokhanov mentions having taken theological courses in Germany and France. Attending lectures given by Adolf von Harnack at the University of Berlin in 1898 and spending a semester at the Faculty of Protestant Theology in Paris gave Prokhanov at least a superficial acquaintance with the European theology of the time. Prokhanov admits that only by the end of his stays in Germany and France could he tolerably speak and understand the respective languages.[52] Taking into account the brevity of his stay in continental Europe, during which time he was working simultaneously on both theological disciplines and language acquisition, the influence of continental theology on Prokhanov and his ministry was minimal, if present at all. Prokhanov mentions in his autobiography that he helped his son learn Greek, Hebrew, and Latin. However, the depth of his own knowledge of the classical languages can also be questioned. There is no sign of consistent personal use of the biblical languages in his ministry.[53] Even though Prokhanov never completed a theological program, his European experience was foundational for the formation of his worldview. He says, "I knew, of course, that the extent of the theological knowledge which I might obtain abroad was very great, and that much more useful knowledge could be attained than I had gained already, but I felt that for the work which was to be done in Russia, the studies which I had pursued were sufficient and there was therefore no need to spend

49. Brackney, *Genetic History of Baptist Thought*, 172–73.

50. Ibid.

51. Prokhanoff, *In the Cauldron of Russia*, 97.

52. Ibid., 102.

53. Only one instance has been found where Prokhanov made use of a Greek word study. *Khristianin* 6 (1924) 79.

more time, and the best plan would be for me to return home as soon as possible.[54]"

After his return to Russia at the end of 1898, Prokhanov had to work full time as an engineer until 1921. He devoted his spare time to organizing, pastoral and educational ministries, and the writing of poetry, as well as to translation and multiple publishing activities.

The Continuity of the Tradition

It is commonly taken for granted that the young Baptist Prokhanov was introduced to the St. Petersburg Gospel tradition after his arrival in the city to study at the Institute of Technology in 1888. However, the correspondence of V. A. Pashkov with Prokhanov's father, Stepan Antonovich, in 1881 suggests a much earlier acquaintance. In one letter, S. A. Prokhanov thanks V. A. Pashkov for some religious literature and books sent from St. Petersburg to Vladikavkaz. It can be surmised from the letter that Pashkov had promised to visit Vladikavkaz in the summer of 1881, and S. A. Prokhanov asks Pashkov to inform him of his arrival date.[55] In a second letter, S. A. Prokhanov informs Pashkov of the receipt of a new shipment of books and of increased oppression from the Orthodox and state authorities who had closed their house of prayer.[56] The correspondence reveals a close cooperation between the Baptist and Evangelical streams during 1881. St. Petersburg aristocrats played an important role as the engine of religious propaganda in Russia. There is no definite information as to the visit of Pashkov to Vladikavkaz in 1881. In any event, the correspondence reveals an earlier acquaintance between Prokhanov and the St. Petersburg movement.

Upon his arrival in Britain in 1895, I. S. Prokhanov established contact with V. A. Pashkov. Pashkov's correspondence contains two letters from I. S. Prokhanov. In his first letter Prokhanov asks Pashkov if he could be given the permanent address of Dr. Baedeker.[57] This may suggest that Pashkov was a key contact for young Prokhanov in Britain. The letter reveals Prokhanov's personal acquaintance with Pashkov's family as well. The second letter to Pashkov was written from Berlin

54. Prokhanoff, *In the Cauldron of Russia*, 103.

55. PP 2/2/277.

56. PP 2/2/293.

57. PP 2/19/1.

in January 1898.[58] It reveals that Pashkov was involved in financial and literary contributions to Prokhanov's newspaper *Beseda* ("The Conversation"). Prokhanov informs Pashkov about the funds he needed for printing the newspaper and thanks him for an article he had sent for publication.[59] This letter contains a snapshot of Prokhanov's worldview which is worth quoting in full.

> As far as philosophy and theology are concerned, I do not consider them necessary for a Christian. Moreover, taking a fancy to these sciences, which are built on the speculation of cold reason, and which put in second place the simple Gospel that revitalizes the mind and heart, I consider a sad mistake. The right place for a Christian is found not in human wisdom, but in revealing the Spirit and power (1 Corinthians 2:4). This is the state of affairs when wisdom, that is science, melts into the background and becomes an instrument. . . . Science for a Christian cannot be the goal but only a means. I feel the call of God to devote all my future life to spreading the "good news" among the Russian people by means of publishing. Printed materials, books, and periodicals should be of four sorts: (1) for the Russian priesthood; (2) for the Russian intelligentsia; (3) for the Russian common people; and (4) for Russian evangelical Christians, with possible influence [as well] on other branches of the schism. The content of the first three sorts of publishing will be the same: the proclamation of salvation to the perishing. The goal of the fourth should be unity, strengthening, and the encouragement of peaceful champions for the kingdom of God. I also realize my holy duty and privilege to work through the living Word, which would have wonderful soil in the Slavic context. I take my being abroad as one of the greatest blessings of the Lord. I am startled by the fact that the diversity of opinions about secondary issues does not ruin, but rather gives special beauty to the spiritual unity of different communities of evangelical Christianity. *It has opened my eyes to see that the foundation of Christian activity should not be made up of dogmatic definitions of faith that might create boundaries, but rather of the requirements of Christ's love, which is greater than all the walls in the world. His life alone is the source of the church's strength on earth. I was led to the path of true Christian freedom by this attitude. There is no greater joy for me than to discover the unity in spirit of God's children behind the curtain of national or ecclesial specificities* [italics added]. As far as Germany is concerned, I

58. PP 2/19/2.

59. Ibid.

> have found much that is instructive about it. The country of the Reformation is experiencing a religious crisis, unfortunately, but there are signs of the future victory of the Galilean. There are many Russian students here, and the Lord gives me opportunities to speak to some of them about "the one thing that is needed." At the conclusion of my long letter, I would like to assure you of my sincere loyalty to you in the Lord.[60]

This letter is important for understanding the nature of Prokhanov's ministry and the identity of the unions that he organized in Russia during the first decade of the twentieth century. Dissatisfaction with Western Protestantism opened for Prokhanov a vista for a neo-Protestant reformation in Russia that would avoid "the mistakes" of the European Classical Reformation.

The Unions

The Russian movement of Evangelical Christians was established through the influence of the Anglo-American revivalist movement of the nineteenth century. It borrowed Western theology, hymnody, ecclesiology, and models of social and literature outreach. It also copied Western evangelical institutions as soon as changes in the Russian political climate allowed this. As early as 1906, Prokhanov began the process of organizing an exact replica of some Western evangelical institutions in Russia. The YMCA of Russia was organized in 1908. This association was an exact copy of the original YMCA that was founded in London in 1844. Prokhanov was elected as its president, and in this capacity he sent greetings to YMCA branches in Germany, Britain, America, and Latvia.[61]

The idea of establishing a Russian Evangelical Alliance was first mentioned in evangelical periodicals in 1906.[62] It was envisioned that this union would become the Russian branch of the World Evangelical Alliance. It would be comprised of individuals who shared evangelical values, regardless of their denominational identity, including Catholics, Orthodox, and Lutherans among others.[63] A concrete proposal about es-

60. Ibid.

61. *Molodoi Vinogradnik*, November (1909) 5.

62. *Bratskii Listok* 9 (1906) 1.

63. *Utrenniaia Zvezda* 1 (1910) 1. Cf. Klibanov, *History of Religious Sectarianism*, 285.

tablishing such a union was made at a conference of Russian Protestants chaired by I. V. Kargel in January 1907.[64] However, history repeated itself and the proposal was not supported by the Baptists, as had been the case during the first such conference in 1884 in St. Petersburg.[65] Pastor Walter Zhak of the Light in the East mission, who became president of the Union of Gospel Christians after Prokhanov's death, concluded that the "the Baptists had no intention of arriving at brotherly cooperation."[66]

In the summer of 1907 Prokhanov and Baron Nikolai visited a conference of the World Evangelical Alliance as representatives of the Russian Evangelical Alliance, even though the alliance had not yet been officially established in Russia.[67] It was officially organized only in January 1909.[68] The alliance was never developed, however, since it was supported by neither the Orthodox nor the Baptists, who became influential during this period,[69] and it disappeared within four years of its launching.

When the first Evangelical church in Russia received its registration in the autumn of 1908, Prokhanov published samples of its registration documents and invited all unregistered congregations in Russia to register and establish a Union of Gospel Christians.[70] This initiative was supported by congregations in various parts of Russia, and in September 1909 the first conference of Evangelical Christians was held in St. Petersburg. Even though Kargel was not able to attend personally, he sent his greetings by telegram.[71] Prokhanov's speech reveals the continuity of the Radstockian tradition:

> All of us belong to different groups of believers in Russia, but we are united on the basis of the following statements of faith. All of

64. *Bratskii Listok* 2 (1907) 7, 21.

65. For a detailed historical account see Wilhelm Kahle, *Evangel'skie Khristiane*, 97–116.

66. Ibid., 114.

67. *Bratskii Listok* 12 (1907) 4.

68. *Bratskii Listok* 1 (1909) 1–13. Among the greetings is a telegram from M. M. Korff, who says that many people in the West do not understand the concept of unity in Christ.

69. Plett, *Istoriia Evangel'skikh Khristian Baptistov*, 24.

70. *Bratskii Listok* 1 (1909) 7–13.

71. Ibid., 11 (1909) 3.

us acknowledge that (1) the only source for knowing God is Holy Scripture, consisting of the Old and New Testaments and nothing else; (2) every person has the right and duty to understand scripture in accordance with the admonition of his free conscience and the infusion of the Holy Spirit, without constraint by anybody or anything; (3) God is one and triune, undivided in his substance; (4) man, created to live a holy life, sinned before God; (5) the Son of God was incarnated, suffered, and died to redeem humanity from sin and was raised for our justification; (6) there is only one mediator between God and people, namely our Lord Jesus Christ; (7) in order to be saved every person needs to have a living faith, personal repentance, regeneration by the Holy Spirit, and an internal testimony about it; (8) all believers are priests to God Most High, a rank received directly from the Lord Jesus Christ, the only High Priest; (9) we believe in the immortality of the soul, the resurrection of the body, the second coming of Christ, the judgment of the living and the dead, and the eternal blessedness of the righteous. What great unity! . . . The Apostle Paul says in 1 Corinthians 11:19: "No doubt there have to be differences among you to show which of you have God's approval." Thus even the competing activity of different churches, if other circumstances do not get involved, can bring only benefit, because it gives opportunity for a spiritual tug and the greater development of gifts. The differences in understanding of some articles of faith in opinions about things of an external nature and about church organization does not break the core unity, but gives every church an opportunity to reveal its individuality. This was the kind of unity desired by Christ when he prayed, "As you, Father, are in me, and I in you, may they also be united in us" (John 17:21). The Father, the Son, and the Spirit are one, but every person of the Trinity has his own individuality. The Father gives birth to the Son. The Spirit comes from the Father. The Father sends the Son and the Spirit. The Son is born of the Father, and he sends the Spirit. The Spirit comes from the Father and is sent by the Father and the Son. This differences in the properties and functions of the three persons do not break their unity. The same can be said with regard to churches and individual believers. Their unity does not absorb their individuality, and their individuality does not break their unity. Unity is not uniformity. Unity includes individuality as an element. Diversity is an element in the beauty of unity. Like [Christ] we should plead with all the strength of our soul and heart, "May all be one". . . . [After

> Prokhanov's speech] the Apostles' Creed was read and repeated with a loud voice by the whole conference.[72]

The nine articles of unity in Prokhanov's speech were taken largely from the basis of unity of the World Evangelical Alliance.[73] However, Prokhanov modified the Western document by adding and removing some articles. The fourth article of the original Western document, "belief in the utter depravity of human nature in consequence of the fall," was translated into Russian as "man, created to live a holy life, sinned before God." The seventh article was modified as well. Prokhanov changed the key Protestant phrase, "the justification of the sinner by faith alone," into a more streamlined sentence: "In order to be saved every person needs to have a living faith, personal repentance, regeneration by the Holy Spirit, and an internal testimony about it." The ninth article, "obligation and perpetuity of the ordinances of baptism and the Lord's Supper," is omitted. Instead, Prokhanov added an emphasized statement about the priesthood of all believers. This modification of the doctrinal platform of Christian unity is telling. While Prokhanov used the statement of the Evangelical Alliance as the foundation for building a distinctly Protestant structure in Russia,[74] the Alliance's basis of unity was not followed strictly, as if it was an unchangeable charter. Doctrinal formulations and theological precision did not play an important role. Prokhanov extended the basis of unity in the Russian context by removing disputable questions concerning the rite of baptism, which could have been a stumbling block for some Protestant bodies in Russia as they considered becoming members of the Union. The rejection of typical Lutheran and Calvinist terminology regarding the utter depravity of man and salvation by faith alone was justified, given the severe Orthodox critique of these doctrines. In line with tendencies in Western evangelicalism,[75] as well as in resonance with the Orthodox mentality, Calvinist terminology was filtered out in the process of transposing the basis of unity. Thus Prokhanov demonstrated continuity with the Western tradition that he was part of, as well as flexibility to adapt to the Russian context.

72. Ibid., 10 (1909) 19–23.

73. PP I/7A.

74. Prokhanoff, *In the Cauldron of Russia,* 104.

75. Bebbington, *Dominance of Evangelicalism,* 125.

Prokhanov built his explanation using the categories of Trinitarian theology and of the Apostles' Creed. He proposed that the dilemma of competing interpretations be solved not on the level of theological arguments, but on the level of pneumatically-driven communities that should demonstrate the validity of their interpretation through the exercise of spiritual gifts. He seems to have understood at this time the hermeneutical nature of the reading communities, which is apparent in his call to unity in diversity. It should also be pointed out that during this period, Prokhanov was not building a Baptist denomination, but was attempting rather to organize a unified evangelical front, held together by evangelical convictions concerning the Romantic key of unity through sentimental devotion to Jesus and concerning biblicism. "The evangelical movement has the goal of renewing the religious life of the Russian nation. In order to achieve this there must be unity among the different branches. What will be the fruit of the evangelical movement: new sectarianism or new reformation? This is a question that depends on the Lord and his servants."[76] The question of rituals was not significant during this period.[77]

An all-Russian reformation by the Spirit that would bring all regenerated Christians together, regardless of their minor differences, had been the vision of the St. Petersburg tradition since the time of Radstock and Pashkov.[78] Unlike the Baptists, who wanted to maintain ties of identity with the world Baptist movement, the Gospel Christians of St. Petersburg believed in a truly Russian evangelical revival that might take a different form from that of the Western Reformation of the sixteenth century.[79]

The Evangelical Periodical *Khristianin* and Its Supplements

The major periodical of the Gospel Christians was *Khristianin*, which was published during the period between 1906 and 1928. Like the first evangelical periodical, the *Russian Workman,* it was named and patterned after its British counterpart. The British non-denominational revivalist newspaper *The Christian* had been published in London since

76. *Bratskii Listok* 9 (1910) 21.

77. Cf. Iartsev, *Sekta*, 5.

78. Ibid., 9 (1906) 1.

79. Ibid., 10 (1910) 24.

1870.[80] Some of the articles were directly translated from *The Christian*. The magazine had several supplements such as *Bratskii Listok* ("The Brotherly Leaflet"), *Molodoi Vinogradnik* ("The Young Vineyard"), and *Detskii Drug* ("The Children's Friend"). The newspaper *Utrenniaia Zvezda* ("The Morning Star") was published weekly beginning in 1910 and was originally intended to be the weekly periodical of the Russian Evangelical Alliance.[81]

The goal of *Khristianin* was succinctly and self-affirmingly expressed in an advertisement published in 1910 in *Utrenniaia Zvezda*:

> This journal has brought a new living stream into Russian spiritual literature, pursuing the goal of implementing the fundamental principles of evangelical teaching apart from any reference to the doctrinal distinctives of the various branches of Christianity. It has significant value for contemporary readers, since it does not touch upon any of the controversial issues promoted by various denominations. Its foundational principle—"in essentials, unity; in doubtful matters, liberty; in all things, love"—colors the content of the journal with the spirit of impartiality and reconcilability; this feature has so far been unknown in Russian spiritual literature. Every sincere believer, whatever confession he might belong to, can subscribe to its essential positions with a clear conscience. Those souls who wish to hear the living word of the *Gospel* without any tincture of later centuries will find in the journal all that is necessary.[82]

The publications *Khristianin, Bratskii Listok,* and *Utrenniaia Zvezda* had three different tasks. The purpose of *Khristianin* was to address the spiritual needs of Christians. *Bratskii Listok* was used as a forum for Christians of different denominations. News from conferences of different denominations such as the Baptists, Molokans, and Gospel Christians, as well as news from Western missionary sources, was continually published in the supplements. The weekly newspaper *Utrenniaia Zvezda* was intended to become the periodical of the Russian Evangelical Alliance. Its goal was to represent the evangelical identity in the public domain. "The main goal of this newspaper is to make heard the voice of the *new progressive-religious Russia* in the chorus of different

80. Bebbington, *Dominance of Evangelicalism*, 186.

81. *Bratskii Listok* 9 (1910) 19.

82. *Utrenniaia Zvezda* 7 (1910) 6.

voices of public life."[83] In order to make a good impression Prokhanov coined a neologism, "New Belief" (*novoverie*). In the issues of *Utrenniaia Zvezda* news about New Believers always appeared following news about Old Believers and Imperial Orthodoxy. This sequence progressed from the old to the new through "worm-eaten" Orthodoxy, which was often one-sidedly represented as the persecutor of all progressive thought. The newspaper did not pass up any opportunity to present the effete condition of the State religion. In contrast, New Belief is always represented as the progressive faith of the new era—the faith that has shaken off all the dusty rags of the past. In Prokhanov's presentation, this new faith was a spiritual movement transforming individuals. It did not contradict human progress or scientific discoveries; instead, it enhanced them.[84] The Romanticism of Radstock's era, with its accent on the emotions, as well as the Modernism of the beginning of the twentieth century, with its accent on progress and the dominance of science, each complementing the other, found their place in the publications of Prokhanov.

These periodicals were the chief means of creating the movement's identity and shaping its theology. The format of Prokhanov's periodicals helped the evangelicals to see themselves as part of a worldwide movement led by the Spirit of God. Every issue of *Khristianin* contained evangelical news from different parts of Russia and the world. It allowed all kinds of Christians to share their testimonies, thoughts, and impressions. The key feature of the periodicals of this period was their tendency toward polyphony. Similar to contemporary Internet forums, where everyone can leave a message, the periodicals sometimes contained contradictory viewpoints.[85]

THE PIETISTIC PROTESTANT AND BYZANTINE PARADIGMS AT THE BEGINNING OF THE TWENTIETH CENTURY

The attitude of the evangelical Christians of this period toward Orthodoxy was no different from that of Radstock. The Orthodox Church was viewed exclusively in terms of religious decadence. It was considered impotent to transform people's lives. "In a word, the Greek Church omitted and

83. Ibid., 6 (1910) 5.

84. *Bratskii Listok* 10 (1906) 1.

85. Cf. Ibid., 9 (1907) 14 and ibid., 12 (1907) 14.

lost the whole Gospel, the source of joy and life, and left its people in the darkness of a hopeless life or spiritual pessimism and everlasting fear, with no salvation and no eternity."[86] Addressing a group of the intelligentsia in 1910, A. Ivanov, a member of the council of the St. Petersburg Evangelical Church, argued that the Gospel was preached in Russia for the first time "not more than 50 years ago."[87] He identified the Gospel Christians as part of the world evangelical movement that was active in all parts of the world. As during the time of Pashkov, a key argument in favor of the primitive form of Christianity was an appeal to the civilized societies of the West, where Protestant countries were more developed than non-Protestant ones. Western Protestant civilization was viewed as a key supporting pillar of Eastern evangelicalism.

However, regardless of his low view of Orthodoxy as a decadent religion that had "left the purity of the gospel teaching,"[88] Prokhanov, like Pashkov, was willing to cooperate with Orthodox believers on the platform of evangelical Christianity. By so doing, he avoided both a direct collision and theological dialogue. His reply to the Orthodox missionary D. Bogoliubov, who had called on him to participate in a public debate in 1909, is revealing: "Christians should not quarrel with each other in front of unbelieving Russia. We should work hand in hand in the ministry of preaching the living Christ and morally renewing our motherland. We invite you cordially to do so."[89] On the one hand, Prokhanov admits that an Orthodox missionary can be a sincere believer and does not deny the possibility of joining in corporate ministry with him. But on the other hand, Prokhanov refuses to talk to Bogoliubov on Orthodox terms, thus evading dialogue. Instead, he proposes his own terms according to which Russia is viewed as an unbelieving country, and evangelicals are presented as preachers of the living Christ who are transforming a pagan country.[90] Neither Orthodox history nor theology are taken into account.

86. Prokhanoff, *In the Cauldron of Russia*, 24.

87. *Bratskii Listok* 4 (1910) 8.

88. Ibid.

89. Ibid., 12 (1909) 17–18.

90. Cf. Duncan, *Russian Messianism*, 14.

THE MESSIANIC IDEA

The Slavophile belief in the messianic role of Russia that had inspired Pashkov played a significant role in Prokhanov's worldview as well. Unlike Pashkov, whose optimism had been based on the possibility of uniting the evangelical movement in Russia before this took place in all the other countries in the world,[91] the messianic inspiration of Prokhanov drew its source from a specific prophecy associated with the names of two highly influential persons in world evangelicalism: Hudson Taylor and D. L. Moody. The prophecy was published in the third issue of *Khristianin* in 1906.[92] It was reproduced from a letter of Taylor found among the correspondence of D. L. Moody not long after Moody's death. According to the prophecy, "There will be a revolution in Russia which will lead to a great revival in the western part of Russia. This revival will spread throughout the earth, and then the Lord will come."[93] Having published this prophecy in 1906, Prokhanov was convinced that Taylor had predicted the events of the Russian Revolution of 1905: "Isn't it joyful for us to look at the future, when the great God is using the Russian Revolution to prepare the soil for revival?"[94] The powerful social cataclysms brought about by the defeat of Russia in the Russian-Japanese war and by the subsequent revolution of 1905 brought to the Gospel Christians not only religious liberty but also a new vision of Russia. According to this vision, the Evangelical Christians of St. Petersburg were obligated to play the most important role in the destiny of both Russia and the world, in light of the second coming of Christ. Russian messianism in its evangelical variation was similar to Marxist eschatological messianism.[95] Like Marxists, evangelicals were convinced of their unique role in transforming the old world order. But unlike Marxists, they believed that this transformation would be brought about by the synergy of believers, with the transcendental breaking in of the Holy Spirit, in line with the great Western revivals of the eighteenth and nineteenth centuries.[96]

91. Cf. Ibid., 52.

92. *Khristianin* 3 (1906) 69.

93. Ibid.

94. Ibid.

95. Duncan, *Russian Messianism*, 52.

96. Iartsev, *Sekta*, 6–7.

THEOLOGICAL DYNAMICS AND BIBLICAL INTERPRETATION

In this section the focus will be on major modifications of the tradition since the time of Pashkov with regard to its theology and biblical interpretation. The key identifiers of evangelicalism—biblicism, crucicentrism, conversionism, and activism—which characterized the movement in the nineteenth century did not suffer any changes.[97] Following the general trend of the Western evangelicalism of the time, Arminian theology was prevalent among Eastern evangelicals as well.[98] The dispensationalist interpretive framework was not articulated or brought onto the stage during this period, which was also characteristic of Moody's revivalist approach.[99] The Russian evangelicals of this time did not have their own statement of faith. Because Kargel and Prokhanov were interested in forming a Christian alliance in Russia, any statement of faith beside the commonly shared Apostles' Creed and broad evangelical values could become a stumbling block to unity in that Orthodox country.

Since the time of Radstock's arrival, the evangelical tradition had been fed on ideas received from the Keswick and independent Brethren movements.[100] The key authors who set the theological tone for *Khristianin* during the first year of its publication were a Brethren revivalist preacher, Grabb,[101] and participants in the Keswick conferences R. A. Torrey,[102] Andrew Murray,[103] and Gregory Mantle.[104] *Khristianin* acquainted the Russian audience with the biographies of evangelical leaders of the nineteenth century such as D. L. Moody,[105] C. H. Spurgeon,[106]

97. Bebbington, *Evangelicalism in Modern Britain*, 3.

98. Idem, *Dominance of Evangelicalism*, 128–30; Klibanov, *History of Religious Sectarianism*, 248.

99. Cf. Marsden, *Fundamentalism and American Culture*, 138.

100. Cf. Sawatsky, *Soviet Evangelicals*, 340; Corrado, *Filosofiia*, 105–10.

101. *Khristianin* 2 (1906) 1; ibid., 4 (1906) 1; ibid., 5 (1906) 7–13; *Bratskii Listok* 4 (1906).

102. *Khristianin* 4 (1906) 30, 70; ibid., 6 (1906) 34; ibid., 8 (1906) 23; ibid., 9 (1906) 7; *Bratskii Listok*, 8 (1906) 13.

103. *Khristianin* 3 (1906) 69; ibid., 5 (1906) 1–6; ibid., 6 (1906) 1; ibid., 7 (1906) 1; ibid., 9 (1906) 1.

104. *Bratskii Listok* 3 (1906) 4; *Khristianin* 5 (1906) 14–19; ibid., 6 (1906) 13–19.

105. *Khristianin* 5 (1906) 74.

106. Ibid., 6 (1906) 60; ibid., 7 (1906) 7; ibid., 8 (1906) 43.

R. A. Torrey,[107] George Müller,[108] and F. Baedeker.[109] These biographies were used as examples of what Christian ministry might look like in the Russian context.[110] The first two books published by the Russian YMCA were *What Do You Think about Christ?* by D. L. Moody and *The First Steps in the Christian Life* by R. A. Torrey.[111] Russian authorship was represented mainly by I. S. Prokhanov and I. V. Kargel. The European Reformation of the sixteenth century is not mentioned in the evangelical periodicals. The movement was self-consciously identified with the Anglo-American revivalism of the second half of the nineteenth century.

The first year of *Khristianin* was characterized by a tense expectation of the final Pentecost of the last days, when the Spirit would be poured out on all flesh.[112] Commenting on news about the Welsh revival led by Evan Roberts, Prokhanov ends his article with this note: "The ministry of Roberts is in full flame, and we will give information about it in *Khristianin* from time to time, because it is concerned with the most important question in the believer's spiritual life, namely the seeking of the Holy Spirit and becoming stronger in him."[113] The teaching of Dr. R. A. Torrey about experiencing the Holy Spirit was dominant during this period.[114] It was a common expectation that the church of the last days would continually pray about the experience of baptism with the Holy Spirit and that it would experience the signs and miracles of the final Pentecost in ever-increasing power.[115] The third issue of *Khristianin* begins with a hymn written by Prokhanov and devoted to the Holy Spirit: "Give us the gifts of healing and the gifts of prophecy. But more than any other blessing give us the gift of your love." This pneumatology is identi-

107. Ibid., 4 (1906) 70.

108. Ibid., 3 (1906) 66–68. Prokhanov does not mention the visit of Müller to Russia in the 1880s.

109. *Bratskii Listok* 10 (1906) 10–12. Prokhanov does not mention in Baedeker's obituary that Radstock and Pashkov had connections with Baedeker.

110. Cf. *Khristianin* 8 (1906) 43 and *Bratskii Listok* 8 (1906) 1–7.

111. *Bratskii Listok* 8 (1906) 13.

112. Ibid., 3 (1906) 5; *Khristianin* 9 (1906) 42 and ibid., 10 (1906) 22.

113. *Khristianin* 2 (1906) 57.

114. Torrey, *Baptism with the Holy Spirit*. See Archer, *Pentecostal Hermeneutics for the Twenty-First Century*, 80–82.

115. Cf. Marsden, *Fundamentalism and American Culture*, 78–80.

cal with that of Pashkov, but it is intensified. It became the ethos of the movement during this period.

The major turn of the tradition is detected in balancing the pneumatological sentimentalism of Radstock and Pashkov with a more systematic approach to the study of scripture, as well as in a more positive evaluation of biblical commentaries and the role of science. Having rejected Orthodox scholarship outright, Eastern evangelicals were left with just one option, namely to depend on Western evangelicalism for ideas, resources, and strategies. Following the Western evangelical tendencies of the time, Prokhanov opened the door to begin moving from the period of Romantic sentimentalism, which had been severely criticized by Leskov and other Orthodox apologists, into the era of Modernity, which was characterized by its optimism and its high view of scientific knowledge.[116]

While the pietistic method of reading scripture was not changed, Prokhanov introduced a more systematic approach to Bible study, having been influenced by the works of D. L. Moody and R. A. Torrey.[117] Moody's *Experiencing Pleasure and Profit in Bible Study* was the first book on biblical interpretation translated into Russian.[118] Readers were encouraged to read the Bible systematically.[119] This systematic approach upheld a high view of the inspiration, unity, and sufficiency of scripture. While the systematic reading of the Bible itself, with a desire to obey its teaching, was preferred over the reading of biblical commentaries and other secondary sources, such secondary books were nevertheless often advertised in the periodicals.

This method of study was based on the Scottish Common Sense philosophy of Thomas Reid.[120] The argument of Common Sense philosophy was that God created the human mind in such a way that it can know the world directly. The human faculties were created by God to be able to know properly the world created by the same God. God has built into human nature first principles that cannot be doubted. "The common sense of mankind, whether of the man behind the plough or the

116. Bebbington, *Dominance of Evangelicalism*, 109.

117. Cf. Moody, *Experiencing Pleasure and Profit in Bible Study*, and Torrey, *How to Study the Bible for the Greatest Profit*.

118. *Utrenniaia Zvezda* 8 (1910) 8.

119. *Khristianin* 3 (1906) 58.

120. Marsden, *Fundamentalism and American Culture*, 15.

man behind the desk, was the surest guide to truth."[121] Taking the Bible as a book of reliable facts, the proponents of common sense realism suggested that any person can understand the Bible directly and correctly. A biblical text taken out of its original historical setting can be properly investigated and understood by any human created in the image of God, regardless of the person's culture, tradition, gender, or education.

The Bible was studied in a variety of ways: structurally, thematically, typologically, biographically, and onomatologically. Structural analysis involved studying large portions of scripture, such as entire books or chapters, in order to understand their key themes and structure. Thematic analysis was concerned with the study of topics such as God's love, peace, sin, salvation, etc. Typological interpretation of the Bible included the study of Old Testament types of Christ, as well as types of various concepts and events (leprosy as a type of sin, etc.). Biographies and names were studied for the purpose of drawing spiritual and moral lessons.

The key genre for theologizing was homilies, together with the occasional translation of Western evangelical books. The method of typological intratextuality was the most common strategy for making sense of the biblical text. An example from Prokhanov's sermon on Psalm 18:35 is typical of this period: "Thou hast also given me the shield of thy salvation; and thy right hand hath holden me up, and thy gentleness hath made me great."

The text of this Psalm is read through the Christocentric prism of the metanarrative of creation-fall-redemption-restoration. The meaning of the text in its original context is not taken into account. Meditating on the word "shield," Prokhanov suggests two dimensions for understanding its meaning. The first is diachronic: the shield of salvation in the past, present, and future. The crucified Christ is our shield of salvation in the past. The risen Christ is the shield of our salvation in the present. And the glorified Christ is the shield of our salvation in the future. The second dimension is synchronic: the shield of salvation against the three enemies of the Christian—the world, the flesh, and the devil. Having read the first clause of the verse through the hermeneutical lens of evangelical Christocentric narrative, Prokhanov proceeds by means of canonical intratextuality. "Thy right hand hath holden me up"—the phrase is linked with Matt 14:31, where Jesus reaches out his hand to

121. Ibid.

the drowning Peter. In the new textual context, Prokhanov focuses on the words of Peter: "Tell me to come to you." Prokhanov comments: "We have the order to live according to the Spirit and the direction to come to you." The next textual item, "the sea," is taken as a hermeneutical springboard: "The one who walks on the sea now will at the end stand upon the sea of glass" (Rev 15:2). Thus the believer is called to walk on the water of life by the power of faith in order to be able to stand on the sea of glass. The call to Peter is the call to us. We should be faithful and victorious.[122] The sentence from the Psalm is used as a springboard to tell the Gospel narrative and theology.

The platform of common sense realism sometimes generated infelicitous interpretations of biblical texts. Thus explaining God's guidance of Joseph through dreams, the author states: "In former times dreams were less frequent than now, because the food and customs of ancient times were simpler than now. For this reason every dream was taken as a significant event, and everyone tried to decipher its meaning. God sometimes sends dreams even *now*, but he usually guides through his word."[123] The author of this explanation is not concerned with substantiating his view by facts or with the logical coherence of his argument. The argument is made up in order to convey the theological conviction that while God formerly guided people through dreams, now the major channel of God's communication is his Word.

The Gospel Christians recognized the hermeneutical problem and the need for an external theological guide to evaluate different interpretations. There is an exchange of views in *Brtatskii Listok* concerning the question of whether believers go to paradise after death. The proponent of the first view argues that scripture clearly teaches that disciples do not go into the presence of the Lord until they have received a reward from him.[124] In reply to this view, another author, Georgii Shipkov, writes: "We need to build our teaching not on separate verses but on the complete teaching of the Old and New Testaments, which is consistently united in meaning." Shipkov admits that the problem consists in the absence of a unifying doctrinal creed "similar to that of the Baptists."[125] Sometimes appeal is made to Western authoritative interpreters. In order to tackle

122. *Khristianin* 2 (1906) 3–10.

123. Ibid., 4 (1906) 69.

124. *Bratskii Listok* 9 (1907) 14.

125. Ibid., 12 (1907) 14.

the teaching of complete sanctification, William Fetler appeals to biblical passages such as Jas 4:2. The Keswick interpretation is supported by reference to such authorities as Spurgeon, Meyer, and Torrey, who did not support the doctrine of the eradication of the sinful nature.[126]

In contrast to the tendency to articulate true biblical teaching on the basis of what Baptist-oriented authors had written, the peculiarly Evangelical attitude was a willingness to drop their own interpretation in order to understand a different interpretation. An Evangelical contributor to the magazine, a certain Mr. Zinov'ev, makes this principle explicit in an article devoted to unity in the Evangelical Alliance:

> Only energized preaching in all the churches about the liberation of everyone from his own self, and especially from his own interpretation of what it means to live in accordance with the Word, can eventually lift us up to our Firstborn from the dead. He died for the purpose that we could die with him to everything and for our subjective [personal] understanding of the Word. Having died with him we have the opportunity to be glad about the understanding of another brother or sister. This opportunity to consider another greater than oneself is given by our dear Firstborn, the Christ. *Freedom from one's own self gives the unity of the two free ones in the third, which is the Son and the Father.*[127]

It is difficult to judge what Zinov'ev meant in this last sentence. But it is clear that he was trying to operate within the framework of Trinitarian theology, arguing for a differential type of interpretation that allows for plurality of meanings.

CONCLUSION

The St. Petersburg Evangelical tradition did not suffer major modifications following its origin in 1874. The key vision of the movement was the organization of an interdenominational Evangelical Alliance, consisting of believers of different confessions, including Orthodoxy, with the goal of arriving at a biblically-based unity. The Alliance was envisioned as a spiritual engine capable of spiritually transforming Russia after the pattern of the leading Protestant countries of the civilized West, and even beyond. It was envisioned that the all-Russian evangelical revival would

126. Ibid., 9 (1907) 6.

127. Ibid., 3 (1909) 1–3.

move Russia to a higher socio-political and religious plane, surpassing even that of the European countries.

Tension between ecclesiological restorationism and pietistic primitivism continued to exist in the movement. The ministry of I. S. Prokhanov during the period between 1894 and 1910 should be viewed as a genuine continuation of Pashkov's vision. Prokhanov and the Gospel Christians not only modeled their identity after Western free evangelicalism, but they also copied Western institutions such as the Evangelical Alliance and the YMCA and relied on Western teachers and preachers, utilizing them as their tuning-fork for the development of theological ideas.

From the theological point of view, the tradition was in continuity with the Anglo-American revivalist movement in general and the Keswick holiness movement in particular. The Evangelical periodicals demonstrate the presence of a significant pneumatological accent in the expectation of a Pentecostal outpouring of the Spirit in the last days. This pneumatological theology was reinforced by a belief in the messianic role of the St. Petersburg movement in the eschatological framework. Prokhanov's way of doing theology was built on Trinitarian foundations and pneumatological intuition. The introduction of the Trinitarian scheme was a new development in the tradition. Pneumatological communities striving for unity in Christ need to exercise their spiritual strength to demonstrate to others that their views are more faithful to the Word. The periodicals provided some space for different voices to be heard and interacted with. Building on the foundation of the World Evangelical Alliance, Prokhanov extended the platform of Christian unity in the Russian context in order to incorporate different sorts of denominations. In an attempt to find a common denominator for different denominations, the periodicals of this period lack an argumentative tone.

The attitude towards Russian Orthodoxy did not change from the time of Radstock. Orthodoxy is viewed as an archaic and impotent religion, bogged down by the weight of dead historical tradition associated with ritualism and authoritarian hierarchism. In principle, the Orthodox are invited to become part of the union, with the expectation that in the course of reading the scriptures they will be re-formed into the Evangelical image.

There is a traceable encroaching of Modernist tendencies on the Romantic nucleus of the tradition. Evangelical Christianity is actively positioned by Prokhanov as pure Christianity, unpolluted by the historical tradition of the past and fully in line with the idea of scientific progress. Prokhanov actively supported the social and political changes taking place in Russia, believing that God encourages a peaceful struggle for freedom.

The approach to biblical interpretation was not changed substantially. Under the influence of revivalist writers such as D. L. Moody and R. A. Torrey, Bible study became more systematized on the proto-fundamentalist basis of the self-sufficiency and self-explanatory nature of the Bible for any reader who is willing to study and obey its message. One's common sense is the surest guide to the correct understanding of scripture. The key trend in Evangelical hermeneutics during this period was a willingness to listen to the other without arguing for one's own biblical interpretation.

We are ready now to turn to the most important period in the history of the tradition, which began with the major socio-political shift in Russian society associated with the events of World War I and the Bolshevik Revolution.

5

The Evangelical Tradition during the Period between 1910 and 1939

"The evangelical movement in Russia is not a native nugget. It was born from the germ brought to us by our believing brothers from abroad at the time of great evangelical revival in Germany, Britain, and America. Our most-used spiritual songs were taken from the same source at the same time, and they have an Anglo-American or German flavor."[1]

INTRODUCTION

The period between the World Wars has been analyzed by different historians of the evangelical movement. The dissertations of Steeves,[2] Kahle,[3] Blane,[4] and Nesdoly[5] contain denominational studies of the tradition. The recently-published book by Heather Coleman demonstrates the rooting of the tradition in the socio-political Russian and Soviet context of the time.[6] The major deficiency of the Western studies is their focus on a specific period of time, without taking into account the development and modifications of the community's self-identity and theology within its specific geopolitical frame of reference. The tradition is unani-

1. *Utrenniaia Zvezda* 3–4–5 (1922) 15.
2. Steeves, "Russian Baptist Union."
3. Kahle, *Evangelische Christen in Russland und der Sowjetunion*.
4. Blane, "Relations between the Russian Protestant Sects and the State."
5. Nesdoly, "Evangelical Sectarianism in Russia."
6. Coleman, *Russian Baptists and Spiritual Revolution*.

mously and uncritically perceived as a species of the Baptist movement and treated as such.[7]

Eastern denominational studies are largely built on the self-identifying narrative, originating in the early Soviet period, that the evangelical movement in Russia was an original and unique spiritual movement brought about by the Spirit of God in Euro-Asia.[8] The origin of this narrative will be discussed in the present chapter. Western scholarship is not interacted with sufficiently in Ukraine because it is not easily accessible.[9] But even when it is mentioned, it is qualified as ideologically biased on certain points, without proper argumentation or facts being given, and even without the supposedly biased points themselves being specified.[10] This state of affairs is due to the embryonic state of the academic research culture of the newly established religious educational institutions in the former Soviet Union.[11] A scholarly monograph written by L. Mitrokhin is the most comprehensive study on the topic available in Russian.[12] Following the Soviet approach to historiography, he frames the tradition

7. Cf. Durasoff, *Russian Protestants*, 55.

8. Reshetnikov and Sannikov, *Obzor Istorii*, 9, 71. Cf. Karetnikova, *Al'manakh po Istorii Russkogo Baptisma*, vy, 1–3; Savinskii, *Istoriia Evangel'skikh Khristian-Baptistov Ukrainy, Rossii, Belorussii (1867–1917)*; *Istoriia Evangel'skikh Khristian-Baptistov Ukrainy, Rossii, Belorussii (1917–1967)*; and Golovashchenko, *Istoriia Evangel'sko-Baptistskogo Dvizheniia v Ukraine*.

9. Reshetnikov and Sannikov, *Obzor Istorii*, 14–15.

10. Ibid., 6–8, 14.

11. I have not been able to locate a single critical book review or an ongoing theological debate on any theological or historical work written by a Post-Soviet Ukrainian author. The academic state of affairs among evangelicals in the former Soviet Union is characterized by a non-dialogical cacophony of local voices in the ocean of the Western, largely fundamentalist literature uncritically translated into Russian with the financial support of various Western institutions. Unfortunately, a recent evaluation of theological education in Euro-Asia does not even mention the problem of the lack of a dialogical and critical research culture. See Kobiakovskii, "Effectiveness of Theological Education in Ukraine." The only document in the public domain is the minutes of a short Internet discussion available in Cherenkov, "Bogoslovskoe Obshchestvo Evrazii Obsuzhdaet." However, this discussion reveals the acknowledgment of the present state of disorientation and a readiness to interact with Western and Eastern scholarship. For a review of the theological state of affairs in Ukraine see Filipovych and Kolodny, "Theology and Religious Studies in the Postcommunist Ukraine." However the authors of this review, who represent the Soviet and Post-Soviet school of religious studies, do not evaluate the quality of research being accomplished in the Ukrainian setting.

12. Mitrokhin, *Baptizm*.

as part of the world Baptist movement, thereby missing the complexity of developments in Anglo-American and Russian evangelicalism.

The goal of this chapter is to demonstrate the modifications of theology and self-identity that took place and to identify the driving forces of the Protestant paradigm and its relationship with Russian Orthodoxy. As in the previous chapter, the modifications of the tradition will be analyzed along the lines of historical identity, theology, and biblical interpretation.

MODIFICATIONS OF THE SELF-IDENTIFYING STORY IN THE HISTORICAL SETTING

A Baptist Denominational Shift

This period of history is characterized by the explicit transition of the Gospel Christians to a more structured ecclesial form.[13] During the second conference of the Gospel Christians in 1910–11 Prokhanov introduced a programmatic statement of faith that caused the amorphous revivalist movement to take on the contours of a Baptist denomination.[14] New members were expected to be baptized upon profession of faith. This transition was conditioned by historical and theological factors. A key historical reason for the this denominational turn was the collapse of the Russian Evangelical Alliance, which had found support from neither the Orthodox nor the Baptists.[15] This move along the route of ecclesiological primitivism was directly connected with the strengthening of the Baptist denomination in Russia, while other dissenting bodies were either being converted by aggressive Baptist missionaries or were massively emigrating from Russia.[16] A confessional denominational expression was also necessary for the State registration of the developing Union of Gospel Christians, in order for it to receive official permission for conferences and publishing activities.[17] From a theological point of view, a doctrinal statement was needed as a leveling device to prevent things from get-

13. For a detailed historical account see Kahle, *Evangel'skie Khristiane*, 121–47.

14. Klibanov, *History of Religious Sectarianism in Russia*, 290.

15. Plett, *Istoria Evangel'skikh Khristian*, 24.

16. Berokoff, *Molokans in America*, 3–20; Woodcock, *Doukhobors*, 10–30; Prokhanoff, *In the Cauldron of Russia*, 126.

17. Lieven, *Evangel'skoe Probuzhdenie*, 105.

ting out of control, given the growing variety of theological voices in the movement.[18] In a self-identifying and programmatic article published prior to one Baptist conference Prokhanov wrote:

> Gospel Christians (*Evangel'skie*) and Gospel Christians-Baptists (Baptists) historically belong to two branches of the same evangelical movement. The *Evangel'skie* movement can trace its origins to St. Petersburg during the time of the famed V. A. Pashkov, while the Baptist movement first appeared in the 1860s in the Caucasus and Malorussia [Ukraine–A. P.]. The difference between them is more in mood and attitude than in dogma. The *Evangel'skie* hold to the principle of church autonomy and the democratic structure of local congregations to a higher degree than do the Baptists.
>
> . . . So what are the dogmas of the *Evangel'skie* and the Baptists? What is new in comparison to Orthodoxy? Once a member of the intelligentsia asked me, "Do you acknowledge the dogmas of the Trinity, the deity of Christ, redemption, and the resurrection of the dead?" I said, "Yes. Even more than that, every one of us can recite nearly the whole Creed with full faith." . . . Thus there is no dogmatic difference with Orthodoxy. What is the difference then? In the Orthodox newspapers they say that the supposed difference lies in our denial of the ritualistic aspect of Orthodoxy. That, however, is not the case. The key innovation in their teaching is that *Evangel'skie* and Baptists take as foundational for the Christian religion the necessity of the *personal conversion of every member*, and their churches include only members who have *consciously* confessed their faith and been baptized. The application of these principles, as they were preached by Christ, restores the church to its original Apostolic perspective. . . . The newness of being baptized upon profession of faith (*verokreshchentsev)* is part of the antiquity of Apostolic times. The meaning of the evangelical movement in Russia is nothing other than the restoration of Apostolic Christianity. In addition to the Russian Baptists and the *Evangel'skie,* there are several other groups that adhere to the same principle: the Mennonites, as well as Latvian and German Baptists.[19]

Prokhanov explained in the article that the *Evangel'skie* (Gospel Christians) were continuing the legacy of V. A. Pashkov with regard to

18. Cf. *Bratskii Listok* 12 (1907) 14.

19. *Utrenniaia Zvezda*, "K S"ezdu Baptistov" 35 (1910).

his vision of uniting the Protestant evangelical bodies.[20] The unity sought by Prokhanov was no different in ethos from the unity envisioned by Pashkov. The major difference was that Prokhanov took the restorationist tendency of the tradition further along the path. According to his proposal, each evangelical body in Russia would retain its autonomy, while a unity committee would be created, consisting of two representatives from each of the five evangelical bodies. The unification of the evangelical front was to be demonstrated in the following ways: (1) setting aside one day each year to pray for unity; (2) launching a common evangelical periodical of the *verokreshchentsy* that would voice their opinions on religious, political, economic, scientific, and other issues in society; (3) establishing a common biblical institute for the preparation of preachers; and (4) acknowledging the YMCA established in Moscow in 1908 as the common union of Christian youth. Besides this, the unity committee was to represent the united evangelical movement before the State authorities.[21]

The subsequent election of Prokhanov in 1911 as a vice president of the Baptist World Alliance, where he presented himself as the leader of general Baptists in Russia,[22] strengthened the process of ecclesiological formation. However, it did not transform the basic vision of the tradition, namely the pursuit of evangelical unity in diversity by creating a united evangelical front in Russia.[23] Prokhanov created a dual self-identity. In the West he positioned himself as a leader of the general Baptists.[24] However, in the East he refused to be called a Baptist but rather employed Russified terminology,[25] in order not to be associated with any Western denomination and therefore to remain faithful to the ethos of the Radstockist-Pashkovite movement.[26] His position in the Baptist World Alliance provided Prokhanov with a platform to influence the dynamically growing Baptist movement. His

20. Prokhanov gave the wrong date for the tragic meeting in St. Petersburg, saying that it was held in 1883.

21. Ibid.

22. Kahle, *Evangel'skie Khristiane*, 58.

23. Durasoff, *Russian Protestants*, 54–55.

24. Kahle, *Evangel'skie Khristiane*, 133.

25. *Khristiane, kreshchenye po vere,* which literally means "Christians baptized upon faith."

26. *Khristianin* 2 (1925) 45.

failed attempts to achieve union with the Baptists over the next twelve years eventually moved Prokhanov to break with them and caused him to look for a new identity that would be faithful to the ethos of the tradition.[27]

On the Way to the New Vision

In the chapter on Pashkov it was demonstrated that the first adherents of the Radstockian worldview and theology were driven by the desire to transform Russia into a civilized country like Great Britain and the United States of America, as well as by the messianic impetus that envisioned the emergence in Russia of a unified, true Apostolic church, made up of the various evangelical denominations, before similar events would take place in all the other countries of the world. The vision of the Slavophiles and Westernizers was thus synthesized during the early stages of the revivalist holiness tradition in Russia. Prokhanov then developed this vision to the ultimate degree.

During the period before the First World War, Prokhanov considered the role of the evangelical movement to be that of a catalyzing agent for the reformation of the Russian Orthodox Church. It was anticipated that the Orthodox Church would be transformed into the exact image of the restored Apostolic church of Pashkov's Romantic dreams, as inspired by the Evangelical Alliance. It was expected that the State Church would be reformed after the pattern of the Western Reformation, with the priests of the Orthodox Church being converted to the true faith, which was identified with primitivist restorationism. In an address to Orthodox priests, Prokhanov wrote: "Reformation truly happens when priests become reformers (Hus, Luther). . . . There is a need for new teaching, rather than a new patch on the old wineskins. . . . You need to cloister yourself with Christ and have a talk with him about the great act of spiritual regeneration. You need to experience it and to become a new man, a new creature in Christ. . . . Without it there is no salvation."[28]

During this period, Prokhanov made unsuccessful attempts to establish a union with the Baptists, taking advantage of his position as Vice President of the Baptist World Alliance. However, the political situation

27. Durasoff, *Russian Protestants*, 61–64. Cf. Sawatsky, *Soviet Evangelicals*, 45.

28. *Utrenniaia Zvezda* 14 (1910) 1. Cf. Klibanov, *History of Religious Sectarianism*, 324.

created by the First World War caused him to distance himself from any connection with the German Baptist denomination, emphasizing that the roots of the movement of Gospel Christians were in the work of Lord Radstock of Britain, a Russian ally in the war. Kahle states that "in 1916 Prokhanov declared in court that the spiritual wealth of his Union was rooted in the British religious treasury—the treasury of a Russian political ally."[29] The February Democratic Revolution was wholeheartedly supported by Prokhanov and by the Christian Democratic Party "Resurrection" which he had organized.[30] This fact was highlighted by Soviet critics of the evangelical movement, while Prokhanov himself never mentioned it during the Soviet period.[31] Prokhanov's desire was to fill the politico-economic transformations in Russia with the spiritual content of his interpretation of primitive Christianity, which he, like all restorationists, identified with the clear teachings of scripture. According to Prokhanov, the worldwide spiritual revolution that was to restore apostolic Christianity would begin in Russia. Then, as it spread around the world, it would change the global outlook according to the pattern of the United States of America, and proceed even further along the restorationist path.[32] He envisioned "the unification of all states into one 'World Union of States,' with suitable organs for regulating global life."[33] Russia was viewed as a new America, a country of new opportunities: "The wealth of the farmer is the foundation on which the national wealth of American millionaires has been based. Shrewd Americans and other foreigners understand very well that Russia in the near future will become, in a commercial and industrial sense, a 'New America,' a new country of 'unlimited possibilities,' and hurry to open their trading and manufacturing enterprises here. We can only welcome all who undertake honest work in Russia, thanks to which our dear fatherland can become a powerful, wealthy, and happy country."[34]

As in the days of Pashkov, the geopolitical gravity of the United States of America was one of the driving forces of the tradition. Being a

29. Kahle, *Evangel'skie Khristiane*, 175.

30. Coleman, *Russian Baptists and Spiritual Revolution*, 144.

31. Cf. Mitrokhin, *Baptizm*, 259–63.

32. Cf. Marsden, *Fundamentalism and American Culture*, 12.

33. *Utrenniaia Zvezda* 1 (1917) 7.

34. *Utrenniaia Zvezda* X/29 (1910) 1.

prolific writer of poetry, Prokhanov devoted a poem to America, which he visited for the first time in 1902.

> . . . For those who fled from persecution
> To seek your shores in days of old
> Brought in their hands the Bible only,
> A gift more precious far than gold.
> As by this Book their lives were ordered
> So let it guide your steps aright,
> And you shall be to all the nations
> A beacon of far reaching light.[35]

Prokhanov made every effort to use the growing evangelical movement as the accelerator of the new spiritual reformation in Russia. Like Pashkov, he desired to overcome the fragmentation of Protestantism that characterized Western countries, presenting the nascent Russian restorationist movement as a lively alternative to the divided Protestantism of Western civilization.[36] The spirit of Russian messianism that energized Pashkov was intensified in the vision of Prokhanov on the wave of the upheaval of civilization. The event of the Bolshevik Revolution, together with the geopolitical crack that it opened, prompted Prokhanov to engage in a creative reinterpretation of the tradition he was leading.

Interpreting the blow to the State Church in 1917 and the dramatic numerical growth[37] of evangelical Christians during the period of the First World War (1914–1918) and the subsequent Civil War (1918–1921) as a prophetic sign of the times, Prokhanov articulated a new master narrative for the tradition.[38] According to the new identity story,

35. Prokhanoff, *In the Cauldron of Russia*, 128.

36. *Evangel'skaia Vera* 1–12 (1935–36) 24.

37. Prokhanov had a tendency to exaggerate numbers. Upon his arrival in America in 1925 he stated the number of baptized evangelical Christians in Russia as five million, including members of their families. See Popov, *Prokhanov*, 120. According to Soviet historians the number of evangelical sectarians was 150,000 by 1917, and this number increased almost five times in the next seven years. See the discussion in Mitrokhin, *Baptizm*, 364.

38. Cf. Coleman, *Russian Baptists and Spiritual Revolution*, 162–63. According to Klibanov there were 31,000 Gospel Christians in Russia by 1912. By December 1926 there were 2,500 registered congregations of Evangelical Christians in the Soviet Union, representing a minimum of 125,000 members, as at least 50 members were required in order for a congregation to be registered. Klibanov, *History of Religious Sectarianism in Russia*, 292.

the tradition of the Gospel Christians did not evolve from the Western revivalist movement. It had been initiated, instead, exclusively by the Holy Spirit. The Russian evangelical movement had been chosen by God to enlighten the world concerning that Apostolic teaching which the European Reformation had not fully recovered. The messianic spirit of Marxist apocalypticism was thus intensifying the messianic ethos of evangelical Christianity.[39] Western civilization ceased to be the gravitational force that provided the momentum. Rather, the ahistorical and universal messianic Spirit active in the exploding Russian evangelical movement, purified of all the weight of past idolatrous tradition, was ready to transform the life of the world in preparation for the messianic Kingdom. The messianic vision of Prokhanov was similar in ethos to that of Alexander I a hundred years earlier who, after the defeat of Napoleon, believed that "he had a holy mission from God to defend Europe from liberals and revolutionaries, whom he considered anti-Christian."[40]

In Prokhanov's understanding, the spiritual vacuum that followed the collapse of the Russian monarchy and the abortion of the embryonic democracy by the onslaught of Bolshevism forced Russia and the world to choose between the evangelical reformation and Marxism.[41] The new reformation needed an image of a new reformer. And from the Gospel Christians' point of view, the only person who could fill that slot was Ivan Prokahnov.[42]

After the arrest of Patriarch Tikhon in May 1922, the Orthodox Church began to disintegrate under the influence of the renovationist movements within Orthodoxy, which were supported and directed by the Bolsheviks.[43] Prokhanov decided to use this opportunity to implement his life vision.[44] The Bolshevik government, being interested in splintering the massive Orthodox Church and steering different religious streams into collision with each other, did not hinder him in his

39. Berdyaev, *Russian Idea*, 262.

40. Duncan, *Russian Messianism*, 17.

41. Prokhanov, *Atheism or the Gospel in Russia, Which?*; Marsden, *Fundamentalism and American Culture*, 156.

42. *Utrenniaia Zvezda* 6–7–8 (1922) 1–14.

43. *Latyshev, Rassekrechennyi Lenin*, 158; Corley, *Religion in the Soviet Union*, 31–32; Shchapov, *Russkaia Pravoslavnaia Tserkov' i Kommunisticheskoe Gosudarstvo*, 156, 160–61; Pospelovskii, *Pravoslavnaia Tserkov' v Istorii Rusi, Rossii i SSSR*, 242–55.

44. Prokhanoff, *In the Cauldron of Russia*, 126.

attempt to put into action his idealistic dreams.[45] Prokhanov's vision was not taken as a serious threat by the new authorities, who were holding the situation under control.[46] The vision began to be implemented in the summer of 1922, with some preparatory steps carried out hurriedly. The magazine *Utrenniaia Zvezda*, edited by Prokhanov, published a long article devoted to the thirty-fifth anniversary of Prokhanov's Christian ministry.[47] The article depicts Prokhanov as the primary leader of the all-Russian and global evangelical movement, "a poet-psalmist, the first and most powerful preacher of the Gospel in Russia, a deep theologian, an ardent champion of the truth, an amazingly powerful speaker, and the giant-reformer [*sic*], our dear brother Ivan Stepanovich Prokhanov."[48] Prokhanov is said to have surpassed Luther as much as Russia surpasses Germany in terms of territory. His literary works are presented as superior to the Russian literary classics by such writers as Pushkin, Nekrasov, and Nadson. Wearing this homemade mantle of neo-European reformer, Prokhanov visited America.[49]

The image of Prokhanov as the leader of the worldwide reformation eclipsed not only the period of Radstock and Pashkov, but also the significance of all European reformations.[50] In his autobiography, Prokhanov recounts the impressive ministry of Pashkov in only three sentences.[51] Radstock is mentioned only once.[52] The long ministry of Dr. Baedeker and his pan-evangelical Russian networking are not mentioned at all, nor is the name of I. V. Kargel mentioned even once in the autobiography.[53] According to the new legend, the history of the

45. Krivova, "Vlast' i Tserkov' v 1922–1925 gg." Cf. Coleman, *Russian Baptists and Spiritual Revolution*, 157–63, 190–92; Regel'son, *Tragediia Russkoi Tserkvi*, ch. 2.

46. Corley, 48, 54.

47. This kind of anniversary does not seem to have been publicly celebrated by anyone else in Russia or elsewhere, either before or after this issue of *Utrenniaia Zvezda*. There is no indication in Prokhanov's autobiography that he had been involved in active Christian ministry in 1887. According to Prokhanov, he was baptized in January 1887 at the age of eighteen. See Prokhanov, *In the Cauldron of Russia*, 48.

48. *Utrenniaia Zvezda* 6–7–8 (1922) 1.

49. Prokhanov, *New Religious Reformation in Russia*; idem, *Awakening Russia Now Seeking God.*

50. *Utrenniaia Zvezda* 6–7–8 (1922) 12–14.

51. Prokhanoff, *In the Cauldron of Russia*, 53–54.

52. Ibid., 53.

53. The name of Kargel is found at the end of "The Resurrection Call" among the

organization and of the theological formation of the evangelical tradition begins with Prokhanov. The pre-Prokhanov period is left vaguely in the background. The pre-Soviet stage of the tradition is left behind the rocket of the new evangelical identity that assumed a worldwide messianic ethos, led by a messianic figure of the restorationist reformation. Prokhanov's autobiography ends with a call to the Christians of the world to reform their lives after the pattern of the primitive church, as exemplified in the movement led by Prokhanov.[54] There is no hint in the document that this Eastern reformer recognized or acknowledged the Western derivation of his primitivist vision.[55]

The Gospel Call

Having in the summer of 1922 posed Prokhanov as the messianic reformer of Russia and the world, the Gospel Christians published an appeal that September addressed to the leaders of the pro-Soviet restorationist movement in the Orthodox Church. One hundred thousand copies of the appeal, entitled "The Gospel Call," were distributed all across Russia. The key thesis of "The Gospel Call" was that the Orthodox Church, without the support of the State, had only one choice, namely to become evangelical in all matters of theology and ecclesiological practice.[56]

The document was written in the spirit of a prophetic appeal from God to the Orthodox Church as a whole, and to the pro-Soviet renovationist movement, "The Living Church," in particular. At the beginning of the document Prokhanov refers to some correspondence he had in 1911 with Archbishop Antonin. Prokhanov had warned the Orthodox Church at that time of God's impending judgment, because of the Synod's refusal to approve his request for permission to print some pocket Bibles. "It was a prophetic voice inspired by God himself. But alas, she [the Orthodox Church] did not recognize the day of his visitation and did not hear his voice. BUT THE VOICE OF THE GOSPEL CHURCH HAS NOT BEEN GAGGED [*sic*]. It appeals with sincere benevolence

names of those who signed the document. See Prokhanoff, *In the Cauldron of Russia*, 268. Kargel's name is incorrectly written in both Russian and English as I. A. Kargel, instead of I. V. Kargel.

54. Prokhanoff, *In the Cauldron of Russia*, 261–70.

55. Hughes, *American Quest for the Primitive Church*, 1–15.

56. See Levitin and Shavrov, *Ocherki po Istorii Russkoi Tserkovnoi Smuty*.

and peace to the newly-organized church."[57] Continuing the address with a prophetic tone he states: "There are two paths before 'The Living Church': (1) she may live for awhile like many 'reviving churches' in the West and then die again, or (2) she may live, grow, and even have life in abundance for an unlimited period of time." In order to follow the path of eternal life and abundance, there is only one simple option, namely to become identical to the Gospel Christians. Prokhanov offers a diagnosis of the present condition of "The Living Church": it is dead as the European Reformation is dead. "The Reformation of Hus, Luther, and others did not make the church alive. . . . [AND] THE SAME DESTINY AWAITS THE RUSSIAN 'LIVING CHURCH'" if it does not choose the path suggested by the prophetic voice of the Gospel Christians.

In "The Gospel Call" Prokhanov creates a new self-identity for the Gospel Christians—a self-identity which has been axiomatic in Russian evangelical historiography right up until the present. In his explanation to the leaders of "The Living Church," the identity of the Gospel Christians is constructed out of thin air, on the Eastern bank of the global political divide. First, the Gospel Church does not have any analogues in the world religious movement, because its name is taken from the Gospel (Mark 1:15; Phil 1:27). This distancing from the Western world is accomplished by a different transliteration of a Western word into Russian. The term "evangelical," when used with reference to the Western free churches, is usually transliterated as *evangelicheskie* Christians, while the Russian evangelical identity is expressed by the Russian term *Evangel'skie* Christians (literally *Gospel* Christians). This variation in Russian translation did not, however, somehow change the theological substance that had been derived from Western sources. It was used rather to create a new identity that implied that there was an essential difference between Western and Eastern evangelical Christianity. The names of Radstock and Pashkov were not mentioned, since the connection with the Western revivalist and restorationist movement was consciously cut off at the rhetorical level and buried in pre-Soviet history.

Second, "The Gospel Church is called to be demotic because it came out of the bosom of the Russian people. The preachers of the Gospel Church are workers and peasants. . . . [I]t is free because it has never been tied to the State. . . . The demotic Evangelical Church is the restored Apostolic church born of the Spirit of God in the womb of the Russian

57. Prokhanov, *Evangelskii Klich.*

people. It grows and lives in accordance with the laws of the Word of God."[58] Key Soviet terms such as "people," "worker," "peasant," and "demotic" are used as ideological pillars for constructing a new Soviet Christian identity. Even though the movement of St. Petersburg Gospel Christians had always been associated with its aristocratic origin, flavor, and financial support, the new identity-constructing myth erased the aristocratic past of the tradition, as it erased its Western origin, with a single stroke of Prokhanov's pen.

Third, "the spirit of the Evangelical Church is UNIVERSAL, ALL-EMBRACING. Being led by this spirit, it greets the movement of 'The Living Church' and is ready to help the new movement to reach the set goals." Thus a particular tradition of ahistorical restorationist primitivism is posed as a divine universal framework that assumes the role of a pedagogue for other, imperfect Christian traditions.[59]

"The Gospel Call" had only limited influence on the renovationist movement of the Orthodox Church. Some ecumenical meetings in several renovationist temples in Moscow and Leningrad were conducted under the banner of the Apostles' Creed,[60] but they did not produce the outcome envisioned by Prokhanov. The fast-growing movement of autocephalic Orthodox churches frightened the Bolsheviks, as it endangered their ability to control the religious processes in that vast country. Thus, instead of sharing the tragic destiny of Nicolas II and his family, Patriarch Tikhon was released in the spring of 1923, which weakened the position of the pro-Soviet Orthodox renovationists. The Bolsheviks preferred to have a centralized and controllable religious structure, and Tikhon was the key person to stabilize the autocephalic processes of decentralization. An ultimatum from the British government also played an important role in Tikhon's release.[61]

At about the same time, Prokhanov was arrested and put in prison for three months. His arrest served multiple purposes.[62] The Bolsheviks used his prominent image as the Reformer of all Russia to divert the sectarians from their pacifist tendencies, to set them against each other,

58. Ibid.

59. Golovashchenko, *Istoriia Evangel'sko-Baptistskogo Dvizheniia*, 6–8.

60. Martsinkovskii, *Zapiski Veruiushchego*, 224–25, 247; Prokhanov, *V Kotle Rossii*, 205–11.

61. Pospelovskii, *Pravoslavnaia Tserkov' v Istorii Rusi, Rossii i SSSR*, 247–48.

62. Prokhanov, *V Kotle Rossii*, 219–22.

and to destroy Prokhanov's prophetic image that was now perceived to be a threat. Prokhanov was forced to change his antimilitaristic position and convince the general conference of the Gospel Christians to accept the Soviet terms.[63]

Since the time of Radstock the Gospel Christians had never been pacifistic in their theology. Indeed, both Radstock and Pashkov had been military officers. During the First World War the Gospel Christians supported the military campaign of Russia, by and large.[64] The issue of pacifism was considered to be a matter for one's own conscience. However, during the civil war that followed the Bolshevik Revolution, the Gospel Christians decided to be neutral and assume a purely pacifist stance. In September 1922 Prokhanov published an appeal entitled "Voice of the East" in which he articulated the new pacifist stance of the Gospel Christians.[65] An excerpt from the Soviet archives is telling. Government officials refer to

> having got down to this work in real earnest and having set ourselves the task of making the sect members recognize for themselves that military service in Soviet Russia should be compulsory, to deprive them of the unity of their organization and with this to check the growth of sectarianism. Having selected for this the most favorable and propitious opportunity—the detention of the leader of one of the most numerous sects of evangelical Christians, Prokhanov, for distributing the antimilitarist appeal "Voice of the East" [September 1922]—we have been able in the process of this detention to win him over to the recognition of military service as compulsory for all evangelicals. With this aim, he wrote a message in this spirit together with five other leading evangelicals. This represented the first shift by the sects away from an anti-militarist position.[66]

As a result of this the Evangelical movement was split, as some of the Gospel Christians could not understand the radical change in Prokhanov's attitude. The image of the great reformer had been damaged. But even though by the exercise of their power over him the Bolsheviks had demonstrated to Prokhanov the naïveté of his vision, he was still inspired by the vision of a global reformation starting from

63. Prokhorov, "'Golden Age' of the Soviet Baptists in the 1920s," 96.

64. Klibanov, *History of Religious Sectarianism in Russia*, 333–34.

65. Coleman, *Russian Baptists and Spiritual Revolution*, 191–93.

66. Corley, *Religion in the Soviet Union*, 48, 54.

Russia. And in order to enhance his vision and secure his position as the Reformer of Russia, Prokhanov decided to be ordained by ministers of the Bohemian Brethren during a visit to Prague at the beginning of 1924.[67] Preparations for the ordination lasted for two months, as the Czech ministers requested confirmation of Prokhanov's identity as the President of the Gospel Christians and the support of the his local congregation in St. Petersburg, as well as that of the Council of the Union.[68] His ordination by the Czechs was intended to symbolize his association with the Slavic reformer John Hus, who was depicted as the forerunner of the Reformation of the sixteenth century. Later, upon his arrival in America in 1925, Prokhanov posed as the Reformer of Russia.[69]

The Resurrection Call

A new strand of self-identity construction is seen in the document entitled "The Resurrection Call," which was written in 1928 and published in 1933 in *Gospel Faith* (*Evangel'skaia Vera).*[70] In "The Resurrection Call," the leaders of the Evangelical Christians appealed to the Christians of the world. A truncated English version of the document was published in Prokhanov's autobiography, which was also printed in 1933.[71] The English version does not, however, convey the messianic ethos and prophetic tone of the original, which would have been incomprehensible in the American context of the time.[72] The basic thesis of the document is identical to that of "The Gospel Call": the reason for the religious decadence so apparent in the world is to be found in the world's alienation from Apostolic teaching in its primitivist interpretation. The new document deepens and dramatizes the development of the myth about the origin of the tradition: "In the era of harsh persecution during the

67. Khale, *Evangel'skie Khristiane*, 124, 429.

68. Archive ECB, 7.3a, 38–41, 47–50. Savinskii, *Istoriia Evangel'skikh Khristian-Baptistov Ukrainy, Rossii, Belorussii (1917–1967)*, 78.

69. Prokhanov, *New Religious Reformation in Russia: A Russian Evangelical Reformer Visits America.* As the Russian language does not have definite or indefinite articles, it can be suggested that Prokhanov viewed himself as *the* Reformer of Russia, taking into account the way he depicted himself in the above-mentioned article in *Utrenniaia Zvezda* 6–7–8 (1922).

70. *Evangel'skaia Vera* 4 (1933) 10–17. Cf. Kahle, *Evangel'skie Khristiane*, 542–96.

71. Prokhanoff, *In the Cauldron of Russia*, 261–68.

72. Marsden, *Fundamentalism and American Culture*, 153–55.

second half of the nineteenth century there was born in Russia a free demotic church as the fruit of the preaching of the Gospel by sacrificial, uneducated, popular preachers."[73] The translation of this passage into English in Prokhanov's autobiography differs from the quoted Russian original. It states: "In spite of the severe persecution of the faithful in the latter half of the century, there arose in Russia a Free Evangelical Church for all the people, and as the direct result of the proclamation of the Gospel through service and sacrifice, there are now a large number of popular preachers, though many of them have had no preparatory training."[74] In the English translation the Russian Evangelical Church is depicted as one of the streams of the Western free church movement that "wants all the Churches throughout the world to share in the knowledge of the events which have transpired up to this time, and the experiences through which it has passed."[75] However, the Russian text of *Evangel'skaia Vera* highlights the new ethos of the new messianic culture that is said to be different from that of all the Christian denominations of the West. Prokhanov depicts the Russian Gospel Church as moving forward independently of Western Christendom.

> The first followers of the Gospel in Russia had fellowship with various representatives of Protestant denominations. Each of these shared their own opinions. However, on all occasions the Russian Gospel Christians acted like the Bereans. They listened to different opinions and "daily examined the scriptures to see if what was said was true" (Acts 17:11). Very often their decisions would not agree with any of the expressed opinions but would cohere with scripture. As was mentioned above, the building of the spiritual house in Russia was not done from the top, as in the West, but from the bottom; that is, it did not start with the priests leading others. Instead, it was done and is done in a more natural way, namely from the depths of the people, as was the case in the time of Christ and the Apostles. The self-sustaining nature of the Evangelical movement explains the fact that it has gone much further than the Western Reformation. As a result of this, the Free Russian Evangelical Church is not identical to any of the religious groups in the world, even though it is akin to many of them. What should we think about all this? Of course, it is a wonderful phenomenon. It means that there is progress in the

73. *Evangel'skaia Vera* 4 (1933) 12.

74. Prokhanoff, *In the Cauldron of Russia*, 265.

75. Ibid., 266.

> work of restoring the Apostolic church. . . . It is natural that the Russian Evangelical movement has taken many steps forward, in comparison with the earlier Reformation. . . . The Russian Evangelical Reformation can say to the earlier Reformation: "I have moved forward along the way which you started to tread, and I want to go even further. Come along!"[76]

The reformation of the Orthodox Church was no longer expected. The Gospel Christians were depicted as builders of a qualitatively new form of Christianity—Resurrection Christianity—that was charging towards the Apostolic golden age ahead of everyone else. This new project could not be identified by the term "reformation," because nothing like it had ever happened in the Western world.[77] Like the Russian Marxists, who created the self-identity of the global locomotive of the communist liberation of the oppressed, Prokhanov presented himself and his movement as the global agent of the resurrection.[78] The ethos and rhetoric of Prokhanov are taken for granted by some contemporary evangelical writers.[79]

Having set aside the idea of reforming the Russian Orthodox Church, Prokhanov began to implement this new vision by attempting to create a worldwide union of Gospel Christians as an alternative to all Western denominations and alliances. Until his death in 1935, he was laboring at establishing a worldwide network of Russian evangelical churches outside of Russia.[80]

As the leader of this progressive worldwide Union, he appeals to the West:

> . . . The spirit of unbelief which is now rampant in Russia in the form of atheism and materialism is the fruit and the creation of the pseudo-science of Western Europe, and, in particular, of

76. *Evangel'skaia Vera* 4 (1933) 15–17. Cf. Hughes and Allen, *Illusions of Innocence*, viii; and Turner, *Churches of the Restoration*, 234.

77. *Evangel'skaia Vera* 4 (1933) 16. Cf. Littell, *Anabaptist View of the Church*, 79–108.

78. *Evangel'skaia Vera* 4 (1933) 15.

79. Popov, *I. S. Prokhanov*, 90.

80. *Evangel'skaia Vera* 1–12 (1935–36) 59–64. By 1935 branches of the Gospel Christians had been established in America, Germany, Latvia, Romania, Estonia, China, Paraguay, Bulgaria, and Canada. The center of the worldwide Union was located in Berlin. According to Prokhanov's will, the chair of the Union was to be the director of the Light in the East mission, Jacob Krecker (p. 61).

> the work of Feuerbach, Buchner, Nietzsche and others, as well as of the faculties of Protestant theological schools, from that of Tubingen down to the present day. We are therefore most deeply convinced that only a spiritual resurrection of the Churches of Western Europe can again conquer the thinking majority of mankind, and produce such a whirlwind of divine power that streams of new spiritual force will flow through the life of all people, with the result that then there will be no place left for unbelief among them. One of the first fruits of the spiritual awakening in Western Europe must be a science which will be defender of the faith, since it will live by faith, and which will fully and irrevocably overcome all the atheistic, materialistic and other theories of unbelief, through the Spirit of Jesus Christ. The Reformation lands, which have produced this unbelief, are under obligation to uncover by means of science all the senselessness, the lack of a sure foundation, which characterized free-thinking, and in the consciousness of their own stupendous responsibility to the civilized world, to demonstrate the fact that Atheism or Free Thinking has never produced and never will be able to produce the power required for that new and exalted future which lies before us. What a glorious and blessed task for the philosophy and science of Western Europe! The highest achievement to be desired along these lines is creation of an Ecumenical Church in the spirit of primitive Christianity. This, however, can be brought about only in one way: "Not by might, not by power, but by my Spirit, says the Lord of Hosts."[81]

Prokhanov dramatically viewed himself as the prophet Jonah for Western civilization. The movement of Gospel Christians was perceived as the fortress of Europe against the barbarism of Asia.[82] The victory of the Gospel in Russia was viewed as salvation for the whole world. Like the Orthodox Slavophile Tutchev, who stated in 1848, "For a long time there have been in Europe only two real powers: the revolution and Russia . . . [and] the life of one means the death of the other,"[83] Prokhanov wrote, "If the Gospel does not win in Russia then others will come, and they will overturn your Western culture." [84] This was the geopolitical Slavophile dictum of Prokhanov.[85]

81. Prokhanoff, *In the Cauldron of Russia*, 267–68.

82. Kahle, *Evangel'skie Khristiane*, 546.

83. Quoted in Duncan, *Russian Messianism*, 26.

84. Kahle, *Evangel'skie Khristiane*, 580.

85. Cf. Marsden, *Fundamentalism and American Culture*, 154–56.

> . . . The leading thinkers of the world predict the approaching collapse of civilization and world culture. For us believers it is clear . . . that it is the result of abandoning God. It is clear to us that if nothing changes, the destruction of civilization is inevitable. But there is a way to salvation. Humanity needs to change direction: not from God but towards God. This change can be brought about only by the Gospel. There was a time when the Roman Empire with its culture was in decay. Then the disciples of Christ, simple fishermen, stepped forward and started to preach the Gospel. This foolishness of preaching regenerated nations . . . and created a new, glorious Christian culture . . . . Preaching nowadays should have just one motto: "*The restoration of Primitive Christianity.*" There is no other Christian organization that could be more prepared for this task than the All-Russian Union of Gospel Christians.[86]

This new identity-making story is characterized not only by the erasure of the Western and Aristocratic periods of the tradition, but also by the erasure of the history of its relationship with the Baptist tradition. In his autobiography, Prokhanov never mentions the fact that he had been elected as a vice president of the Baptist World Alliance.[87] Writing about his family, Prokhanov emphasizes their Molokan origin. Even though he mentions that his father was converted from Molokanism in 1876, Prokhanov chooses not to specify the new faith of his father. He simply says that his father started to attend "a local church of the brothers"[88]

The fact that his father Stepan Antonovich was an influential Baptist minister is muted.[89] Referring to his own conversion, Prokhanov also manages to avoid his own association with the Bapitsts: "On the 17th of January, 1887, I joined the local group of Christian believers, having been baptized in the river Terek at Vladikavkaz."[90] Prokhanov does not mention even once the long history of attempts to achieve unity with the

86. *Evangel'skaia Vera* 1–12 (1935–36) 60.

87. The Russian translation of Prokhanov's autobiography was accomplished by the President of the AUCECB, Alexei Bychkov, who edited the English original. Bychkov wrote an introductory article in which he mentioned the fact that Prokhanov was a Vice President of the Baptist Union and added the word "Baptist," where Prokhanov had simply written "Gospel Christians." See Prokhanov, *V Kotle Rossii*, 7–9, 128, 255, 259, 262.

88. Prokhanoff, *In the Cauldron of Russia*, 160.

89. PP 2/2/293.

90. Prokhanoff, *In the Cauldron of Russia*, 48.

Baptist Union during the period between 1907 and 1923. This conscious separation from the Baptist movement stands in stark contrast to his purely Baptist self-identification in 1922, when he posed himself "as a Baptist working among the Gospel Christians."[91] According to his earlier biography, the key task of Prokhanov's ministry was to bring about unity between the evangelical and Baptist movements. His selective recollection of the past suggests that his major interest in writing his autobiography was not in history per se.

Historical Mistakes in Prokhanov's Autobiography

The key sources for understanding Prokhanov's life are his autobiography, written in 1933 in New York; his biography printed in *Utrenniaia Zvezda* in 1922; and an issue of *Evangel'skaia Vera* published shortly after his death in 1935.[92] A comparison of these sources suggests that Prokhanov was not concerned about historical accuracy or consistency. He managed to date incorrectly some events from his personal life. He claimed that he studied in Berlin in the fall of 1896 and that he studied in Paris during the first half of 1897.[93] However, his original letters containing a detailed description of the courses he was taking in Berlin and outlining his future plans to visit Paris were written to Pashkov in January of 1898,[94] and the official record of Bristol Bible College supports the original correspondence with Pashkov. It states, "I. Prokhanoff, a refugee from Russia (1895), did not return in 1897 because the climate affected his health."[95] Prokhanov began his studies in Bristol at the end of 1895. A letter to Pashkov, written from Bristol, is dated December 15, 1895.[96] He spent one year in Bristol and moved to London in 1897. After his uncompleted studies in the Congregational college there, he moved to Berlin at the end of 1897. Mistakes in dating are made, as well, with regard to events in the public domain. For example, Prokhanov mistak-

91. *Utrenniaia Zvezda*, 6–7–8 (1922) 3.

92. Ibid., 1–14; *Evangel'skaia Vera*, 1–12 (1935–36) 4–60.

93. Prokhanoff, *In the Cauldron of Russia*, 101–2.

94. PP 2/19/1–2.

95. From a personal letter of Shirley Shire, a librarian at Bristol Baptist College, January 31, 2005.

96. PP 2/19/1.

enly dates the death of Leo Tolstoy as having taken place on November 11, 1911, while Tolstoy actually died a year earlier.[97]

Considering that Prokhanov wrote his autobiography at the same time that he wrote his will for the Worldwide Union of Gospel Christians,[98] it seems reasonable to suggest that his autobiography is better viewed as a preface to his will concerning the establishment of that Union.[99] This vision was intended to become his magnum opus. But his premature death in 1935 and the Second World War put an end to this "illusion of innocence."

THEOLOGY

The Restorationist Holiness Movement: From the Middle Course between Liberalism and Fundamentalism towards the Latter

The American trajectory, from the revivalism of D. L. Moody to the fundamentalism of R. A. Torrey, had its parallel in the Russian evangelical movement through direct contacts with representatives of the Moody Bible Institute.[100] Prokhanov visited R. A. Torrey and A. C. Gaebelein in 1925 and participated in several Bible conferences.[101] Prokhanov's attitude toward fundamentalist teaching and his general understanding of the religious discourses of the times are expressed in his report, which is worth quoting at length:

> [Conferences] play an important role in defending pure biblical teaching against various wrong teachings that have appeared in the past and are springing up at the present time *in America* (italics added). One of these teachings is so-called *modernism.* This teaching tries to deny the inspiration of the Bible, as well as [the doctrine of] redemption, the fact of Christ's resurrection, etc. The influence of modernism is being experienced by all the main American Christian groups. Theologians such as Dr. Torrey

97. Prokhanoff, *In the Cauldron of Russia*, 80. Tolstoy died on November 7 (Nov. 20, New Style), 1910. He was buried on November 9, 1910. Notably, the Russian translation of the text by Bychkov contains the same historical mistakes found in Prokhanov's original.

98. *Evangel'skaia Vera*, 1–12 (1935–36) 59.

99. Ibid., 60–64.

100. Cf. Ware, *Restorationism in the Holiness Movement*, 34–51.

101. *Khristianin* 2 (1926) 49–59.

> devote themselves to explaining the basics of the purest Gospel teaching, or the Apostolic spiritual worldview. These basics are called "The Fundamentals." For this reason the followers of pure biblical-evangelical teaching in all the churches are called *fundamentalists.* With great enthusiasm they proclaim "the testimony of Christ" which will undoubtedly triumph over all deviations from the truth.
>
> Modernism is a delayed and weakened reflection of the German rationalism of Strauss and Bauer on American and British soil. Germany is recovering from the consequences of its rationalism and at the present time is returning to pure Gospel teaching, being guided by A. Harnack and others. But the old yeast is producing its effects in the British and American lands in strange and incomprehensible ways. The old struggle over the faith between human wisdom and the "foolishness of preaching" spoken of by Paul is being repeated here [in America].[102]

Having presented the fundamentalist R. A. Torrey and the foremost German advocate of the liberal theological program, Adolf von Harnack, as representatives of essentially the same theological camp in America and Germany respectively may suggest that Prokhanov did not properly understand either the theological discourse of both liberalism and fundamentalism or the rationality behind them.[103] It may also be concluded that he had not read *The Fundamentals,* since the one of the first articles in the first volume includes a severe critique of Harnack.[104] Prokhanov's utmost concern was for the restoration of a primitivist form of Christianity uncorrupted by the weight of church tradition. That was the common ground that united Harnack and Torrey in Prokhanov's non-systematized worldview.[105] Having been converted into and shaped by the holiness tradition that steered a middle course between liberalism and evolving fundamentalism, Prokhanov equally emphasized the doctrinally orthodox formulations of the fundamentalists (such as the doctrines of the Trinity, the deity of Christ, etc.) and Harnack's rejection of tradition in favor of an emphasis on practical and experiential Christianity, which denied or reinterpreted those doctrines.[106] The in-

102. Ibid., 51–52.

103. Cf. Murphy, *Beyond Liberalism and Fundamentalism*, 4–7.

104. Bettex, "Bible and Modern Criticism," 88.

105. Cf. Mitrokhin, *Baptizm*, 375.

106. Cf. Marsden, "Everyone One's Own Interpreter," 95.

clusion of names such as Bauer, Strauss, and Harnack in the article was rather a rhetorical device, intended to give some weight to Prokhanov's opinions among the largely uneducated Russian evangelical audience. There is no evidence that Prokhanov was versed in either classical or liberal Protestant literature. Prokhanov's grasp of theological discourse is seen in his autobiography, written eight years after the article in *Kristianin*:

> After mature acquaintance [*sic*] with the theories of Harnack, I came to the conclusion that he, and theologians generally of the new Tubingen School, took a considerably milder position toward the question of the origin of the books of the New Testament than I had expected. In fact, they came close to the traditional view. . . . [N]o disputes against the affirmations of the critics are necessary, for they contradict each other, and the safest approach is to stick to the general data of the universal church. Since [the] time [of my studies in Germany], whatever I have read has not caused me to change my mind. . . . At first I could not follow the lectures, but I studied the languages very diligently, as well as keeping up my studies in theology.[107]

Prokhanov never worked out why he preferred the testimony of the "universal church" concerning the issue of dating the books of scripture, while rejecting the Patristic theological tradition and taking sides with Harnack. He used both liberal and Orthodox sources pragmatically to enhance his primitivist vision, without much intellectual contemplation or rigorous research. Unlike in the West, where "Fundamentalism, dispensational premillennialism, the Higher Life movement and Pentecostalism were all evangelical strategies of survival in response to religious crises of the late nineteenth century,"[108] the restorationist holiness movement in Russia had the ethos of a proactive movement. It was creating its identity as a new, advanced Western civilization in the old Byzantine country on the wave of the great socio-political upheavals of the first two decades of the twentieth century. Both liberal and fundamentalist intuitions, grounded in the tradition-denying rationality of modernity, could be united in Prokhanov's vision to subvert the Eastern Orthodox paradigm. The unfortunate pairing of Torrey and Harnack

107. Prokhanoff, *In the Cauldron of Russia*, 102. As was stated earlier, Prokhanov studied in Berlin for six months.

108. Noll, *Scandal of the Evangelical Mind*, 24.

suggests that the modernist core of Prokhanov's worldview was neither fundamentalist nor liberal.

Following a middle course between religious liberalism, with its emphasis on the religious experience of the divine, and nascent academic fundamentalism, with its grounding in the common sense realism philosophy of Thomas Reid and the inductive approach of Francis Bacon, the revivalist tradition of Radstock emphasized the importance of the experience of the Spirit. It had a high view of scripture without using it for the purpose of objective investigation.[109] Religious experience was provocatively generated within the context of the worshipping community by means of homilies, testimonies, singing, poetry, and prayers invoking divine intervention manifested in physical healing and spiritual regeneration.[110] As Mark Noll succinctly puts it: "As in the popular romanticism of the mid-century, the subjective personal experience was also accentuated without denying the objective authority of Scripture and the transcendental reality of God. Personal experience of the supernatural was sufficient proof to authenticate Christianity. This experience confirmed that the Bible was supernaturally inspired—no further argumentation was necessary."[111]

The fundamentalist-liberal debates were heard of in the Soviet Union as a distant echo. Russian liberalism as represented by Tregubov did not have wide influence in the Russian context.[112] Anti-liberal rhetoric in the 1920s was directed exclusively against the Western liberal tendencies that denied the doctrine of redemption.[113] The liberal tendencies in American evangelicalism were taken as another proof that the Gospel Christian movement was closer to the Christianity of the Apostolic Age than was the evangelical movement in the leading evangelical nation. Because the modernist worldview took a radical atheistic and anti-transcendental form in Russia, the disputes between Communists and Christians were conducted in the vein of theistic/atheistic discourse.[114] However, the evangelicals, by and large, were not prepared for dialogue

109. Cf. Abraham, *Canon and Criterion in Christian Theology.*

110. Cf. Coleman, *Russian Baptists*, 47–64.

111. Noll, "Primitivism in Fundamentalism and American Biblical Scholarship," 95.

112. *Utrenniaia Zvezda* 48 (1910) 6; Cf. *Utrenniaia Zvezda*, 31 (1910) 2.

113. *Khristianin* 2 (1926) 49–51.

114. Martsinkovskii, *Zapiski Veruiushchego*, 88–94.

with educated atheistic lectors. A small number of well-educated representatives of the evangelically-minded intelligentsia did participate in public debates.[115] It was impossible, however, for evangelical apologetics to be effective in the long run, as the Bolsheviks spewed forth a massive amount of anti-religious propaganda backed by the State, while banishing or imprisoning their theistic opponents.[116] In order to resist the atheistic onslaught of the Bolsheviks, the Gospel Christians had to rely on Western sources—until their printing activities were banned. Eventually, during the Soviet period right up until the collapse of the Communist global experiment, any sort of theology was pronounced to be unscientific and speculative.

Theological Creeds

The first theological creed we know about was circulated among some of the St. Petersburg Pashkovites in 1897.[117] This creed was of a reactive nature, supporting the key values of the Evangelical Alliance. The restorationist wing of the Pashkovites denied the value of icons and of attending the Orthodox liturgy. But because we are aware of only one written reference to this creed, there is no indication that it was widely disseminated or even known about by many of the St. Petersburg Pashkovites.

Prokhanov wrote his theological creed in 1910 and emphasized its native Russian origin. "This project creed was prepared by R u s s i a n f o r c e s [spacing in the original] independently, with the help of the Bible and a concordance."[118] The primitivist methodology of the Anglo-American holiness movement for creating a doctrinal statement with the help only of the Bible and a concordance is, a priori, viewed as a universal normative practice. Kenneth Archer points out that this type of Bible reading with the help of a biblical concordance was a commonly-practiced popular interpretive method, used by both laity and pas-

115. Ibid., 112–23.

116. Peris, *Storming the Heavens*.

117. *Pashkovshina*; *Missionerskoe Obozrenie*, September-October, Book 1 (1897) 797–806.

118. Archive ECB, 11. e 25. 19, 9. Prokhanov, *Verouchenie Evangel'skikh Khristian*. Cf. Weber, "The Two-Edged Sword," 111. See also Moody, *Pleasure and Profit In Bible Study*, 50.

tors to such an extent that it functioned in service as a "fundamentalist liturgy."[119]

The creed was necessitated by the registration of the Union of Gospel Christians with the State.[120] Prokhanov explicitly stated that the creed was needed for "people who require a reason for [their] hope. But the true guide for evangelical Christians always and everywhere," he wrote, "is the Word of God and the inner revelation which agrees with the written Word."[121] Churches with other creeds could be part of the evangelical movement if their creed did not contradict the creed of the Gospel Christians.[122] The tension between the normalizing and secondary roles of the creed was left unresolved, as was the case with many other things in the tradition initiated by Radstock.

The project of the creed was presented during the second conference of the Evangelical Christians in 1910–1911 and was accepted during a single session without any theological refinements.[123] Regardless of its poorly organized structure, it was fairly comprehensive and answered the key theological and practical questions of the day. The most discussed issue was that of marriage and divorce, while the dogmatic section did not give rise to *any* discussions.

The first article of the creed is devoted to the doctrine of the Triune God. In this article Prokhanov emphasizes the equality of the persons of the Trinity, while excluding any reference to the word *homoousion*, which is found in the Apostles' Creed. The first article is followed by an article on the creation of the visible and invisible world. The third article discusses the means of knowing eternal truth. Prokhanov emphasizes that this article makes the Russian Gospel Christians different from their Western counterparts.[124]

According to Prokhanov the first means of knowing truth is "internal, unwritten revelation," which is followed by "external written revelation." Attempting to explain the primary role of internal revelation, he states: "According to the Holy Scriptures, internal revelation is

119. Archer, *Pentecostal Hermeneutics*, 46.

120. Archive ECB, 11. e 25. 19. A copy of *Utrenniaia Zvezda* 1–2 (1911). Cf. Lieven, *Evangel'skoe Probuzhdenie*, 105–6.

121. Archive ECB, 11. e 25. 19. A copy of *Utrenniaia Zvezda*, 1–2 (1911) 9.

122. Ibid., 6.

123. Ibid. There were 46 delegates at the conference.

124. Ibid., 9. Cf. Archer, *Pentecostal Hermeneutics*, 40.

'an anointing from the Holy One' (1 John 2:20–27) which abides in the believer. Without this internal revelation a person has no access to external revelation—that is, to the written Word of God (Luke 24:45); but internal revelation cannot contradict external revelation. Thus if internal revelation contradicts the written Word of God, then it is not true (1 Cor 4:6; Gal 1:8)."

The dialectical tension between the primacy of the internal experience of the Spirit, resulting in the unlocking of the meaning of scripture, and the testing role of the external scriptures, which can nullify the spiritual drive of the interpreter, is neither solved nor questioned. By default, it is assumed that the interpreter cannot understand scripture without having been regenerated by the Spirit. The model originally suggested by Prokhanov retained the key elements of Radstock and Pashkov's approach to the pneumatological reading of the canonical text. Even though Prokhanov was convinced of the uniqueness of this approach to reading scripture, due to his rather limited understanding of the theological map of the time, it was, in fact, no different than the romantic sort of reading characteristic of the revivalist holiness tradition: "The Bible appealed to the deepest emotions and was a down-to-earth guide to holy living. Through Scripture the Holy Spirit worked. These emphases were especially apparent in the new holiness movement emerging in the mid-decades of the century in both the Methodist and Reformed traditions. Subjective personal experience of God, 'the Baptism with the Holy Spirit,' confirmed objective proofs of the Bible's authority. For many simple believers the subjective experience was sufficient."[125]

A potential solution to the problem of competing interpretations is found in the minutes of the conference, which state that dogmatic issues are discussed at general conferences of the union and that officials positions are declared only upon the affirmation of at least two-thirds of the participants.[126] Furthermore, twenty-two years later Prokhanov emphasized that decisions of the general conference are only recommendations for local congregations, which retain final authority to make up their own mind with regard to dogmatic issues.[127] As an example of an unbiblical teaching that does not correspond to the Word of God, Prokhanov cites the Reformed teaching on predestination: "[C]oncerning God's

125. Marsden, "Everyone One's Own Interpreter," 85.

126. Ibid.

127. *Evangel'skaia Vera* 4 (1933): 13.

plan for the salvation of man and predestination . . . the most commonly held view on predestination is the so called 'Calvinistic one.'[128] But this view, based on unconditional predestination, diverges from the Word of God, because the grace of God is offered to all people and not only to those predestined to eternal salvation. Predestination is based only on God's foreknowledge."[129]

This programmatic creed, written in the spirit of Wesleyan restorationist primitivism and pronounced with authority by the charismatic leader, does not seem to have played a normalizing role in the local churches or even to have been widely known among them. It was never republished, discussed, or referred to in Russia or the Soviet Union. However, the method of doing theology is telling, as the conference was apparently totally satisfied with the creed's authoritative interpretation.

An alternative creed written by I. V. Kargel is dated 1913.[130] It is much shorter and better organized. The fundamental theological difference between the two creeds is that Prokhanov held to postmillennial theology (Article 18), while Kargel was a proponent of the premillennialist dispensationalist thought of the Darby school, which was first explicitly articulated in the creed that he wrote. Prokhanov's postmillennialism was a significant modification of the tradition, compared with the time of Radstock. However, this modification did not create a new tradition but only a variation within the holiness movement, as was also the case in the West. In the Western holiness movement, postmillennialism preceded romantic premillennialism. But the Eastern evangelical movement, intellectually dependent on Western sources, was acquiring theological tendencies in reverse order. The religious atmosphere of Great Britain at the end of the nineteenth century, when Prokhanov studied in Bristol and London, was largely dominated by postmillennial views.[131] Steven Ware writes:

> The holiness movement began in the late nineteenth century with the largely postmillennialist vision it had received from its

128. The works of Calvin (or of any other Protestant theologian, for that matter) were unfamiliar to the audience. The foreign title was given with quotation marks because the discourse of the classical Reformation was foreign to the Russian ear.

129. Ibid., 10.

130. The creed was analyzed by Chalandeau, "Theology of the Evangelical Christians-Baptists in the USSR," 82–85.

131. Bebbington, *Dominance of Evangelicalism*, 182.

> Methodist forebears—the conviction that a pure Church could convert the entire world and therefore initiate the millennium—a one-thousand-year period of peace and prosperity which would end with the return of Christ. By the beginning of the twentieth century, however, a premillennialist vision had begun to become predominant among holiness leaders—a vision which retained hope for changing the world through the conversion of individuals to the lifestyle of Christian holiness, but largely avoided political involvement and shifted ultimate responsibility for changing the world to Christ at his return.[132]

Prokhanov's postmillennialism harmonized well with the modernistic tendencies of his theology and served as an engine for his social and political activity. The revolution of the Spirit and the triumph of true science and progress that he envisioned were supported by his postmillennial theology. The apex of Prokhanov's postmillennial vision was revealed in his desire to build an evangelical "City of the Sun" in Siberia that would reflect the ideal of Christian communal life governed by restored Apostolic Christianity.[133] The immediate return of Christ was not part of Prokhanov's vision.[134]

Johann Kargel, who remained in the shadow of Prokhanov, promoted a futurist interpretation of the book of Revelation, under the direct influence of dispensationalist writers.[135] He expected the second, invisible coming of Christ at any moment. This expectation resulted in a change in the dynamics of spiritual life for all premillennialists everywhere. "The shortness of time before the end of the age gave a heightened significance to everyday life and an added urgency to evangelism."[136] Unlike Prokhanov, who envisioned building a new city in Siberia, Kargel supported the vision of Baptist minister William Fetler, a graduate of

132. Ware, *Restorationism*, 56.

133. Bourdeaux, *Opium of the People*, 152–53. It should be mentioned that Prokhanov wanted to build the city with funds from Western evangelicals. See Iartsev, *Sekta*, 28, Sawatsky, *Soviet Evangelicals*, 37.

134. Cf. *Evangel'skaia Vera*, 5 (1933) 27–29. Prokhanov believed that atheistic ideology would collapse and that there would be an evangelical era. "After the thirteenth chapter of Revelation come the fourteenth and fifteenth. We should not stop at the thirteenth chapter."

135. In his book *Svet iz Teni Buduiushchikh Blag*, originally published in Russian in 1908, Kargel mentions in the introduction the names of some dispensationalist writers whose works he used.

136. Bebbington, *Dominance of Evangelicalism*, 180.

Spurgeon's Bible college, of starting a monastic order within the evangelical movement. A depth of spiritual life in the vein of the Keswickian premillennialist tradition was to be the key focus of this order.[137]

The Concept of Christian History in the Tradition

The Gospel Christians' view of Christian history was most clearly presented by Iaroslav Prokhanov, the son of Ivan Prokhanov, in 1925.[138] His presentation was totally in line with the historiographical views of the Western free churches.[139] According to primitivist historiography, genuine Christianity lost its potency as a result of the mixing in of Hellenistic philosophy and culture. In the wake of the Constantinian shift in the relationship between church and state, the condition of the former was corrupted. The use of icons and the veneration of saints are viewed not in terms of cultural reception, contextualization, or theological development, but of pagan corruption. However, the merit of the "dead historical churches" was in their preservation of the Gospel. Following the Western primitivist canons, Ia. Prokhanov views the evangelical tradition as standing in the vein of the Western church father Augustine and the Western Reformers. At the end of the article, Ia. Prokhanov appeals to the reader: "Let us lift the banner of primitive Christianity in our country. Let us learn not only from its victories but also from its defeats."[140] Ware succinctly expresses the general attitude of the tradition:

> In summary, it may be said that the radical holiness leaders of the late nineteenth century felt that they had been given the privilege of witnessing the fulfillment of prophetic scripture and, therefore, the advance of God's eschatological design for human history. . . . The history of Protestantism had been in reality the story of the progressive restoration of the Church's original doctrine, polity, and especially its piety. That process of restoration had met its completion as all of these factors had coalesced in the holiness movement. It is no wonder, then, that Herbert Riggle concluded

137. Klibanov, *History of Religious Sectarianism*, 309. See also Nichols, "Ivan Kargel and the Pietistic Community of Late Imperial Russia," 71–87.

138. *Khristianin* 11 (1925) 37.

139. Williams, *Retrieving the Tradition and Renewing Evangelicalism*, 107–19. Hill, "Comparing Three Approaches to Restorationism," 232–37.

140. *Khristianin* 11 (1925) 37.

> his exposition of Zechariah's prophecy by exclaiming, "Thank God we have reached that time."[141]

Ia. Prokhanov's view was developed at length in Rogozin's book, published a decade later.[142] The articles written by Gospel Christians during this period demonstrate a typically Western structure of thought and argumentation, derived from the Western evangelical sources that had been used for their education.

Bible Courses

Bible courses were organized several times in St. Petersburg. The first one, a six-week course, was conducted in 1906.[143] The most stable period was between 1924 and 1928. During this period the Gospel Christians made their first attempts to interact with early church history and the early Church Fathers using sources published in Russia.[144]

Iaroslav Prokhanov, in an article entitled "Gnosticism and the Mortification of the Church," interacted with Irenaeus' work *Against Heresies* and made reference to a range of other early Church Fathers. The younger Prokhanov argued that, as a result of the Church Fathers' attempt to contextualize the Gospel for the Hellenistic culture in reaction against Gnostic doctrines, the church "lost [its] spiritual life . . . as the creed took the place of living faith. Teaching about Christ replaced the teachings of Christ."[145] Even though this short article is full of sweeping generalizations and unwarranted conclusions, it demonstrates the presence of a historical consciousness and an attempt to work with written theological sources. However, due to the persecutions that soon followed and the subsequent closure of the Bible school, this theological trajectory, present in the Gospel Christian tradition since the time of Vladimirov, was never developed.

Having rejected outright the validity of Orthodox theological scholarship, the course lecturers were forced to rely on books and notes from

141. Ware, *Restorationism*, 103.

142. *Evangel'skaia Vera*, 1–3 (1939) 24.

143. *Khristianin* 2 (1906) 32.

144. Ibid. 11 (1925) 31–37.

145. Ibid., 33, 36.

Western evangelical sources.[146] The Baptist archive in Moscow contains a manuscript written by Ivan Prokhanov on homiletics and Bible introduction. It reflects the backbone of conservative evangelical scholarship of the time.[147] Prokhanov produced a substantial compilation, including a survey of the Old and New Testaments and their historical background, the geography of the Holy Land, textual criticism, general and special hermeneutics, and the history of the Russian Bible.[148] Even though it was probably the most comprehensive resource compiled by any Russian evangelical, it had no chance to influence the tradition since it was never published.[149] The only book Prokhanov wrote on homiletics was published before the Bolshevik Revolution and was used during the Soviet period.[150] In this book, Prokhanov upholds the conservative evangelical ethos and homiletical approaches, giving as examples sermons of C. H. Spurgeon, F. B. Meyer,[151] and his own. Not only did Prokhanov transmit evangelical homiletics but, being a gifted writer of poetry, he translated from English evangelical sources 413 songs, which became the core of Eastern evangelical worship.[152]

Christian education in the Bible school had a distinctively pragmatic purpose, preparing effective ministers to spread the Gospel in its restorationist interpretation. Prokhanov explicitly points out the dangers of biblical studies that lead to "cold-minded Christianity approaching death."[153] A rationalistic knowledge of the biblical text unsupported by life experience is reproached.[154] However, unlike the Romantic Radstock

146. Archive ECB, 7.1v.

147. Ibid., 7.1v–14.

148. Unfortunately Prokhanov did not mention any written sources that he used for this compilation of evangelical scholarship. It can be suggested that he prepared the compilation after his return from America in 1925, where he met with the leaders of the Moody Bible Institute.

149. See a list of literature published by Prokhanov in *Evangel'skaia Vera* 1–2 (1935–36) 19–22.

150. Prokhanov, *Kratkoe Uchenie o Propovedi.*

151. Cf. Fullerton, *No Ordinary Man.* Meyer played an important role in the Keswick holiness tradition. Prokhanov indirectly and directly borrowed his ideas from representatives of the holiness tradition. Cf. Prokhanov's sermon on "Spiritual Geography" in *Bratskii Vestnik* 3 (1945), and Knapp, *Out of Egypt into Canaan or Lessons in Spiritual Geography,* quoted in Ware, *Restorationism*, 136.

152. Prokhanov, *V Kotle Rossii*, 144.

153. *Khristianin* 4 (1924) 15–16.

154. Ibid., 36.

and Pashkov, he introduced an intellectual stream into the tradition by pointing out the importance of "pure science," which he identified as "a collection of useful knowledge."[155] Prokhanov encouraged his students to study the general sciences, including history, philosophy, languages, and medicine, as well as the theological disciplines, in order to be better prepared for ministry. In his autobiography, Prokhanov points out that he tried to give his sons the best university education and even invited a Christian governess from London to teach them English.[156]

His attitude toward science and scripture was in accord with the American fundamentalist teaching on the relationship between science and evangelical faith.[157] Despite his recommendations regarding the use of one's intellectual faculties, his core convictions were basically fideistic, as can be seen from his attitude towards the Synoptic problem: "There is no reason to think that the Gospel writers borrowed information from each other or from other sources. The real author of the Gospels is the Holy Spirit."[158] The fundamentalist leanings in the tradition can be seen in an article on the Bible published in *Khristianin* in 1926. The authors of the article presented some ideas of F. Bettex, a contributor to *The Fundamentals*.[159] The Bible is viewed, in a rather Islamic way, as a copy of the heavenly book of "true scripture" (Daniel 10:21), which is the original: "The Bible is its imprint given to humanity. God would not have left the entire Christian world in the state of ignorance for eighteen long centuries concerning the history of Babylon, Assyria, [and] Egypt . . . had the correct understanding of holy scripture depended only on historical discoveries and geographical and archeological investigations."[160]

INTERPRETATION

Exegesis

In the mid-1920s the editors of *Khristianin* noticed the growing entropy in biblical interpretation among the Gospel Christians and decided to

155. Prokhanov, *Kratkoe Uchenie*, 79.
156. Idem, *V Kotle Rossii*, 157.
157. Cf. Orr, "Science and Christian Faith," 334–47.
158. *Evangel'skaia Vera*, 13 (1932) 8.
159. Bettex, "Bible and Modern Criticism," 76–93.
160. *Khrisitianin* 8 (1926) 44–45.

print a systematic introduction to the Bible in order to homogenize their theology. This introduction consisted of basic outlines of the biblical books and brief historical information about their origin and setting.[161] These materials were intended to unify biblical study among the congregations. This systematic turn was in line with the method of inductive Bible study promoted by the Moody Bible Institute.[162]

Prokhanov's compilation on biblical interpretation, found in his unpublished manuscript, is the most comprehensive, as well as indicative, treatment of the topic, and provides insight into the worldview of the rector of St. Petersburg Bible Institute.[163] Being faithful to the intuition of the holiness tradition, Prokhanov begins his teaching by saying that scripture cannot be understood by a person who is not spiritually prepared to read it.[164] However, his subsequent treatment of biblical hermeneutics attempts to make a significant shift away from the simplicity of pietistic reading that had characterized the tradition up to that point. Unlike the praxis-oriented Bible reading of Pashkov, he tries to articulate a system of hermeneutics by giving rules for reading the Bible and defining what approaches are correct and incorrect in reading scripture.

The first approach to the study of scripture is that of grammatical reading. Prokhanov teaches that "the meaning of scripture depends on the meaning of individual words . . . which can have general and particular senses."[165] The task of the reader is to determine the particular sense of the word intended by the author, located in a specific historical context.[166] In order to do that one needs to study the word in different contexts within the same book in particular, and in the Bible in general. And Prokhanov teaches that in the process of doing that, the reader should keep in mind the presence in scripture of Hebraisms and semi-Hebraisms, samples of which he generously provides.[167]

161. *Khristianin* 4 (1924) 37.

162. Inductive Bible study will be discussed in the next chapter.

163. Archive ECB, 7. 1v.–14.

164. Ibid., XXVI–XXVIII. Cf. Torrey, *How to Pray*, 155–57.

165. Archive ECB, 7.1v.–14, XXVII.

166. Cf. Torrey, *How to Pray*, 98–99.

167. Archive ECB, 7.1v.–14, XXVIII–XXXI. As Hebrew was not taught in the Bible Institute in any depth the relevance and practicality of Prokhanov's samples were doubtful. Prokhanov stated that the text he and his students are working with is the Synodal translation of the Bible as the most trustworthy translation. "Synodal translation means to us what the daughter of Pharaoh meant to Moses." Archive ECB, 7. 1v.–14, XXVI.

The second approach is to study the various connotations of selectively chosen words in different biblical passages (flesh, blood, faith, grace, etc).[168] Having set forth the foundation for a high level of biblical interpretation, borrowed from unreferenced sources, Prokhanov interpolates his own ideas, immediately giving himself away. Having highlighted the word "context" as a new heading, he defines it as "comrade" (!) and teaches that to read texts in context means to read various scriptural texts that deal with a common idea. Thus, according to this "contextual" approach to reading, the word "mature" has the same meaning in Heb 5:14, 1 Cor 2:6, Phil 3:15, etc.[169] Having explained the meaning of contextual reading, Prokhanov highlights a new subsection, "Parenthetical Clauses and Particles." This section begins as follows: "To understand some books it is necessary to accept their structure and plan. [But] they can be different: sometimes a book develops one and the same thought, but sometimes there is a deviation from it. This is done for clarification."[170] In the next paragraph of six short sentences Prokhanov gives samples of what he considers to be parenthetical clauses that deviate from the idea of the book. However, the particles mentioned in the heading are not discussed or even mentioned before the end of this short section.

The third approach to biblical interpretation is to study the general plan of a book and determine its main subject.[171] "For example, in order to become acquainted with the Epistle to the Romans, it is necessary to find a verse which points to the general meaning of the epistle; in this case it is Rom 3:28."[172]

The fourth approach is to compare scripture with scripture.[173] Having pointed out the importance of studying scripture in the original languages, Prokhanov moves on to the procedures to be followed in interpreting figures of speech in the Bible.[174] He mentions the following types of figures of speech: parables, types and antitypes, symbols, allegory, prophecy, and poetry. He also discusses the use of the Old

168. Cf. Torrey, *How to Pray*, 100–101.

169. Archive ECB, 7.1v.–14, XXXIII.

170. Ibid., XXXV.

171. Cf. Torrey, *How to Pray*, 94–96.

172. Archive ECB, 7.1v.–14, XXXV.

173. Cf. Torrey, *How to Pray*, 101–2.

174. Archive ECB, 7.1v.–14, XLI.

Testament in the New Testament. Homemade rules are suggested for the interpretation of each of the kinds of figures of speech. For example, writing about the interpretation of allegories, Prokhanov teaches:

> In order to establish a correct attitude toward allegories, one must remember the composite sense of scripture. Certain parts of scripture can have three senses: (1) literal, (2) moral, and (3) figurative or allegorical. We need to determine the literal sense of the text first and only after that bring out the moral and allegorical senses. Consider, for example, Genesis 24: (1) how Abraham sent [his servant]; (2) how a man can find a godly wife for himself by means of prayer; (3) how Abraham's sending of the slave symbolizes the sending of the Holy Spirit to prepare the Church. The truth [is found] when the three senses cohere. . . . When we come to an allegory, we must ask ourselves how to interpret it. In Matthew 22:2 it says: "A marriage feast was prepared for a king's son." Here we need to take the context into account: John 3:29 says that it is the bridegroom of the soul who unites with her. In the book of Revelation we read about the marriage of the Lamb. Thus in our passage we need to understand that the king's son stands for Jesus Christ. From this [example] is derived the method for interpreting allegories: we need to find a parallel text and determine the main sense. Then we will be able to understand the meaning of the allegory. If parallel texts are absent, then we need to recall the general meaning of the book. For example, in the Gospel of Matthew the general meaning of the book is that "Christ has come to find and save the lost," and so he invites them to the marriage feast.[175]

Prokhanov writes that "there are two types of difficulties in biblical interpretation. The first one is imaginary and can easily be resolved by means of more detailed study. The second one is real. It can be resolved by means of more detailed study, by correcting imprecise translations, and by acquainting oneself with the customs of biblical lands and more broadly applying historical facts.[176] The goal of the Bible is to present the divine plan for the salvation of humankind."[177]

As can be seen from the passages quoted above, Prokhanov's hermeneutical approach was in line with his misunderstanding of Torrey and Harnack, with whom he had become acquainted personally. One needs

175. Ibid., XLIV.

176. Archive ECB, 7.1v.–14, LX.

177. Ibid., LXIII.

to remember that during the time of his studies, Prokhanov was insufficiently fluent in English, German, or French to be able to understand sympathetically the promising structure implied by his headings or to fully grasp the meaning of what he was learning.

Even though Prokhanov's manual on hermeneutics is muddled and arbitrary in nature, it reveals his awareness of three hermeneutical traditions. First, the atomistic approach to biblical words and parallel texts and the focus on book structure display a dependence on the inductive methodology of the Moody Bible Institute. Second, in his discussion of the historical narrative in Genesis 24, Prokhanov reveals an acquaintance with the Alexandrian hermeneutical principle of the triple sense of scripture. Third, Prokhanov places a significant accent on the need to be aware of biblical culture and history in order to resolve scriptural problems, reflecting the intuitions of liberal scholarship. Prokhanov's departure from Russia in 1928 prevented him from ever systematizing his hermeneutical thinking.

In 1926 there appeared a short article written by V. Bykov, who was one of the lecturers at St. Petersburg Bible Institute. The article was entitled "Exegesis: The Primary Methodology for the Interpretation of Holy Scripture."[178] It was republished in 1970, without any mention of the author's name.[179] The method of Bible study presented by Bykov was practiced in evangelical churches until finally being squeezed out by the more developed method of inductive Bible study that was introduced shortly before the collapse of the Soviet Union in 1991. Bykov made selective use of a book by the Catholic professor F. Vigouroux, *Manuel biblique: ou, cours d'écriture sainte a l'usage des seminaries*, which had been edited by V. V. Vorontsov and published in Russian in 1915.[180]

At the beginning of his article, Bykov classifies the Bible as divinely inspired scripture that needs to be interpreted through a Christocentric prism, in an attempt to discover testimony specifically about Christ (Luke 24:25–27; John 5:39). "Thus Holy Scripture, being exceedingly deep, is composed according to a wonderful plan whose purpose is to testify about Jesus Christ. The exegete should look for Jesus. The exegete is like a child who assembles his blocks, having a certain picture before

178. *Khristianin* 3 (1926) 26–32.

179. *Kratkii Kurs po Gomiletike i Ekzegetike.*

180. Vigouroux, *Manuel Biblique.*

himself."[181] Having described the Christocentric purpose of reading scripture, Bykov discusses the literal and spiritual meaning of every biblical passage. The literal meaning of a text is associated with its historical meaning, which Bykov calls *the direct* meaning. "The words of Scripture should be understood according to their simple meaning and their usual sense without over-intellectualizing."[182] However, according to Bykov, a rigidly literalistic reading can be misleading. He then presents a number of texts that cannot be read and obeyed literally (Matt 16:24; John 8:12; Matt 5:29–30). Thus a text can also have a spiritual meaning, as can be seen in the use of the Old Testament in the New (1 Cor 9:9). Bykov points out that the spiritual meaning consists of figures of speech and typology, which are also prominent in the New Testament. The two meanings of a text are not set against each other, but are viewed as a complementary pair. Bykov writes that "due to the limitations of human nature, people usually choose [only] one of these approaches to biblical interpretation, resulting in a one-sided, limping [unbalanced] interpretation. Representatives of the most important schools of exegesis are: (1) Origen, a great exegete of ancient times who interpreted everything spiritually; (2) Russian Molokans, called 'spiritual Christians,' [whose approach to interpretation is] the same as that of Origen; and (3) Russian Orthodoxy, which adheres to the literal interpretation of scripture—for example, its interpretation of the Eucharist and [its belief in] regeneration through paedobaptism."

Unlike these "one-sided approaches," according to Bykov the Gospel Christians should master both the literal and spiritual interpretation of scripture.[183] He provides examples of biblical exegesis which he considers to represent a balanced approach. He writes, for example, about Mark 9:1–8, the Transfiguration of Christ. Literally, the text is to be understood as referring to a historical event on the Mount of Transfiguration that reveals the deity of Christ. But Bykov takes the spiritual meaning of the text to be "personal growth in knowledge of the glorified Christ." Thus two modes of reading this text are practiced simultaneously and complementarily, and the spiritual meaning of the passage is grounded in the individualistic, pietistic spiritual knowledge of the reader.

181. *Khristianin* 3 (1926) 26–27.

182. Ibid.

183. Ibid., 31.

In order to understand better the meaning of a text, Bykov suggests paying attention to its context—using the word "context" in its usual sense. However, the most important condition for correctly interpreting a text is the subjective condition of the interpreter.[184] The interpreter should be a regenerated and spiritually-experienced person. Without having been spiritually regenerated, an interpreter cannot understand the meaning of scripture. Bykov writes:

1. The genuineness of the interpreter's regeneration is a crucial factor in biblical interpretation.
2. The unique personal experience of the interpreter plays a crucial role, inasmuch as the experiences of different people in *the process of regeneration* are not identical.
3. The level of spiritual maturity of the interpreter also plays a crucial role in the interpretation of scripture.
4. Disagreements with regard to interpretation often serve the divine goals, prompting people to explore certain issues more thoroughly: 1 Corinthians 11:19.[185]

Even though the exegetical methodology of Bykov does justice neither to Origen and the Molokans nor to the Russian Orthodox Church, it reflects the shift in the tradition that was noted in the historical article by Iaroslav Prokhanov and in the hermeneutics of Ivan Prokhanov. The Gospel Christians became open to interaction with other historical traditions and with printed materials even from Catholic sources. Even though this interaction was carried out in a spirit of spiritual arrogance while reflecting intellectual frailty, it demonstrated the emergence of a primitive research culture.

This shift did not disrupt the tradition initiated by Radstock. The pneumatological starting point for interpreting scripture, as well as the literal and typological pietistic approach to interpretation, had not changed since the origin of the tradition. However, the tradition began to take a more cautious posture towards the excesses of pneumatic enthusiasm, in light of the development of the Pentecostal movement, which had branched off from the Gospel Christians under the influence of Western missionaries.

184. *Khristianin* 3 (1926) 32.

185. Ibid.

Reaction to the Pentecostal Movement: An Example of Theological Interpretation

The early issues of *Khristianin* and its supplements contain articles emphasizing the importance of the activity of the Holy Spirit and the eschatological outpouring of the Spirit. It is suggested the Spirit is as active in the present as he had been in the Apostolic period, and that all the gifts of the Spirit are still operative. One article in particular emphasizes the necessity of the gift of speaking in tongues.[186] Prophecies, visions, and faith healings are considered normal Christian experience.[187]

This attitude eventually changed, however, as a result of the development of the Pentecostal movement, which branched out from the core of the Gospel Christian tradition in 1910, under the influence of A. I. Ivanov, who had been an active minister among the Gospel Christians.[188] Over the course of several years the Pentecostal ferment within the tradition led to the development of a separate movement, which drew new adherents from other evangelical traditions, as well. The Gospel Christians realized that they needed to develop a new interpretive strategy to separate themselves from the growing Pentecostal movement.[189] The attitude of the Pentecostals towards the Gospel Christians was similar to that of the latter towards the Orthodox Church: the absence of a certain spiritual experience taken to be normative was considered a sign of a low spiritual condition. The reaction of the Gospel Christians towards the Pentecostals was also similar to the way the Orthodox reacted to them: the Pentecostals were branded as heretics who were destroying the unity of the true Church through their false teaching.[190] The enthusiasm of Pentecostalism, with its emotional excesses, was interpreted as the activity of a false spirit.[191]

Prokhanov's theological interpretation, on the crest of the anti-Pentecostal campaign, is demonstrated in his evaluation of the theology of R. A. Torrey, who had originally been viewed as an evangelical

186. *Utrenniaia Zvezda* 19 (1910) 5.

187. *Khristianin* 2 (1906) 55–57.

188. Klibanov, *History of Religious Sectarianism*, 304–5; Franchuk, *Prosila Rossiia Dozhdia u Gospoda*, vol. 1, 300–310.

189. Karetnikova, *Al'manakh po Istorii Russkogo Baptizma*, vyp. 3, 5–61.

190. *Khristianin* 2 (1925) 64. See also Prokhanov, "Dukh Sviatoi, Ego Dary i Deistviia" and Kargel, "Ob Uchenii Piatidesiatnikov."

191. Ibid.

authority. Torrey, like V. A. Pashkov, differentiated between the experience of regeneration and that of baptism with the Holy Spirit. While in America, Prokhanov wrote an article for a Russian journal attacking Torrey's views[192]:

> Dr. Torrey holds the right position on many issues except one. That is the issue of baptism with the Holy Spirit. As I wrote in my booklet about the Holy Spirit, Torrey's teaching that baptism with the Holy Spirit is something different from regeneration does not correspond to the teaching of Scripture. . . . Dr. Torrey has made a mistake with regard to the terminology of experience. . . . He believes that before the drastic change in his life, he had already been regenerated, and that the change had been brought about by his being baptized with the Holy Spirit. In reality, however, he had not been regenerated before this experience, but had only been *revived* [italics added]. The drastic change in his life was indeed brought about by regeneration, which is the same as baptism with the Holy Spirit.[193]

Prokhanov claims that a "believer" in Christ, while still in an unregenerate state, can experience a certain level of activity of the Spirit, which he terms "being revived." He claims that this perspective is based on biblical teaching, even though the term "being revived" is never used in the Synodal translation of the Russian Bible. Prokhanov denies the present reality of the gift of speaking in tongues because, according to his interpretation of Acts 2, the gift was originally given for the proclamation of the Gospel among the nations. When the canon of scripture became complete, this gift was abolished. He supports this interpretation by means of testimonies from different parts of Russia concerning the harmful nature of the Pentecostal movement.[194] However, he emphasizes that all the other gifts of the Spirit are operative in the churches of the Gospel Christians, including those of healing and prophecy. Earlier, Prokhanov had argued for the necessity of a Trinitarian approach to the understanding of scripture, on the basis of our unity in Christ. Fifteen years later he speaks as a prophet who has the correct keys to biblical

192. Cf. Torrey, *Baptism with the Holy Spirit*. Torrey rejected the Pentecostal interpretation of the Spirit's baptism, taking a distinctively Keswickian interpretation of baptism with the Spirit as the empowerment for Christian service. See Archer, *Pentecostal Hermeneutics*, 81.

193. *Khristianin* 2 (1926) 50–51.

194. Ibid.

interpretation. And the pendulum began to swing even further away from Pentecostalism. In 1926, for example, Ia. Khoduch wrote an article arguing for the cessation of all miraculous gifts except that of wisdom.[195]

CONCLUSION

During the period between 1910 and 1939 the holiness tradition of the Gospel Christians was modified with regard to the story of its self-identity, its theology, and its approach to biblical interpretation. As a result of the geopolitical shift after the Bolshevik revolution, the tradition's new identity was built on the Eastern bank of the civilizational divide. Facts about the Western origin of the tradition, as well as it aristocratic period, were suppressed. The Anglo-American holiness tradition was presented as an indigenous demotic movement. The Russian messianic spirit that energized the Bolsheviks amplified the theological drive of the restorationist wing of the movement, as represented by Prokhanov. Because of the failure to reform the Orthodox Church and find unity with the Baptists, Prokhanov modified the identity of the movement, together with his own identity, by reconfiguring the story of the previous relationships with the Baptist movement. The movement was now envisioned as the worldwide union of a qualitatively new Christianity, different from Western denominations, because it claimed to have restored the primitive Christianity of the Apostolic church. Prokhanov perceived himself as a new reformer who headed a new worldwide reformation of restored Christianity. From the point of view of the Protestant Paradigm, Orthodox Christianity had to be demolished and made to conform to the image represented by the restorationist movement.

The theology of the Gospel Christians was slightly modified as the movement progressed further along the restorationist railroad track. However, the Trinitarian, Christocentric, and pneumatic framework of the tradition suffered no changes. Prokhanov explicitly articulated his postmillennial, Arminian stance, which deviated from the original premillennial outlook of Radstock. I. V. Kargel retained the premillennialism of Radstock but introduced the dispensationalist interpretive scheme, which had not been followed during the earlier period. However, due to the high standing of Prokhanov as the native leader of the movement

195. *Khristianin* 3 (1926) 48–53. The editors of the magazine point out that the article reflects only the opinion of the author.

during the period between 1910 and 1928 and as the rector of the Bible Institute, who claimed to have received a European theological education, the position of Kargel was very much a minority view. Thus the modernistic component of Prokhanov's theology began to shine through the original Romantic core of the tradition. This rationalistic shift is observable in the articles written by lecturers from St. Petersburg Bible Institute, who began to interact with printed sources and make their own arguments. However, no ongoing theological discourse was established.

The tradition continued to move along the trajectory of Anglo-American evangelicalism, borrowing its historiography, printed resources, hymnography, and inductive Bible study methods, as well as its finances. Personal contacts between the leaders of both movements took place in 1925. The survey of Prokhanov's hermeneutics displays the state of theological confusion and the presence of divergent hermeneutical traditions in his unsystematic thinking. The major difference between Russian evangelicalism and Anglo-American mainstream evangelicalism was that the former emphasized the unquestionable authority of the charismatic leader, regardless of the quality of his arguments, while the latter was developing a rationalist theological program in the vein of common sense realism. Pietism was still the core of the tradition.

There was a shift in biblical interpretation, as lecturers at St. Petersburg Bible Institute tried to articulate rationally an evangelical hermeneutical method, superficially interacting with different hermeneutical traditions. Prokhanov demonstrated an arbitrary and confused hermeneutics with the presence in his thinking of the inductive Bible study method, the triple sense of scripture of the Alexandrian school, and the liberal intuition concerning the necessity of a historical understanding of the text and of its human author. However, Prokhanov's sermons and articles demonstrate that he took an anti-intellectual position towards higher criticism and interpreted scripture in the vein of the holiness tradition. The Christocentric exegetical methodology of Bykov is in line with this, as he argued for the necessity of both literal and spiritual interpretation. As in the case of Radstock, the key for the correct understanding of scripture is the subjective experience of the Holy Spirit.

In the next chapter we will conclude the narrative of the self-identity, theology, and hermeneutics of the Gospel Christians, preparing the ground for theological construction.

6

The Gospel Christians between 1944 and 2008

"The fact that major changes in the way we view the past usually correspond to major social transformations that affect entire mnemonic communities, as shown in many studies of changes in attitudes to the past in post-communist countries after the collapse of communism, also provides the evidence that remembering is more than just a personal act and the nature of political power can influence the content of our memories."[1]

INTRODUCTION

In this concluding historical chapter I will examine the development of historical identities, theology, and biblical interpretation during the period from World War II until the present time. This period of time has been chosen somewhat arbitrarily for the purposes of the present research, as it provides the necessary framework for identifying and describing fluctuations in the tradition. My argument is that geopolitical forces were shaping the identity narrative and theological practices of the tradition, culminating in the post-Soviet crisis discussed in the introductory chapter. Due to the underdeveloped field of inquiry, my presentation of this period will be done in rather broad strokes. Further research is needed to improve the resolution of the historical and theological picture given in this chapter.

As in the previous chapters, I develop my argument utilizing Hans Küng's theory of theological paradigms and Alasdair MacIntyre's theory of tradition-based rationality. In the present chapter Küng and MacIntyre

1. Misztal, *Theories of Social Remembering*, 12.

are present rather tacitly. Küng's theory emphasizes the fact that theological paradigm shifts happen as a result of geopolitical upheavals. In this respect I continue to consider the tradition of the Gospel Christians as part of the Protestant Paradigm that was undergoing change as a result of the geopolitical shifts of the twentieth century. It will be demonstrated that the Modernist paradigm of theology was introduced to the tradition through Western evangelical missionary activity in Ukraine following the collapse of the Soviet Union. But despite these theological transformations under the influence of Western missions, the heirs of the Gospel Christians produced a narrative identity against the backdrop of the resurgent Russian Orthodox civilization. MacIntyre's project is present in the discussion of the tradition's narrative and its practice of theology and biblical interpretation. Having established the contemporary state of historical and theological affairs in the fragmentized tradition of the Gospel Christians in Ukraine, we will prepare a platform for a paradigmatic transformation of the tradition in the post-Soviet context in the constructive chapter of this book.

HISTORICAL IDENTITIES

During World War II it became obvious that the ideology of international communism was not powerful enough to unite the Soviet Empire and hold it together in the midst of the existential crisis brought about by the German invasion. In his recent study on the religious question during this period of Soviet history, Steven Miner analyzed strategies developed by the Kremlin to overcome its existential and political predicament, as the Bolshevik internationalist ideology proved to be deficient in solving the multifaceted problems brought about by the War. Miner has demonstrated that the relationship between the church and the state had a complex character, as the religious question was inseparably interwoven with politics, state security, diplomacy, and propaganda: "The evolution of the Soviet regime's wartime approach to religion can . . . only be fully understood in the context of Russian History and traditions, Soviet ideology and practice, the specific and shifting circumstances of the war against the Nazis, and the demands of the wartime alliance with the Western democracies."[2]

2. Miner, *Stalin's Holy War*, 3.

Miner has argued that, like the Russian Orthodox tsars, the Soviet leaders used the Russian Orthodox Church as an effective tool for russification and for dethroning nationalistic and anti-Soviet tendencies on the western borders of the Soviet Union. Stalin used the church to deal with nationalist drives that were supported by local nationalist priests in the newly-recovered regions. The Orthodox Church helped the Kremlin establish order amidst the chaos produced by the changing tide of the war. Miner points out the importance of the international dimensions of the question of religion, as the Soviet regime sought to secure the support of its Western democratic allies. "Throughout the war . . . Moscow and its agents abroad would work tirelessly to eradicate the memory of pre-war Soviet religious repression and to replace it with a new image of the USSR as the defender of Christian civilization."[3] The establishment of the Moscow Patriarchy in 1943 was followed by the establishment of the All-Union Council of Evangelical (Gospel) Christians-Baptists in 1944.[4] The address of the leaders of the Gospel Christians and the Baptists to Soviet believers in 1942 demonstrates the ethos of the time when the Union was about to be established: "In our day, Europe has been shaken under the wheels of the military machine of Hitler's Germany. It has inscribed on its banner: 'The Conquest of the World! The Enslavement of Humanity.' . . . There is great danger for the work of the Gospel. . . . Three great powers, Russia, Britain, and the United States, have joined their forces to rebuff the threat . . . and deliver Europe from the impending danger of enslavement."[5]

The patriotic call to support the Soviet motherland during a time of crisis was the backdrop for the establishment of the new Protestant Union.

The history of the AUCECB has been discussed in several historical monographs.[6] It is beyond the scope of the present research to examine historical details studied elsewhere. For the purpose of our research interest, it is sufficient simply to note several undisputed facts, so that we may proceed with our study of historical identities, theology, and bibli-

3. Ibid., 12.

4. AUCECB hereafter.

5. Savinskii et al., *Istoriia Evangel'skikh Khristian-Baptistov v SSSR*, 229.

6. Sawatsky, *Soviet Evangelicals Since World War II*; Mitrokhin, *Baptizm*; Tatiana Nikol'skaia, "Istoriia Dvizheniia Baptistov-Initsiativnikov"; Savinskii, *Istoriia Evangel'skikh Khristian-Baptistov Ukrainy, Rossii, Belorussii (1917–1967)*.

cal interpretation in the tradition of the Gospel Christians.[7] First, the newly-established Union was a pro-Soviet institution that supported the Soviet government in matters of internal and external affairs.[8] Second, within a year of its establishment the Union included Pentecostal churches, without ever mentioning the anti-Pentecostal campaign of the 1920s. Third, from its very beginning, the Union had a strongly hierarchical centralized structure that was a channel for state control over the local churches.[9] Unlike the vision of Pashkov and the early Prokhanov, who dreamed of the free association of free individuals and churches, the Union was built from the top down. It was thoroughly controlled by the State, which can be seen in the history of the split in the 1960s, when the leadership of the Union sent out to the churches restrictive instructions that caused a schism in the artificially-created body.[10] In the present discussion, our focus will be on the mainline historiography in the tradition.

A. V. Karev

Alexander Vasil'evich Karev can be considered the key shaper of Soviet denominational historiography and the key architect of Soviet evangelical identity during the period of the Cold War.[11] Born in 1894, Karev was educated in Lutheran institutions and obtained a good command of German before beginning his studies, which he never completed, at St. Petersburg Technical Institute. Having been converted to evangelical Christianity in 1913, Karev became a member of the YMCA, which was led by Baron Nikolai, a close associate of Ivan Prokhanov. Nearly two years after his conversion Karev was baptized in a church of the Gospel Christians led by Johannes Kargel. Beginning in 1922 he worked in the Union of Gospel Christians, substituting on occasion for Ivan Prokhanov, and teaching a course at the Bible institute. The official biography of Karev is silent

7. Cf. Mitrokhin, *Baptizm*, 396–410.

8. Gordon William Carlson, "Russian Protestants and American Evangelicals Since the Death of Stalin," 164, 166, 289–90, 428–29, 443–44.

9. Sawatsky, "Re-Positioning of Evangelical Christians-Baptists and Sister Church Unions between 1980 and 2005," 191–92.

10. Nikol'skaia, "Istoriia Dvizheniia Baptistov-Initsiativnikov," 65–78; Michael Bourdeaux, "Religious Liberty in the Soviet Union," 119–32.

11. Karev, *Izbrannye Stat'i.*

about the fact that he was imprisoned in the 1930s.[12] When the AUCECB was created in October 1944, Karev was elected as the General Secretary of the Union, holding this position for the next twenty-seven years. He was also the chief editor of *Bratskii Vestnik* (*The Brotherly Herald*), which was the official journal of the newly-created religious body. This journal was the key means for shaping the movement's theology and identity.[13] At a conference in 1963 Karev expressed his view of the journal, writing: "In the old journals, especially in *Khristianin*, profound articles by foreign preachers were published. But now *Bratskii Vestnik* publishes articles written by our own brothers. Our journal is acknowledged by many international theologians, who have sent many letters about the matter, to be the most spiritual of all such journals."[14]

During the Cold War, Karev was a representative of the Soviet Union in various international organizations, including the World Peace Council, the Soviet Council of Peace, The Peace Trust, the Institute of Soviet-American Relations, and the World Council of Churches.[15] The programmatic article, "Russkoe Evangel'sko-Baptistskoe Dvizhenie" ("The Russian Evangelical-Baptist Movement"), which was published during this period in *Bratskii Vestnik,* provides a new narrative of the origin and history of the AUCECB.[16]

The article, written by Karev, was crafted in such a way as to give a historical account of the AUCECB. As such, it lacks all the sharp corners of the past, suggesting instead a distinctively Western origin for the evangelical movement in Russia, which reached its evolutionary climax in the AUCECB. Karev particularly points out that the newly-created Union is part of the world Baptist movement with which the leadership of the AUCECB established relations immediately after its organization. The structure and content of Karev's article is similar to that employed by the German Baptist historiographer Waldemar Gutsche, whose book was published a year earlier.[17]

According to Karev, the evangelical movement began in Russia at the time of Catherine II, who invited foreigners to settle in Russia by

12. Ibid, 12.

13. De Chalandeau, "Theology of the Evangelical Christians-Baptists in the USSR."

14. Archive ECB, 11e.–3.15, 15.

15. De Chalandeau, "The Theology," 218–32.

16. *Bratskii Vestnik* 3–4 (1957).

17. Gutsche, *Westliche Quellen.*

her manifestos of 1762 and 1763. Settlements of German Mennonites became the cradle of the evangelical movement. As Russian peasants started working in the German settlements, they became acquainted with the teachings of Pietistic preachers who came from Germany. Thus the Mennonites, Lutherans, and Reformed Christians were responsible for sowing the seeds of the Gospel in Russia. According to Karev, the Orthodox Church did not give spiritual life to the Russians, but it did produce a spiritual thirst among Russian God-seekers, who were fascinated by Bible study, which was not sufficiently provided by Russian Orthodoxy. Under the influence of the German Baptists, Russian workers in German colonies were converted to the Baptist movement. Karev, following Gutsche, emphasized the German origin of the Baptist movement in Southern Russia, given the names of many German people and Western institutions that were part of the foundation of the movement.

The second stream of the evangelical movement, according to Karev, came from the Caucasus region. He points out that the pioneer of the evangelical revival there was the Scotsman John Melville. The other two leading figures of the revival in the Caucasus were the Syrian missionary Jacob Yakub and Lithuanian Baptist Martin Kalveit. Karev emphasizes that the Molokans, whom he calls Russian Quakers, many of whom became followers of the evangelical movement, could not understand the Gospel until Baptist preachers explained it to them.

The story of the St. Petersburg stream of the evangelical movement begins with the German Protestant Johannes Gossner, who went to Russia in 1812 and ministered there until 1825. Even though the name of Gossner had never previously appeared in the consciousness of the tradition, Karev devotes a significant amount of space to a description of the Gossner's revivalist ministry in St. Petersburg.[18] The revivalist ministry of Lord Radstock is referred to as the second spiritual revival in St. Petersburg. Karev draws parallels between Radstock's ministry and that of Gossner at the beginning of the nineteenth century. As he describes developments within Radstock's ministry in St. Petersburg, Karev, following Gutsche, demonstrates his acquaintance with the writings of Leskov, Leo Tolstoy, and Dostoevskii and their views on the Radstockist movement. His description of the St. Petersburg revival is supported by

18. It is worth pointing out that ten years later Karev eliminated the ministry of Gossner from his story of the origin of the St. Petersburg revival. See *Bratskii Vestnik* 4 (1967).

the published testimonies of Korff and Lieven, as well as the work of Latimer on the ministry of Dr. Baedecker in Russia. Having mentioned that Johannes Kargel served as an interpreter for Dr. Baedeker in Russia, Karev then tells about Kargel's own ministry. Karev also points out that Kargel had been educated at a German Baptist seminary. After describing the times of Orthodox oppression under K. P. Pobedonostsev, Karev focuses on the multiple attempts of the Gospel Christians and Baptists to unite. His main thesis is that the Gospel Christians were a species of the British Baptist tradition, which "was not often recognized by the elder Russian sibling, born of the German Baptist tradition. . . . However, this failure was remedied in 1944 when the two brothers threw themselves together and embraced each other in brotherly love." Karev does not mention the Soviet persecution; instead he praises the Soviet Government for giving the evangelicals the freedom they lacked during Tsarist times.

The narrative provided by the chief editor of *Bratskii Vestnik* was the key identifying story during the time of the Cold War. Karev demonstrated a highly selective approach to reading the history of the movement. The interpretation of the past was done exclusively through the grid of the newly-established AUCECB, with the purpose of supporting the artificially-created Union. The atmosphere of the Cold War necessitated a complete association of the Union with the well-established Western Baptist tradition, which created a platform for the leaders of the AUCECB to be ambassadors in the West of the Soviet political program. "On all his trips, besides the preaching of the Gospel and fellowship with brothers and sisters, there was set a great and noble goal, namely the bringing together of the West and the East, the relief of world tension, and the defense of peace."[19] On the other hand, Karev was a promulgator of the Communist myth concerning the superiority of the Soviet order over Western civilization. In his article entitled "The Birth of the New World," Karev glorified Lenin and the Soviet order as a new epoch in the history of the world, praising the Soviets for the religious freedom given to believers.[20] Even though the Union was brought into being as a result of complex political and geopolitical processes that imposed upon scattered congregations a particularly Baptist identity, the messianic

19. Karev, *Izbrannye Stat'i*, 13–14. Cf., "Iubileinoe Poslanie Vsem Khristianam Mira" in *Bratskii Vestnik* 4 (1967).

20. Karev, *Izbrannye Stat'i*, 167–70.

Slavophile spirit had not disappeared but took a new form. Its presence is detectable in the report delivered by Karev at the fortieth All-Union conference in 1969.[21] Karev writes:

> The Reformation of the sixteenth century gave birth to the so-called Protestantism that is a great protest movement against the deviations of the Catholic Church from the central truths of the Gospel. The Protestantism of the sixteenth century became a great river which flowed in four main riverbeds: Lutheranism, Calvinism, Zwinglianism, and Anabaptism. The seventeenth and eighteenth centuries gave birth to a fifth riverbed, which is called "free evangelical churches." To this movement belong the Congregationalists, Baptists, Mennonites, and Methodists. To these free churches the twentieth century added the Pentecostal churches. The brotherhood of Gospel Christians-Baptists belongs to the world Baptist movement, but at the same time it occupies a completely different place among the other free churches. What is the difference between the brotherhood of Gospel Christians-Baptists and the rest of the free churches and the world Baptist movement? To answer this question in short we say: the brotherhood of Gospel Christians-Baptists is the bearer of restored Apostolic Christianity, and in this respect there is no other church in the world similar to it. We should say directly that the "pastoral system" and the elimination of the concept of the "priesthood of all believers" has removed the contemporary free evangelical churches from the ideal of Apostolic Christianity. Only the churches of Gospel Christians-Baptists have continued to maintain the spirit of the Apostolic churches during the one hundred years of their existence. At the time of the ninetieth anniversary of our brotherhood in 1957, it was said: "We have made a long journey along the stream of the Evangelical-Baptist river, starting from its sources in the South and North of Russia and continuing to its current state. And we can say with deep gratitude to God that the Russian Gospel Christians-Baptists have taken first place among the evangelicals in Europe. However, it is not only the number of people in our membership that causes us to thank God, who is adding those who are being saved every day. It is also that the inner spiritual substance of this movement is causing world Christianity to utter the greatest praise and thankfulness to God for the Russian Gospel Christian-Baptist movement as the bearer of Apostolic Christianity, which cannot be said about the Christian churches in the West. The saddest fact of

21. Archive ECB, 11e–4.1.

> contemporary Western Christianity, including the world Baptist movement, is the loss of the spirit of Apostolic Christianity, the spirit of the first love of Christ, the spirit of witness, the spirit of the priesthood of all believers, and the spirit of Apostolic simplicity. As a result of this, anyone wishing to find around the globe a country in which the church resembles the churches of Apostolic times, with all the attributes of primitive Christianity, one should point to the USSR, where Gospel Christians-Baptists have kept, until the present moment, the spirit and structure of the Apostolic churches. Without any pride or conceit we can say that the church of Gospel Christians-Baptists in the USSR is the Apostolic Church of the twentieth century.[22]

In his account, Karev presents the Soviet evangelical movement as the best representative of Western evangelicalism or even of Christianity in the world. The story told by Karev had significant similarities and dissimilarities to the story invented by Prokhanov. Unlike the later Prokhonov, who tended to remove the tradition from European religious processes in the eighteenth and nineteenth centuries, Karev correctly roots the tradition in the Protestant Paradigm of free church evangelicalism. However, following Prokhanov's vector, he builds the identity on the Eastern bank of the geopolitical divide, identifying the USSR as the most advanced country in the world and the Soviet evangelical movement as representing the most advanced example of restored Apostolic Christianity. Similar to Prokhanov, he argues that the Christians of the Soviet Union should engage with the world of atheism. However, unlike Prokhanov, who perceived Communism as a threat to Western civilization, Karev took the role of promoter of Soviet propaganda. Following the steps of the later Prokhanov, he was not interested in the present state of the Orthodox Church. From a theological point of view, Russian Orthodoxy simply does not appear on the horizon of Karev's story.

The Post-Cold War Turn in Historiography

The subsequent evangelical historiography moved along the general trajectory developed by Gutsche and Karev, but with one significant change. As the period of the Cold War was coming to an end during the period of Gorbachev's reforms in the mid-1980s, a shift occurred

22. Archive ECB, 11.e–4.1, 1–3.

in the self-identifying narrative of the tradition. Influenced by the context of increasing freedom initiated by *Glasnost* and *Perestroika*, Soviet evangelicals immediately reacted to changes in the geopolitical force field and the rebirth of Orthodox consciousness, as the tottering Soviet Union was about to celebrate the 1000th anniversary of Russia's baptism in 1988.[23]

This change was characterized by a return to and modification of the later Prokhanov's view of the non-Western origin of the tradition, developed in the Slavophile key. Using the term *samobytnost'*, which had been employed by the Slavophiles of the nineteenth century to describe the original path of Russia's development as different from that of Europe,[24] the compilers of the most prominent Soviet evangelical historiography argued for the unique origin and development of the tradition.[25] The authors of the volume applied the Soviet evolutionary concept of changing social formations to the religious formations in Russia, with the evolution reaching its climax in the AUCECB:

> In the history of the evangelical revival of the Russian and Ukrainian people we can find many specific and unique (*samobytnyi)* features which cannot be found among other nations. In the search for God's truth and salvation, the Russian and Ukrainian nations have come a long way from the first doubts concerning the truthfulness of the ritualistic teaching of the Greek-Byzantine Church, to conversion to Christianity of the first Apostolic church, as revealed in the holy Gospel. . . . Believers perceive the history of the evangelical revival of our people as having been produced by the activity of the Holy Spirit. . . . The appearance of the first congregations of Gospel Christians-Baptists in Russia was not the fruit of foreign missions. It was not a random event, "infused into people from the outside," as has been presented by Orthodox researchers.[26]

Even though the compilers of the volume claim that the change in their views concerning the origin of the Russian evangelical movement took place after "rigorous research,"[27] this assertion is really more rhetorical in style, as is acknowledged at the beginning of the volume: "This

23. Il'icheva, *Tysiacheletie Kreshcheniia Rusi.*

24. Zenkovskii, *Russian Thinkers and Europe*, 40.

25. Savinskii et al., *Istoriia Evangel'skikh Khristian-Baptistov v SSSR*, 13.

26. Ibid., 12–13.

27. Ibid., 13.

book is written by enthusiasts, and we are therefore in debt to demanding readers [i.e., we ask for their indulgence] for some deviations from the [normal] professional style of presenting such material."[28] In light of the previous chapters of this research, it is obvious that the change in rhetoric of the self-identifying story was bound to result in inconsistencies. Thus to justify their claims about the Eastern origin of the Gospel Christians, the late Soviet Baptist historians assert that "the appearance in St. Petersburg of 'the congregation of revival and holiness' among the aristocracy started from the conversion of E. I. Chertkova and N. F. Lieven. They underwent a conversion experience before the arrival of Lord Radstock in St. Petersburg from England."[29] However, several pages later, while discussing the conversion of the above-mentioned women, the compilers of this volume point out that both of them, in fact, experienced spiritual rebirth while in Western Europe. Chertkova was converted following a sermon of Radstock, while Lieven experienced conversion during a prayer meeting at the home of a former minster, a certain Mr. Blackwood, in England.[30] Realizing the flaw in their thesis, the architects of the new evangelical identity were forced to admit: "Lord Radstock is the exception. His sermons in aristocratic salons in English and French laid the foundation for the great revival, which eventually acquired its independence and penetrated all strata of society."[31]

The drastic modification of the self-identifying story was a survival strategy, in light of the impending geopolitical changes that would reshape the configuration of the world and the nature of Orthodox consciousness in Euro-Asia. Having presented themselves as the apex of the evolution of Christian consciousness, the architects of the new story excised their tradition from the developments of European Protestantism in the nineteenth century. One will search in vain for any discussion of the holiness movement or the theological location of the founder of the tradition on the theological map of Anglo-American evangelicalism at the end of the nineteenth century. The subsequent discussions of Russian and Ukrainian self-identity develop this rhetorical turn to the indigenous roots of the evangelical movement. This modification of the self-identifying narrative of the Gospel Christians-Baptists illustrates the

28. Ibid., 7.

29. Ibid., 14.

30. Ibid., 80–81.

31. Ibid., 95.

gravitational pull of the emerging Orthodox paradigm, which is tacitly acknowledged in all evangelical reconstructions following the collapse of the Soviet Union.

M. S. Karetnikova

M. S. Karetnikova, a self-taught historian of the AUCECB, has attempted to argue that the Christianity that was brought to Russia at the turn of the tenth century contained two streams, which have been present in Russia ever since.[32] Taking as her starting point the fact that Cyril and Methodius translated the scriptures into the Slavonic language, she proposes the thesis that "from the very beginning of Christianity in Russia, there was the possibility of it being developed in either ritualistic or evangelical forms." [33] Even though Karetnikova demonstrates the presence of historical awareness in her attempt to tell the story of indigenous evangelical Christianity in Russia, she does not succeed in offering any substantial argumentation for her grand thesis. Her arguments can be boiled down to the fact that there were diverging groups in Russian Orthodoxy that often deviated from the State Church, which was prone to cooperate with the state authorities and which was ritualistically rigid. Selectively describing some of the dissenting bodies throughout Russian history, she suggests that the Spirit was preparing Russia to be enlightened by the light of the Gospel in the nineteenth century. In order to tell the story of Russia's enlightenment with "the pure Gospel," which "had never before been preached in Russia,"[34] Karetnikova provides the full version of the article written by Karev in 1957![35] In so doing, Karetnikova tries to kill two birds with one stone. On the one hand, she tries to maintain continuity with the tradition's historiography. On the other hand, she locates Karev's article in the broader framework of her own construction. However, the two birds are killed at a precious price. First, Karetnikova fails to discuss the genesis of shifts in the tradition's

32. In a telephone conversation in March 2006, M. S. Karetnikova admitted that neither she nor any other evangelical historian known to her in Russia was trained to perform historiographic research in public archives. Nor did she know of anybody accomplishing this sort of research. However, as exceptions, she mentioned Sharyl Corrado and Tatiana Nikol'skaia, whose works were referred to earlier.

33. Karetnikova, *Al'manakh po Istorii Russkogo Baptizma*, 11.

34. Ibid., 3–4.

35. Ibid., 85–192.

historiography. Prokhanov's shift during the Soviet period towards the "indigenous" origin of the movement, as well as Karev's "Westernizing" historiographic shift, are neither analyzed nor explained. Second, Karetnikova presents the historically contingent restorationist segment of the Protestant Paradigm in the absolute terms of "the pure Gospel." This primitivist move, universalizing a historically contingent form of life, has disastrous consequences. It nurtures an attitude of superiority, which prevents genuine dialogue with those who are outside this recent historical tradition. It also erects obstacles to genuine and critical retrospection by insiders. In trying to find a quick fix for the tottering tradition, Karetnikova utilizes the simplest ideological tool available: the Hegelian rationality of Soviet ideology, which perceived Soviet socialist formation as the apex of the evolution of social formations. To view the tradition of the Gospel Christians-Baptists as the apex of spiritual evolution on the graph of Orthodox dissent is to give to the Hegelian spirit, which had departed from the corpse of the Soviet system, a new home in a religious body.

V. A. Bachinin

In a recent book, V. A. Bachinin, a representative of the Russian movement of Gospel Christians, stretches this tendency to its limit.[36] Following Karetnikova, Bachinin identifies the presence of two tendencies in Russian Orthodoxy, one of which is associated with Byzantine ritualism and the other with "evangelicalism." He takes St. Joseph of Volotsk (1440–1515) as the key representative of the first type, while taking St. Nil of Sorsk (1433–1508) as a representative of the second type. The brief story of the two tendencies within Orthodoxy is read in a highly selective way. In the process of his discussion, Bachinin neglects to mention the role of St. Sergius of Radonezh (d.1392), whose life and spirituality reflected an organic balance between the two tendencies, before their separation following his death.[37] Besides presenting a selective and overly generalized schematic reading of the Orthodox tradition, Bachinin fails to demonstrate how the newly-reconstructed

36. Bachinin, *Evangel'skie Tsennosti v Grazhdanskom Obshchestve*, 49–74.

37. Cf. Zernov, *St. Sergius—Builder Of Russia*, 72–80. Zernov calls these tendencies in Orthodoxy priestly and prophetic respectively. He makes a strong argument, pointing out that in the life of St. Sergius these tendencies were found in delicate balance.

historical consciousness of evangelical Orthodoxy is connected with the distinctively Western origin and self-identity of the tradition of the Gospel Christians in Russia and the Soviet Union. In fact, in his discussion of the historical consciousness of the Gospel Christians in Russia, Bachinin never even mentions the tradition originated by Radstock! This sort of identity construction reflects a deep crisis in the tradition, which is attempting to reconfigure the story of its own past in light of its immediate experiences. It is introducing a new storyline rhetorically constructed by means of a selective reading of the highly complex and multifaceted Orthodox tradition, which has become the dominant force in the cultural context. Aggressive Western missionary involvement in the former Soviet Union seems to have been a significant contributor to this changing identity, as well.[38] The newly-invented story does not seem to be promising, since it is based on erasures and, as a result, lacks scholarly rigor, internal consistency, or explanatory power.

Iu. Reshetnikov and S. Sannikov[39]

The book written by Reshetnikov and Sannikov is an important historico-theological study in the Ukrainian theological context, as it is used as a textbook in theological schools for understanding the historical and theological trajectories of what came to be known as the Evangelical-Baptist movement.[40] For a number of reasons, it is difficult to review the argument of this important self-identifying work. Having undertaken the task of surveying the theology and history of the diverse Evangelical-Baptist movement in Ukraine from its beginning until the present time, against the backdrop of Western Protestantism, the authors had to be highly selective and brief in their presentation of the vast subject matter.[41] They often do not present a coherent argument, but rather express their views abruptly without providing any support for their often questionable and sometimes erroneous interpretations.[42] Even though

38. Cf. Neill, *Western Saints in Holy Russia*, 61–81.

39. Reshetnikov and Sannikov, *Obzor Istorii Evangel'sko-Baptistskogo Bratstva na Ukraine*.

40. The word "Evangelical" originally referred to the tradition of the "Gospel Christians."

41. The book consists of 223 pages.

42. For one instance among many, the authors claim that Arminian theology was

the book contains a massive bibliography, it does not include the most important doctoral studies undertaken in Western universities and seminaries during the past forty years.[43] Although the authors refer to some important Soviet studies on sectarianism, the content of those studies is largely ignored. The book also lacks a systematic approach to referencing, which makes it difficult to understand the sources of the authors' ideas or material. There is no clear evidence that the authors have critically interacted with evangelical periodicals, which are indispensable primary sources, in order to rectify or explain the historiographic shifts of the Soviet period. It is surprising and telling that the very same material was published without noticeable modifications as an academic project by the Ukrainian Academy of Sciences.[44]

The proposal made by Reshetnikov and Sannikov is based on an appropriation of Western evangelical resources and Eastern Soviet evangelical historiography. However, the authors use the material of previous scholarship selectively in order to create a new identity story likely to satisfy both Western sponsors and partners and concerned Easterners with regard to the Western sects and denominations imported to Ukraine following the collapse of the Soviet Union. The argument is based on the assumption that evangelical Christianity in Ukraine is a unique synthesis of the Western Protestant tradition and a spiritual movement within Orthodoxy.[45] The authors state that Western Protestantism shaped the movement ideologically and ecclesiologically (organizationally), while

influential in the northern wing of the movement partly because of the influence of the British Darbyism and that of General Baptist doctrine (31). However, Darby was a Calvinist and the Arminian tendency was present in the tradition since its inception.

43. Cf. Filipovych and Kolodny "Theology and Religious Studies in the Postcommunist Ukraine," 92. In a private conversation, Iu. Reshetnikov admitted that he was not familiar with the content of many of the Western sources cited in the bibliography, even though he knew of their existence.

44. Iarotskii, *Istoriia Religii v Ukraiini*, vol. 5, *Protestantism v Ukraiini*, 241–420. See a penetrating critique of the Ukrainian Academy as a whole in "Slow train coming: Reform of Ukraine's archaic research system is needed sooner rather than later," *Nature* 440, 7081 (2006) 128–30, 132. Theological studies are in an embryonic state in Ukraine, as theology had been excluded from the registry of the Ministry of Education until June 2005. According to Professor V. M. Zhukovskii of Ostroh Academy there is no theological department in any of the universities of Ukraine at present. Zhukovsky made this statement in private e-mail correspondence on April 3, 2006.

45. Reshetnikov and Sannikov, *Obzor Istorii*, 9.

the theological influence of Orthodoxy is "impossible not to notice."[46] In this respect Reshetnikov and Sannikov are trying to achieve a more balanced synthesis of the late Prokhanov story of the native origin of the movement and Karev's story of its Western derivation, while taking into account the newly-important Orthodox background. According to their thesis, the Spirit led the evangelicals out of the Orthodox Church (Karetnikova's thesis) and later equipped the indigenous Eastern movement with resources developed in Western Protestantism. However, this argument is flawed from the very outset of the project, as no clear example of the influence of Orthodox theology is provided in the entire book.[47] Neither do the writers resolve the obvious contradictions of their own narrative that result from the rhetorical nature of their project. For example, the writers state that the evangelical movement[48] originated

46. Ibid.

47. Cf. Greenfeld, "Eastern Orthodox Influence on Russian Evangelical Ecclessiology." Greenfeld does not provide a single example of Orthodox influence on the tradition of "the Gospel Christians," mistakenly locating Lord Radstock in the General Baptist tradition (95). Similar argumentation is used by Kolomiytsev, "Sources of Authority in Russian Evangelical Theology," 52–71. However, because Kolomiytsev builds his argument for a Reformed fundamentalist post-Soviet theology on Soviet scholarship, he does not take into account the origin of the holiness tradition and mistakenly attributes its key characteristics, such as Arminian theology, experiential pneumatology, etc., exclusively to Orthodox influences. Sawatsky, *Soviet Evangelicals*, 341–42, is probably the author responsible for the historical confusion. Sawatsky erroneously attributes the non-systematic reasoning and emphasis on emotions to Orthodox influence, without taking into account the proto-Pentecostal Romantic paradigm which was planted by the charismatic mystic Radstock in St. Petersburg. This non-rationalistic pneumatic approach of Radstock and his worldview is a better alternative explanation for the theological imprecision and the imaginative approach to reality. It was demonstrated earlier that Radstock openly rejected Orthodox theology, spirituality, and practices, and that his followers emulated even minute aspects of his ministry. Sawatsky is also incorrect in claiming that the teaching of Darby played a vital role in the birth of the evangelical movement (341). Sawatsky is correct, however, in stating that "the most significant influence from Orthodoxy was the negative stimulus it provided" (342). Cf. Elliott, "Eastern Orthodox and Slavic Evangelicals," 15–16. Elliott does not define the term "Western evangelicalism" in his presentation; this makes his list questionable. It would have been fairer to compare the Eastern evangelical movement with respective Western holiness traditions. Elliott is right in noticing that Eastern evangelicalism has more in common theologically with freewill Nazarenes than with most U.S. Southern Baptists (15).

48. The term "evangelical movement" is used in the traditional Soviet sense. The authors do not focus on the differences between Gospel Christians, Baptists, Stundists, Mennonites, etc.

by Divine Providence without Western influence.[49] But in the following paragraph they note that a revival among Ukrainian peasants in Kherson Province began in a *German colony*, where the Russian peasant Onischenko worked as a hired hand for German Protestants.[50] The writers declare that the "Evangelical-Baptist movement is one of the branches of the radical Reformation, or Protestantism."[51] Yet several pages later they emphasize that although "[there is] an opinion that the movement originated as a result of German propaganda . . . that it was something brought in from the outside . . . [t]his opinion does not correspond to reality."[52] Instead of providing argumentation for the indigenous origin of the movement by engaging in a theological, ecclesiological, or hymnodic comparative analysis of the primary sources, the writers follow the Hegelian post-Cold War Soviet Baptist historiography in describing various movements within Orthodoxy, sometimes noting that certain dynamics in Orthodoxy were brought about by means of Western influences.[53] The fact that Orthodoxy was dynamic and experienced various influences does not necessarily serve as an argument that the so called Evangelical-Baptist movement was not a direct result of Western presence. The Western self-identity of the early evangelical movement, as well as the proselytizing activity of Western missionaries, is well documented in doctoral dissertations written in Ukraine and America.[54] The Baptist authors do not provide a satisfactory answer to the question of how a religious movement that began in German colonies in Ukraine and that ended up with a distinct Protestant theology, ecclesiology, hymnography, and Western self-identity within the first three decades of its existence could be interpreted ingenuously and not as a conversion from what was considered to be an archaic and deficient form of historic Christianity sullied by paganism.

49. Reshetnikov and Sannikov, *Obzor Istorii*, 75. Cf. 70.

50. Ibid. Cf. Hominuke, "Evangelical Christianity among the Ukrainians," 91: "This much could be said, that in 1850 [Onischenko] was attending regularly the German Evangelical Church, having adopted even their colonists' garb."

51. Reshetnikov and Sannikov, *Obzor Istorii*, 50.

52. Ibid., 59.

53. Ibid., 61–63.

54. Beznosova, "Pozdnee Protestantskoe Sektantstvo Iuga Ukrainy," 57–129; Zhuk, *Russia's Lost Reformation*, 275–76. Cf. Coleman, *Russian Baptists and Spiritual Revolution*, 14–17.

Even though the writers argue that, unlike all previous research projects,[55] they are presenting an objective study, the surprising omissions make it clear that, in constructing a new historical identity in the public domain of post-Soviet Ukraine, they are promoting a certain perspective that causes them to make highly subjective decisions as to which material to include or exclude from their presentation. One of the most striking omissions of the book is the erasure of the tradition of the Gospel Christians that originated with Radstock and Pashkov, the presence of which was felt in Ukraine early on. In their sketch of Western Protestant theology the authors describe the Protestant Reformation (ch. 1) and the Radical Reformation in Europe, with a specific focus on the Baptist tradition (ch. 2). The historical and theological roots of the movement in the revivalist paradigm of Radstock, Baedecker, and Pashkov are not brought into view.[56] Although the key leaders of the Gospel Christians are mentioned, their theological and historical identity is either erased[57] or is given a denominational Baptist outlook through selective referencing.[58] The clear Western derivation of the Gospel Christians and their well-recorded tradition creates a problem for the myth of the indigenous origin of the evangelical movement and is consequently removed from the process of constructing a new identity.

In their attempt to create a new identity, the authors express their uneasiness about the fact that the Gospel Christians and Baptists have usually been referred to in Orthodox and Soviet scholarship as "sectarians."[59] In order to restore the dignity of the movement, they argue that "in contemporary religious studies the term 'sect' is used to describe a religious group that has not been formed into a church, that lacks a hierarchy, institutes of authority, and professional education. The contemporary Ukrainian Baptist movement cannot be defined as a sect," they argue, "because it has all the characteristics of a church: clear doctrine, a structure of subordination, [and] a corpus of professional pastors."[60]

55. Reshetnikov and Sannikov, *Obzor Istorii*, 6–15.

56. Ibid., 32.

57. Ibid., 139.

58. Ibid., 140.

59. Ibid., 11. Cf. Negrov and Nikol'skaia, "Baptists as a Symbol of Sectarianism in Soviet and Post-Soviet Russia," 133–42.

60. Ibid.

As usual, the authors do not provide the source of their definition, while bypassing Ernst Troeltch's classic differentiation between "church" and "sect."[61] It is beyond the scope of the present research to discuss the "church-sect" typology, although there is obvious pertinence to this study in the typology's contrast between the voluntary nature of membership of the "sect" type and the "inherited" membership of the "church" type.

My intention is to point out the highly rhetorical and superficial nature of the work of the denominational writers. The definition advocated by Reshetniov and Sannikov is problematic on its own terms. According to their definition, the early history of the Gospel Christian movement was distinctively sectarian, while some of the religious bodies not traditionally associated with church typology, such as the Jehovah Witnesses, can be characterized as churches. In light of the definition newly established by the Baptist writers, the intuition of the militant atheist Yartsev, writing in 1928, sounds almost prophetic:

> . . . The Baptists do not mind oscillating in this regard: they either render tribute to democracy or bypass it. They follow the path of centralization and delegation of authority down the hierarchical ladder. The Gospel Christians follow the same route. This path has been trodden by Russian Orthodoxy and all other religions. . . . The office of presbyter was introduced among the Gospel Christians not long ago . . . but its future is brighter than that of the bastard democracy under whose façade all decisions are made by a group of *apparatchiki* and *kulaks*.[62]

A similar critique of the Russian sects was made by the Russian philosopher Nikolai Berdiaev, who wrote one year before the Bolshevik Revolution: "The sects begin with a spiritual burning and spiritual revival, but at the end they develop a self-sufficient sectarian mode of life, fossilized, cold, and enclosed. The spirit of the Baptists is the most repelling; they come into the circle of their sect and consider themselves to be saved, while the rest of the world is buried in darkness and perdition. This element is present in all sects."[63]

61. Troeltsch, *Social Teaching of the Christian Churches*, 331–35. Cf. Nesdoly, "Evangelical Sectarianism in Russia," 1–44. Nesdoly's dissertation is built upon critical engagement with Troeltsch's classical work. Troeltsch's book is available in Russian.

62. Iartsev, *Sekta*, 14–15.

63. Berdiaev, "Dukhovnoe Khristianstvo i Sektantstvo v Rossii," 454. See 441–62.

The later Pashkov's original vision of interdenominational ecumenical unity based on devotion to Christ and mutual love in the Spirit, rather than on a doctrinal system or organization with professional ministers, is not discussed or even mentioned in the work of these Baptist history writers. According to their definition, the interdenominational movement of Gospel Christians was sectarian until it became institutionalized in the power structure of the Baptist Union. The self-identity of the movement is presented reactively against the backdrop of the National Church, whose theology is misrepresented by oversimplification or sheer omission.[64]

Thus the historical identity constructed by Reshetnikov and Sannikov is deeply problematic. It is made possible only by a selective reading of the complex tradition and selective interaction with scholarship from a specifically denominational point of view, as well as by creating new definitions detached from established scholarship. The authors do not demonstrate the presence of Orthodox theology in the Evangelical-Baptist tradition. Neither are they successful in demonstrating the Orthodox origins of the movement, nor do they differentiate between the distinctively revivalist pan-evangelical and pro-ecumenical tradition of the Gospel Christians and the narrowly denominational viewpoint resisted by the first generation of Gospel Christians. They perpetuate Prokhanov's interpretation of the indigenous origins of the evangelical movement, which he developed after the Bolshevik Revolution. The new element appearing in the work is that the authors have depicted Slavic evangelicalism not only against the background of Orthodoxy but also against that of the European Reformation, thereby attempting to synthesize the Western self-description of Karev and the Eastern self-identity of the later Prokhanov and of the post-Cold War denominational historians. This synthesis is not worked out, however, but is rather imposed on the reader without any argumentation.

The Gospel Christian identity is suppressed, as the authors pursue the distinctly organized identity of a modern denomination that stands as an institutional rival to the Byzantine Orthodox Church. By creating a

64. In their discussion of the relationship between scripture and tradition, the authors manage not to present the Orthodox view on the issue (see pp. 19–20). Sannikov makes no reference to the work of Alister E. McGrath, *Reformation Thought*, from which he derived his material. This omission is surprising, as Sannikov wrote an introduction to the Russian translation of this book: Alister Magrat, *Bogoslovskaia Mysl' Reformatsii* (Odessa: Bogomyslie, 1994).

hybridized "Eastern-Western" self-identity, represented as an organized religious institution, Sannikov and Reshetnikov present the heirs of the AUCECB as the outgrowth of an Orthodox spiritual movement which at the same time is identical to some of the traditions of the Radical Reformation of the West. This move makes the tradition appear compatible with a variety of Western Protestant bodies that perceive ecclesiastical restorationism as the apex of spiritual evolution. As in the case of Karetnikova, one of the major deficiencies of this identity construction is that it gives assurance of the superiority of a primitivist form of Christianity (in this case, the Protestant Paradigm in general which is brought into view) over Orthodoxy (the Byzantine Paradigm), which is implicitly perceived as an archaic form of Christianity that needs simply to be overcome, rather than engaged through dialogue. As a result, no dialogue or even any attempts at dialogue with Orthodoxy seem to be taking place in Ukraine.[65] Like Bachinin's identity construction, the construction of Reshetnikov and Sannikov is made possible only by means of a series of historical erasures and a lack of interaction with the primary sources of the tradition, as well as with established scholarship.

V. I. Davidiuk

V. I. Davidiuk has for a number of years been the President of the Ukrainian branch of the Light in the East Mission and the council chairman of the Association of Missionary Churches of Gospel Christians of Ukraine.[66] In the interview recounted below, Davidiuk said that by the end of the Soviet period he had become strongly dissatisfied with his personal experience in the local Baptist Church. He was concerned "why so few people from the world" came to church and why "some

65. In my interview with the Rector of the Ukrainian Orthodox Spiritual Academy of the Kiev Patriarchy, Bishop Dmytro Rudiuk, he pointed out that no dialogue is taking place between evangelicals and the Orthodox in Ukraine. While acknowledging the difficult state of religious affairs in Ukraine with regard to the split Orthodox Church, the Bishop confirmed an openness to cooperate with evangelicals in educational and theological projects. The interview was conducted on April 19, 2007.

66. See www.amcecu.org and www.sns.org.ua. The Association of Missionary Churches of Gospel Christians of Ukraine is one of many evangelical bodies that associate themselves with the Gospel Christians usually associated with the name of I. S. Prokhanov.

questions are answered because 'it is done this way in our denomination' and not because the solution has a scriptural ground."

Under the inspiration of the interdenominational Russian-speaking radio evangelist Earl Poysti, a graduate of National Bible College and New York University, Davidiuk organized a Bible study in his church to promote the teachings of Poysti and the printed materials of the Navigators'. Conducting unsanctioned rival Bible study meetings was not welcomed by the official leaders of his Baptist church, and because of this activity Davidiuk was even threatened with possible excommunication. While these meetings brought about consolidation among some church members, they were seen as unpredictable by the church leadership.

However, after giving his word to the leaders of his local congregation that he was not going to cause a schism, Davidiuk was allowed to leave in peace. "I knew where I was coming from, but I did not know where I was going; I had a group of about forty people that was meeting in my house. I made several attempts to assimilate this group of new believers into my local congregation but it was of no avail. The only thing I knew was that there were thousands of people around me who needed the simple Gospel message. I clearly saw that educated people of the late Soviet period were not attracted to the Baptist church. A new church was formed out of this group of new converts. I thus kept my word given to the leadership of the Baptist church that I would not cause a schism within the church."

The following years were devoted to multiple missionary and pastoral activities in Ukraine. Davidiuk made international as well as national contacts by participating in the International Congress on World Evangelization held in Manila in 1989 (under the auspices of the Lausanne Movement), and several months prior to that by becoming part of the first indigenous missionary association in the USSR, called the *Light of the Gospel.* This association united likeminded Soviet evangelicals of the new generation who were inspired by the vision of starting new churches in the USSR in light of the new missionary opportunities and freedoms. Through international contacts made in the Philippines by representatives of the *Light of the Gospel* mission, a Bible college was started in Donetsk, which was later renamed Donetsk Christian University. It was envisioned that this educational center would play a crucial role for mission in the Soviet Union. As a result of the activities of the *Light of the Gospel*, many churches were planted in various countries of the CIS.

Being among the leaders of this then-growing missionary movement, Davidiuk served as a member of the Board of Trustees of Donetsk Christian University and actively participated in the planting of new churches in Ukraine. According to Davidiuk's testimony, when he started his first church he did not want to be associated with any denomination.

> We just wanted to help people understand the Gospel message and experience the transforming power of God in their lives. When we were ready to register our first congregation, we were told that we needed to have a name. We decided therefore to be called "Gospel Christians." I never studied history. I just somehow knew that the Gospel Christians associated with the name of Prokhanov were freer than the Baptists. Thus in our church any member of the congregation was allowed to baptize or administer communion if the entire congregation had authorized that member for these activities. We welcomed people from different denominational backgrounds. We were ready to extend our fellowship to any person whose thoughts and deeds were devoted to Christ.

Contacts were made in 1990 with the German *Light in the East* mission. Even though the history of this mission is inseparably intertwined with that of the Gospel Christians of Prokhanov's time, and especially of the time after Prokhanov's death, when one of the founders of *Light in the East*, Pastor Walter Zhak, took Prokhanov's place, Davidiuk pays little attention to these historical trajectories. At the same time, he does not deny that some people may indeed see a historical succession, given the establishment of the Association of Missionary Churches of Gospel Christians of Ukraine in 1999. This Association unites evangelical churches of various doctrinal and ecclesiological shades on the basis of key evangelical values.

However, the poles of unity with regard to essential evangelical values and diversity in the area of doctrine create dynamics in the Association that make it rather unstable, as some of the member churches would prefer the more centralized structure and doctrinal clarity that a denomination would provide. The present self-identification of the Gospel Christians is world evangelicalism according to its Bebbingtonian definition. The Pentecostal and charismatic movements are viewed with suspicion, as was the case during the later Prokhanov period. According to its official historiography, the roots of the Association go back to 1988, when the door for missionary outreach began to open in the Soviet Union. Thus the historic identities of the evangelical movement during the Russian and Soviet periods do not seem to play a significant role in the construction of a Post-Soviet identity. A number of churches started by various Western evangelical agencies have become part of the Association. At present, the Association consists of forty-seven churches and five mission agencies located in different parts of Ukraine. Total church membership in 2007 was 2460 people, which represents a slight decline in membership since 2005.[67] After nearly two decades of massive missionary activity in the former Soviet Union, the Association of Gospel Christians has come to a place where it is beginning to reflect on its self-identity and theology. The change of tide of the Western presence in the country makes it crucial that the past, present, and future of the Association be reevaluated.

THEOLOGY

Alexander de Chalandeau on the Theology of *Bratskii Vestnik*: The Soviet Period

Alexander de Chalandeau undertook an analysis of the theology of *Bratskii Vestnik*.[68] His work is the only available study on this topic. As his dissertation was written during the Cold War, Chalandeau lacked the necessary primary sources, and the historical part of his dissertation uncritically repeats the historiography of *Bratskii Vestnik*.[69] However, unlike Karev, he identifies the Gospel Christians with the Plymouth Brethren, without specifying the nature of this identification.[70] His work is based on the assumption that the AUCECB has an indigenous theology that needs to be studied and systematized.[71] The author does not seem to be aware that the materials published in *Bratskii Vestnik* were actually derived from distinctively Western sources and were intended for purposes other than theological systematization through the

67. In 2005 there were 2505 members.

68. De Chalandeau, "Theology of the Evangelical Christians-Baptists in the USSR."

69. Ibid., 1–58.

70. Ibid., xii, 62.

71. Ibid., x.

theological grid of the fundamentalist theology used in the analysis. As Chalandeau did not have access to the materials used in the Bible courses offered in Moscow since 1967, his study seems to be somewhat incomplete and under-researched. Chalandeau does not seem to have been aware that the academic dean for this program, V. A. Mitskevich, was a recent graduate of Spurgeon's College or that the dogmatic theology course taught in the Bible school had been compiled from works by the American authors William Evans[72] and Edgar Young Mullins.[73] By means of their international contacts, Soviet evangelicals had access to certain English-language resources. Having established contact with the Moody Bible Institute in the 1920s, they continued to rely on the scholarship of this evangelical institution. Despite its obvious deficiencies, Chalandeau's study confirms that the treatment of theological themes in *Bratskii Vestnik* was in line with Anglo-American conservative evangelical theology. Chalandeau seems to have had two major frustrations with the tradition he analyzed. First, from his strictly fundamentalist point of view the quality of the theology that appeared in *Bratskii Vestnik* was becoming more muddled under the new leadership in the Union.[74] Second, Chalandeau noted that due to the heterogeneous nature of the Union, Soviet evangelicals were unable to grasp fine theological points, since mutually-exclusive theological positions could be preached in the same churches by different preachers without any seeming conflict.[75] It was the nature of the AUCECB to support theological polyphony, without establishing a research culture with rational theological discourse that would facilitate reflection on diverse theological positions.

The major theological turbulence, which Chalandeau did not detect, took place with regard to the doctrine of eschatology. Due to their harsh experiences in the 1930s, the Soviet evangelicals rejected the Modernist postmillennialism of Prokhanov, appropriating instead the dispensational Romantic premillennialism of Kargel as their default teaching.[76] This theological dynamic is understandable in light of the

72. Evans, *Great Doctrines of the Bible.*

73. Mullins, *Baptist Beliefs.* See Savinskii et al., *Istoriia Evangel'skikh Khristian-Baptistov v SSSR*, 269.

74. De Chalandeau, "Theology of the Evangelical Christians-Baptists in the USSR," 107.

75. Ibid., 105.

76. Ibid., 141–53.

atheistic context that suppressed all forms of religion, as well as the restoration of the state of Israel in 1948. The heated atmosphere of the Cold War and the danger of nuclear engagement between the world superpowers established dispensational premillennialism as an undisputed doctrine during the Soviet period. This premillennial turn was fully in line with the trajectory represented by the Moody Bible Institute.

Except for the premillennial turn, the theological riverbed did not undergo any abrupt modifications from the time of Prokhanov and Kargel, as the Soviet evangelicals were forced to rely on printed materials from the 1920s. The acceptance of Pentecostals into the Union caused the leadership of the tradition to be more careful with regard to their teaching on pneumatology. Karev was a promoter of the Keswickian spirituality of Kargel and Prokhanov, interpreting baptism with the Holy Spirit in terms of spiritual rebirth.[77] However, the sharp anti-Pentecostal rhetoric of his teachers is absent from the pages of *Bratskii Vestnik*. It did not take long, however, for the critical articles written by Kargel and Prokhanov in the 1920s to be republished and widely distributed after 1991.

Chalandeau did not pay attention to the fact that in 1946 the Soviet evangelicals claimed that their theological statement of faith was nothing other than the Apostles' Creed.[78] "This Apostles' Creed is of value to us, because it expresses in condensed form the very essence of our teaching."[79] The earlier creeds written by Prokhanov and Kargel were not mentioned until two decades later.[80] It is likely that the artificially-created heterogeneous Union did not have any resources for producing a unifying statement, while the previous evangelical creeds were probably either unknown or forgotten. Thus the Apostles' Creed served as the foundation for unity for a number of years. However, their subsequent participation in ecumenical organizations pressed the leadership of the Union to appropriate creeds of a distinctly evangelical origin.

Biblical interpretation during the Soviet period did not undergo many changes from the 1920s. However, one article written by a prominent contributor to *Bratskii Vestnik*, Ivan Motorin, added a new dimension to the established Christocentric literalist-typological interpretation

77. Cf. ibid., 126–40.

78. *Bratskii Vestnik*, "Vo Chto my Verim," 3 (1946).

79. Ibid.

80. *Bratskii Vestnik*, "Verouchenie Evangel'skikh Khristian Baptistov," 4 (1966).

of scripture practiced since the days of Radstock and Moody.[81] On the one hand, Motorin was aware of the modernistic tendency in Western seminaries to read scripture in ways that shifted the focus from Christ as Savior to Christ as a messenger of universal salvation. "The central vice of some contemporary theologians is that they approach the Bible as a rich human book, which lacks the spirit of divine life. . . . They read it as they do any other human book."[82] Having given some recommendations as to how to read scripture according to the approach to inductive Bible study followed by Torrey and Moody, Motorin provides an insight that had previously been absent in the tradition. He writes:

> In studying scripture in the light of scripture, we should refer to the spiritual heritage given to us by men of faith and ministers in the vineyard of the Lord. Their works contain many valuable and precious things. The history of the church includes many names of men who knew the Bible in depth and who effectively ministered by preaching its message and interpreting its content. We find these names both during the time of the Apostles and in our own time. Thus gifted authors such as Tertullian, Origen, Basil, Gregory, Chrysostom, Jerome, Augustine, and others left a rich heritage. In our time, the names of Spurgeon, Moody, Torrey, Kargel, and Prokhanov are known. All of these are luminaries of evangelical thought, which cannot be bypassed if we want to study the Bible seriously, know it, and be effective in our ministry. We must remember that the experience of men of faith of the past, their knowledge and heritage, should not only be thoroughly appropriated, but every believer should try to multiply these unsearchable riches of Christ. The truth of the Gospel has never been revealed in all its fullness to any prophet, apostle, or man of faith. Everyone has known it only in part. Only the church universal, which is the gathering of all the saints and is the pillar and foundation of the truth, is the bearer of revelation and knowledge of the will of Christ. She is the holder of the great treasury into which every man of faith, every male or female minister of God, drops their coins according to the gift of Christ. . . . Only in fellowship with all the saints do we approach the understanding of the fullness of his will in greater measure.[83]

81. Idem, "Kak Izuchat' Bibliiu," 1 (1947).

82. Ibid.

83. Ibid.

Motorin's vision reflects insight into the Orthodox concept of *sobornost'*. According to this concept, the world of scripture can be understood only within the framework of the church universal. However, this vision of Motorin has never been developed in the tradition, partly due to the lack of access to the spiritual heritage of the past, and partly due to the lack of educated theologians and historians who would be able to pursue such a vision.

The Post-Soviet Theological Vision in Ukraine in the Work of Reshetnikov and Sannikov: A Conservative Trajectory

The erasure of portions of the history of the tradition of the Gospel Christians resulted in the omission of its foundational theological themes. The Baptist writers manage not to mention the Keswickian roots of the evangelical movement or identify divergent theological streams in the artificially unified tradition of the Gospel Christians and Baptists. Much attention is paid to the clash between Arminian and Calvinistic theological streams, which seems to be more an issue of post-Soviet evangelical struggles than of struggles within the Baptist or Evangelical traditions of the past.[84] The authors do not seem to notice the tensions or differences between the theology of Kargel and that of Prokhanov. The theological construction is as selective as is the proposed construction of the historical identity. Following the fundamentalist trajectory of the late Soviet Baptists, the authors begin their discussion of theology not with God or the work of the Spirit, but with the principle of *sola scriptura*,[85] thus solidifying the shift from the theocentric pneumatological theology of Prokhanov and Kargel to a rationalistic Bible-centered approach common to the conservative mainstream of American evangelicalism. In their brief discussion of the Trinity the authors demonstrate their awareness of the *filioque* issue, but make an excuse for not developing Trinitarian theology by stating: "It is clear that the indigenous Baptist movement had no desire to step into this highly difficult discussion in

84. Reshetnikov and Sannikov, *Obzor Istorii*, 24–32. Sometimes the Calvinist-Arminian polemic among Ukrainian evangelicals is more of a pragmatic than a theological nature, as some Western sponsors require that their Ukrainian partners hold to the same Reformed doctrines that they do in order to receive financial support for their projects. This was pointed out to me in many private and confidential conversations with different evangelical leaders in Ukraine.

85. Ibid., 18–22.

Orthodox canonical territories. . . . [T]his issue has almost never been discussed."[86] The authors do not take into account the fact that any form of abstract metaphysical theologizing was consciously suppressed in the primitivist holiness tradition whose spirituality was shared by the Baptists and the Gospel Christians. The issue of Orthodox canonical territories as an excuse for not developing Trinitarian theology is not advanced any further so as to provide a critique, but the very presence of this idea indicates a tacit awareness of Orthodox civilization.

A significant theological shift is made by the authors which has had important ramifications for the development of post-Soviet theology and incipient academia in Ukraine. The writers identify with American theological fundamentalism the pious and "nearly mystical" attitude of Russian and Ukrainian evangelicals towards the scriptures as the inspired Word of God. "Biblical conservatism and fundamentalism influenced nearly one hundred percent of this religious group."[87] The authors use the high view of scripture in the tradition to develop their fundamentalist discourse, utilizing scripture as the epistemological instrument for objective and scientific knowledge of God's truth. The nature of the fundamentalist discourse is seen in their sketchy discussion of the Bible and biblical interpretation.

The writers do not attempt to undertake a diachronical survey of biblical interpretation in the tradition. Instead, they adopt definitions of American conservative theology with regard to biblical interpretation. The following sort of theological language was unfamiliar in the pietistic communities in Ukraine before the collapse of the Soviet Union: "The Bible has a dual authorship and nature (divine and human). . . . This means that God gave to humankind an ahistorical . . . revelation and preserved it in copies and translations which are the Word of God to the degree that they are faithful to the autograph. . . . This dual nature of the Bible requires prayerful literal grammatico-historical interpretation, under the illuminating influence of the Holy Spirit."[88]

The switch to discourse identical to that of the old Princeton theology of Hodge and Warfield occurs without any introduction, comment, or road sign.[89] By not telling the reader about the theological origin of

86. Reshetnikov and Sannikov, *Obzor Istorii*, 23. Italics added.

87. Ibid., 21.

88. Ibid., 22.

89. Sandeen, *Roots of Fundamentalism*, 128. Cf. Dayton, *Discovering an Evangelical*

the quoted definition, the authors give the impression that these views originated in the Ukrainian-Russian evangelical tradition.[90] One of the reasons the authors do not mention the Keswickian roots of Slavic evangelical spirituality common to the Baptists and Gospel Christians may be their unarticulated conviction that doing theology in the key of rationalistic foundationalism, which does not seem to be easily compatible with experiential nature of the Keswickian holiness tradition, is the path on which post-Soviet evangelical theology should tread.[91] However, the authors do not develop a theological discourse that would enable one to come to more definite conclusions.

The Post-Soviet Theological Vision Presented in the Work of Mikhail Cherenkov: A Liberal Trajectory

The recently-published dissertation of M. N. Cherenkov was written under the supervision of Professor P. L. Iarotskii.[92] In contrast to the discourse of American fundamentalism, Cherenkov's work develops the liberal trajectory of Adolf von Harnack,[93] which had been latently present in the worldview of Prokhanov. Unlike Reshetnikov and Sannikov, whose theological worldview was shaped under the influence of conservative American professors at Odessa Theological Seminary, Cherenkov has not been educated within the context of a theological tradition. The modality of his thought and form of argumentation reflects the historically contingent intellectual tradition cultivated at the secular universities of post-Soviet Ukraine.

As with Reshetnikov's dissertation, Cherenkov's work is difficult to analyze because of the extremely broad scope of his research and his inadequate interaction with his sources as a result. One gets the impression that the sources are chosen randomly, simply on the basis of their accessibility in the Ukrainian context. The author does not present a coherent argument but overwhelms the reader with various theories, none of which receives sufficient analysis and critique. The author does not explain why he chooses specific dialogue partners, nor does he dem-

Heritage, 121–35. See also Barr, *Fundamentalism*.

90. Reshetnikov and Sannikov, *Obzor Istorii*, 21.

91. See the critique of the holiness movement in Warfield, *Perfectionism*.

92. M. N. Cherenkov, *Evropeiska Reformatsia*.

93. Cf. ibid., 113, 155–56, 274–75.

onstrate adequate acquaintance with the critical analysis of theories in the context of the respective discourses in the Western academy, even though he includes in his bibliography more than twenty somewhat random English titles. The dissertation is built largely on publicly available translations of English-language works into Russian. However, it does not give the sense that its author is aware of the intellectual traditions and contexts out of which these fragments of Western discourses are taken. The bibliography does not contain a single reference to any doctoral dissertation in the field, which explains the author's lack of awareness of Western academic standards for interacting with primary and secondary sources, as well as with selected dialogical partners in a clearly defined field of appropriate size, in order to be able to make an original contribution to knowledge in a particular field.

Representatives of this segment of the Ukrainian academy seem to prefer to establish their own standards. The number of cited sources and the use of complex scientific nomenclature seem to be of greatest value within this interpretive community. The approach to nomenclature in Cherenkov's work could be classified as "terrorist obscurantism." As Michael Foucault said of Derrida: "He writes so obscurely you can't tell what he's saying, that's the obscurantism part, and then when you criticize him, he can always say, 'You didn't understand me; you're an idiot.' That's the terrorism part."[94] Even though the main thesis (or, to be more precise, one of the many main theses) of Cherenkov's work may be boiled down to "the necessity of consolidating around the universals of European culture and . . . of entering the European space as a full and responsible subject, having overcome cross-cultural and interdenominational alienation . . . , "[95] this very work reflects a misunderstanding of the basic standards for academic argumentation within the context of heterogeneous European academic tradition.

I will provide a couple of examples among many to demonstrate the point. The author writes: "The universality of Protestantism as a metahistorical spiritual paradigm includes as its condition the unity of its archetype and the diversity of national traditions, as well as their dialogue, synthesis, and borrowing."[96] Nowhere in the work is it properly argued that Protestantism is a universal metahistoriacal and spiritual

94. Postrel and Feser, "Reality Principles," 2.

95. Cherenkov, *Evropeiska Reformatsia*, 453.

96. Ibid., 32.

paradigm, nor am I sure that this thesis could be argued for, as it is nonsensical if the words are used in their conventional sense. Protestantism is a historical, not a metahistorical, paradigm that has its roots in very specific historical circumstances, and as such is a socially and politically contingent phenomenon. The author continues: "The ecumenical theologian Hans Küng broadens the Reformation paradigm so as to include the whole of church history. He makes reference to a series of revolutions whose leaders were reformers—people like the Apostle Paul, Origen, Luther, Shleiermacher, and Karl Barth. According to this approach the Reformation is viewed not only as a distinct phenomenon, but also as a regularity of church history."[97] While this perspective is attributed to Küng, the Ukrainian author neglects to provide a reference as to where Küng supposedly expresses this view of church history. The Russian translation of Küng's book, *The Great Christian Thinkers*, cited in Cherenkov's bibliography, neither discusses metahistorical paradigms nor extends the Reformation paradigm to include all of church history. If Cherenkov takes "the Reformation" to mean the dialectical process of constant change in the Christian tradition that leads to different paradigms, he should have argued for a new definition of the term, which has a stable conventional meaning in the West. It does not seem sufficient simply to state that "the Reformation may be viewed as a principle of spiritual life common to all Christians."[98] This thesis should be argued for, as the dialectic of change is also found in all living traditions outside of Christianity. To build on this thesis without proper argumentation for it is to build a castle of sand on the seashore. The same can be said about the term "Protestantism," because, Cherenkov continues, "Protestantism does not endanger the dogmatic basis of the Russian Orthodox faith but rather can be viewed as the critical method of theology common to all confessions of faith. So we should not speak about theological incommensurability but about differences in methods and forms of preaching."[99] This statement seems to be meaningless, as well, because "Protestantism" conventionally stands for a heterogeneous religious movement in Western Christianity under whose umbrella there is a variety of religious groups with respective theological methods institutionalized in different establishments. This confusion, which may

97. Ibid., 48.

98. Ibid., 113.

99. Ibid., 112.

be attributed to the theological incompetence of the research institution at which the dissertation was examined, can be better understood in light of the Christological understanding of the Ukrainian author of this obscure piece of work.

In the following analysis of Cherenkov's dissertation, my aim is to identify its theological platform and to point to its theological trajectory within the theological narrative of the tradition of the Gospel Christians. This aim will be achieved through a study of the Christology reflected in Cherenkov's works. However, before doing this I would like to say something about his understanding of the historical identity of the Gospel Christians, as reflected in his dissertation.

Even though the name of Paul Ricoeur, who argues that identity is formed by means of narratives,[100] is briefly mentioned, the dissertation does not attempt to analyze in any depth the various self-identifying narratives of Ukrainian evangelicals. According to the author's definition, the evangelical churches "are all late Protestant communities (except for the Jehovah's Witnesses), unlike in Western Protestantism, where the term 'evangelicals' usually refers only to the Baptists and the Pentecostals.'"[101] In light of this definition, which ignores major Western studies of evangelicalism, all the historical constructions of different periods disappear from the research focus of his work. However, the dissertation fully supports the extreme historical reconstruction of Bachinin discussed earlier.[102]

The study of Christology in the works of Cherenkov should begin with his candidate dissertation done in the Department of Philosophy at Donetsk National University.[103] The main thesis of this work is that "atheistic I-humanism should be replaced by the humanism of the Other" on the platform of "universal values and the will and potential to continue human history."[104] The word "Other" in the philosophical work of Cherenkov signifies a whole range of related terms: "The concept of 'the Other' (another person, life, being, transcendence) is a key term in the contemporary study of humanism."[105] Because this humanistic

100. Ibid., 86.

101. Ibid., 13.

102. Ibid., 165.

103. Cherenkov, *Filosofsko-istoricheskoe Pereosmyslenie.*

104. Ibid., 5.

105. Ibid., 173.

ideology is viewed in terms of "objectivity" and of a "scientific project," the scriptures and biblical revelation play no epistemological role in this work. Although the Old and New Testaments are discussed in the second chapter of the dissertation, he does not refer to them at all in his main conclusions at the end of the chapter. According to Cherenkov, "Universalistic tendencies, which had been implicitly present in the Old Testament corpus, were formed and found their perfection in the teaching of Christ (or that of the Christians)."[106] In the author's view, this "teaching of Christ (or that of the Christians)" is the climax of humanism. Jesus, in Cherenkov's understanding, "preached, lived, and thought almost exclusively within the frame of understanding of the Jewish religion of the first century. However, in certain directions he transcended that frame and opened for his followers opportunities to creatively develop his logic, to interpret and reinterpret those ideas in which the tension between 'old' and 'new,' between Jewish and Christian, was *felt*."[107] Jesus is presented in purely humanistic terms: he is a first-century Jew who provided the hermeneutical key for establishing a universal religion (or rather ideology), which was shaped and reshaped later by his disciples. The work does not depict Jesus as being the unique Son of God, nor does it use the language of the Trinitarian ontology of God employed in the Apostolic witness.[108] Instead, the concept of divine sonship is transposed and applied to all of humanity. "The son of God" is not the preexistent and incarnate Logos, but humanity in general:

> God reveals himself to humanity not as a natural force or an absolute idea, but as a person, the Father, who calls humankind his son. Christianity enabled the transcendent God to be close to humankind and established a family relationship between them. It recognized the kindred connection of humankind with the celestial world. The divine-human relationship is realized from now on *in a single human dimension*. . . . The fullness of the fatherly relationship of God with humankind is revealed in the New Testament. Humankind is not only created by God but also born of him. Humankind is thought of as God's own son (even though he is called a "prodigal son") and the rightful heir. In this

106. Ibid., 88.
107. Ibid.
108. Cf. Wright, *What Saint Paul Really Said*, ch. 4.

> sense we can say that *God and humankind are counted as equal in terms of their origin and potential.*[109]

Because in Cherenkov's construction the language of the ontological uniqueness of Jesus' sonship is transposed to a humanistic frame of reference, the redemption Jesus accomplished is not mentioned in the dissertation and is omitted from his presentation of the biblical drama of "creation–fall–redemption–glorification" as something irrelevant: "To summarize, we can say that the biblical authors, in their attempt to create a holistic and historical concept of humankind's journey from the creation of the world to the Day of Judgment, were faced with problems that were unresolved and that are still relevant for contemporary thinkers. . . . Perhaps the diversity of biblical understandings can be explained by the absence of one single exhaustive answer."[110] In order to emphasize the diversity and openness of Christian discourse, Cherenkov refers to the work of James Dunn on unity and diversity in the New Testament, which has been translated into Russian. He neglects to mention, however, that the concept of unity in Dunn's presentation is attached to the apostolic kerygma that presents the narrative identity of Jesus as the Son of God who was crucified for the sins of the world and rose on the third day.[111] In light of this transposition, it is not surprising that the main method for biblical interpretation adopted by Cherenkov is the existentialist method of "demythologization" developed by Rudolf Bultmann.[112]

The Christology expressed in Cherenkov's candidate dissertation on humanism does not seem to undergo any significant changes in the doctoral dissertation he wrote on the European Reformation and evangelical Christianity in Ukraine. Even though he often mentions that evangelical Christians adhere to the conservative theological position of "*sola scriptura, sola fide, sola gratia*" and that they believe in the inspiration of scripture, his main dialogue partners throughout the work are liberal theologians and humanistic philosophers. Their philosophical programs and epistemological assumptions are neither discussed nor critiqued, nor is the conservative critique of liberal trends analyzed in

109. Cherenkov, *Filosofsko-istoricheskoe Pereosmyslenie*, 98. Italics mine.

110. Ibid., 104.

111. Dunn, *Unity and Diversity in the New Testament.*

112. Cherenkov, *Filosofsko-istoricheskoe Pereosmyslenie*, 47.

any depth. The conservative theology and expressions of evangelical leaders of the past and present are assimilated and absorbed into the purely humanistic and somewhat random discourse of the author:

> The revelation of the New Testament cannot be found in a complete form because the very actualization, continuation, and creative reproduction of the faith of Christ and the Apostles reveals more completely the nature of the Gospel. According to this understanding, the source of theology is not so much Holy Scripture as a historical-theological document as it is the living actuality of faith, the events of spiritual life. Protestant evangelical theology, unlike the Orthodox and Catholic traditions, does not perceive revelation to be part of church tradition, which sets boundaries and serves as a key to interpretation.[113]

Having made this incorrect statement about evangelical theology—which unlike liberal thought holds that divine revelation is found in the person of God's Son, Jesus Christ, and in the canonical text of scripture—Cherenkov reflects in his dissertation his misunderstanding of evangelicalism. One may find it surprising that in a dissertation devoted to evangelicalism the author makes no mention or use of books on evangelical theology that are widely available in Russian.[114]

For now, I will forego any discussion of the concept of revelation in Patristic and Reformed theology. The point will be made sufficiently by analyzing the meaning of the clause "the . . . actualization . . . of the faith of Christ and the Apostles reveals more completely the nature of the Gospel" in the quotation above. In their understanding of the Apostolic kerygma, neither the European Reformers nor Ukrainian Gospel Christians have ever seen the phrase "the faith of Christ" as being purely subjective genitive. Instead, the genitive has always been viewed as objective (or as a genitive of mystery, a subjective-objective genitive). As an objective genitive, the phrase means that Christ is the object of faith. So they view Christ as the object of faith (and as the originator of faith in the genitive of mystery), while Cherenkov argues that Christians actualize the subjective faith of Jesus. The faith of the Apostles, the Church Fathers, the Reformers, and Eastern Gospel Christians is faith in Christ and his redemptive work. This understanding is fixed in the

113. Cherenkov, *Evropeiska Reformatsiia*, 185.

114. Cf. McGrath, *Christian Theology*, published in Russian in 1998; and Erickson, *Christian Theology*, published in Russian in 1999.

Apostles' Creed. In contrast, the Ukrainian author's homemade definition, unsupported by any argument, reflects the individualistic mindset of the humanistic Enlightenment. He sees no qualitative difference in the faith of Christ, the faith of the Apostles, and the faith of the following generations of Christians. According to this reading, Jesus Christ is not God's unique Son, but only the founder of the "faith." For this reason, the definition refers not to faith in Christ but to "the faith of Christ and apostles"—that is, to the faith that Jesus and the Apostles had. Thus the nature of the Gospel is found, not in the Apostolic witness about Christ, which is sealed by the Spirit in the biblical canon, but in the "actualization" by other individuals "of the faith of Christ and the Apostles." This statement views Christ, the Apostles, and other believers on the same level: The Apostles and ordinary believers are different from Christ only in degree, rather than in nature, and have the same potential for the creative reproduction of this faith. Quoting the work of Joachim Jeremias, written four decades ago, the author argues without any critique or comments: "According to the reconstruction of Jeremias, the sermon of Jesus was eschatological. Jesus expected the end of the world to come in his lifetime. . . . According to Jeremias the image of Christ was too human and apocalyptic, so the Apostles made corrections to his teaching, in which Easter as metahistorical event replaced eschatology."[115]

In the rest of the work, the dated method of demythologization is utilized as the primary method of biblical interpretation.[116] The author reveals his lack of knowledge of the field of New Testament studies over the past forty years, despite the fact that some important works have been translated into Russian and are widely available in the Ukrainian context.[117] However, for one reason or another they are neither mentioned nor referred to in this highly selective work.[118]

A clear example of demythologization or "the actualization of the faith of Christ and the Apostles" is seen in Cherenkov's interpretation of the Christmas event:

115. Cherenkov, *Evropeiska Reformatsiia*, 185.

116. Cf. ibid., 156, 239, 276, 280.

117. Wright, *Jesus and the Victory of God*, published in Russian in 2004.

118. To name a few: Blomberg, *Interpreting the Parables*, published in Russian in 2005; Ladd, *Theology of the New Testament*, published in Russian in 2003; and Morris, *New Testament Theology*, published in Russian in 1996.

> "We are born to make a tale to be a true story." These words from a song of the Soviet era are probably not known to younger readers. And their author was perhaps not thinking about what I am thinking of. What I am thinking is this: we lack a tale in our life, a tale that would change this life, that would make it interesting and happy. Christmas for many people is simply a tale far removed from reality. But for me it is a TALE which *can* become a true story. So you live in the pitch darkness of loneliness . . . and suddenly God comes . . . as a cute baby, as the incarnation of goodness and love. . . . During this time of financial and spiritual crisis, when people do not believe anyone, the tale of Christmas may soften the heart, cause a kind smile, and give hope.[119]

In his book *The Third Truth*, published by the evangelical Association for Spiritual Renewal, Cherenkov builds on the material of his candidate dissertation.[120] From the first sentences of the book, where the author writes that "a human being always starts with the self," to its last pages, where the author exalts humanism, he accomplishes the transposition of biblical concepts into a humanistic frame, while intertextually and superficially interacting with a large number of heterogeneous sources. This book is a clear manifestation of the postmodernist subject being torn apart in an ocean of textual fragments and random quotations. The key terms whose conventional meaning among evangelicals is radically changed are "revelation" and "God." According to this book, the reader should come to an understanding of the "third truth," which is the truth of God. The first truth is one's own truth (or worldview), while the second truth is the worldview of the other (that is, other human beings). However, when the reader arrives at the shortest chapter of the book, the title of which is identical to the title of the book itself, she discovers that the author has nothing to say other than to make the rather trivial statement that truth belongs to God.[121] In the following chapter the author clarifies where the revelation of God should be found: "The mystery of meeting and fellowship, of friendship and love. This *is* the revelation: when the other reveals me myself, and when in the face of the other is revealed the Third. If two people love each other, then God abides between them. And this mystery is great indeed."[122] Thus revelation is

119. Cherenkov, "My Rozdeny chtob Skazku Sdelat' Byl'iu," 50.

120. Idem, *Tret'ia Pravda*.

121. Ibid., 78.

122. Ibid., 81.

found not in the person of the incarnate Son of God or in the inspired witness about him, but in human relationships of love and friendship. In light of this changing of the connotation of the term "revelation," it becomes obvious that the phrase "biblical God" also suffers a transformation. In the chapter "The Biblical God: The One and Only," there is no hint that, as the Apostle John says, the biblical God is revealed in the person of Jesus Christ: "No one has ever seen God, but God the One and Only, who is at the Father's side, has made him known" (John 1:18). Neither can one find any trace of understanding of Christian pneumatology or Trinitarian doctrine. The center of Cherenkov's message is not the Apostolic kerygma about the revelation of God in the person of the crucified and resurrected Jesus, but a humanistic message of the "One": "The One God rules the world; he knows all the complexities and contradictions of life and perceives the destinies of everyone. Faith in such a God calms a person in the midst of what appears to be the triumph of evil. Only when the world is understood as created and cared for by the One can it be perceived as morally just and fair. Faith in the One God is faith in the ultimate victory of goodness and in the ultimate meaning and harmonious beauty of the universe."[123] The narrative identity of Christ, grounded in the Apostolic witness, plays no role in the Ukrainian author's liberal reconstruction.

The rejection of Chalcedonian Christology and the Nicene Creed, which play crucial roles as hermeneutical lenses in Patristic and Reformed theology, is the reason why such concepts as "metahistorical" and "universal," which are grounded in the ontology of the Incarnate Logos in the language of evangelical discourse, are transposed and applied to the historically contingent phenomena of the sixteenth century. "The Reformation" and "Protestantism" become "metahistorical" and "universal" at the expense of the historical particularization of Jesus as a first-century Jew, "who preached, lived, and thought almost exclusively in the frame of understanding of the Jewish religion of the first century," and whose major contribution was to open "for his followers opportunities to creatively develop his logic." The historical phenomena become "metahistorical" due to brazen theological linguistic disruption. The language of the unique deity and humanity of Jesus is torn asunder to signify the divinity of the Father and the universal humanity. It is in the love and friendship of human beings that the Third One is revealed. It

123. Ibid., 92.

should be noted, however, that the One of the humanistic tradition is different from the One of more ancient religions such as Judaism and Islam. In this newer religion, "*God and humankind are counted as equal in terms of their origin and potential.*" In the thought of this Ukrainian philosopher, the humanistic One is not the omnipotent Creator who is ontologically different from creation, nor "The Father" of humankind, but rather "The Big Brother" who may sometimes be speaking with a somewhat louder voice. Even though Cherenkov references the Russian translation of *Dogmatics in Outline* by Karl Barth in both his candidate and doctoral dissertations, Barth's main argument, which is set within the boundaries of the Apostles' Creed, is ignored and not interacted with in these works.

One may hope that eventually Dr. Cherenkov and the new theological school of Professor Iarotskii will be able to produce a coherent argument to support their insights, taking into account the conventional standards of the European theological community and of established and ongoing academic discourses. In particular, one would wish to see a clear argument for the necessity of switching from the evangelical way of theologizing within the frame of the Apostles' Creed to the existential mode that takes European cultural processes as its major criterion and gauge. However, taking into account two factors—the financing of these research programs by the state and state licensing of the degrees—one would not be surprised if this neo-monotheistic religion of the Enlightenment takes the course of expanding and multiplying research projects of this sort of quality, with its local standards, instead of investing finances and intellectual efforts into integrating with the Western theological community in a tradition-continuous way when a particular religious tradition is studied.

Cherenkov writes that "to be a humanist means to row upstream by resisting conventional opinions, the inertia of the masses, and the current state of affairs. Humanism is always a critical position from which humankind and the world are viewed ideally—a position that is independent of state authority and the stereotypes it imposes as well as of the dominating traditions."[124] Yet, despite his high opinion of humanism, for one reason or another Cherenkov decided not to critically analyze the philosophical shifts of the humanistic tradition of his supervisor, P. Iarotskii. In the bibliography of his doctoral dissertation Cherenkov lists

124. Ibid., 205.

only the works of Iarotskii written during the post-Soviet period. Half a century ago, the Institute of Philosophy of the Ukrainian Academy of Sciences was not a neutral institution, nor has it become ideologically neutral now, despite its claims to "objectivity." Cherenkov's dissertation reveals that the humanistic tradition, which is institutionalized in this educational establishment, is consistent in its promotion of the ideology of the ruling authorities. In Soviet times, Professor Iarotskii was a disseminator of Soviet anti-liberal ideology.[125] After the collapse of the Soviet Union he became a supervisor of research projects in the area of "objective" and "scientific" religious studies that promote pro-European Ukrainian aspirations and integration into liberal capitalist civilization. One will not find in Cherenkov's dissertation any critical reflection on these ideological shifts and turns in this historically contingent institution, whose standards and methodology he naïvely takes to be "objective." Neither will one find any criticism of "liberal democracy," with its ideologies and myths, in light of the metahistorical drama of Easter. If such self-reflection has not been accomplished, the best dialogical partners for this sort of project may be St. Augustine and Alasdair MacIntyre.[126]

Because Cherenkov's dissertation was published by an evangelical organization, one may conclude that in the Eastern evangelical movement, the liberal trajectory, which had been latently present in the worldview of Prokhanov, has now explicitly appeared. This may be attributed to liberal sources newly translated into the Russian language and mediated by secular institutions that inherited from the Soviet era their monopoly in the domain of licensed education. The appearance of this mode of thought has not resulted in any serious discussions among evangelicals in the Ukraine, which may partly be explained by the lack of theological competence among evangelical leaders and communities.

125. P. L. Iarotskii, *Klerikal'nyi Antisovetizm*, 250–78; *Antikomunistichna sutnist' Uniats'ko-natsionalistichnoi fal'sifikatsii istorii ukrain'skogo narodu*, 9, 189. See also *Antikomunizm Social'no-Politichnoi Doctriny Egovizmy*; *Krisis Iegovizma*; *Evolutisia Sovremennogo Iegovizma*; and *Uniatstvo i Klerikal'nyi Antikomunizm*.

126. Augustine, *Confessions*, and Alasdair MacIntyre, *Marxism and Christianity*.

THE POST-SOVIET PRACTICE OF BIBLICAL INTERPRETATION

The historiographic erasures characteristic of the work of Reshetnikov and Sannikov can be detected in the practice of biblical interpretation in the tradition since the collapse of the Soviet Union. At this juncture our main interlocutor is Vitalii Tkachuk.[127] Tkachuk was born in 1942 and began pastoring an AUCECB church in Odessa in 1975. Between 1989 and 1994 he served as the superintendant of the AUCECB in the Odessa region. Then in 1994 he moved to Kiev and for a number of years served as vice-president of the Ukrainian Union of Gospel Christians-Baptists. Tkachuk graduated from the Correspondence Bible Course in Moscow in 1985 and from the Odessa Bible School in 1993. He received his doctoral degree by completing an unaccredited doctor of ministry program offered jointly by Kiev Theological Seminary and Odessa Theological Seminary.[128] Tkachuk's work is chosen for several reasons. First, the author's credentials qualify him as one of the best representatives of current evangelical thought in Ukraine. Second, the bibliographical references included in Tkachuk's book reflect almost all the sources on hermeneutics and exegesis translated from English that are widely used in evangelical seminaries in Ukraine. As such, the book is the best example of the practice of biblical interpretation in the tradition of the Gospel Christians-Baptists in Ukraine at the beginning of the twenty-first century. My task in reviewing Tkachuk's book is largely descriptive. I seek to demonstrate the shift that took place in the practice of biblical interpretation without going into an in-depth critique of it. In a future research project I will attempt to reconstruct the practice of biblical interpretation, taking into account its diachronic development.

The structure and much of the content of Tkachuk's book mirrors that of Henry A. Virkler's text on evangelical hermeneutics.[129] As a result of Tkachuk's heavy dependence on Western texts recently translated from English into Russian, one will search in vain for any discussion of biblical interpretation in the tradition's past. The names and works of the key shapers of the tradition's practice—people such as Prokhanov,

127. Tkachuk, *Metody i Printsipy Tolkovania Sviashchennogo Pisania.*

128. The above-mentioned S. V. Sannikov is also a graduate of this program. There is no accredited doctoral program in theology in Ukraine.

129. Virkler, *Hermeneutics.*

Kargel, and Bykov—are missing from the bibliographical list. Following a typically fundamentalist trajectory, Tkachuk starts his bibliography with Scofield's reference Bible, which was translated into Russian and has been widely distributed during the post-Soviet era.

Joining the chorus of mainline American evangelicals and fundamentalists, Tkachuk glorifies the inductive Bible study method: "Hermeneutics is considered as science because it has rules which can be systematized. The rules and principles of this science are not arbitrary, since they were not established by church councils or synods. They are genuinely scientific because they are *obvious*, comprehensive, and inductive in nature."[130]

However, despite his claims regarding the scientific nature of the project, it suffers from an abundance of sweeping generalizations and a lack of interaction with or references to primary and secondary sources or to the critiques of "scientific methodology" by such giants of twentieth-century hermeneutics as Gadamer and Ricoeur.[131] In his presentation, Tkachuk does not build a scholarly argument but imposes his views by means of a rather arbitrary differentiation between "healthy" and "unhealthy" hermeneutics.[132] Argumentation seems to be unnecessary, as the hermeneutical theory is presented as *obvious*. Healthy hermeneutics is said to be built on the "grammatico-historical" method of interpretation. Tkachuk states: "This healthy kind of biblical interpretation . . . can be found in the early Christian history of the first century. Later it can be found in the Syrian-Antiochian school and later yet in the works of Nicolas of Lyra and Erasmus, Luther, and Calvin. They interpreted the Bible historically, according to 'the rules of grammar and facts of history.'"[133] In saying this, Tkachuk does not actually interact with the works of the authorities mentioned or with secondary works on their hermeneutics. He continues: "Unhealthy hermeneutics, on the other hand, is characterized by the following features: (1) stretching the text

130. Tkachuk, *Metody i Printsipy*, 4. Italics added.

131. The classical work of Gadamer, *Truth and Method*, was published in Russian early on. See G. G. Gadamer, *Istina i Metod* (Moskva: Progress, 1988). Paul Ricouer's *The Conflict of Interpretations* was published under the title *Konflikt Interpretatsii: Ocherki o Germenevtike* (Moskva: Kanon, 1995). But these works are not mentioned in Tkachuk's book. There is no indication in the text that he was aware of these hermeneutical theories and the critique they provide for the "scientific" approach in hermeneutics.

132. Cf. Bray, *Biblical Interpretation*, 354–55.

133. Tkachuk, *Metody i Printsipy*, 32.

to fit one's preferred interpretation—it is the text that should "bend" the interpreter, and not the other way around; (2) shallow interpretation—the interpreter should not improvise when interpreting texts but rather should work hard to apply the principles of healthy hermeneutics; and (3) allegorical interpretation."[134]

In contrast to these unhealthy approaches, Tkachuk provides six principles of healthy interpretation drawn from the Western evangelical textbooks on hermeneutics cited in his bibliography, which includes only references to texts available in Russian: (1) The Principle of Literal Interpretation. Literal interpretation is commonsensical. The text should be taken at face value. Literal interpretation stands in contrast to allegorical interpretation.[135] (2) The Grammatical Principle. According to this principle one should read the text in its immediate context. One needs to understand the grammar of a sentence well in order to produce a healthy interpretation. The meaning of every individual word can be determined by consulting a good dictionary and paying attention to its context. "Many words in the Bible have a single meaning which is context-independent."[136] (3) The Literary Principle. In this longest section Tkachuk discusses different genres of scripture and provides rules for interpreting various kinds of figures of speech, including metaphor, irony, and synecdoche.[137] (4) The Historical Principle. In order to understand the text properly, one needs to know the events "behind" the text. To know who the authors and their audiences were, as well as the circumstances of the text's composition, is crucial for understanding its meaning.[138] (5) The Principle of Synthesis. This principle is built on the assumption of the unity of scripture. Thus no interpretation should contradict the obvious meaning of other scriptural texts. The New Testament has priority over the Old Testament, and the Gospels are to be interpreted in light of the Epistles. No interpretation should contradict the analogy of faith—the harmonious system of truths that is said to characterize scripture. Each truth in the system has a different value, depending on the number of references to that truth, the unity of

134. Ibid., 33–36.

135. Ibid., 37–40.

136. Ibid., 41–44.

137. Ibid., 49–80.

138. Ibid., 81–87.

the references within their contexts, their clarity, and their diversity.[139] (6) The Principle of Practical Application. Scripture should not only be interpreted but also applied. The application of biblical texts is built on the ability of the interpreter to *imagine* herself as the author or original addressee. Having empathetically imagined herself in the situation of the author, the interpreter is encouraged to express the meaning in her own words for her own context.[140] A given text of scripture should be applied personally to the interpreter on the basis of 2 Tim 3:16–17. In the process of application, the interpreter should remember the historical nature of some of the biblical commandments. In a rather arbitrary manner, Tkachuk provides a set of supposedly obvious and common-sensical principles that should guide the interpreter in the process of cultural transposition. For example, Tkachuk interprets the recommendation Paul gave to Timothy in 1 Tim 5:23 concerning the consumption of wine as a local and non-transitive cultural prescription.[141] According to this reading, "This prescription was given to Timothy for his own individual use. When doctors issue a prescription, they write the name of a particular patient, and other individuals are forbidden to make use of a prescription written for someone else."[142] Tkachuk is not concerned about providing any thorough argumentation or criteria for his "rules." In this case, he seems to be quite comfortable using contemporary medical practice as an obvious and universal framework for filtering out what he does not consider to be transcultural in Paul's epistle to Timothy. Tkachuk does not develop his interpretation any further, so as to come to any definite conclusions as to exactly how he desires to make use of this interpretive framework and produce meaning for his theological system. This example illustrates how easy it is to take historically contingent practices such as the writing of medical prescriptions and derive or construct "obvious" universal principles without any further argumentation.

Tkachuk's hermeneutical text can be reduced to a rather static algorithmic methodology for an individualistic discovery of supposedly objective truths from the Bible with the help of a dictionary and lexicon. His uncritical adaptation of the universal framework of Western evan-

139. Ibid., 87–93.

140. Ibid., 93.

141. Ibid., 93–101, 98.

142. Ibid., 98.

gelical scholarship erased the history of the practice of biblical interpretation in the tradition and eliminated the historical particularity of the Gospel Christians in the post-Soviet context. This elimination of the historical horizon of a distinctive community of readers results in a rather arbitrary imposition of interpretive rules. In this respect, Tkachuk, like Reshetnikov and Sannikov, continues the tradition of authoritarian and radical transformations of theology and theological practices in the community. Instead of developing a narrative that could facilitate changes to the tradition's practices, he rather arbitrarily eliminates the past and uncritically makes use of Western textbooks to transform the practice of biblical interpretation. It is easier to create "a rule" establishing the need to interpret the Gospel narrative in light of the didactic material in the Epistles than it is to provide a rational argument as to why this must be and on what criteria this rule is built.[143] Tkachuk's rule in this particular case is based on the assumption that a narrative is not an appropriate means for shaping the theology and identity of the community. Instead, the propositional truths of didactic material are given priority. To suggest the priority of the Epistles over the Gospels is to forget that "the Bible is not primarily a book of timeless doctrines or a book of moral law. It is primarily a story. . . . Story is the overarching category in which [other genres] are contextualized."[144]

Despite its claims to scientific rigor, Tkachuk's approach does not attempt to explain the disarray of competing "objective" interpretations found in different scholarly commentaries that fragmentize and splinter evangelical groups, both in Ukraine and in other parts of the world, over a number of issues, including Arminian vs. Calvinist theology, charismatic practices vs. cessationism, and evolutionary theory vs. creationism, to name a few. Neither does it demonstrate a rigorous evaluation of the criteria used to formulate the rules of "healthy interpretation." It naively assumes that an individual researcher, armed with evangelical dictionaries and lexicons recently translated into Russian, can uniformly reconstruct the "behind-the-text" setting, which is of crucial importance for "correct" interpretation. No less naïvely, it assumes that every interpreter who simply follows Tkachuk's healthy rules will imagine the historical setting of the text in the same way, or will come to the same conclusion with regard to the genre and literary details of the text in

143. Ibid., 88.

144. Bauckham, *Scripture and Authority Today*, 10.

view. Despite his claims to objectivity, the rules of cultural transposition produced by Tkachuk open the door for incommensurable and arbitrary interpretations. Given the lack of rigorous argumentation and interaction with established scholarship, Tkachuk's work claims authority on the basis only of his personal preferences with regard to distinguishing between "healthy" and "unhealthy" hermeneutics. Thus on Tkachuk's account, the Patristic and medieval practice of biblical interpretation, as well as that of the Gospel Christians in Ukraine prior to 1991, is "unhealthy" by default. Every community that does not practice this "healthy" sort of interpretation needs to be "healed" through conversion, rather than being engaged through dialogue. The historic fathers of the Gospel Christians are slaughtered and eliminated by their sons from the memory of the tradition, because the former had been dead wrong in interpreting scripture, not having taken into account the latter's standards based on the historico-grammatical method. This authoritarian rationality that claims universal objectivity does not seem to be different in essence from the "scientific," "objective," and "obvious" nature of the Marxist ideology that dominated the Soviet context for a number of decades.

Despite his desire to erase the previous methodology of biblical interpretation, Tkachuk's approach is, in fact, built on an assumption articulated by Bykov, who was more realistic with regard to interpretive differences. According to Bykov, the correct interpretation of a given passage of scripture is that which is held by whoever is more spiritually mature. And it often happens that the people who occupy this privileged slot are the representatives of ecclesial hierarchies who control educational institutions, accrediting agencies, and publishing houses. If there are any conflicts in interpretation, it is *their* version of "objective" reconstruction that will be counted as truly "objective" and "scientific," despite the fact that a rival tradition may use the very same methodology but calibrate the historic and linguistic data differently.[145]

145. One tragic illustration of such an interpretive collision was the clash of vision over the nature of spiritual leadership at Donetsk Christian University in 2002. As a result of the interpretive conflict, the President and Academic Dean as well as many faculty members left the university. The new leadership of DCU was not able to launch the already-validated MTh program in Contextual Theology mentioned in the introductory chapter, and the number of full-time students dropped from 120 in 2000 to eight in 2008.

Tkachuk's book does not make it clear why lay members of Christian communities should read the Bible or do inductive study themselves, as suggested by the interpretive methodology, rather than simply reading the works of experts who are more knowledgeable in ancient languages and historical studies. It would seem that commentaries by experts who have followed the rules of healthy hermeneutics should be considered more valuable than the rough and uninterpreted material found directly in the scriptures. Tkachuk's work on hermeneutics does not explain why ordinary church members should read his work, rather than reading inductively-produced Bible commentaries and correcting their understanding of the Bible by aligning their thinking with that reflected in more objective scholarly volumes. And from an academic point of view, it is not clear why Tkachuk produced this work, since Henry Virkler's book, which was translated into Russian earlier, presents a more coherent and scholarly account of inductive Bible study. Tkachuk's work does not seem to have much academic or ecclesial value. In light of this research, it does, however, have significant hi/storical value. It demonstrates a recent shift in the practice of biblical interpretation: leading Ukrainian evangelicals have switched to the "objective" and scientific methodology introduced by North American missionaries without looking back into their own past, and without looking around in search of more appropriate dialogue partners.

CONCLUSION

Under the tremendous pressures of the Soviet period, the tradition of the Gospel Christians had to adjust its identity, theology, and biblical interpretation to the state of the geopolitical force field between East and West. During the Cold War its identity was rooted in a distinctively Protestant framework, while during the post-Cold War period its identity has been presented either in terms of the evolutionary development of Russian Orthodoxy or as an organic synthesis of a purified Russian Orthodoxy and Western Protestantism. This evolutionary and reactive perspective creates a false sense of pious superiority which prevents theological dialogue between the Protestant and Orthodox paradigms. And the Slavophile messianic drive shifted along the lines of the modified narrative. During the Cold War period the tradition was presented as the best and most unique representative of free evangelicalism in the world. Following the Cold War it was rhetorically represented as the unique synthesis of Orthodoxy and Protestantism. As a result of the acute institutionalization of the tradition during the Soviet period, it took on a Baptist self-identity that was relevant for representing Soviet Protestantism internationally. However, the collapse of the Soviet system led toward separation from the institutionalized Baptist Union. The newly-established association of Gospel Christians in Ukraine, represented by V. I. Davidiuk, identifies itself with the worldwide evangelical movement, without attempting to construct a unique Eastern self-identity or theology.

This overview of theological developments has demonstrated that evangelical theology in Ukraine depends on the input of Western conservative evangelical theology, which is not always sufficiently or critically understood or even acknowledged by Eastern evangelicals. The shift from the postmillennialism of Prokhanov to the premillennialism of Kargel was the major theological development during the period. This theological turn prepared the tradition for total absorption by the mainstream of Western conservative evangelical theology. Because the AUCECB was brought into existence by the state authorities during World War II, this heterogeneous Protestant body was held together for several decades on the platform of the Apostles' Creed and by the practice of tolerance toward diverse Biblical interpretations. The apex of differential Biblical interpretation is found in the article by Motorin, who suggested that scripture be read in light of the insights of the masters of Christian tradition, both past and present. Systematic articulation of theology was not possible, however, due to the heterogeneous nature of the communities and the artificial bonds that united them. The sudden collapse of the Soviet Union did not give time to establish a hermeneutical horizon for developing consistent and comprehensive tradition-continuous theologies or practices. As the work of Reshetnikov and Sannikov demonstrates, the tradition-continuous survival strategy was found in uncritical dependence on the unreferenced importation of conservative Anglo-American discourse, as well as in selective readings of past theological and historical fragments.

The work of M. N. Cherenkov demonstrates the emergence of a liberal tendency in the Eastern evangelical movement. This may be attributed to the influence of secularism in the non-church-related educational establishments of Ukraine, which have a monopoly on licensed education in this domain. However, it is too early to talk about the level of influence or even of acceptance of this trajectory, which had been latent in the evangelical interpretive community in the worldview of Prokhanov.

The tradition's practice of biblical interpretation underwent radical modification under the intense influence of Western missions. Just as its narrative self-identity was modified by a series of selective readings from the past, its practice of biblical interpretation was modified in a rather radical way. As has been noted, Vitalii Tkachuk does not deal with developments in the practice of biblical interpretation within his own tradition. Instead, he uncritically adopts conservative Western hermeneutics, which is characterized by claims to universality and by the rather arbitrary imposition of algorithmic "rules" for reading scripture along grammatico-historical lines. The authoritarian nature of this shift can be well understood against the backdrop of two major factors. First, the lack of indigenous scholarship resulted in the simplest solution possible: to erase the past and to borrow Western resources that were flooding the country. Second, the centrifugal processes that were splintering the AUCECB needed to be resisted. The radical diversity of biblical interpretation that had characterized the tradition before the collapse of the Soviet Union was exchanged for the radical homogeneity of interpretation provided by the algorithmic inductive method of conservative Western hermeneutics. This "scientific" turn in biblical interpretation provided the necessary centripetal forces for homogenizing the tradition. One of the side effects of the radical switch in the tradition's narrative identity, theology, and practice of biblical interpretation is the lack of a genuine research culture and scholarly dialogical interaction, the appearance of which threatens the structures of authority that freely create narratives and modify practices.

In the following theological and hermeneutical reconstruction I suggest that the way out of the current crisis of identity and theology should not be sought in the authoritative imposition of criteria that claim universality, obviousness, and "healthiness" by eliminating the community's past identity, theology, and practices. Reversing the process of absorption by universal and ahistorical Western evangelical theology, influenced by the rationality of modernity, I will pursue a postmodern realist and particularistic reconstruction of the identity and theology of the historically contingent tradition.

7

The Gospel Christians: On the Way to a New Theological Framework and a New Identity

"Lack of justice, lack of truthfulness, lack of courage, lack of the relevant intellectual virtues—these corrupt traditions, just as they do those institutions and practices which derive their life from the traditions of which they are the contemporary embodiments."[1]

INTRODUCTION

It was demonstrated in the previous chapters that the tradition of the Gospel Christians followed the theological lead of the fundamentalist wing of Anglo-American evangelicalism. In light of this discovery we are in a position to extrapolate this trajectory by bringing it into critical dialogue with selected contemporary trends in Western evangelical theology. In this chapter I will explore the critical realist and holistic (coherentist) realist programs that have found their way into the Ukrainian evangelical milieu. After critically evaluating these approaches, I will demonstrate the applicability of the holistic realist program for resolving the current epistemic crisis in the tradition. This theological engagement will accomplish two goals: (1) it will reconstruct the post-Soviet self-identity of the Gospel Christians in Ukraine, and (2) by accomplishing the first goal, it will demonstrate the applicability of holistic realist theology. This reconstruction will open the door for doing post-Soviet evangelical theology within the emerging postmodern paradigm originally discussed by Hans Küng.

1. McIntyre, *After Virtue*, 207.

ON THE WAY TO RESOLVING THE PENDING ISSUE OF THE SELF-IDENTITY OF THE GOSPEL CHRISTIANS

Articulating the identity of the Ukrainian Gospel Christians is the most important task to be accomplished by this research, as the practices of the tradition will not be effective without a clear and coherent self-identifying narrative that is able to explain the current experiences of the community. In the historical part of our research it was demonstrated that previous self-identifying narratives were dependent on the frequent changes in the configuration of both Western and Eastern civilization. Creative leaders of the tradition constructed every new self-identifying narrative to re-establish lost coherence and relevance. And this same geopolitical factor plays an important role in the painful process of finding a particular historical identity in the present, as well. As Ukrainian society balances between the Euro-Asian Orthodox and Western poles, so do the Gospel Christians. In the previous chapter it was argued that the post-Soviet historical reconstructions of self-identity depict Gospel Christians both as part of worldwide evangelicalism and as an indigenous outgrowth of Orthodoxy, given the prominence of Orthodox culture.

However, in the process of reconstructing the identity of the movement, one needs to remember that the current configuration of both the Orthodox and Western civilizations is different than it was either at the time of the inception of the tradition or in the aftermath of the Bolshevik revolution. It was demonstrated earlier that the conversion of some of Radstock's followers to the Protestant paradigm occurred in part in response to the decadence of Orthodox civilization, against the background of the superior Western civilization of the time. The present situation looks rather different, however. The culture of the pre-modern Orthodox civilization that has reappeared stands out as a viable option against the background of the collapse of the Enlightenment Project in the West and the poor performance of Western Christendom in its attempts to cope with the post-modern situation.[2]

But while the resuscitated world of Orthodoxy promises an alternative path of development, it is too early to make any judgments about its performance in the post-Soviet context.[3] Its rich liturgy and the

2. Cf. Oden, *Two Worlds*.

3. See an insightful collection of essays in Witte and Bourdeaux, *Proselytism and Orthodoxy in Russia*, 56–61.

mystical orientation of its apophatic theology, as represented by bright saints, scientists, philosophers, and theologians, looks attractive to some in the post-modern milieu of the West, as well as to many in the East.[4] Its gravitational pull has moved some evangelicals in both Ukraine and America to full-fledged conversion,[5] while less mesmerized evangelicals are attempting to contextualize their outlook, as well as their methods of evangelism, within the Orthodox milieu, without abandoning their fundamental Protestant convictions and theology.[6] However, the majority of Ukrainian Gospel Christians have changed neither the appearance nor the practices of their form of life. Their survival strategy of disengagement from the culture and its own heritage has contributed significantly to the contemporary crisis, especially in light of the Western retreat following nearly two decades of intensive, massive, but not very efficacious activity.[7] This is the rough and shifting contextual background against which the theological construction will be developed in this chapter. Unfortunately, I have no choice but to proceed with this construction during a notorious season of bad roads in Russia and Ukraine, when the ground, or rather mud, is continually causing one's foot to slip. There is no sign that this theological season is going to change anytime soon.

Before taking the first step towards a constructive reworking of the tradition's narrative, I need to bring into focus the major findings of my historical research. It was demonstrated earlier that, despite the emic story of its indigenous origin, the DNA test of the tradition is positive with regard to its belonging to the Anglo-American revivalist evangelicalism of the late nineteenth century. As such, the tradition cannot change its theological framework even if it attempts to reconstruct its trajectory beginning with the time of St. Vladimir, or the times of Cyril and Methodius, by means of an imaginative interpolation on the diachronic graph of Orthodox dissent. Neither can it present a single work of indigenous theology to establish its Eastern credentials, as it has been continually and uncritically adjusting throughout the years of

4. Cf. Oden, *Rebirth of Orthodoxy*; Tanner and Hall, *Ancient and Postmodern Christianity*.

5. Kobzar', *Pochemu ia ne mogy Ostavat'sia Baptistom i Protestantom voobshche*. Cf. Clendenin, *Eastern Orthodox Christianity*, 164–67.

6. Andriy Murzin, "As an Orthodox among Orthodox."

7. Cf. Turlac, "Crisis in Evangelical Christian-Baptist Theological Education in the Former Soviet Union."

its existence to the sound of the conservative evangelical tuning fork. The inappropriate use of imagination and/or biased scholarship produce incoherence in the historical narratives or do injustice to the past, or both. It was the burden of the historical part of our research to clear the blockage caused by Soviet and post-Soviet denominational historiography. The following discussion is built on the premise that the tradition of Russian/Ukrainian Gospel Christians, which was thrown into existence by the surging wave of Anglo-American revivalism, has been organically connected with the world of Western evangelicalism ever since.

The historical and theological analysis included in the previous chapters has created a hermeneutical situation that allows for the making a number of interpretive moves, many of which were intuitively suggested by earlier researchers. One possible strategy is a synchronic dialogue with the competitive tradition of Russian Orthodoxy. This is the strategy that was attempted by Donald Fairbairn.[8] However, even though this route will eventually be inevitable, it seems premature in the current situation. Taking into account the present unresolved differences within local evangelicalism and the divided state of Ukrainian Orthodoxy, direct and official dialogue may not be fruitful. In order to be able to enter into meaningful dialogue with those outside the Protestant paradigm, Ukrainian evangelicals need to process and reflect upon their fragmentized and mercurial past and present. For the same reason, the strategy suggested by Darrell Cosden of dialoguing with other local traditions throughout the world seems premature, as well.[9] In his article, Cosden used the metaphor of a growing child who needs to come of age and articulate her own thoughts and perspectives by dialoguing with others. He applied this figure of speech to Eastern evangelicalism which as "the youngest child . . . seeks to establish her own identity and uniqueness in relationship with and in contrast to her more dominant brothers and sisters."[10] I would suggest, however, that this metaphor is unfortunate, inasmuch as it is grounded in dated historiography. Ukrainian evangelicals need to overcome not so much a puberty crisis as the middle-age crisis of a person who has spent most of his life in prison. Now is the moment in his life when he comes to the realization that he has awakened

8. Fairbairn, *Eastern Orthodoxy through Western Eyes*. Cf. Sawatsky, "Slavic Evangelicals in Mission within the Commonwealth of Independent States," 203.

9. Cosden, "Coming of Age," 319.

10. Ibid., 323.

in a new world, whose language and structure he does not understand. The variable set of glorious stories about his life that he often told both before and during his imprisonment needs to be reevaluated in light of scripture, tradition, reason, and present experience. The naïve excitement of his illusions, in which he perceived himself to be the hero of the world, has evaporated. The old world is gone, and the old language of the tradition cannot piece together either the broken fragments of the past or the threatening diversity of the present.

In light of the changed metaphor, I suggest a strategy of recollection and contemplation of the fragmentized narratives and theological practices of the past. This recollection should not be conducted, however, in narcissistic seclusion, but rather while listening to the theological dialogues taking place within the family of Anglo-American evangelical theologies. This approach will organically continue the trajectory of reliance on Anglo-American theological discourse, but with the important difference that it will be done in a critical mode. The self-critical and critical components will constantly be supported by the incoherent past of the tradition, as well as by the failure of the Western mission since the collapse of the Soviet Union to persuade Eastern Europeans to embrace the Western paradigm. This ongoing conversation in the "parent directory" will provide Ukrainian evangelicals with the necessary background, as well as with discourse in the post-modern global village. In order to proceed with our construction we need to take into account some of the developments in Western evangelicalism that brought the Slavic evangelical tradition into being.

SOME DEVELOPMENTS IN WESTERN EVANGELICALISM

The discussions and debates in the Anglo-American theological discourse of the post-modern period are immense.[11] The growing cacophony of voices and the subtleties of these debates can be bewildering, as one crosses the linguistic wall between the former Soviet Union and the West.[12] However, the porous linguistic barrier dividing the cultures may serve as a navigating device for guiding and developing the discourse. In the following analysis I will concentrate on two modes of evangelical

11. Cf. Vanhoozer, *Cambridge Companion to Postmodern Theology*.

12. Cf. Levison and Pope-Levison, *Return to Babel*.

theology that have penetrated the Ukrainian evangelical tradition since the collapse of the Soviet Union.

The Fundamentalist Trajectory

In his article, Cosden points out that conservative Anglo-American evangelical theology is considered an attractive model by many Ukrainian evangelicals.[13] This is not surprising, as nearly all theological resources available in the country were translated from English with the generous financial assistance of Western evangelical Institutions following the collapse of the Soviet Union.[14] However, Cosden goes a step further by demonstrating the contextual nature of conservative Anglo-American theology and by asking whether that particular contextual form is the best model to be emulated in the Ukrainian context.[15] Even though his article presents an oversimplified perspective on the development of trajectories in both the Western and Eastern branches of Protestantism, it pushes the question in the right direction, in light of the growing crisis in theological education in Ukraine.[16]

In contrast to Cosden's conventional understanding of the indigenous development of the tradition as "the younger sibling," we demonstrated that the Gospel Christian movement is not a sibling but a child of Western evangelicalism, whose tradition has moved along the conservative evangelical trajectory from the beginning. We saw that Prokhanov became personally acquainted with the leaders of the evangelical fundamentalist movement in 1925, and that he highly commended their writings as "pure evangelicalism," without fully understanding the nature of their discourse. One can only guess how the trajectory might have developed within the milieu of Communism, had it not been stopped by the brutal force of militant atheism. A recent MA thesis by A. Kolomiytsev, a graduate of a fundamentalist institution, provides a clue.

Kolomiytsev critiques Prokhanov for his experiential pneumatic approach and argues for the full-fledged conversion of the tradition to the

13. Cosden, "Coming of Age," 319.

14. Penner, "Critical Evaluation of Recent Developments in the Commonwealth of Independent States," 18–19.

15. Cosden, "Coming of Age," 325–29.

16. Turlac, "The Crisis."

contemporary fundamentalist mold.[17] Despite his highly critical attitude towards evangelical beginnings in Russia and Ukraine, Kolomiytsev has taken to its logical conclusion the tendency that Prokhanov himself introduced into the evangelical movement in Russia. We have demonstrated that unlike the Romantic Radstock, Pashkov, and Kargel, Prokhanov cherished nineteenth-century Modernist optimism about science and the scientific method. This vector of theological development is not surprising, since the objective scientific reasoning of fundamentalism reflects the same sort of rationality found in the Soviet school system, with its naïve realism[18] and its belief in the inductive method and objective scientific study. Thus fundamentalist rationality is easily understood in the post-Soviet milieu.[19] Its simplicity and resultant clarity give many evangelicals the feeling that they are standing on firm ground with clear safety boundaries in the dizzying vortex of socio-political and cultural motion.

In light of contemporary developments in North American culture in general, and in the philosophy of science and theology in particular, Cosden points out that the mainstream of conservative American evangelicalism is a contextualized form of Christianity significantly impacted by Enlightenment rationality.[20] Nancey Murphy has demonstrated the line of development in both conservative evangelicalism and liberalism in America. According to Murphy's thesis, both conservative evangelicalism and its rival, liberalism, are grounded in the individualistic rationality initiated by René Descartes, who began the lonely search for universal and undeniable foundations for certain knowledge.[21] Tracing the trajectory of philosophical development, Murphy convincingly demonstrates that conservative evangelical theology, represented by Princeton theologians Warfield and Hodge, relies on the Common Sense philosophy of Thomas Reid and the inductive method of Francis Bacon, further developed by John Stuart Mill.[22]

17. Kolomiytsev, *Sources of Authority in Russian Evangelical Theology*.

18. Berdiaev, *Tsarstvo Dukha i Tsarstvo Kesaria*, 112. Berdiaev points out that Lenin was a naïve realist in his understanding of materialism.

19. Cf. Oden, *Two Worlds*, 50–52.

20. Cosden, "Coming of Age," 328.

21. Murphy, *Beyond Liberalism and Fundamentalism*, 15–22.

22. Ibid., 32–35. See also Noll, *Princeton Theology*, 30–35.

Taking scripture scientifically as the foundation for the objective study of the inerrant data of divine truth, the fundamentalist theologians of the Old Princeton School applied the inductive method to scripture in search of the universal objective facts revealed therein. As a result of this enterprise, the study of scripture was turned into a scientific project in which the goal of the theologian was to scrutinize the text of scripture, severed from tradition and experience, for the purpose of extracting its propositional content. The extracted propositions were, in turn, assembled by means of logic into doctrinal systems that were assumed to be universally applicable.[23] And the resultant universal body of doctrine was claimed to represent divine reality as it truly is, with the qualification that further scientific analysis of scripture might improve even more the resolution of the mental picture. Thus by taking scripture as the foundation for knowledge and applying the inductive method to it, fundamentalist theologians generated a highly cognitive product which was claimed to be an ahistorical and universal representation of divine truth.[24] Stanley Grenz points out that the fundamentalist project muted the diverse and complex text of scripture, as the study of propositional theologies under the guidance of theological experts shifted the focus from scripture itself, with its multiple genres, to cognitive doctrinal systems.[25] The fundamentalist approach not only fails to do justice to the literary diversity of scripture, but it also diminishes scripture's communitarian aspects, as well as its reflection of social praxis. At the end of the day, it leads to enclosed and watertight theological systems narcissistically detached from history and culture, as well as from genuine dialogue with other historical traditions.[26]

A broader spectrum of evangelical culture was introduced into the post-Soviet context with the establishment in 1997 of the Euro-Asian Accrediting Association of Evangelical Schools.[27] This Association was founded as a replica of similar evangelical associations in the West, adopting their documentation and standards.[28] By uniting leading

23. Grenz, *Revisioning Evangelical Theology*, 65.

24. Grenz, *Renewing the Center*, 220–29.

25. Grenz and Franke, *Beyond Foundationalism*, 37.

26. Barr, *Fundamentalism*, 328–37.

27. Brown, "Progress and Challenge in Theological Education in Central and Eastern Europe," 6–7. See www.e-aaa.org.

28. Penner, "Critical Evaluation of Recent Developments in the Commonwealth of

representatives of various theological schools, many of whom were graduates of Western evangelical institutions, the Association became a major channel for transporting conservative evangelical scholarship and ethos into the former Soviet Union. The key evangelical texts typically used in American evangelical seminaries were translated into Russian. By copying and pasting Anglo-American theological culture into the post-Soviet context, the EAAA transplanted a fragmentized approach to the structuring of theological studies in Ukraine.[29] And as a result of its overdependence on the West, the EAAA became a channel for the transmission of post-fundamentalist theological discourse.

Post-Fundamentalist Evangelical Developments in the Former Soviet Union

Even though American evangelicalism is still dominated by the Enlightenment paradigm, some evangelicals have critically embraced the post-modern cultural shift and have proceeded with the development of post-foundational forms of theology.[30] The penetration of distinctively post-foundational theologizing into the post-Soviet context occurred relatively late.[31] An article written in 2000 by Nikolai Kornilov derived its spin from recent contributions by Stanley Grenz, Roger Olson, and Trevor Hart, who represent evangelical engagement with the post-modernist cultural shift.[32] In his article, Kornilov fleshed out some of the key problems in Russian evangelicalism and suggested possible directions for their solution. His argument, or rather appeal, begins with an acknowledgment that the evangelical movement in the former Soviet Union has not had a written theological culture, nor has it had theologians who were able to utilize their rational abilities to formulate and resolve problems posed by contemporary circumstances both inside and outside the church.[33] Thus the practice of doing theology and fostering

Independent States," 22.

29. Charter, "Theological Education for New Protestant Churches of Russia," 152–68.

30. J. G. Stackhouse, *Evangelical Futures*; Bartholomew et al., *Futures of Evangelicalism*. See the discussion on foundationalism and post-foundationalism below.

31. Kornilov, "Kakogo Roda Bogoslovie nam Nuzhno?," 5–17.

32. Grenz and Olson, *Who Needs Theology?*; Hart, *Faith Thinking*.

33. Kornilov, "Kakogo Roda Bogoslovie nam Nuzhno?," 12.

written theological discourse has been absent in the evangelical church in the East.[34] In order to break the impasse, Kornilov recommends that Eastern evangelicals become acquainted with both the Eastern Orthodox and Western Protestant traditions, as well as take an introspective look at their own past.[35] The key to resolving the problems of identity and theology is to be found in re-evaluating past history, as well as in shortening the distance between the newly-established evangelical educational institutions and the church. Following the lead of non-foundationalist evangelicals, Kornilov emphasizes the primary importance of the Gospel narrative, read within the context of local tradition, and open to dialogue with others.[36] The major thrust of Kornilov's appeal is to engage with scripture and culture in new and refreshing ways.[37]

Even though Kornilov's contribution did not lead to any ongoing discussion in the former Soviet Union, his appeal provided a necessary opening for doing Eastern evangelical theology in a non-foundational key.[38] In the present theological construction, I will follow the stream introduced by Kornilov, focusing exclusively on one aspect briefly touched upon in his presentation, namely self-critical introspection of the tradition of the Gospel Christians.

Beyond Foundationalism

Basically, non-foundationalism is a philosophical reaction against the Cartesian turn toward universal foundations for knowledge adopted by fundamentalist theologians.[39] The guiding metaphor of foundational-

34. Ibid., 13.

35. Ibid., 15.

36. Ibid., 15.

37. Ibid., 16.

38. Cf. Negrov, "Hermeneutics in Transition," 33–55. This article demonstrates that the author is struggling with many contemporary issues and searching for answers in philosophical hermeneutics, while having been taken captive by Soviet and post-Soviet historiography. It is yet to be seen how the author will resolve the host of problems that he marked out in this highly vague article that contains a number of sweeping generalizations concerning Orthodox and Protestant theologies. However, the overall impression is that he seems to be moving towards foundationalism in its revisionist form, trusting rigorous historical-critical methodology and searching for a universal hermeneutical system. If this is the case, Negrov is on the way to developing the Harnackian trajectory that was latently present in Prokhanov, as well.

39. Phillips, *Faith after Foundationalism*; Thiel, *Nonfoundationalism*.

ism is that of building a house. According to this metaphor, one needs to establish a self-evident foundation in order to proceed with building a body of truth.[40] It has been pointed out that foundationalism is self-contradictory, as belief in the existence of universal and self-evident foundations is not itself self-evident.[41] The fragmentizing developments of the twentieth century revealed the naïveté of the Cartesian program. Jay Wood describes the current epistemic conditions: "Kuhn's discussions of 'paradigms,' Wittgenstein's talk of 'language games' and Dilthey's 'life categories,' as well as Gadamer's discussion of 'horizons' all underscore the essential embeddedness of our thinking in concrete historical/cultural situations, from which it is fantasy to suppose we can extricate ourselves."[42]

In our discussion of evangelical developments since the collapse of foundationalism, we will focus on two approaches that have found their way into the Ukrainian context, either through the translation of relevant works into Russian, or through the appropriation of such ideas by local evangelicals through English-language sources or contacts.

Alister McGrath is a prominent representative of the critical realist approach.[43] His new theological program seems to have much promise in the Anglo-American evangelical milieu.[44] McGrath acknowledges that "the best we can hope after the demise of foundationalism is a tradition-specific rationality which reaches beyond that tradition in its explanatory potency."[45] The key feature of critical realism is a strong conviction of the existence of reality outside of the knowing subject, and of her ability to come to know reality as it discloses itself. By using appropriate tools, the observer, who belongs to a living tradition of investigation, comes to know a particular reality, adjusting his language for the discovery and description of that reality. The theories, models, and concepts are always open to revision.[46] Even though the knower does not construct reality,

40. Audi, *Epistemology*, 188.

41. Wood, *Epistemology*, 89.

42. Ibid., 97.

43. McGrath, *Christian Theology*.

44. McGrath, *Science of God*. Cf. Wright, *New Testament and the People of God*, 31–44.

45. McGrath, *Scientific Theology*, vol. 2, *Reality*, 101.

46. McGrath, *Reality*, 195.

she affects what can be known in the process of observation.[47] The existing reality is given priority in the process of knowing, as the "methodology is determined by ontology" *a posteriori*.[48] McGrath argues for the "critical importance of both extra-systemic reference and intra-systemic consistency."[49] By emphasizing a correspondence theory of truth and the referential nature of language, the proponents of critical realism in theology place emphasis on the process of discovering objective reality by means of a nuanced and flexible methodology or set of methodologies.

Other evangelical theologians, some of whom inspired Kornilov's article, have gone further along the non-foundationalist path in science, adopting more holistic forms of theology.[50] The holistic turn in theology is signified by the adoption of coherence and pragmatic theories of truth.[51] Alister McGrath's epistemology is more suitable for use in the natural sciences, whose major objects of investigation are inanimate. Holistic epistemology is successfully employed in the social sciences, which deal with creative agents who, being part of created reality, not only discover but also construct certain aspects of reality.[52] The metaphor for holism is not a foundation, but a web of interconnected beliefs viewed as a whole. Murphy states: "Justification consists in showing that problematic beliefs are closely tied to beliefs that we have no good reason to call into question. So the coherence of the web is crucial for justification. When inconsistencies appear—conflicts within the web or with 'recalcitrant experience'—there are always a number of ways to revise in order to restore consistency. The choices that will be made here are in a sense pragmatic: how to mend the web with as little disturbance to the whole as possible."[53]

47. Ibid., 205.

48. Ibid., 223.

49. Ibid., 19.

50. Murphy and Kallenberg, "Anglo-American Post-Modernity"; Yoder, *Politics of Jesus*; Lash, *Theology on the Way to Emmaus*; Abraham, *Canon and Criterion in Christian Theology*; McClendon, *Systematic Theology*, vol. 1, *Ethics*; Grenz, *Theology for the Community of God*; idem, "Articulating the Christian Belief-Mosaic"; Grenz and Franke, *Beyond Foundationalism*; Fowl and Jones, *Reading in Communion*.

51. However, in adopting pragmatic and coherence theories of truth these evangelicals do not deny either the revelatory nature of scripture or realism as such.

52. Tanner, *Theories of Culture*.

53. Murphy, *Beyond Liberalism and Fundamentalism*, 94.

Thus the web of beliefs is not founded on anything but is in a constant process of modification, as the community-and-tradition-based investigation of reality continues. The changing web takes into account not only realities that are there to be discovered, but also those which are being constructed or reconstructed. While reality is assumed to be there, the focus is not so much on describing the correspondence between the web and reality as much as on the holistic pragmatic performance of the coherent web. The explanatory power of the web is fortified by the diachronic historical dimension of the tradition in line with MacIntyre's project discussed in the introductory chapter. Thus a tradition which is able (1) to give a rational and non-contradictory account of the current experience of reality without self-contradiction and (2) to resolve its own epistemological crises, as well as (3) to demonstrate more explanatory power than its rivals, can have higher claims for truthfulness. McGrath adopts a similar perspective, borrowed from the writings of Otto von Neurath: "We are like sailors who, on the open sea, must reconstruct their ship but are never able to start afresh from the bottom. Where a beam is taken away, a new one must at once be put there, and for this the rest of the ship is used as support. In this way, by using the old beams and driftwood, the ship can be shaped entirely anew, but only by gradual reconstruction."[54]

Despite their many similarities, there are at least two crucial differences between the critical realist approach and realist holist approach. First, unlike critical realists, who make a distinction between discovery and construction in the process of knowing reality, representatives of the realist holist paradigm point out that reality—or at least some aspects of reality—is not only discovered *but also* constructed by means of creative linguistic input.[55] This constructive component of evangelical holists has far-reaching consequences for doing theology. A major evangelical representative of the holist program, Stanley Grenz, writes:

> Similar to the so-called "critical realists," Christian theology maintains a certain undeniable givenness to the universe. But this givenness is not that of a static actuality existing outside of, and co-temporally with, our socially and linguistically constructed reality. It is not the objectivity of what some might call

54. McGrath, *Science of God*, 228–29.

55. Patterson, *Realist Christian Theology in a Post-modern Age*, 19. The constructive aspect is eschatologically closured in this form of realist theology.

> "the world as it is." Rather, the objectivity set forth in the biblical narrative is the objectivity of the world as God wills it. . . . Rather than being antithetical to the social constructionist insight, the "eschatological realism" . . . takes it a crucial step forward. . . . We participate with God as through the constructive power of language we inhabit a present linguistic world that sees all reality from the perspective of the future, real world that God is bringing to pass.[56]

Second, holistic realists are concerned that critical realists tend to shift the focus from holistic participation in the Christian form of life in its totality to participation in a discourse about the extratextual referent that brought this form of life into being.[57] This shift in focus has the potential of producing a modified foundationalist theology, founded on a modified general theory, namely a correspondence theory of truth.[58] As a result, critical realists may be standing on the slippery slope of cognitivism, which highlights cognitive systems of theology rather than the performance of the form of life as a whole. Scripture and tradition may be used to a great extent as authoritative materials for a theological discourse governed by extratextual criteria derived from a general theory.

In light of these critiques, McGrath's critical realist approach does not seem to be self-consistent on its own terms. We have seen that according to McGrath, the methodology of critical realism depends *a posteriori* on ontology. However, McGrath does not discuss the question of *how* one determines ontology or stratifies reality in the first place, as the question itself presupposes the primacy of a linguistically-mediated tacit methodology of a certain tradition-based community. The philosophy of internal realism developed by Hilary Putnam addresses this issue. Putnam points out that "[objects] do not exist independently of conceptual schemes. We cut up the world into objects when we introduce one or another scheme of description. Since the objects and the signs are alike internal to the scheme of description, it is possible to say what matches what."[59] However, Putnam makes it clear that not all stratifications of reality are acceptable:

56. Grenz, "Articulating the Christian Belief-Mosaic," 136. See the discussion in Cosden, *Theology of Work*, 144–76.

57. Murphy and Kallenberg, "Anglo-American Post-Modernity," 40–41. See also Murphy, *Anglo-American Postmodernity*, 113–29.

58. Patterson, *Realist Christian Theology*, 31.

59. Putnam, *Reason, Truth, and History*, 52.

> Denying that it makes sense to ask whether our concepts "match" something totally uncontaminated by conceptualization is one thing; but to hold that every conceptual system is therefore just as good as every other would be something else. If anyone really believed that, and if they were foolish enough to pick a conceptual system that told them they could fly and to act upon it by jumping out of the window, they would, if they were lucky enough to survive, see the weakness of the latter view at once. Internalism does not deny that there are experiential *inputs* to knowledge; knowledge is not a story with no constraints except *internal* coherence; *but it does deny that there are any inputs which are not themselves to some extent shaped by our concepts*[60] [italics original].

Thus by assuming ontological primacy as universally self-evident, McGrath seems to smuggle in a local linguistic input built on a general correspondence theory of truth. Critical realism does not have access to the universal point of view from which one can determine ontology or correctly stratify all of reality from God's point of view before the eschatological consummation.[61] Therefore epistemology and ontology cannot be neatly separated from each other, since fluid objects, especially those of constructed social reality, are not available apart from the linguistic mediation of creative subjects. McGrath seems to misread the agenda of the post-foundational holistic theological program, engaging in a black-and-white division of epistemology into realist and anti-realist categories.[62] By not considering a mediating internal realist position that accommodates both realism and language-riddenness, McGrath downplays the organic interpenetration of reality and language. In his new project, McGrath fails to discuss the constructive role of language performed by the socio-linguistic community of the church in the process of reshaping the present reality into the form of the eschatological blueprint presented in scripture. In failing to do so he eventually dimin-

60. Ibid., 54. As it stands on its own, Putnam's philosophy represents a sort of conceptual anti-realism. But when incorporated into the canonical framework of divine revelation, it provides a strong realist explanatory grid for understanding how the extra-textual world can be cut up through the prism of the redeemed world, projected by inspired scripture. Thus the final stratification of reality will be accomplished in the future, while in the present the church is involved in the process of the creative reconstruction of the present reality.

61. See the discussion in Patterson, *Realist Christian Theology*, 1–32.

62. Hensley, "Are Postliberals Necessarily Antirealists?," 69–81.

ishes the role of the Incarnation that made these constructive processes possible, as the Divine Word took on the human flesh to transform the present state of affairs (1 Corinthians 15:47–49).[63] In light of the historical investigation, which demonstrates the highly creative and fluid nature of the socially constructed tradition formed in the hurly-burly of life, I will proceed along the holist realist lines of post-foundationalist evangelicalism.[64]

A CULTURAL-LINGUISTIC MODEL

Evangelical holist theologizing was inspired by the development of post-liberalism, which was initiated by theologians associated with Yale Divinity School.[65] In his programmatic work on the nature of doctrine, George Lindbeck attempted to make an advance in ecumenical dialogue by proposing a mediating cultural-linguistic model that was supposed to overcome the deficiencies of the conservative "cognitive-propositional" and liberal "experiential-expressive" approaches.[66] In the years since the publication of his book, there have been intense ongoing discussions over Lindbeck's proposal.[67] In my treatment of the post-liberal program I will focus on the most important features of his proposal.

Driven by the post-liberal insights of the theology of Karl Barth, as well as relying on the philosophy of language of Ludwig Wittgenstein, the ethnography of Clifford Geertz, the social theory of Peter Berger, and the epistemology of Michael Polanyi, Lindbeck suggested that religions should be perceived as cultures and their respective doctrines

63. McGrath is oriented towards the past even when he mentions "transformations of the present and the construction of the future." Cf. McGrath, *Genesis of Doctrine*, 1. However, the aspects of transformation and construction are not developed in McGrath's theology, and the eschatological dimension is downplayed and rarely mentioned, as is the role of the community in transforming the social reality.

64. On the social construction of reality, see Berger, *Social Reality of Religion*; *Rumor of Angels*; Berger and Luckmann, *Social Construction of Reality*; and Finn, *Social Reality*. See comments on the theological appropriation of social construction theory in Milbank, *Theology and Social Theory*, 133–36.

65. Grenz and Franke, *Beyond Foundationalism*, ix. See Fodor, "Postliberal Theology."

66. Lindbeck, *Nature of Doctrine*.

67. See the recent evaluations of postliberal theology in Goh, *Christian Tradition Today*; Vidu, *Postliberal Theological Method*; and DeHart, *Trial of Witnesses*.

as languages of those cultures.[68] Instead of viewing religions as expressing a common-core experience of the divine through different symbols (expressivism), or arguing that theological language makes propositional truth claims about reality (cognitivism), religions should rather be perceived as different forms of life and their languages as correlating to those forms. According to this view, Christian doctrines function as second-order grammatical rules for first-order biblical writings and Christian practices.[69] According to Lindbeck, second-order rules do not necessarily make truth claims about ontological referents but rather demarcate what is acceptable or not acceptable for Christian talk about God: "Rule theory does not prohibit speculations on the possible correspondence of the Trinitarian pattern of Christian language to the metaphysical structure of the Godhead, but simply says that these are not doctrinally necessary and cannot be binding."[70]

Even though the largest part of Lindbeck's book targets the "expressivist" form of liberal theology, conservatives are critiqued for being preoccupied with cognitive systems of propositional truths that are claimed to correspond to divine reality. In his evaluation of conservative evangelical theology, Lindbeck points out that propositional truths expressed in language cannot be considered as universal or as referring to an extratextual reality, since propositions can be pronounced in an incorrect context, producing speech-acts incoherent with the form of life as a whole.[71] The proposition "Christ is Lord" is false "when used to authorize [crusaders] cleaving the skull of the infidel."[72] In Lindbeck's view, cognitivist theologians tend to simplify the issue of correspondence, perceiving it in terms of mental correspondence of concepts to a rather static objectified reality outside of language. Without denying either extratextual realism or the importance of propositions in theological discourse, Lindbeck points out that correspondence to the divine should be viewed in terms of the whole form of life performed by a religion:

> A religion thought of as comparable to a cultural system, as a set of language games correlated with a form of life, may as a

68. Lindbeck, *Nature of Doctrine*, 32–33.
69. Pecknold, *Transforming Postliberal Theology*.
70. Lindbeck, *Nature of Doctrine*, 106.
71. Ibid., 63–69.
72. Ibid., 64.

> whole correspond or not correspond to what a theist called God's being and will. As actually lived, a religion may be pictured as a single gigantic proposition. It is a true proposition to the extent that its objectives are interiorized and exercised by groups and individuals in such a way as to conform in some measure in the various dimensions of their existence to the ultimate reality and goodness that lies at the heart of things. It is a false proposition to the extent that this does not happen. . . . A map, let us stipulate, becomes a proposition, an affirmation about how to travel from one place to another, only when actually utilized in the course of a journey. To the extent that the map is misread or misused, it is a part of a false proposition no matter how accurate it may be in itself. Conversely, even if it is in many ways in error . . . it becomes constitutive of a true proposition when it guides the traveler rightly. A map of imaginary space, in contrast, cannot be used (because it is categorially false) to formulate ontologically true or false propositions, but only meaningless ones. The categorially and unsurpassably true religion is capable of being rightly utilized, of guiding thought, passions, and action in a way that corresponds to ultimate reality, and of thus being ontologically (and "propositionally") true, but is not always and perhaps not even usually so employed.[73]

Lindbeck's cultural-linguistic model opened the door for an intensive and constructive dialogue between evangelicals and post-liberals.[74] The complex text of *The Nature of Doctrine* was received by evangelicals as a Wittgensteinian duck-rabbit picture, which may well have been the intention of the author. Some evangelicals saw in it a self-enclosed relativism lacking propositional truth claims about extratextual reality,[75] while others perceived it in realistic terms as a path for evangelicals to explore critically.[76] Choosing the company of the latter, I now turn to the critical evaluation of the theological heart of the supposedly pre-theological program of *The Nature of Doctrine*.

73. Ibid., 51–52.

74. Phillips and Okholm, *Nature of Confession*.

75. Cf. McGrath, "Evangelical Evaluation of Postliberalism," 23–44; Wilson, "Toward a New Evangelical Paradigm of Biblical Authority," 151–61.

76. Wilson, "Toward a New Evangelical Paradigm," 151–61; Hensley, "Are Postliberals Necessarily Antirealists?," 69–80.

Scripture "Absorbs" the World

At the end of this slim volume, Lindbeck makes a proposal for a postliberal theology. According to the cultural-linguistic model, doctrines should be perceived as second-order rules that define the correct use of language in the Christian form of life. "It is in this sense that theological description in the cultural-linguistic mode is intra-semiotic or intratextual."[77] By saying this, Lindbeck means that religions should be studied on their own terms without trying to put them into the procrustean bed of an external standard. The most direct outcome of the ethnographic approach to religions is a way of reading and interpreting the sacred texts that constitute and project the symbolic universe of a religion. Sacred texts should be studied on their own terms from within the practicing community, without using interpretive frameworks extracted from other semiotic systems, especially those that claim universality.[78] Lindbeck points out that the canonical texts of religious communities produce a hermeneutical lens through which the world is viewed: "For those who are steeped in them, no world is more real than the ones they create. A scriptural world is thus able to absorb the universe. It supplies the interpretive framework within which believers seek to live their lives and understand reality."[79] Lindbeck goes on to say that every sacred text of a particular religion requires specific interpretive techniques in order to interpret reality through the prism of that sacred text, or to absorb the world, using Lindbeck's idiom.[80] Having established this premise, Lindbeck takes Christianity as an example and demonstrates that it was the classical approach throughout church history to read the world through the framework of scripture. "Traditional exegetical procedures assume that the Scripture creates its own domain of meaning and that the task of interpretation is to extend this over the whole of reality."[81]

Lindbeck borrowed from the influential works of Hans Frei and Erich Auerbach the metaphor of absorbing the world by the text of

77. Lindbeck, *Nature of Doctrine*, 114.

78. See the discussion in Goh, *Christian Tradition Today*, 187–202.

79. Lindbeck, *Nature of Doctrine*, 117.

80. Ibid. The metaphor of world absorbing is used by Lindbeck to signify the prioritization of the canonical narrative and its types that then are used to interpret and frame events and processes in the world.

81. Ibid.

scripture .[82] Erich Auerbach demonstrated that the Old Testament, unlike the classical writings of the Greeks, seeks to overcome the reality of the reader. "Far from seeking, like Homer, merely to make us forget our own reality for a few hours, it seeks to overcome our reality: we are to fit our own life into its world, feel ourselves to be elements in its structure of universal history."[83] Auerbach points out that the biblical story of the Old Testament, which starts with creation and ends with prophecies of judgment, includes the interpretation of other realities, such as Assyrian, Babylonian, Persian, and Roman history.[84] Analogously, Christian writers sought to incorporate the external world into the story of canonical scripture: "Augustine did not describe his work in the categories we are employing, but the whole of his theological production can be understood as a progressive, even if not always successful, struggle to insert everything from Platonism and the Pelagian problem to the fall of Rome into the world of the Bible."[85]

The engine for the redescription of the world through a scriptural framework is typological interpretation that connects types found in scripture with extra-scriptural events or persons in history.

> It is important to note the direction of interpretation. Typology does not make scriptural contents into metaphors for extratextual realities, but the other way around. It does not suggest, as is often said in our day, that believers find their stories in the Bible, but rather they make the story of the Bible their story. Intratextual theology redescribes reality within the scriptural framework rather than translating Scripture into extra-scriptural categories. It is the text, so to speak, which absorbs the world, rather than the world the text. . . . As the work of Hans Frei shows, the situation has changed radically in recent centuries, and new difficulties have arisen. Typological interpretation collapsed under the combined onslaughts of rationalistic, pietistic, and historical-critical developments. Scripture ceased to function as the lens through which theologians viewed the world and instead became primarily an object of study whose religiously significant or literal meaning was located outside itself. The primarily literary approaches of the past, with their affinities to informal ways of reading the classics in their own terms, were replaced by fun-

82. Frei, *Eclipse of Biblical Narrative.*

83. Auerbach, *Mimesis*, 15.

84. Ibid., 16.

85. Lindbeck, *Nature of Doctrine*, 117.

> damentalist, historico-critical, and expressivist preoccupations with facticity or experience.[86]

Thus Lindbeck's argument is to demonstrate the incommensurability of different interpretive frameworks.[87] Each interpretive framework belongs to a particular paradigm and a particular life world. A foreign semiotic system as well as new experience should be inserted into the Christian life world by means of pre-critical typological hermeneutics and supported by historical-critical scholarship.[88] Foreign interpretive frameworks, being products of different narrative worlds, have the potential of absorbing and disfiguring the original stories and the identities presented in them. Lindbeck provides an example of such a transformation in Hellenistic Gnosticism: "The Jewish rabbi, who is the crucified and resurrected Messiah of the New Testament accounts, was transformed into a mythological figure illustrative of thoroughly non-scriptural meanings."[89] However, Lindbeck does not argue for strong incommensurability, where paradigms are viewed as watertight worlds. In his reply to Donald Davidson's argument, according to which the theory of incommensurability is incoherent, as some degree of commonality is needed to recognize instances of incommensurability, Lindbeck clarifies his position.[90] "My use of the term [refers] to what Charles Peirce would perhaps call a 'vague' sign determinable only by its context and its use."[91] Referring to MacIntyre, Lindbeck points out that there is no need to have a common communicative meta-system to recognize what is untranslatable from one system into another as the interpreter acquires skills in a second language.[92] Consequently, competing paradigms can be compared by performance and by their assimilative power to absorb reality without internal contradiction.[93]

A major criticism of Lindbeck's pragmatic approach has been his presentation of truth as represented in the canon, as he stresses the

86. Ibid., 118–19.

87. See the discussion in Marshall, *Trinity and Truth*, 160–69.

88. Lindbeck, *Church in a Postliberal Age*, 241–42.

89. Ibid., 118.

90. Davidson, *Inquiries into Truth and Interpretation*, 37–54.

91. Lindbeck, *Church in a Postliberal Age*, 231.

92. Ibid. See the discussion in Goh, *Christian Tradition Today*, ch. 5.

93. Lindbeck, *Nature of Doctrine*, 131.

semiotic code rather than what is encoded.[94] Lindbeck persuasively demonstrates that before modernity, scripture was used as the lens to interpret the whole of life. However, he takes for granted the existence of religious life forms without tracing their geneses.[95] Why should one trust the Christian scriptures as the world absorber if their content may be pure fiction? Why not be absorbed by the world or by other religious life forms? Historically, Christians did not believe in the Old Testament and produce the New Testament because these semiotic systems demonstrated superiority over their competitors in absorbing reality. Rather, the scriptures were born as a result of historical events and experiences of reality that preceded them. As Francis Watson writes:

> . . . [E]mphasis on the autonomy of the text in its final form can easily lead to the conclusion that the "pre-textual" reality of Jesus is hermeneutically irrelevant. Instead of claiming that the reality of Jesus is textually *mediated*, ought we not to state that it is textually *constructed*? The word became not flesh but text. But the denial of the enfleshment of the word has been characteristic of every form of docetism. . . . The difference between Jesus and a spirit is that he has hands and feet, flesh, and bones, and is capable—even in his risen form—of eating fish (Luke 24:39–43). But if this risen Jesus is *purely* the creation of the narrator, then he is a being not of flesh and bones but of words, incorporeal as a spirit. In other words, to read this narrative as self-enclosed is to fall prey to precisely the docetism that it so emphatically opposes.[96]

The incarnation of the Logos textually mediated, and the form of life initiated by his life, ministry, death, and resurrection, is the locus of world-absorption, and not the semiotic system that mediates this reality. However, acknowledging the priority of encoded reality over the semiotic code, one does not need to assume that this reality is humanly accessible outside of the semiotic system embedded in and produced by the historic tradition which supplied the rules for deciphering the code. As Sue Patterson argues: "Truth can only be both internal and external if divine truth is revealed; transcendent truth is also couched incarnationally as human truth. On this reckoning an expression of agnosticism

94. Patterson, *Realist Christian Theology*, 41.

95. McGrath, *Genesis of Doctrine*, 32–34.

96. Watson, *Text, Church and World*, 224, 292. Cf. Berdyaev, *Freedom and the Spirit*, 34, 61.

about the degree of correspondence to external truth is an attribution of unconvertedness or unredeemedness to the Church's representation of incarnational reality. . . . If the text . . . is inextricably part of the revelation it mediates, then the notion of an extra-biblical referent becomes a category mistake."[97]

Even though Lindbeck did not spell out his views on the historicity of the Gospels and the extratextual reality mediated by the text, in his more recent contribution he clearly demonstrates his realist position and the importance of exiting the text.[98]

The Lindbeckian model has also been critiqued for its rather homogeneous understanding of intratextuality. The intratextual approach tends to depict the semiotic universe of scripture as a static, determinate, and coherent system detached from traditions of interpretation. However, the Christian life world is more heterogeneous, and the canonical content is too diverse to allow for such a static and enclosed view.[99] Volf has pointed out that it is impossible to separate the extratextual and intratextual traffic.[100] Even though Lindbeck did not articulate explicitly what constituted the dividing line between intratextuality and extratextuality, he did so implicitly. In discussing the absorption of scripture by Hellenistic Gnosticism, Lindbeck provided the criterion that separates the intra from the extra, namely the narrative identity of Jesus presented in the canon.[101] As long as the process of world absorption does not change the image of the king into that of a fox, to use the language of Irenaeus, so long the community can develop its intratextual web of beliefs and perfect its performance. [102] "[T]he controlling *sensus literalis* is the narrative meaning of the stories about Jesus. Meanings contrary to this sense must be excluded. Thus when the biblical narrational understanding of the Church engenders meanings with the Jesus story, the narrative must be altered or abandoned."[103] The following appropriation of Lindbeck's proposal is taken along the lines of minimalist

97. Patterson, *Realist Christian Theology*, 41, 47.

98. Lindbeck, "Post-Critical Canonical Interpretation," 49.

99. DeHart, *Trial of Witnesses*, 182–84.

100. Volf, "Theology, Meaning, & Power," 45–66.

101. Lindbeck, *Nature of Doctrine*, 118. Cf. Frei, *Identity of Jesus Christ.*

102. Irenaeus *Adv. Haer.* I.9.4.

103. Lindbeck, "Story-Shaped Church," 46–47.

interpretation of intratextuality, based on the narrative identity of Christ as revealed in the final form of Christian scripture.

In the process of absorbing extratextual reality through the church's life in the world, the Christian semiotic system does not remain the same.[104] When an extratextual reality is absorbed, it becomes part of the semiotic system and sheds new light on the text that has absorbed it. In a sense, the text itself expands and illuminates its own depth, having shown the capacity to swallow the extratextual reality.[105] Kenneth Surin has pointed out that in the constant process of absorbing Christians and newcomers into the Christian life world, there is always present a dynamic that challenges the existing tradition:

> The church is the gospel-shaped "narrative space" where Christians learn to "sacrifice" themselves, over and over again, to the community's narrative texts, to the "new" language. This they do by consenting to be interrogated by those texts in such a way that they learn, slowly, laboriously and sometimes painfully, to live the way of Jesus. This interrogation—which is fundamental to the church's "pedagogy of discipleship"—may, depending on historical circumstances, have the consequence of actually decomposing, as opposed to reinforcing, certain already existing patterns of "Christian identity." These alternative "identities" will be articulated in a language which gives speech to all that is denominated by the category of the "other." It will be a language capable of undermining the filiative and affiliative bonds which sustain the unredeemed order.[106]

The dynamics of the world absorption explicated by Surin can be illustrated by the historical narrative of the first part of our research. It was established that during the first five years of their existence, the Gospel Christians of St. Petersburg maintained their Orthodox identity while listening to the evangelical expositions of Lord Radstock. However, over the course of time their Orthodox identity began to decompose, as Pashkov, Korff, and others were becoming part of the life world of Western evangelicalism through association with the World Evangelical Alliance. By reading scripture through the hermeneutical filter of Victorian evangelicalism, which denied the importance of

104. Marshall, *Trinity and Truth*, 149–53.

105. Cf. Vandevelde, *Task of the Interpreter*, 138. And cf. the discussion in Marshall, *Trinity and Truth*, 147–49.

106. Surin, *Turnings of Darkness and Light*, 217–18.

the Patristic tradition, the emerging Russian evangelicals came to see certain doctrines and practices of the Orthodox Church as unbiblical. As a result of the inadequate performance of the Byzantine paradigm in the spiritual, social, and political spheres, its symbolic universe was reconfigured among some of the followers of Radstock, resulting in their spiritual conversion. This paradigm shift took place as the canonical text, as interpreted by Radstock, "contracted and eschewed" the previous absorptions of the world that had become part of the Orthodox tradition over the course of its history. Through the "hermeneutical contraction" of the canonical text was born a life world of the Gospel Christians that began to move along the restorationist trajectory of Western evangelicalism. The Protestant paradigm of reading the Bible in a primitivist, pre-critical way was perceived as more coherent by Radstock's followers at that time. The new form of life represented by Radstock provided for the first Russian evangelicals not only simplicity and seeming internal consistency, but also a new worldwide vision, as well as a new narrative, new theological language, new experiences, new international contacts, and a sense of mission. The subsequent story and experiences of the tradition over the course of more than a hundred years destabilized it, bringing it into a state of internal incoherence and partial identity loss. The proposed solution for the tradition to regain its coherence is to be absorbed by the gravity of the Logos, textually mediated through scripture.

Scripture "Absorbs" the Story of the Gospel Christians

Having established the trajectory of post-Soviet evangelicalism, I have suggested that the ancient theological method of absorbing the world by scripture, reintroduced in the programmatic works of post-liberal theologians, could be a viable theological option for Eastern evangelicals to consider. In the rest of the chapter I will apply this method to the story of the Gospel Christians by reading it through the hermeneutical lens of scripture. In so doing, I will attempt to forge a new self-identifying story for the post-Soviet context. The path I intend to tread is influenced by the insights of the North American post-liberal ethicist, Stanley Hauerwas, who writes: "The constructive theological task remains primary. Our concern must be to understand better how to live appropriate to the God whom we find in the narratives of Israel and Jesus, and how these stories help provide the means for recognizing and critically appropriating other stories enmeshed in many histories—of our families, of Texas, America, European civilization, and so on—each of which is constituted by many interrelated and confusing story lines. The moral task consists in acquiring the skills, i.e., the character, which enable us to negotiate these many kinds and levels of narrative in a truthful manner."[107]

Following the Barthian dictum of post-liberalism, the story of the Gospel Christians will be viewed from within the story of scripture, and not the other way around. In the following paragraph I will specify which levels of narrative derived from the historical part of the present research will be taken for the construction of a new identity for the tradition. As has been demonstrated, the tradition of the Gospel Christians periodically changed its identity, depending on the configuration of the geopolitical forces between the Eastern (capitalist Orthodox, Soviet Marxist-Leninist, neo-capitalist Orthodox) and Western (Protestant capitalist) civilizations. The self-identity of the Gospel Christians fluctuated in the direction of the more powerful political force and was in part inspired by Russian messianism. As a result of this changing self-identity, the content of the tradition's memory and the direction of its imagination changed as well. The collapse of a world superpower brought the Gospel Christians to a severe identity crisis and to a reconfiguration of the tradition's shared memory and imagination. It was demonstrated earlier that the latest identity construction imitated the evolutionary Hegelian Marxist rationality of the fallen world power: it was claimed that the Gospel Christians are a historic product of the work of the Holy Spirit, who was active both in the West and in the East in the process of restoring Apostolic Christianity. This partially correct reading, despite its incoherence with previous identities, helps the Gospel Christians to sustain their new indigenized identity within the revived Orthodox cultural milieu. In the following theological reconstruction of the tradition, I will attempt to "out-narrate" the political and nationalist forces that shaped the evangelical identity during the Russian, Soviet, and post-Soviet periods.

Post-liberal theologians along with evangelicals follow the ancient Patristic and Reformed tradition of reading scripture as a unified text

107. Hauerwas, *Community of Character*, 96. On Hauerwas and his theology, see Jones et al., *God, Truth, and Witness*; Thomson, *Ecclesiology of Stanley Hauerwas*; and Hauerwas and Berkman, *Hauerwas Reader*.

that narrates one story with a center.[108] The center of the overarching Christian story of God, which begins with the creation of the universe and ends with its eschatological re-creation in Christ, is found in the event of the Jewish Messiah.[109] More particularly, it is centered on his incarnation, life, death, and resurrection.[110] Some modern theologians consider it problematic to view scripture in this way, due to the multiplicity of biblical narratives and genres.[111] However, Gerard Loughlin has argued that the church, from its earliest times, beginning with Augustine (or even earlier) and continuing until Barth and Lindbeck in the West, has had no problem identifying the story and its center.[112] Even though Loughlin's argument may be unimpressive for those who approach the text with a different interpretive framework, it demonstrates the logic of the post-liberal *ad hoc* apologetic: the practice of scriptural reading is part of the form of life of an ancient tradition, which uses internal rather than external criteria for its performance.[113] Richard Bauckham has recently demonstrated that despite scripture's polyphonic nature and the different versions it gives of the story, "much of the recent scholarship has tended to exaggerate biblical diversity."[114] The historical event narrated as the unifying center of scripture not only provides the identity of Christ,[115] but also serves as a trans-contextual meta-critique: "The cross and resurrection stand not only as a critique of human self-affirmation and power, but also as a *meta-critique which assesses other criteria, and*

108. Loughlin, *Telling God's Story*, 44–45; Lash, *Believing Three Ways in One God*, 8.

109. Williams, *Open to Judgment*, 160.

110. McGrath, *Enigma of the Cross*, 17–34; Moltmann, *Crucified God*, 1–6; Stott, *Cross of Christ.*

111. Wiles, "Scriptural Authority and Theological Construction," 42–58.

112. Loughlin, *Telling God's Story*, 45. See also Watson, *Text and Truth*, 18–28, 287–88; and Webster, *Holy Scripture*. In the Eastern Orthodox civilization in general and Eastern evangelicalism in particular the Bible is not viewed in any other way. Due to the absence of liberal theological departments in the country and to identification either with Orthodoxy or evangelicalism, this view is not only ecclesial but also a public norm in the post-Soviet context.

113. Cf. Watson, "Are There Still Four Gospels?," 116.

114. Bauckham, "Reading Scripture as a Coherent Story," 43. See also Bartholomew and Goheen, "Story and Biblilcal Theology," 158–68.

115. Frei, *Theology and Narrative*, 59.

which transforms the very concept of power. The power of the cross lies *precisely not in rhetorical self-assertion or manipulation.*"[116]

As Bauckham puts it, "Only the human who has thus himself been identified irrevocably with the lowest of the low can be entrusted with the power that God exercises characteristically on their behalf. Distortion of the biblical story into an ideology of oppression has to suppress the biblical meaning of the cross."[117] In the following section we will evaluate the formative forces that shaped the identity of the Gospel Christians in the light of scripture's center.

Christ and the Powers

Our main interlocutor at this juncture is the Mennonite theologian John Howard Yoder.[118] In his influential cross-disciplinary study on New Testament social ethics Yoder advanced a reinterpretation of the relationship between the cross of Christ and the powers of this world.[119] The angle of Yoder's engagement with the topic was significantly influenced by the socio-political context of his writing. At the time of his writing, the Western church was contemplating the "power of evil that [had] been seen breaking through the crust of the most civilized societies" in the events that took place between 1930 and 1950.[120] It was also a time of strong geopolitical tension between the two world superpowers. Yoder quoted in his epigraph the words of C. H. Dodd, written in 1940: "The Gospel is firmly rooted in a story of that which once happened. The story is familiar. But we should observe that the situation into which Jesus Christ came was genuinely typical. . . . The forces with which he came into contact were such as are permanent factors in history: government, institutional religion, nationalism, social unrest."[121]

Rejecting the individualistic interpretations promoted in pietistic and existentialist scholarly circles, Yoder suggested reading the New

116. Thiselton, *New Horizons in Hermeneutics*, 615. Italics original.

117. Bauckham, "Reading Scripture as a Coherent Story," 52.

118. Nation, *John Howard Yoder*.

119. Yoder, *Politics of Jesus*, 135–62. Cf. Barth, *Church Dogmatics*, vol. 4, *Christian Life*, 220–33.

120. Ibid., 141.

121. Dodd, "Kingdom of God and the Present Situation," quoted in Yoder, *Politics of Jesus*, 2.

Testament, and specifically the ministries of Jesus and Paul, through the prism of social ethics.[122] Richard Hays summarizes the content of Yoder's book by saying, "Yoder argues for three fundamental theses: (1) that the New Testament consistently bears witness to Jesus' renunciation of violence and coercive power; (2) that the example of Jesus is directly relevant and normatively binding for the Christian community; (3) that faithfulness to the example of Jesus is a political choice, not a withdrawal from the realm of politics."[123]

According to Yoder, the Christian is called to imitate Jesus in peaceful resistance to participation in the power games of this world: "Servanthood replaces dominion, forgiveness absorbs hostility. Thus—and only thus—are we bound by New Testament thought to be like Jesus."[124] In light of our research focus, we will concentrate on one particular aspect of Yoder's work that touches on the attitude of Christ toward the powers of this world, which played such a crucial role in forming the identity of the Gospel Christians.

Following the lead of Hendrikus Berkhof, whose work he translated into English, Yoder concentrates on those New Testament texts that refer to principalities and powers, authorities, and rulers (Rom 8:38; 13:1; Gal 4:3–5; Eph 2:2; Col 2:20).[125] According to Berkhof and Yoder, the Apostle Paul demythologized the ancient concept of principalities and powers, perceiving them as power structures that had originally been created by God to prevent human life and society from entering into chaos.[126] In line with this approach, Grenz provides the following definition of these structures: "Structures of existence are those larger, suprahuman aspects or dimensions of reality which form the inescapable context for human life and which therefore condition individual and corporate human existence."[127] Yoder lists different types of power structures that govern human social existence: "We have here an inclusive vision of religious

122. Yoder, *Politics of Jesus*, 135.

123. Hays, *Moral Vision of the New Testament*, 239–40.

124. Yoder, *Politics of Jesus*, 134.

125. Berkhof, *Christ and the Powers*, 33. Berkhof is not the only scholar who influenced Yoder. See the bibliography in Yoder, Politics, 142 n.4. For the list of terms in Pauline texts, see Arnold, *Powers of Darkness*, 218. Reid, "Principalities and Powers," 747–49.

126. Berkhof, *Christ and Powers*, 30.

127. Grenz, *Theology for the Community*, 228.

structures . . . intellectual structures ('-ologies' and '-isms'), moral structures (codes and customs), political structures (the tyrant, the market, the school, the courts, race, and nation). The totality is overwhelmingly broad."[128] Even though these power structures are built into the matrix of human existence and to a certain degree are constructed by humans, they cannot be said to be purely human constructs. Power structures enjoy a quasi-independent existence as they lie beyond human control.[129] On the one hand human beings cannot live without structures of some sort; on the other, "no specific group of individuals has the ability to alter greatly the structures in the context of which we live."[130] Grenz points out that the fact that structures exist beyond human control indicates that they are not only quasi-independent but also quasi-personal, being mysterious and incomprehensible in their core.[131] The structures serve the divine purposes, and they can be manipulated by the spiritual forces of evil. While being human structures of existence, they are not closed off from the supernatural realm. When they are influenced by evil, they become oppressive and lead away from the recognition and worship of the true God. The powers, however, can be used by God. Grenz provides examples of the Roman government as the instrument of God's justice (Rom 13:1–7) and as demonic when persecuting God's people (Revelation 17).[132] In his discussion of the powers, Yoder arrives at the following conclusions: (1) The powers are a good creation of God. *We cannot live without them.* (2) However, because the powers are fallen, they do not serve people but enslave them. *We cannot live with them.* (3) Being dependent on the powers, people await the redeeming work of God.[133]

Yoder goes on to discuss the redeeming work of Christ with respect to the powers. According to Yoder, to be human is to be subordinate to these power structures, without which there would be "no history nor society nor humanity." Thus in order to redeem people, Christ had to break the sovereignty of the fallen powers that enslaved them, as these powers could not be ignored or set aside. "This is what Jesus did,

128. Yoder, *Politics of Jesus*, 145.

129. Grenz, *Theology for the Community*, 230.

130. Ibid.

131. Ibid.

132. Ibid., 233–35.

133. Yoder, *Politics of Jesus*, 146.

concretely and historically, by living among men a genuinely free and human existence."[134] And this brought him to the cross. "In his death, the Powers—in this case the most worthy, weighty representatives of Jewish religion and Roman politics—acted in collusion."[135] Having voluntarily chosen the way of non-violent submission to the powers and thus fulfilling the will of the Father, Jesus broke their rule "by refusing to support them in their self-glorification; and that is why they killed him. Preaching and incorporating a greater righteousness than that of the Pharisees, and a vision of an order of social human relations more universal than the Pax Romana, he permitted the Jews to profane a holy day (refuting thereby their own moral pretensions) and permitted the Romans to deny their vaunted respect for law as they proceeded illegally against him."[136]

Through his obedience and non-violence Jesus became the first-fruits of the new creation, which derived its strength directly from God. Yoder draws extensively from Berkhof's exegesis of Col 2:13–15: "Christ has disarmed the principalities and powers and made a public example of them." On the cross the true nature of the powers was revealed, as previously they had been taken to be "the most basic and ultimate realities." Both Jewish and Roman authorities failed to do justice to this revealed truth (1 Cor 2:8). By his resurrection from the dead Jesus demonstrated that he had triumphed over the powers, having revealed their true nature.[137]

Yoder takes the next step by taking into account Berkhof's exposition of Eph 3:8–11. As a result of Jesus' victory over the powers, the messianic community, composed of both Jews and Gentiles, is called to demonstrate to the powers the wisdom of God. The community formed by the Apostolic preaching of the Gospel reveals "the unsearchable wealth of Christ" by its sheer existence in the world as the new humanity that lives a life of freedom in Christ.[138] Thus the church is called to be a restored society that demonstrates to the world the new configuration of restored and tamed powers (social, cultural, religious, intellectual, etc.) under the rule of Christ. "The Church must be a sample kind of hu-

134. Ibid.,147.

135. Ibid.

136. Ibid., 148.

137. Ibid., 149–50.

138. Ibid., 151.

manity within which, for example, economic and racial differences are surmounted. Only then will she have anything to say to the society that surrounds her about how those differences must be dealt with."[139]

Even though this exposition of Christ and the powers as represented by Yoder has not been unanimously accepted by New Testament scholarship, it has secured a well-grounded position in the unsettled debate over principalities and powers.[140] Walter Wink's extensive study is the most prominent scholarly work in this field.[141] In many respects Wink's analysis supports Yoder's interpretation. According to Wink, the powers are good, fallen, and will be redeemed through the work of Christ.[142] However, in his research Wink rejects the idea of the powers as supernatural entities that can exist apart from material manifestations of power.[143] According to Wink, "The Powers are simultaneously the outer and inner aspects of one and the same indivisible concretion of power."[144] In taking this position, Wink conflates the material agents of power with the realm of spiritual forces. He internalizes the spiritual realm as "the interiority of earthly institutions."[145] Marva Dawn has recently criticized Wink for this reductionist interpretation.[146] According to Wink, victory over the powers is accomplished through the church's singing of the heavenly chorus of Rev 11:15: "The kingdom of the world has become the kingdom of our Lord and of his Messiah, and he shall reign for ever and ever." Commenting on Wink's assertion that "singing about is a way of bringing about,"[147] Dawn correctly points out that Wink has downplayed the objective role of the Messiah as the Victor

139. Ibid., 154.

140. For a recent exposition along the lines of Yoder and an overview of the scholarship, see Dawn, "Powers and Principalities," 609–12; *Powers, Weakness, and the Tabernacling of God*; "Biblical Concept of the 'Principalities and Powers'"; Harink, *Paul among the Postliberals*, 105–49; and Wright, *What Saint Paul Really Said*, 153–56, 160–61.

141. Wink, *The Powers*, vol. 1: *Naming the Powers*; *The Powers*, vol. 2: *Unmasking the Powers*; *The Powers*, vol. 3: *Engaging the Powers*; *When the Powers Fall*; *The Powers That Be*.

142. Wink, *Engaging the Powers*, 65–74.

143. Wink, *Naming the Powers*, 104.

144. Ibid., 107.

145. Wink, *Engaging the Powers*, 164.

146. For the critique see Dawn, *Powers*, 15–19.

147. Wink, *Engaging the Powers*, 324.

over the powers.[148] She writes: "He is right about singing, but nowhere does Wink recognize that the Messiah, Jesus Christ, *has brought about* his Kingdom in the Triune work of atonement and will ultimately bring it about in the recapitulation of the cosmos that Revelation describes. . . . Wink's reduction of God makes his victory feeble; he loses the Joy of *Christ's* triumph over the powers at the cross and empty tomb."[149]

Conservative evangelicals, on the other hand, tend to view principalities and powers exclusively in terms of angelic beings who influence individuals and who may work through social structures.[150] Douglas Harink has pointed out that these expositors do not take seriously into account the consistently apocalyptic language of Pauline texts on the powers.[151] The apocalyptic perspective on the powers provides not only an individual, but also a cosmic scale of Christ's victory that involves both redeemed humanity and the rest of the created cosmos.

Yoder's approach takes this perspective seriously and provides a new link between Christology and the doctrine of creation.[152] Apocalyptic theology centered on Christ and his community demonstrates that the Christ event initiated a cosmic transformation of the entire universe, including the fallen powers. The eschatological community of the church, through its participation in the eschatological gift of the Spirit, is the channel for taming and redeeming fallen powers.

> All the idolatry, disorder, and dissolution of earthly and heavenly reality . . . can no longer be any *final* threat to the community's destiny of becoming conformed to the image of God's Son. The powers, though often disordered, threatening, and destructive, are already subject to God's purposes in Christ. They serve God's purposes even in their power to kill God's servants, for in this the conquest of the Lamb/lambs . . . is most directly revealed, and the conformity to Christ in his death and resurrection is made evident—in fact, made possible! Yet powers too, with all creation, or rather, intrinsic to the very reality of creation (they are all identified as "creatures" Rom 8:39), await their final redemption.[153]

148. Dawn, *Power, Weakness, and the Tabernacling of God*, 18.

149. Ibid. Italics original.

150. O'Brien, "Principalities and Powers: Opponents of the Church"; Arnold, *Powers of Darkness*.

151. Harink, *Paul among the Postliberals*, 118–19.

152. Ibid., 119, 120.

153. Ibid., 123. See the reading of Rom 8:12–39 by Harink on 121–25.

This apocalyptic theology is thoroughly grounded in the biblical framework of creation-fall-redemption-glorification, having the cross of Christ at its center. Through his death and resurrection, Christ, the incarnate Logos, has become the door to the new order, the presence of which is revealed through his community, which extends the accomplished redemption to the creation, which includes the powers. In light of this understanding of scripture's center, we are ready to read the story of the Gospel Christians.

Gospel Christians and the Powers: Constructing a New Identity

In this final section I intend to reconstruct the self-identifying narrative of the tradition of the Gospel Christians. This task will be accomplished by reflecting on the historical narrative of the tradition and on its historiography in light of the discussion of Christ and the powers. The story of the Gospel Christians is intended to be read not only in correlation with the central narrative of scripture, which centers on the cross of Christ, but also in correlation with the storylines of Russian Orthodoxy and of the socio-political context. The new construction intends to locate the tradition of the Gospel Christians on the map of free church evangelicalism in the Orthodox, Soviet, and post-Soviet contexts, as well as to out-narrate the forces that have shaped the tradition throughout its existence and that eventually brought it to incoherence, resulting in an identity crisis.

The movement of Gospel Christians in Imperial Russia was born in the Orthodox Church, which had been under the control of the State since the time of Peter the Great.[154] The poor performance of Russian Orthodoxy, which became the policing instrument of imperial and nationalistic politics, created a deep crisis in the Russian society of the nineteenth century. The spiritual movement initiated by a British revivalist preacher was aimed at restoring the primacy of Gospel ethics and morality in the Orthodox Church and beyond, in light of the impending return of Christ. This movement was set on the Protestant rails of Victorian evangelicalism by means of reading scripture through the prism of its founder's evangelical tradition in the vein of the early Keswick holiness movement. Led by the St. Petersburg aristocracy, the new movement displayed the emergence of a new culture which attempted to

154. Zernov, *Russians and Their Church*, 113–32.

untangle the boundaries between different strata of society and different Christian denominations. It attempted to unite Christians of different backgrounds around the scriptures, in the hope of achieving the unity of the primitive church through the hermeneutics of "Bible reading" and mutual love. In the beginning, the movement did not consciously intend to challenge the spiritual authority of either the Orthodox Church or the Russian Monarchy, striving exclusively for the restoration of the Apostolic spirituality of the primitive church. Eventually, however, the Russian leaders of the movement, who had begun to pursue the vision of the restoration of primitive ecclesiology, endeavored also to transform the political structure of Russian society according to the pattern of advanced Western post-Reformed liberal civilization. In so doing, they were challenging the power structure of the pre-modern Imperial Church by being a counter example of a new form of life. Within a single decade the movement was drawn by the forces of Western civilization, which were amplified by the drives of Russian messianism. This was an unconscious synthesis of the Westernizers' and Slavophiles' ideologies manifested in the society of the time. The influence of this ideological component went largely unrecognized, but it was present in the movement from that time on. The changes of identity that followed were the direct result of the changing configurations of geopolitical forces. The Soviet period of the tradition is the most representative, as the identity was changing flexibly, depending on the configuration of the geopolitical force field. The power of Russian messianism had been present since the time of Pashkov, who wanted to establish the first nationwide restored primitivist church to be found anywhere in the world. The climax of the messianic drive is seen in the ministry of Prokhanov, who took the mantle of John Hus and was proclaimed the New Reformer of the final Reformation that was to start from the East. During the time of the Cold War, a flip-flopping of these two constitutive powers took place. Unlike Prokhanov, who took an anti-Soviet political stand and assumed an indigenous Eastern identity, Karev took a pro-Soviet political stand and assumed the Western identity of the Baptist movement. Such changing configurations can be understood against the background of the geopolitical forces of the respective historical periods. Post-Soviet evangelical developments have been characterized by the swiftly changing identity that followed the vectors of the new geopolitical force field. By the exercise of historic imagination, late Soviet and post-Soviet historiographers developed a quasi-Orthodox identity, thereby carving out a place in the new Orthodox culture as a developed and institutionalized religious structure of native origin. The messianic component was reconfigured and manifested in the claim of a "unique synthesis" of Western and Eastern Christianity whose roots go deep into both Orthodoxy and Protestantism. However, despite forging a quasi-Orthodox identity, the Gospel Christians-Baptists did not change their Protestant practices or abandon their continual dependence on conservative Western theology.

By allowing themselves to be shaped by geopolitical forces, the Gospel Christians created a series of epistemic crises. These crises had previously been resolved by erasing or reconfiguring the memory of the past and projecting an imaginative symbolic universe that often distorted the vision of the cross in the Russian and Ukrainian contexts.[155] The post-Soviet brand of Gospel Christians, represented by the Association of Missionary Churches of Gospel Christians of Ukraine, forges its identity in association with Western free church evangelicalism, being uncritically dependent intellectually and often financially on Western resources. A solution to the current crisis of the evangelical traditions in Ukraine, which has been brought about by the failure and withdrawal of the Western mission, may be sought in a critical re-evaluation of the previous historical constructions of identity and theological practices, in light of the Logos, textually mediated by the canon.

CONCLUSION

Having traced the developments in the theological tradition of the Gospel Christians since the collapse of the Soviet Union, we have demonstrated that holist realist theology, influenced by the post-liberal program, is a pragmatically useful approach for solving the current epistemic crisis of the tradition. The holist approach demonstrates sufficient explanatory power to account for the past epistemic crises in the tradition and clears the way for further reconstruction. Being grounded in the Patristic and Reformation approach of reading the world through the lens of scripture, it is in line with the pre-critical communitarian and pragmatic nature of the Christocentric tradition initiated by Radstock. By reading the narrative of the tradition through the lens of scripture's center, namely the

155. Cf. Volf, *End of Memory*, ch. 5.

cross of Christ, I have demonstrated a way to deal with the inconsistencies of the previous identity constructions.

So who are the Gospel Christians in Ukraine? They are members of the Protestant theological paradigm in general and of its branch of Anglo-American free evangelicalism in particular, whose theology and vision was originally shaped by the holiness proto-Pentecostal currents of the late nineteenth century. This theological paradigm, influenced by the Romantic and Modernist currents of its time, was introduced from the West and promised to be superior to the older Byzantine Paradigm brought to Russia from the South nine hundred years earlier. It has always depended intellectually on the Western evangelical movement, even during those times when it was separated from the rest of the world by the Iron Curtain. From its inception, the tradition did not cultivate intellectual virtues or a research culture, thus absolutizing and universalizing its historically contingent form of life as shaped and modified by its authoritative leaders. By allowing itself to be dominated by political and nationalist powers, the paradigm experienced radical modifications of its self-identifying narrative and eventually became an institutionalized religious structure. As this happened, certain groups of Gospel Christians left these structures in pursuit of less rigid Christian expressions. The movement's association with the world of free church evangelicalism continued, and it retained its previous reservations towards Pentecostalism, Orthodoxy, Catholicism, and liberal Protestantism.

What is the solution to the current crises of theology and identity? The solution is to be found in the cross of Christ and in the creative reconstruction of the narratives and practices of this historically contingent tradition in light of the cross. Resisting the efforts of the fallen powers to shape their identity, the Gospel Christians must *remember* their past in the light of the cross and strive to become an eschatological community that demonstrates the life of Christ's victory over the powers.[156] One way of demonstrating this victory can be through refusing to take part in the current political battles between the Orthodox and Western civilizations, which represent prominent power structures in

156. Yoder, *Original Revolution*, 113–31; Hauerwas, *Peaceable Kingdom*, 96–115. Cf. McClendon, *Systematic Theology*, vol. 1, *Ethics*, 31. McClendon's "Baptist vision" of "the present Christian community as the primitive community and the eschatological community" is in line with my narrative construction. See also Volf, *After Our Likeness*, as an example of ecclesiological construction along these lines.

today's world. Consequently the tradition needs to resist the waves of Ukrainian or Russian nationalism that accompanies those structures.[157] Taking into consideration their historical contingency and their past naïveté, the Gospel Christians should self-critically evaluate their practices. And this evaluation needs to be accomplished in dialogical company with other Christian traditions populating the Ukrainian context. As Loughlin puts it:

> The biblically formed narratives of Christ and his Church become the story which literally makes the world; it goes all the way down. One can develop Lindbeck's idea by saying that when a person enters the scriptural story he or she does so by entering the Church's performance of that story: he or she is baptized into a biblical and ecclesial drama. It is not so much being written into a book as taking part in a play, a play that has to be improvised on the spot. As Rowan Williams puts it, people are invited to "create" themselves in finding a place within this drama—an improvisation in the theatre workshop, but one that purports to be about a comprehensive truth affecting one's identity and future.[158]

The "place" that Loughlin and Williams are talking about is not a *tabula rasa*. It is a public and historic stage, constructed of a complex interaction of multiple and competing traditions. So in the process of reading and improvising, the performers not only create themselves but also reconstruct the public stage by interpreting it through the Christocentric grid of the biblical canon and in light of the narratives of the tradition.

157. Cf. Storkey, *Jesus and Politics*, ch. 12.

158. Loughlin, *Telling God's Story*, 20. Cf. Vanhoozer, *Drama of Doctrine*.

Conclusion

SUMMARY

The principal aim of this project was to resolve the contemporary crises of identity and theology in the tradition of the Gospel Christians in Ukraine. Having sketched the diachronic development of the tradition's identifying narrative and the dynamics of its historical memory, its theological vectors, and its practice of biblical interpretation, I proposed a strategy for reconstructing the tradition's identity and practices along the lines of the emerging post-modern realist theology.

In the first chapter we focused on the biography and theology of Lord Radstock, the revivalist founder of the tradition. It was demonstrated that his theology and his practice of biblical interpretation can be properly understood in light of theological and socio-political developments in the British Isles, Europe, and America since the Reformation. Contrary to the tendency of Radstock's biographers to present him either in a non-denominational ecumenical light or in strictly sectarian terms during the time of his stay in Russia, it was proposed that Radstock be seen as an Anglican evangelical of the Victorian and Romantic eras who had been influenced by the Brethren movement. Instead of looking at Radstock through the grid of "neutral biblicism" or of the Orthodox power reaction to "Bible Christianity," it was suggested that Radstock's mission in Imperial Russia be considered as a clash between the Byzantine and Protestant paradigms. Each of these paradigms had its own theology, hermeneutics, ecclesial practices, and geopolitical charges. The analysis of Lord Radstock's practice of biblical interpretation was in line with his historical identity. Radstock appropriated typological, Christocentric, literalist, and pneumatic theological hermeneutics typical of the emerging holiness paradigm of the early Keswick movement. Being anti-intellectual and sentimental, Radstock absolutized his evangelical theology and practices. This resulted in his non-dialogical stance during his Russian ministry.

In chapter two we demonstrated the presence of two theological paradigms coexisting side by side without entering into dialogue with each other. The first followers of Radstock retained their Orthodox identity and many of its practices. However, Radstockian theology and his approach to the practice of biblical interpretation were creating ferment within the movement, with their emphasis on a theology of conversion and on personal assurance of salvation. It was demonstrated that the aristocratic Radstockists appropriated narrative as the major genre for promoting their pietistic concerns.

In the third chapter we observed the separation of the paradigms and a split in the emerging Russian evangelical movement. V. A. Pashkov was the focus of our study. It was demonstrated that Pashkov was converted into the Revivalist Paradigm and that he envisioned Russia as part of Western civilization. He introduced and developed strong connections with Western evangelical institutions such as the Evangelical Alliance and intended to reform Russia on the evangelical platform. Having moved along the lines of restorationist currents, Pashkov desired not only to restore Apostolic piety in Russia, but also the primitive church, inspired by the Evangelical Alliance and the emerging Keswick movement. Unlike the Orthodox Paradigm that envisioned the unity of the Church on the platform of Apostolic succession and Patristic tradition, the emerging evangelicals envisioned the unity of the church on the platform of primitivist theology and conversionism. However, not all members of the movement supported Pashkov's ecclesial restorationism. The majority of the aristocracy did not go beyond the restoration of Apostolic piety, as was demonstrated in our analysis of the second period of the *Russian Workman*.

In the fourth chapter we explored the continuity of the evangelical tradition in the new socio-political context of Russia at the beginning of the twentieth century. After the failure to establish a branch of the Evangelical Alliance in Russia, ecclesial restorationism became the mainstream of Russian evangelicalism. Pietistic restorationism moved to the margins and eventually disappeared. In contrast to the dominant Orthodoxy and Old Belief, evangelicals identified themselves as the New Belief—a progressive Christian movement fully in line with the modernist currents of the times, with a belief in science and progress.

Theologically, the Russian evangelicals of this period relied heavily on proto-fundamentalist Western Anglo-American evangelicalism, cloning Western evangelical institutions, translating books from the West, and publishing Western articles. The holiness movement and experience-oriented Keswick theology were the most prominent theological shapers of the tradition.

The fifth chapter demonstrated the impact of the socio-political process on the formation of the self-identifying narrative and historical consciousness and memory of the heterogeneous Gospel Christian tradition. After the failure to establish the growing evangelical movement on the Baptist platform and the subsequent failure to convert Orthodoxy into the primitivist mold, the leader of the Gospel Christians, Ivan Prokhanov, created a story that emphasized the Eastern origins of the tradition, which he envisioned as the locomotive for the restoration of Apostolic Christianity, which in turn was envisioned as being able to save Western civilization from militant atheism. However, despite the new narrative identity, Prokhanov and his Bible institute relied largely on Western evangelical sources representing the emerging fundamentalist movement. In reaction to these rationalizing tendencies, the Pentecostal movement sprang out of the midst of the Gospel Christians, resulting in severe criticism by the established authorities of the tradition. Russian evangelicals were unable to establish a research culture in the vortex of these socio-political upheavals. To solve the crises that beset the tradition, the pietistic communities had to rely on the authority of their leaders, democratic councils, and Western sources.

In chapter six we analyzed developments in the tradition between 1944 and the present time. It was demonstrated that the Soviet identity of the Gospel Christians was formed by the socio-political forces dominant during World War II. During the Cold War, the Gospel Christians-Baptists presented themselves as the most advanced evangelicals in the world, engaged in restoring the purity of the golden Apostolic age better than any other Protestant body anywhere. The creators of the post-Cold War identity attempted to present the tradition as an evolutionary development of Eastern Christianity, through the agency of the Holy Spirit, from Orthodoxy to restorationism. In the process of this reconstruction, they utilized the Hegelian rationality of the tottering Soviet system. In response to the severe institutionalization of the tradition, certain groups left the religious structure in search of freer evangelical expression in association with global evangelicalism. It was demonstrated that people associated with the tradition of the Gospel Christians have always relied on theological developments in Anglo-American evangelicalism. However, due to its isolation from the rest of the world by the Iron Curtain, the tradition began to base its unity on the Apostles' Creed and supported that unity by developing a tolerance toward different theological views. Due to the lack of a genuine research culture, current leaders of the tradition tend to introduce Western theologies as if they were indigenous developments within the Eastern evangelical tradition. It is clear that Anglo-American fundamentalism has been playing the most influential role in reshaping the identity, theology, and practices of the tradition during the post-Soviet period. It was demonstrated that a liberal stream has appeared in the Eastern evangelical movement in the twenty-first century, which can be seen in various evangelical publications. This development is relatively new and is due to the influence of secular interpretive communities that inherited a monopoly over licensed education in the departments of religious studies at the state universities.

In the seventh chapter, utilizing the resources of holist realist theology influenced by post-liberal insights, I suggested a reconstruction of the historical identity of the Gospel Christians. The holist approach demonstrates sufficient explanatory power to account for the past epistemic crises in the tradition and clears the way for further reconstruction. Grounded as it is in the Patristic and Reformation approach of reading the world through the lens of scripture, it is in line with the pre-critical communitarian and pragmatic nature of the Christocentric tradition initiated by Radstock. By reading the narrative of the tradition through the lens of scripture's center, namely the cross of Christ, I demonstrated a way to deal with the inconsistencies of the previous identity constructions. It was suggested that the Gospel Christians should view themselves as an eschatological community formed and shaped by complex historical processes. By adopting the insights of MacIntyre, Küng, Lindbeck, and Yoder, I demonstrated a way of doing Eastern evangelical public theology in the post-modern realist way.

CONTRIBUTIONS OF THIS STUDY

In this study I have attempted to bring together themes and topics that have previously been separated from each other. Its major contribution is to provide a thick description and reconstruction of a particular historical tradition by analyzing it from different perspectives, and by bringing it into dialogue with different fragments of relevant scholarship. First, the tradition of the Gospel Christians was located on the map of Christian theology by appropriating Hans Küng's theory of paradigms. In the present work, Pashkov's papers and other archival documents were scrutinized for the first time from a theological point of view. Second, it was argued that the theological and historiographic developments of the tradition should be understood against the dynamic backdrop of the socio-political context. I demonstrated that contextual forces such as messianism and the contemporary ideologies of the Slavophiles and Westernizers, as well as deep currents of Modernism and Romanticism, tacitly influenced, shaped, and drove the tradition. Third, it was argued that the tradition did not experience abrupt denominational shifts, as had been argued in previous scholarly works which diminished continuities and exaggerated diachronic differences. In line with MacIntyre's diachronic justification, I attempted to provide a coherent narrative account for the differences, continuities, and myth-making in denominational historiographies. Fourth, I demonstrated that the social memory and imagination of the tradition are historically contingent. Memory and imagination are shaped by the survival strategies developed by authoritative leaders in order to resolve new crises caused by new experiences. Fifth, drawing on the resources of Western evangelicalism and post-liberalism, I suggested a new solution to the contemporary crises of identity and theology. The proposed reconstruction enables both historians and theologians to participate in established Western scholarship and discourses that have not previously been introduced or systematically dealt with in Ukraine or Russia.

IMPLICATIONS AND NEW QUESTIONS RAISED BY THE STUDY

Historical Identity Issues

First, in the present work I have focused on the tradition of the Gospel Christians as represented only by its key leaders. Further archival work needs to be done, however, to explore other historical constructions that may have been present in this heterogeneous tradition. Second, in order to improve the resolution of the historical picture, the Baptist tradition and its historiography should be critically explored in search of diachronic constructions of the particularly Baptist denominational identity. Third, it was demonstrated that the tradition of the Gospel Christians can and should be understood against the background of the disputes between the Slavophiles and Westernizers. Further research is needed to understand the impact of these cultural tendencies on the tradition. In line with this research, the Russian cultural and mental "maps" of the nineteenth and early twentieth centuries should be revised, as they do not include such impressive emotion-, piety-, and practice-oriented religious movements as the Gospel Christians. These movements occupy a middle position between those of the Slavophiles (Orthodox) and the Westernizers (humanists). It was demonstrated that intellectuals such as Vladimirov, who is never mentioned in the standard historiographies, envisioned and rationalized a third, religious solution to the crumbling Russian identity that was different from those proposed by the Slavophiles and the Westernizers.

Theology

The present research should help Ukrainian students of theology understand that no theological construction is possible without taking historical contingency into account. It opens a way for shaping and molding Ukrainian evangelical theology in dialogue with current discourses that are taking place in the Anglo-American and Continental academy. However, any theological construction should be done in line with the historical identity of the tradition.

Practices

In the present work I have provided a diachronic description of the development of the practice of biblical interpretation. In future research I will attempt to reconstruct, in a tradition-continuous way, the practice of biblical interpretation for the twenty-first century. The practice will be reconstructed in light of recent developments in semiotics and theological hermeneutics. The reconstruction of the practice should be in line with the new historical identity and theology of the Ukrainian Gospel Christians. And, if necessary, other practices of the tradition will also need to undergo the same kind of diachronic evaluation and reconstruction.

Culture

The present research has demonstrated that the Gospel Christian tradition was drastically shaped by the political processes taking place in society. The Ukrainian Gospel Christians must be involved in the complex dialogical process of forming Ukraine's post-Soviet cultural identity, while being aware of the ideological currents in the midst of which they find themselves. They can do so by participating in academic discussions that create, shape, and articulate values in the public life of Ukraine, while remembering and not denying their own past. The drive of Western fundamentalism that marginalizes the tradition by its separatist attitudes should be resisted and exorcized by exposing its ideological frameworks. Through participation in ongoing dialogue in the public sphere of Ukraine, the Gospel Christians should strive to develop an academic research culture in true dialogue with other participants who come from other traditions that populate the public sphere in Ukraine. In particular, it is inevitable that the Gospel Christians will begin to enter into genuine dialogue with the most influential religious tradition in Ukraine—Eastern Orthodoxy. It is hoped that the present research may be a helpful tool for locating and developing points of commensurability between theological paradigms that have never before been in real dialogue in Ukraine.

Glossary

Practice: Any coherent and complex form of socially established cooperative human activity through which goods internal to that form of activity are realized in the course of trying to achieve those standards of excellence which are appropriate to, and partially definitive of, that form of activity, with the result that human powers to achieve excellence, and human conceptions of the ends and goods involved, are systematically extended.[1]

Virtue: An acquired human quality the possession and exercise of which tends to enable us to achieve those goods which are internal to practices and the lack of which effectively prevents us from achieving any such goods.[2]

Tradition: A historically extended, socially embodied argument, and an argument precisely in part about the goods which constitute that tradition. Within a tradition the pursuit of goods extends through generations, sometimes though many generations. Hence the individual's search for his or her good is generally and characteristically conducted within a context defined by those traditions of which the individual's life is a part, and this is true both of those goods which are internal to practices and the goods of a single life.[3]

Identifying narrative: A story a community tells about its historical origin and its past and present experiences and goals.[4]

1. MacIntyre, *After Virtue*, 175.
2. Ibid., 178.
3. Ibid., 207.
4. See the discussion of personal identities shaped by narrative in MacIntyre, *After Virtue*, 195–207.

Restorationism/Primitivism: An effort to deny history and to return to the time before time, to the golden age that preceded the corruptions of life in history. Spiritual restorationism is focused on matters of piety, faith, and doctrine. Ecclesiastical restorationism is focused on issues of church polity, ordinances, and offices.[5]

Messianism: Belief in an exclusive calling, a calling which is religious and universal in its significance and which sees in a given people the bearer of the messianic spirit. The given people are God's chosen messianic people.[6]

Civilization: The highest cultural grouping of a people and the broadest level of cultural identity. It is defined both by common objective elements such as language, history, religion, customs, and institutions, and by the subjective self-identification of a people.[7]

5. Ware, *Restorationism in the Holiness Movement in the Late Nineteenth and Early Twentieth Centuries*, 34–35.

6. Definition by Berdyaev, quoted in Duncan, *Russian Messianism*, 7.

7. Huntington, *Clash*, 43.

Bibliography

PRINTED SOURCES

Abraham, William J. *Canon and Criterion in Christian Theology*. New York: Oxford University Press, 1998.

———. "I Believe in One, Holy, Catholic and Apostolic Church." In *Nicene Christianity*, edited by Christopher Seitz et al., 177–87. Grand Rapids: Brazos, 2001.

Adam, A. K. M. *Faithful Interpretation: Reading the Bible in a Postmodern World*. Minneapolis: Fortress, 2006.

———. *Making Sense of New Testament Theology: "Modern" Problems and Prospects*. Studies in American Biblical Hermeneutics. 1995. Reprint, Eugene, OR: Wipf & Stock, 2005.

———. *What is Postmodern Biblical Criticism?* Guides to Biblical Scholarship. New Testament Series. Minneapolis: Fortress, 1995.

Anderson, Vladimir. *Staroobriadchestvo i Sektantstvo: Istoricheskii Ocherk Russkogo Religioznogo Raznomysliia*. St. Petersburg: Izdanie V. I. Gubinskogo, 1908.

Archer, Kenneth J. *A Pentecostal Hermeneutics for the Twenty-First Century: Spirit, Scripture, and Community*. New York: T. & T. Clark, 2004.

Arnold, Clinton. *Powers of Darkness: Principalities and Powers in Paul's Letters*. Downers Grove, IL: InterVarsity, 1992.

Aslund, Anders, and Michael McFaul, editors. *Revolution in Orange: The Origins of Ukraine's Democratic Breakthrough*. Washington: Carnegie Endowment for International Peace, 2006.

Augustine. *Confessions*. Translated by R. S. Pine-Coffin. London: Penguin, 1961.

Audi, Robert. *Epistemology: A Contemporary Introduction to the Theory of Knowledge*. New York: Routledge, 1998.

Auerbach, Erich. *Mimesis: The Representation of Reality in Western Literature*. Translated by Willard R. Trask. Princeton: Princeton University Press, 1953.

Bachinin, V. *Evangel'skie Tsennosti v Grazhdanskom Obshchestve*. St. Petersburg: Aleteia, 2006.

———. *Khristianskaia Mysl': Sotsiologia, Politicheskaia Teologia, Kul'turologia*. Vol. 2. St. Petersburg: Novoe i Staroe, 2004.

———. "Lord G. Radstock." Online: http://www.archipelag.ru/authors/bachinin/?library=1337.

Baker, Peter, and Susan Glasser. *Kremlin Rising: Vladimir Putin's Russia and the End of Revolution*. New York: Scribner, 2005.

Ball, Terrence. "History: Critique and Irony." In *The Cambridge Companion to Marx*, edited by Terrell Carver, 124–42. Cambridge: Cambridge University Press, 1991.

Barabas, Steven. *So Great Salvation: The History and Message of the Keswick Convention*. London: Marshall, Morgan & Scott, 1952.

Barr, James. *The Bible in the Modern World*. London: SCM, 1972.

———. *Fundamentalism*. London: SCM, 1977.

Barry, Randall K., editor. *ALA-LC Romanization Tables: Transliteration Schemes for Non-Roman Scripts*. Washington: Library of Congress, 1997.

Barsukov, I. P. *Mitropolit Moskovskii i Kolomenskii po ego Sochineniiam, Pis'mam i Rasskazam Sovremennikov*. Moscow, 1883.

Barsukova, Z. N. *Prosvetitel' Sibirskikh Stran*. St. Petersburg, 1901.

Barth, Karl. *Church Dogmatics*. Vol. 4, *The Christian Life*. Translated by Geoffrey W. Bromiley. Grand Rapids: Eerdmans, 1981.

Bartholomew, Craig G., and Michael W. Goheen. *The Drama of Scripture: Finding Our Place in the Biblical Story*. Grand Rapids: Baker, 2004.

———. "Story and Biblilcal Theology." In *Out of Egypt: Biblical Theology and Biblical Interpretation*, edited by Craig Bartholomew et al., 144–71. Grand Rapids: Zondervan, 2004.

Bartholomew, Craig, Robin Parry, and Andrew West, editors. *The Futures of Evangelicalism*. Grand Rapids: Kregel, 2003.

Bauckham, Richard. "Reading Scripture as a Coherent Story." In *The Art of Reading Scripture*, edited by Ellen F. Davis and Richard B. Hays, 38–53. Grand Rapids: Eerdmans, 2003.

Bebbington, D. W. *The Dominance of Evangelicalism*. Downers Grove, IL: InterVarsity, 2005.

———. *Evangelicalism in Modern Britain: A History from the 1730s to the 1980s*. New York: Routledge, 1989.

———. *Holiness in Nineteenth-Century England*. Carlisle, UK: Paternoster, 2000.

———. *The Nonconformist Conscience*. Boston: Allen & Unwin, 1982.

Bediako, Kwame. *Theology and Identity*. Oxford: Regnum, 1992.

Benham, Stephen John. "Music Education as Identity Construction: An Investigation of the Church Music Schools of the All-Ukrainian Union of Associations of Evangelical Christian-Baptists." PhD diss., University of Rochester, 2004.

Berdiaev, Nikolai. "Dukhovnoe Khristianstvo i Sektantstvo v Rossii." In *Sobranie Sochenenii*, vol. 3, *Tipy Religioznoi Mysli v Rossii*. Paris: YMCA, 1989.

———. *Freedom and the Spirit*. London: Centenary, 1935.

———. *Istoki i Smysl Russkogo Kommunisma*. Paris: YMCA, 1955.

———. *The Origin of Russian Communism*. Ann Arbor: University of Michigan Press, 1960.

———. *The Russian Idea*. Herndon, VA: Lindisfarne, 1992.

———. *Vekhi: Landmarks*. Armonk, NY: Sharpe, 1994.

Berger, Peter. *A Rumor of Angels: Modern Society and the Rediscovery of the Supernatural*. New York: Doubleday, 1990.

———. *The Social Reality of Religion*. London: Penguin, 1973.

Berger, P. L., and T. Luckman. *The Social Construction of Reality: A Treatise in the Sociology of Knowledge*. New York: Doubleday, 1966.

Berkhof, Hendrikus. *Christ and the Powers*. Translated by John Howard Yoder. Scottdale, PA: Herald, 1962.

Berokoff, John K. *Molokans in America*. Los Angeles: Stockton-Doty Trade, 1969.

Bettex, F. "The Bible and Modern Criticism." In *The Fundamentals*, edited by R. A. Torrey et al., vol. 1, 76–93. Grand Rapids: Baker, 2003.

Bevan, Daisy. "Odd Memories of an Ordinary Person." In Bevan Collection. London: School of Slavonic and East-European Studies.

Bevans, Stephen B. *Models of Contextual Theology*. Maryknoll, NY: Orbis, 2002.

Beznosova, Oksana Vladimirovna. *Pozdnee Protestantskoe Sektantstvo Iũga Ukrainy, 1850–1905*. Kandidat Istoricheskikh Nauk diss., Dnepropetrovskii Gosudarstvennyi Universitet, 2001.

Binfield, Clyde. "Jews in Evangelical Dissent: The British Society, the Herschell Connection and the Pre-Millennial Thread." In *Prophecy and Eschatology*, edited by Michael Wilks. Oxford: Blackwell, 1994.

Blane, Andrew. *Georges Florovsky, Russian Intellectual and Orthodox Churchman*. New York: St. Vladimir's Seminary Press, 1994.

———. "The Relations between the Russian Protestant Sects and the State, 1900–1921." PhD diss., Duke University, 1964.

Blomberg, Craig L. *Interpreting the Parables*. Downers Grove, IL: InterVarsity, 1990.

Bogdanovich, E. *Otkrytye Pis'ma Starosty Isaakievskogo Sobora g. Pashkovu*. St. Petersburg, 1883.

Bogoliubov, D. I. *Kto Eto—Pashkovtsy, Baptisty i Adventisty*. Saint Petersburg, 1912.

———. "Pashkovtsy, ili Khristiane Evangelicheskogo Ispovedania." In *Russkie Sektanty, ikh Uchenie, Kul't i Sposoby Propagandy*, edited by M. A. Kal'nev, 99–110. Odessa, 1911.

Bourdeaux, Michael. *Opium of the People: The Christian Religion in the USSR*. Oxford: Mowbrays, 1965.

———, editor. *The Politics of Religion in Russia and the New States of Euroasia*. London: Sharpe, 1995.

———. "Religious Liberty in the Soviet Union: Baptists in the Early Days of Protest (1960–1966)." In *Eastern European Baptist History: New Perspectives*, edited by Sharyl Corrado and Toivo Pilli, 119–32. Prague: International Baptist Theological Seminary, 2007.

Braaten, Carl E., and Robert W. Jenson, editors. *A Map of Twentieth-Century Theology*. Minneapolis: Fortress, 1995.

Brackney, William H. *A Genetic History of Baptist Thought*. Macon, GA: Mercer University Press, 2004.

Bray, Gerald Lewis. *Biblical Interpretation*. Downers Grove, IL: InterVarsity, 1996.

Breyfogle, Nicholas B. *Heretics and Colonizers: Forging Russia's Empire in the South Caucasus*. Ithaca, NY: Cornell University Press, 2005.

Brown, Cheryl, and Wes Brown. "Progress and Challenge in Theological Education in Central and Eastern Europe." *Transformation* 20 (2003) 1–12.

Busch, Eberhard. *Karl Barth and the Pietists: The Young Karl Barth's Critique of Pietism and Its Response*. Downers Grove, IL: InterVarsity, 2004.

Bushkovitch, Paul. "What Is Russia? Russian National Identity and the State, 1500–1917." In *Culture, Nation, and Identity*, edited by Andreas Kappeler et al. Toronto: Canadian Institute of Ukrainian Studies Press, 2003.

Butkevich, T. I. *Obzor Russkikh Sekt*. St. Petersburg: Tuzov, 1915.

Callahan, James Patrick. *Primitivist Piety: The Ecclesiology of the Early Plymouth Brethren*. Lanham, MD: Scarecrow, 1996.

Campbell, Ted A. *The Religion of the Heart: A Study of European Religious Life in the Seventeenth and Eighteenth Centuries*. Columbia: University of South Carolina Press, 1991.

Carlson, Gordon William. "Russian Protestants and American Evangelicals Since the Death of Stalin: Patterns of Interaction and Response." PhD diss., University of Minnesota. 1986.

Carter, Grayson. *Anglican Evangelicals: Protestant Secessions from the Via Media, c. 1800–1850*. Oxford: Oxford University Press, 2001.

Carwardine, Richard. "Revivalism." In *The Oxford Companion to Christian Thought*, edited by Adrian Hastings et al., 622–23. Oxford: Oxford University Press, 2000.

Chadwick, Owen. *The Victorian Church*. London: Adam & Charles Black, 1966.

Charry, Ellen T. *By the Renewing of Your Minds: The Pastoral Function of Christian Doctrine*. New York: Oxford University Press, 1997.

Charter, Miriam L. "Theological Education for New Protestant Churches of Russia: Indigenous Judgments on the Appropriateness of Educational Methods and Styles." PhD diss., Trinity Evangelical Divinity School, 1997.

Cherenkov, M., editor. *Bogoslovie i Bogoslovskoe Obrazovanie v Sovremennom Obschestve: Aktual'nye Voprosy Teorii i Praktiki*. Odessa: Euro-Asian Accrediting Association and Bogoslovskoe Obshchestvo Evrazii, 2002.

———, moderator. "Bogoslovskoe Obshchestvo Evrazii Obsuzhdaet: Kto My, Evraziiskie Protestanty?" In *Fenomen Evraziiskogo Protestantizma: Materialy Konferentsii Bogoslovskogo Obshchestva Evrazii*, edited by M. Cherenkov. Odessa: Bogoslovskoe Obshchestvo Evrazii, 2003.

———. *Evropeiska reformatsia ta ukrains'kii evangel'skii protestantizm.*Kyiv: Connect International and Assotsiatsia "Dukhovne vidrodzhennia," 2008.

———, editor. *Fenomen Evraziiskogo Protestantizma: Materialy Konferentsii Bogoslovskogo Obschestva Evrazii*. Odessa: Bogoslovskoe Obshchestvo Evrazii, 2003.

———. "Filosofsko-istoricheskoe pereosmyslenie evropeiskogo gumanizma." Dissertatsia na soiskanie uchenoi stepeni kandidata filosofskikh nauk, Donetskii Natsional'nyi Universitet, 2003.

———. "My Rozhdeny chtob skazku sdelat' Byl'iu." *Lingua Franca* 11 (2009) 50.

———. "Opyt Teologii Osvobozhdeniia i Problema Stanovleniia Natsional'nogo Bogosloviia." In *Fenomen Evraziiskogo Protestantizma: Materialy Konferentsii Bogoslovskogo Obshchestva Evrazii*, edited by M. Cherenkov. Odessa: Bogoslovskoe Obshchestvo Evrazii, 2003.

———. *Tret'ia Pravda*. Moscow: Dukhovnoe Vozrozhdenie, 2006.

Chistovich, I. A. *Istoria Perevoda Biblii na Russkii Iazyk*. St. Petersburg, 1899.

Christoff, Peter K. *An Introduction to the Ninteenth-Century Russian Slavophilism*. Boulder, CO: Westview, 1991.

Clendenin, Daniel B. *Eastern Orthodox Theology*. Grand Rapids: Baker , 2003.

Clowes, Edith W., Samuel D. Kassow, and James L. West, editors. *Between Tsar and People: Educated Society and the Quest for Public Identity in Late Imperial Russia*. Princeton, NJ: Princeton University Press, 1991.

Coad, F. Roy. *A History of the Brethren Movement*. Vancouver: Regent College Publishing, 1968.

Coady, C. A. J. *Testimony: A Philosophical Study*. Oxford: Clarendon, 1992.

Coleman, Heather Jean. "The Most Dangerous Sect: Baptists in Tsarist and Soviet Russia, 1905–1929." PhD diss., University of Illinois, 1998.

———. *Russian Baptists and Spiritual Revolution, 1905–1929*. Bloomington: Indiana University Press, 2005.

Collin, Finn. *Social Reality*. New York: Routledge, 1997.

Connerton, Paul. *How Societies Remember*. Cambridge: Cambridge University Press, 1989.

Copleston, Frederick. *A History of Philosophy*. Vol. 10, *Russian Philosophy*. New York: Continuum, 2003.

Corley, Felix. *Religion in the Soviet Union: An Archival Reader*. London: Macmillan, 1996.

Corrado, Sharyl. *Filosofiia Sluzheniia Polkovnika Pashkova*. St. Petersburg: Vsekh, 2005.

———. "The Gospel in Society: Pashkovite Social Outreach in Late Imperial Russia." In *Eastern European Baptist History: New Perspectives*, edited by Sharyl Corrado and Toivo Pilli, 52–70. Prague: International Baptist Theological Seminary, 2007.

———. "The Philosophy of Ministry of Colonel Vasiliy Pashkov." MA thesis, Wheaton College, 2000.

Cosden, Darrell. "Christian Morality in a Pluralistic Society: Perspectives for Post-Soviet Cultures." *Evangelical Review of Theology* 22 (1998) 337–45.

———. "Coming of Age: The Future of a Post-Soviet Evangelical Theology." *Evangelical Review of Theology* 26 (2002) 319–36.

———. "Contextual Theological Education among Post-Soviet Protestants." *Transformation* 18 (2001) 125–28.

———. *A Theology of Work: Work and the New Creation*. Carlisle, UK: Paternoster, 2004.

Croatto, J. Severino. *Biblical Hermeneutics*. Maryknoll, NY: Orbis, 1987.

Dann, Robert Bernard. *Father of Faith Missions: The Life and Times of Anthony Norris Groves*. Waynesboro, GA: Authentic Media, 2004.

Davidson, Donald. *Inquiries into Truth and Interpretation*. Oxford: Clarendon, 1985.

———. *Subjective, Intersubjective, Objective*. Oxford: Clarendon , 2001.

Davies, Horton. *Worship and Theology in England: From Newman to Martineau, 1850–1900*. Princeton, NJ: Princeton University Press, 1962.

Davis, Ellen F., and Richard B. Hays, editors. *The Art of Reading Scripture*. Grand Rapids: Eerdmans, 2003.

Dawn, Marva. "The Biblical Concept of the 'Principalities and Powers': John Yoder points to Jacques Ellul." In *The Wisdom of the Cross: Essays in Honor of John Howard Yoder*, edited by Stanley Hauerwas et al., 168–80. 1999. Reprint, Eugene, OR: Wipf & Stock, 2005.

———. "Powers and Principalities." In *Dictionary for Theological Interpretation of the Bible*, edited by Kevin J. Vanhoozer, 609–12. Grand Rapids: Baker, 2005.

———. *Powers, Weakness, and the Tabernacling of God*. Grand Rapids: Eerdmans, 2001.

Dayton, Donald W. *Discovering an Evangelical Heritage*. New York: Harper & Row, 1976.

———. *Theological Roots of Pentecostalism*. Peabody, MA: Hendrickson, 1991.

De Chalandeau, Alexander. *The Theology of the Evangelical Christians-Baptists in the USSR*. ThD diss., Universite des Sciences Humaines de Strasbourg, Faculte de Theologie Protestante, 1978.

DeHart, Paul J. *Trial of Witnesses: The Rise and Decline of Post-Liberal Theology*. Oxford: Blackwell, 2006.

Devlin, Judith. *Slavophiles and Commissars: Enemies of Democracy in Modern Russia*. New York: St. Martin's, 1999.

Deyneka, Peter. *The Life and Suffering of Christians in Solovki and Siberia, Russia*. Grand Rapids: Zondervan, n.d.

Dietrich, Walter, and Ulrich Luz, editors. *The Bible in a World Context*. Grand Rapids: Eerdmans, 2002.

Dockery, David S. *Biblical Interpretation Then and Now*. Grand Rapids: Baker, 1992.

Dolbilov, M. D. "Konstruirovanie Obrazov Miatezha: Politika M. N. Murav'eva v Litovsko-Belorusskom Krae v 1863–1865 gg. Kak Ob'ekt Istoriko-Antropologicheskogo Analiza." In *Actio Nova 2000*, 338–408. Moscow: Globus, 2000.

Dolina, Oleg, *An Examination of Ukrainian Protestant/Baptist Church History with Particular Reference to Its Origin and Development until 1939*. MPhil diss., University of Wales, Lampeter, 1996.

Dugin, A. G. *Osnovy Geopolitiki*. Moscow: Arktogeya, 2000.

Duncan, Peter J. S. *Russian Messianism: Third Rome, Revolution, Communism, and After*. London: Routledge, 2000.

Dunn, James D. G. *Unity and Diversity in the New Testament*. 2nd ed. London: SCM, 1997.

Durasoff, Steve. *The Russian Protestants: Evangelicals in the Soviet Union: 1944–1964*. Rutherford, NJ: Fairleigh Dickinson University Press, 1969.

Dyck, Johannes. "Fresh Skins for New Wine: On the Structure of the First Russian Baptist Congregations in South Russia." In *Eastern European Baptist History: New Perspectives*, edited by Sharyl Corrado and Toivo Pilli, 34–51. Prague: International Baptist Theological Seminary, 2007.

Erickson, Millard J. *Christian Theology*. Grand Rapids: Baker, 1983.

Elliott, Mark. "Eastern Orthodox and Slavic Evangelicals: What Sets Them Both Apart from Western Evangelicals." *East-West Church and Ministry Report* 3 (1995) 15–16.

Ellis, Geoffrey H. *The Other Revolution: Russian Evangelical Awakenings*. Abilene, TX: ACU Press, 1996.

Evans, William. *The Great Doctrines of the Bible*. Chicago: Moody, 1964.

Fairbairn, Donald. *Eastern Orthodoxy through Western Eyes*. Louisville: Westminster John Knox, 2002.

Fidler, Stephen, et al., "Ever Eastward? A Divided NATO Pauses at Russia's Red Lines." Online: http://www.ft.com/cms/s/0/8bc3ccd0-0007-11dd-825a-000077b07658.html?nclick_check=1.

Filipovych, Lyudmyla, and Anatoly Kolodny. "Theology and Religious Studies in the Postcommunist Ukraine: History, Modern Status, Perspectives." *Numen* 51 (2004) 78–93.

Findlay, James F. *Dwight L. Moody: American Evangelist, 1837–1899*. Chicago: University of Chicago Press, 1969.

Fletcher, William C. *Christianity in the Soviet Union*. Los Angeles: University of Southern California Press, 1963.

Florovskii, Georgii. *Puti Russkogo Bogosloviia*. Minsk: Izdatel'stvo Belorusskogo Ekzarkhata, 2006.

Florovsky, Georges. *Bible, Church and Tradition: An Eastern Orthodox View*. Belmont, MA: Nordland, 1972.

———. *The Ecumenical World of Orthodox Civilization*. The Hague, Netherlands: Mouton, 1974.

———. "The Orthodox Churches and the Ecumenical Movement Prior to 1910." In *A History of the Ecumenical Movement 1517–1948*, edited by Ruth Rose and Stephen Charles Neill, 169–215. London: SPCK, 1954.

Fodor, James. "Post-Liberal Theology." In *Modern Theologians: An Introduction to Christian Theology since 1918*, 3rd ed., edited by David F. Ford, 229–48. Oxford: Blackwell, 2005.

Forbes, Chris. "Pauline Demonology and/or Cosmology? Principalities, Powers and the Elements of the World in their Hellenistic Context." *Journal for the Study of the New Testament* 24 (2002) 51–73.

———. "Paul's Principalities and Powers: Demythologizing Apocalyptic?" *Journal for the Study of the New Testament* 82 (2001) 61–88.

Ford, David F. "System, Story, Performance: Proposal about the Role of Narrative in Christian Systematic Theology." In *Why Narrative?*, edited by Stanley Hauerwas and L. Gregory Jones, 191–215. Grand Rapids: Eerdmans, 1989.

Fountain, David. *Lord Radstock and the Russian Awakening*. Southampton, UK: Mayflower Christian, 1988.

Fowl, Stephen E. *Engaging Scripture: A Model for Theological Interpretation*. Challenges in Contemporary Theology. Oxford: Blackwell, 1998.

———. "Learning to Narrate Our Lives in Christ." In *Theological Exegesis: Essays in Honor of Brevard S. Childs*, edited by Christopher R. Seitz and Kathryn Greene-McCreight, 339–54. Grand Rapids: Eerdmans, 1999.

Fowl, Stephen E., and Gregory L. Jones. *Reading in Communion: Scripture and Ethics in Christian Life*. 1991. Reprint, Eugene, OR: Wipf & Stock, 1998.

Franchuk, V. I. *Prosila Rossia Dozhdia u Gospoda*. Kiev: Svitankova Zoria, 2002.

Freeman, Curtis W., et al. *Baptist Roots: A Reader in the Theology of a Christian People*. Valley Forge, PA: Judson, 1999.

Frei, Hans W. *The Eclipse of Biblical Narrative: A Study in Eighteenth and Nineteenth Century Hermeneutics*. New Haven: Yale University Press, 1974.

———. *The Identity of Jesus Christ: The Hermeneutical Bases of Dogmatic Theology*. Philadelphia: Fortress, 1975.

———. "Response to 'Narrative Theology: An Evangelical Appraisal.'" *Trinity Journal* 8 (1987) 21–24.

———. *Theology and Narrative: Selected Essays*. Edited by William C. Placher and George Hunsinger. Oxford: Oxford University Press, 1993.

———. *Types of Christian Theology*. New Haven: Yale University Press, 1992.

Fuller, W. Harold. *People of the Mandate*. London: Paternoster, 1996.

Fullerton, W. Y. *No Ordinary Man: A Remarkable Life of F. B. Meyer*. Minneapolis: Ambassador, 1993.

Gadamer, Hans-Georg. *Truth and Method*. 2nd ed. Revised by Joel Weinsheimer and Donald G. Marshall. New York: Continuum, 2004.

Garadzha, V. I. *Religiovedenie*. Moscow: Aspekt, 1995.
Geertz, Clifford. *The Interpretation of Cultures: Selected Essays*. New York: Basic, 1973.
Geraci, Robert, and Michael Khodarkovsky, editors. *On Religion and Empire: Missions, Conversions, and Tolerance in Tsarist Russia*. Ithaca, NY: Cornell University Press, 2001.
Glover, Willis B. *Evangelical Nonconformists and Higher Criticism*. London: Independent, 1954.
Goh, Jeffrey C. K. *Christian Tradition Today*. Louvain: Peeters, 2000.
Gololob, G. "Nasledstvo Navufeia ili o Natsional'nom Dukhovnom Samoopredelenii." In *Fenomen Evraziiskogo Protestantizma: Materialy Konferentsii Bogoslovskogo Obshchestva Evrazii*, edited by M. Cherenkov, 15–49. Odessa: Bogoslovskoe Obshchestvo Evrazii, 2003.
———. "Oshibka Rovoama, ili Sud'ba Otechestvennogo Bogoslovia." In *Bogoslovie i Bogoslovskoe Obrazovanie v Sovremennom Obshchestve*, edited by M. Cherenkov, 125–39. Odessa: Euro-Asian Accrediting Association and Bogoslovskoe Obshchestvo Evrazii, 2002.
Golovashchenko, S., sostavitel'. *Istoria Evangel'sko-Baptistskogo Dvizhenia v Ukraine*. Odessa: Bogomyslie, 1998.
Gray, James M. "The Inspiration of the Bible—Definition, Extent and Proof." In *The Fundamentals*, edited by R. A. Torrey et al., vol. 2, 9–43. Grand Rapids: Baker, 2003.
Green, Garrett. *Imagining God: Theology and the Religious Imagination*. San Francisco: Harper & Row, 1989.
———. *Theology, Hermeneutics and Imagination: The Crisis of Interpretation at the End of Modernity*. Cambridge: Cambridge University Press, 2000.
Green, Joel B. *Hearing the New Testament*. Grand Rapids: Eerdmans, 1995.
Greenfeld, Lev. *Eastern Orthodox Influence on Russian Evangelical Ecclesiology*. ThM diss., University of South Africa, 2001.
Grenz, Stanley J. "Articulating the Christian Belief-Mosaic: Theological Method after the Demise of Foundationalism." In *Evangelical Futures: A Conversation on Theological Method*, edited by John G. Stackhouse Jr., 107–38. Grand Rapids: Baker, 2000.
———. *Revisioning Evangelical Theology*. Downers Grove, IL: InterVarsity, 1993.
———. *Theology for the Community of God*. Nashville: Broadman & Holman, 1994.
———. *Renewing the Center*. Grand Rapids: Baker, 2000.
———. *Rediscovering the Triune God: The Trinity in Contemporary Theology*. Minneapolis: Fortress, 2004.
———. *The Named God and the Question of Being: A Trinitarian Theo-Ontology*. Louisville: Westminster John Knox, 2005.
———. *The Social God and the Relational Self*. Louisville: Westminster John Knox, 2001.
Grenz, Stanley, and John R. Franke. *Beyond Foundationalism*. Louisville: Westminster John Knox, 2001.
Grenz, Stanley J., and Roger E. Olson, editors. *Twentieth Century Theology: God and the World in a Transitional Age*. Downers Grove, IL: InterVarsity, 1992.
———. *Who Needs Theology?* Downers Grove, IL: InterVarsity, 1996.

Gribben, Crawford, and Timothy C. F. Stunt. *Prisoners of Hope? Aspects of Evangelical Millennialism in Britain and Ireland, 1800–1880*. Carlisle, UK: Paternoster, 2005.

Gunton, Colin E. *The Actuality of Atonement: A Study of Metaphor, Rationality and Christian Tradition*. London: T. & T. Clark, 1988.

———, editor. *Cambridge Companion to Christian Doctrine*. Cambridge: Cambridge University Press, 1997.

———. *The Promise of Trinitarian Theology*. Edinburgh: T. & T. Clark, 1991.

Gunton, Colin E., Stephen R. Holmes, and Murray A. Rae, editors. *The Practice of Theology: A Reader*. London: SCM, 2001.

Gutsche, Waldemar. *Westliche Quellen des russischen Stundismus: Anfaenge der evangelischen Bewegung in Russland*. Kassel, Germany: Oncken, 1957.

Harink, Douglas. *Paul among the Postliberals: Pauline Theology Beyond Christendom and Modernity*. Grand Rapids: Brazos, 2003.

Harris, Marvin. *Cultural Materialism: The Struggle for a Science of Culture*. New York: Vintage, 1980.

Hart, Trevor. *Faith Thinking: The Dynamics of Christian Theology*. Downers Grove, IL: InterVarsity, 1995.

———. "Tradition, Authority, and a Christian Approach to the Bible as Scripture." In *Between Two Horizons: Spanning New Testament Studies and Systematic Theology*, edited by Joel B. Green and Max Turner, 183–204. Grand Rapids: Eerdmans, 2000.

Hatch, Nathan O. "Sola Scriptura and Novus Ordo Seclorum." In *The Bible in America: Essays in Cultural History*, edited by N. Hatch and M. Noll, 59–78. New York: Oxford University Press, 1982.

Hauerwas, Stanley. *A Community of Character: Toward a Constructive Christian Social Ethics*. Notre Dame, IN: University of Notre Dame Press, 1981.

———. *The Peaceable Kingdom: A Primer on Christian Ethics*. Notre Dame, IN: University of Notre Dame Press, 1983.

———. *Wilderness Wanderings: Probing Twentieth-Century Theology and Philosophy*. Boulder, CO: Westview, 1997.

Hauerwas, Stanley, and John Berkman. *The Hauerwas Reader*. Durham: Duke University Press, 2001.

Hauerwas, Stanley, and Gregory L. Jones, editors. *Why Narrative? Readings in Narrative Theology*. Grand Rapids: Eerdmans, 1989.

Hays, Richard B. *The Conversion of the Imagination*. Grand Rapids: Eerdmans, 2005.

———. *Echoes of Scripture in the Letters of Paul*. New Haven: Yale University Press, 1989.

———. *The Moral Vision of the New Testament*. Edinburgh: T. & T. Clark, 1996.

Heidegger, Martin. *Being and Time*. Translated by J. Macquarrie and E. Robinson. London: SCM, 1962.

Heier, Edmund. *Religious Schism in the Russian Aristocracy, 1860–1900: Radstockism and Pashkovism*. The Hague, Netherlands: Martinus Nijhoff, 1970.

Hensley, Jeffrey. "Are Postliberals Necessarily Antirealists? Reexamining the Metaphysics of Lindbeck's Postliberal Theology." In *The Nature of Confession: Evangelicals and Postliberals in Conversation*, edited by Timothy R. Phillips and Dennis L. Okholm, 69–80. Downers Grove, IL: InterVarsity, 1996.

Herrlinger, Kimberly Page. "Class, Piety, and Politics: Workers, Orthodoxy, and the Problem of Religious Identity in Russia, 1881–1914." PhD diss., University of California, Berkeley, 1996.

Higgins, Gregory C. *The Tapestry of Christian Theology: Modern Minds on the Biblical Narrative*. New York: Paulist, 2003.

Higton, M. A. "Hans Frei and David Tracy on the Ordinary and the Extraordinary in Christianity." *Journal of Religion* 79 (1999) 566–91.

Hill, Samuel S. "Comparing Three Approaches to Restorationism: A Response." In *The American Quest for the Primitive Church,* edited by Richard T. Hughes, 232–38. Urbana: University of Illinois Press, 1988.

Hominuke, James. *The Evangelical Christianity among the Ukrainians*. BD diss., Northern Baptist Theological Seminary, 1943.

Horton, John, and Susan Mendus, editors. *After MacIntyre*. Cambridge: Polity, 1996.

Hudson, Winthrop S. *American Protestantism*. Chicago: University of Chicago Press, 1961.

Hudspith, Sarah. *Dostoevsky and the Idea of Russianness: A New Perspective on Unity and Brotherhood*. London: Routledge, 2003.

Hughes, Richard T., editor. *The American Quest for the Primitive Church*. Urbana: University of Illinois Press, 1988.

Hughes, Richard T., and C. Leonard Allen. *Illusions of Innocence: Protestant Primitivism in America, 1630–1875*. Chicago: University of Chicago Press, 1988.

Huntington, Samuel P. *The Clash of Civilizations and the Remaking of World Order*. London: Free, 2002.

Ianyshev, Ioann, and V. A. Pashkov, "Sushchnost Ucheniya g. Pashkova, Izlozhennaya im Samim." *Tserkovnyi Vestnik* 19 (May 10, 1880) 4–7.

Iarotskii, P. L. *Antikomunistichna Sutnist' Uniats'ko-Natsionalistichnoi Fal'sifikatsii Istorii Ukrain'skogo Narodu*. Kyiv: Vyscha Shkola, 1984.

———. *Antikomunizm Social'no-Politichnoi Doctriny Egovizmy*. Kyiv: Naukova Dumka, 1976.

———. *Evolutisia Sovremennogo Iegovizma*. Kiev: Izdatel'stvo Politicheskoi Literatury Ukrainy, 1981.

———, editor. *Istoriia Religii v Ukraiini*. Vol. 5. *Protestantizm v Ukraiini*. Kyiv: Svit Znan', 2002.

———. *Klerikal'nyi Antisovetizm: Sistema Ideologicheskikh Diversii*. Kiev: Izdatel'stvo Politicheskoi Literatury Ukrainy, 1984.

———. *Krisis Iegovizma: Kriticheskii Analiz Ideologii i Evolutsii Obydennogo Religioznogo Soznania*. Kyiv: Naukova Dumka, 1979.

———. *Uniatstvo i Klerikal'nyi Antikomunizm*. Kyiv: Vydavnitstvo Politychnoi Literatury Ukrainy, 1982.

Iartsev, A. *Sekta Evangel'skikh Khristian*. Moscow: Bezbozhnik, 1928.

Ignatkov, V. "Novye Gorizonty." In *Bogoslovie i Bogoslovskoe Obrazovanie v Sovremennom Obshchestve*, edited by M. Cherenkov, 9–22. Odessa: Euro-Asian Accrediting Association and Bogoslovskoe Obshchestvo Evrazii, 2002.

Il'icheva, N., editor. *Tysiacheletie Kreshcheniia Rusi*. Moscow: Izdatel'stvo Moskovskoi Patriarkhii, 1988.

Jakim, Boris, and Robert Bird, editors. *On Spiritual Unity: A Slavophile Reader*. Hudson, NY: Lindisfarne, 1998.

Jeanrond, Werner G. "The Rationality of Faith: On Theological Methodology." In *Hans Küng: New Horizons for Faith and Thought*, edited by Karl-Joseph Kuschel and Hermann Haring, 105–21. London: SCM, 1993.

Jenson, Robert W. *Systematic Theology*. Vol. 1, *The Triune God*. Oxford: Oxford University Press, 1997.

Jones, Charles Edwin. *The Keswick Movement: A Comprehensive Guide*. Lanham, MD: Scarecrow, 2006.

Jones, Gregory L., Reinhard Hütter, and C. Rosalee Velloso Ewell, editors. *God, Truth, and Witness: Engaging Stanley Hauerwas*. Grand Rapids: Brazos, 2005.

Kahle, Wilhelm. *Evangelische Christen in Russland und der Sowjetunion*. Wuppertal, Germany: Oncken-Verlag, 1978.

Kappeler, Andreas, Zenon E. Kohut, Frank E. Sysysn, and Mark von Hagen, editors. *Culture, Nation, and Identity: The Ukrainian-Russian Encounter, 1600–1945*. Edmonton: Canadian Institute of Ukrainian Studies Press, 2003.

Karetnikova, M. S. *Al'manakh po Istorii Russkogo Baptizma*. St. Petersburg: Vsekh, 1999.

———. *Al'manakh po Istorii Russkogo Baptizma*. Vyp. 2. St. Petersburg: Vsekh, 2002.

———. *Al'manakh po Istorii Russkogo Baptizma*. Vyp. 3. St. Petersburg: Vsekh, 2004.

———. "Ivan Veniaminovich Kargel." In I.V. Kargel, *Sobranie Sochinenii*, 684–88. St. Petersburg: Biblia dlia Vsekh, 2002.

Karev, A. V. *Izbrannye Stat'i*. Moscow: Izdanie Vsesoiũznogo Soveta Evangel'skikh-Khristian Baptistov, 1977.

———. *The Russian Evangelical Baptist Movement, or, Under His Cross in Soviet Russia*. 1960.

Kargel', I. V. "Ob Uchenii Piatidesiatnikov." Online: http://rus-baptist.narod.ru/pozicia/03.htm.

———. *Svet iz Teni Budushchikh Blag*. St. Petersburg: Biblia dlia Vsekh, 1998.

———. *Sobranie Sochinenii*. St. Petersburg: Biblia dlia Vsekh, 2002.

Kartashev, A. V. *Ocherki po Istorii Russkoi Tserkvi*. 2 vols. Moscow: Nauka, 1991.

Keene, Timothy Charles. "The Use of Narrative to Facilitate the Reading of Paul's Ethics." PhD diss., University of Wales, Lampeter, 2007.

Kent, John. *Holding the Fort: Studies in Victorian Revivalism*. London: Epworth, 1978.

Kerr, Fergus. "The Reception of Wittgenstein's Philosophy by Theologians." In *Religion and Wittgenstein's Legacy*, edited by D. Z. Phillips and Mario Von Der Ruhr, 253–72. Aldershot, UK: Ashgate, 2005.

———. *Theology after Wittgenstein*. Oxford: Blackwell, 1986.

Kessler, J. B. A. *A Study of the Evangelical Alliance in Great Britain*. Goes, Netherlands: Oosterbaan & Le Cointre, 1968.

Khomiakov, Alexei S. *The Church is One*. London: The Fellowship of St. Alban and St. Sergius, 1968.

Klibanov, A. I. *History of Religious Sectarianism in Russia (1860s–1917)*. Oxford: Pergamon, 1982.

Kobiakovskii, Igor. "The Effectiveness of Theological Education in Ukraine: A Research Project." *Theological Reflections* 7 (2006) 178–204.

Kobzar', Sergei. *Pochemu ia ne mogy Ostavat'sia Baptistom i Protestantom voobshche*. Slavyansk, Ukraine: Pechatnyi Dvor, 2002.

Kolarz, Walter. *Religion in the Soviet Union*. London: Macmillan, 1961.

Kolomiytsev, Alexey. *Sources of Authority in Russian Evangelical Theology*. ThM diss., Master's Seminary, 2005.

Korff, M. M. *Am Zarenhof*. Giessen, Germany: Brunnen-Verlag, 1956.

Kornilov, Nikolai. "Kakogo Roda Bogoslovie nam Nuzhno?" *Put' Bogopoznaniia* 6 (2000) 5–17.

Korogodskii, Iurii. "Kosovski Vyklyky Ukraiiny." *Politika*, Ukrainian. Online: http://www.pravda.com.ua/news/2008/2/22/72041.htm.

Korsunskii, I. N. *Mitropolit Moskovskii i Kolomenskii*. Kharkov, 1898.

Krapivin, M. Y., A. J. Leikin, and A. G. Dalgatov. *Sud'by Khristianskogo Sektantstva v Sovetskoi Rossii*. St. Petersburg: SPbGU, 2003.

Krivova, N. A. *Vlast' i Tserkov' v 1922–1925 gg*. Moscow: AIRO-XX, 1997.

Krushelnycky, Askold. *An Orange Revolution: A Personal Journey Through Ukrainian History*. London: Harvill Secker, 2006.

Kuhn, T. S. *The Structure of Scientific Revolutions*. Chicago: University of Chicago Press, 1970.

Küng, Hans. *Christianity: Essence, History and Future*. London: SCM, 1995.

———. *Global Responsibility: In Search of a New World Ethic*. London: SCM, 1991.

———. *Great Christian Thinkers*. London: SCM, 1994.

———. *Theology for the Third Millennium: An Ecumenical View*. London: Harper Collins, 1991.

———. *Tracing the Way: Spiritual Dimensions of the World Religions*. London: Continuum, 2002.

Küng, Hans, and David Tracy, editors. *Paradigm Change in Theology*. Edinburgh: T. & T. Clark, 1989.

Kuzio, Taras. *Ukraine: Perestroika to Independence*. New York: St. Martin's, 2000.

LaCugna, Catherine Mowry. *The Theological Methodology of Hans Küng*. New York: Scholars, 1982.

Ladd, George Eldon. *A Theology of the New Testament*. Grand Rapids: Eerdmans, 1993.

Lakatos, Imre, "Falsification and the Methodology of Scientific Research Programmes." In *The Methodology of Scientific Research Programmes: Philosophical Papers*, vol. 1, edited by John Worrall and Gregory Currie. Cambridge: Cambridge University Press, 1978.

Lampert, Evgueny. *Nicolas Berdyaev and the New Middle Ages*. London: Clarke, 1945.

Land, Steven J. *Pentecostal Spirituality: A Passion for the Kingdom*. Sheffield, UK: Sheffield Academic Press, 1993.

Landow, George P. *Victorian Types, Victorian Shadows*. Boston: Routledge & Kegan Paul, 1980.

Lash, Nicholas. *Believing Three Ways in One God*. London: SCM, 1992.

———. *Theology on the Way to Emmaus*. London: SCM, 1986.

Latimer, Robert Sloan. *Dr. Baedeker and His Apostolic Work in Russia*. London: Morgan & Scott, 1907.

———. *Under Three Tsars: Liberty of Conscience in Russia 1856–1909*. London: Morgan & Scott, 1909.

Latyshev, A. G. *Rassekrechennyi Lenin*. Moscow: Mart, 1996.

Lehrer, Keith. *Theory of Knowledge*. Boulder: Westview, 1990.

Lennox, Stephen John. "Biblical Interpretation in the American Holiness Movement, 1875–1920." PhD diss., Drew University, 1992.

Leskov, Nikolai. *Schism in High Society: Lord Radstock and His Followers*. Translated by James Yeoman Muckle. Nottingham: Bramcote, 1995.

Levison, John R., and Priscilla Pope-Levison, editors. *Return to Babel*. Louisville: Westminster John Knox, 1999.

Levitin, Anatolii, and Vadim Shavrov. *Ocherki po Istorii Russkoi Tserkovnoi Smuty*. Moscow: Krutitskoe Patriarshee Podvor'e, 1996.

Liakhu, V. "K Voprosu o Vzaimodeistvii Teologii, Bogosluzheniia i Teologii Kul'tury v Liturgicheskom Opyte Neoprotestantisma." In *Bogoslovie i Bogoslovskoe Obrazovanie v Sovremennom Obshchestve*, edited by M. Cherenkov, 44–69. Odessa: Euro-Asian Accrediting Association and Bogoslovskoe Obshchestvo Evrazii, 2002.

Lindbeck, George A. *The Church in a Postliberal Age*. Edited by James J. Buckley. London: SCM, 2003.

———. *The Nature of Doctrine: Religion and Theology in a Postliberal Age*. London: SPCK, 1984.

———. "Post-Critical Canonical Interpretation: Three modes of Retrieval." In *Theological Exegesis: Essays in Honor of Brevard S. Childs*, edited by Christopher Seitz and Kathryn Greene-McCreight, 26–51. Grand Rapids: Eerdmans, 1999.

———. "The Story-Shaped Church: Critical Exegesis and Theological Interpretation." In *The Theological Interpretation of Scripture: Classic and Contemporary Readings*, edited by Stephen E. Fowl, 39–52. Oxford: Blackwell, 1997.

Lindheim, Ralph, and George S. N. Luckyj, editors. *Towards an Intellectual History of Ukraine: An Anthology of Ukrainian Thought from 1710 to 1995*. Toronto: University of Toronto Press, 1996.

Lints, Richard. "The Postpositivist Choice: Tracy or Lindbeck?" *Journal of the American Academy of Religion* 61 (1993) 655–77.

Littell, Franklin Hamlin. *The Anabaptist View of the Church*. Boston: Starr King, 1958.

Liubashchenko, V. "Otechestvennaia Shkola Bogosloviia: Metodologiia, Problemy, Perspektivy." In *Bogoslovie i Bogoslovskoe Obrazovanie v Sovremennom Obschestve*, edited by M. Cherenkov, 37–43. Odessa: Euro-Asian Accrediting Association and Bogoslovskoe Obshchestvo Evrazii, 2002.

———. "Problema Natsional'nogo Bogosloviia: Za i Protiv." In *Bogoslovie i Bogoslovskoe Obrazovanie v Sovremennom Obshchestve*, edited by M. Cherenkov, 180–91. Odessa: Euro-Asian Accrediting Association and Bogoslovskoe Obshchestvo Evrazii, 2002.

Lieven, Sofia. *Evangel'skoe Probuzhdenie v Rossii*. Korntal, Germany: Svet na Vostoke, 1967.

Losskii, N. O. *Istoriia Russkoi Filosofii*. Moscow: Sovetskii Pisatel', 1991.

Losskii, V. N. *Ocherk Mistischeskogo Bogosloviia Vostochnoi Tserkvi*. Moscow: Tsentr "SEI," 1991.

Loughlin, Gerard. *Telling God's Story: Bible, Church and Narrative Theology*. Cambridge: Cambridge University Press, 1996.

Lowith, Karl. *Max Weber and Karl Marx*. London: Routledge, 1993.

Lowrie, Donald Alexander. *Rebellious Prophet: A Life of Nikolai Berdyaev*. New York: Harper, 1960.

Lundin, Roger, Anthony C. Thiselton, and Clarence Walhout. *The Promise of Hermeneutics*. Grand Rapids: Eerdmans, 1999.

Lyotard, Jean-Francois. *The Postmodern Condition*. Translated by G. Bennington and B. Massumi. Minneapolis: University of Minnesota Press, 1984.

Mackintosh, C. H. "The First 50 Years: A History." Online: http://www.mybrethren.org/history/framchm.htm.

MacIntyre, Alasdair C. *After Virtue: A Study in Moral Theory*. London: Duckworth, 1981.

———. *After Virtue: A Study in Moral Theory*. 2nd ed. Notre Dame: University of Notre Dame Press, 1984.

———. "Epistemological Crises, Dramatic Narrative, and the Philosophy of Science." In *Why Narrative? Readings in Narrative Theology*, edited by Stanley Hauerwas and L. Gregory Jones, 138–57. Grand Rapids: Eerdmans, 1989.

———. *Marxism and Christianity*. 3rd ed. London: Duckworth, 2008.

———. *Three Rival Versions of Moral Enquiry: Encyclopedia, Genealogy and Tradition*. London: Duckworth, 1990.

———. *Whose Justice? Which Rationality?* London: Duckworth, 1988.

Marsden, George M. "Everyone One's Own Interpreter?: The Bible, Science, and Authority in Mid-Nineteenth-Century America." In *The Bible in America: Essays in Cultural History*, edited by N. Hatch and M. Noll, 79–100. New York: Oxford University Press, 1982.

———. *Fundamentalism and American Culture*. New York: Oxford University Press, 1980.

———. *The Outrageous Idea of Christian Scholarship*. New York: Oxford University Press, 1997.

———. *Understanding Fundamentalism and Evangelicalism*. Grand Rapids: Eerdmans, 1991.

Marshall, Bruce D. *Trinity and Truth*. Cambridge: Cambridge University Press, 2002.

Martsinkovskii, V. F. *Zapiski Veruiūshchego*. St. Petersburg: Bibliia dlia Vsekh, 1995.

McCarthy, Mark Myers. "Religious Conflict and Social Order in Nineteenth-Century Russia: Orthodoxy and the Protestant Challenge, 1812–1905." PhD diss., University of Notre Dame, 2004.

McClendon, James, Jr. *Biography as Theology*. Nashville: Abingdon, 1974.

———. *Convictions: Defusing Religious Relativism*. Valley Forge, PA: Trinity, 1994.

———. *Systematic Theology*. Vol. 1, *Ethics*. Nashville: Abingdon, 1986.

———. *Systematic Theology*. Vol. 2, *Doctrine*. Nashville: Abingdon, 1994.

———. *Systematic Theology*. Vol. 3, *Witness*. Nashville: Abingdon, 2000.

McGrath, Alister E. *Christian Theology: An Introduction*. Oxford: Blackwell, 2001.

———. *The Enigma of the Cross*. London: Hodder & Stoughton, 1987.

———. "An Evangelical Evaluation of Postliberalism." In *The Nature of Confession*, edited by Timothy R. Phillips and Dennis L. Okholm, 23–44. Downers Grove, IL: InterVarsity, 1996.

———. *The Genesis of Doctrine: A Study in the Foundations of Doctrinal Criticism*. Grand Rapids: Eerdmans, 1997.

———. *Reformation Thought: An Introduction*. Oxford: Blackwell, 1993.

———. *The Science of God: An Introduction to Scientific Theology*. New York: T. & T. Clark, 2004.

———. *A Scientific Theology*. Vol. 2, *Reality*. New York: T. & T. Clark, 2002.

McNeill, John. *Western Saints in Holy Russia*. Pasadena: Mandate, 2002.

Mearsheimer, John J. "The Case for a Nuclear Deterrent." *Foreign Affairs* 72 (Summer 1993) 50–66.

Mel'gunov, S. *Tserkov' i Gosudarstvo v Rossii: Sbornik Statei*. Moscow: Sytin, 1906.

Men', Alexander. *Kak Chitat' Bibliiu*. Kaliningrad, Russia: FOM, 2002.

Meyendorff, John. *Byzantine Theology: Historical Trends and Doctrinal Themes*. Bronx: Fordham University Press, 1979.

Milbank, John. *Theology and Social Theory*. Oxford: Blackwell, 1990.

Miner, Steven Merritt. *Stalin's Holy War*. Chapel Hill: University of North Carolina Press, 2003.

Misztal, Barbara A. *Theories of Social Remembering*. Philadelphia: Open University Press, 2003.

Mitrokhin, L. N. *Baptizm: Istoriia i Sovremennost'*. St. Petersburg: Izdatel'stvo Russkogo Khristianskogo Gumanitarnogo Instituta, 1997.

Moltmann, Jürgen. *The Crucified God: The Cross of Christ as the Foundation and Criticism of Christian Theology*. Translated by R. A. Wilson and John Bowden. London: SCM, 1974.

———. *Experiences in Theology: Ways and Forms of Christian Theology*. Translated by Margaret Kohl. Minneapolis: Fortress, 2000.

Moody, D. L. *Experiencing Pleasure and Profit in Bible Study*. Chicago: Moody, 1895, 2001.

———. *Sovereign Grace: Its Source, Its Nature, and Its Effects*. Chicago: Bible Institute Colportage Association, 1891.

Moody, William R. *The Life of Dwight L. Moody, by his son*. New York: Revell, 1900.

Moon, Norman S. *Education for Ministry: Bristol Baptist College, 1679–1979*. Bristol, UK: Bristol Baptist College, 1979.

Morris, Leon. *New Testament Theology*. Grand Rapids: Zondervan, 1990.

Morton, Adam, editor. *A Guide through the Theory of Knowledge*. Oxford: Blackwell, 2003.

Muckle, James Y. *Nikolai Leskov and the "Spirit of Protestantism."* Birmingham, UK: Department of Russian Language and Literature, University of Birmingham, 1978.

Mueller II, Alfred G. *In The Name Of God: Rhetoric, Religion, and Identity in Post-Soviet Ukraine*. Bloomington, IN: AuthorHouse, 2004.

Müller, George. *Autobiography of George Müller*. London: J. Nisbet, 1906.

Mullins, Edgar Young. *Baptist Beliefs*. Valley Forge, PA: Judson, 1962.

Murphy, Nancey C. *Anglo-American Postmodernity*. Boulder, CO: Westview, 1997.

———. *Beyond Liberalism and Fundamentalism*. Valley Forge, PA: Trinity, 1996.

———. *Reconciling Theology and Science*. Kitchener, Ontario: Pandora, 1997.

———. "Scientific Realism and Postmodern Philosophy." *British Journal for the Philosophy of Science* 41 (1990) 291–303.

———. *Theology in the Age of Scientific Reasoning*. Ithaca, NY: Cornell University Press, 1990.

Murphy, Nancey, and George F. R. Ellis. *On the Moral Nature of the Universe: Theology, Cosmology, and Ethics*. Philadelphia: Fortress, 1996.

Murphy, Nancey, and Brad J. Kallenberg. "Anglo-American Post-Modernity: A Theology of Communal Practice." In *The Cambridge Companion to Post-Modern Theology*, edited by Kevin J. Vanhoozer, 26–41. Cambridge: Cambridge University Press, 2003.

Murphy, Nancey, Brad J. Kallenberg, and Mark Thiessen Nation, editors. *Virtues & Practices in the Christian Tradition*. Notre Dame, IN: University of Notre Dame Press, 1997.

Murphy, Nancy, and James Wm. McClendon Jr., "Distinguishing Modern and Postmodern Theologies." *Modern Theology* 5 (1989) 199–212.

Murray, Stuart. *Biblical Interpretation in the Anabaptist Tradition*. Kitchener, Ontario: Pandora, 2000.

Murzin, Andriy. *As an Orthodox among Orthodox: Towards Contextualized Evangelical Theology and Practice in Russia/Ukraine*. ThM diss., Reformed Theological Seminary, Jackson, Mississippi, 2003.

Nassif, Bradley. "Eastern Orthodoxy and Evangelicalism: The Status of an Emerging Global Dialogue." In *Eastern Orthodox Theology: A Contemporary Reader*, edited by Daniel B. Clendenin, 211–48. Grand Rapids: Baker, 2003.

Nation, Mark Thiessen. *John Howard Yoder: Mennonite Patience, Evangelical Witness, Catholic Convictions*. Grand Rapids: Eerdmans, 2006.

Nee, Watchman. *The Normal Christian Life*. Uhrichsville, OH: Barbour, 2000.

Negrov, Alexander I. "Biblical Interpretation in the Russian Orthodox Church: A Historical and Hermeneutical Perspective." PhD diss., University of Pretoria, 2001.

———. "Hermeneutics in Transition: Three Hermeneutical Horizons of Slavic Evangelicals in the Post-Soviet Period." *Theological Reflections* 4 (2004) 33–55.

Negrov, Alexander, and Tat'iana Nikol'skaia, "Baptists as a Symbol of Sectarianism in Soviet and Post-Soviet Russia." In *Eastern European Baptist History: New Perspectives,* edited by Sharyl Corrado and Toivo Pilli, 133–42. Prague: International Baptist Theological Seminary, 2007.

Nesdoly, Samuel J. *Among the Soviet Evangelicals*. Edinburgh: The Banner of Truth Trust, 1986.

———. "Evangelical Sectarianism in Russia: A Study of the Stundists, Baptists, Pashkovites, and Evangelical Christians, 1855–1917." PhD diss., Queens University, 1972.

Nichols, Gregory. "Ivan Kargel and the Pietistic Community of Late Imperial Russia." In *Eastern European Baptist History: New Perspectives*, edited by Sharyl Corrado and Toivo Pilli, 71–87. Prague: International Baptist Theological Seminary, 2007.

———. *Pashkovism: Nineteenth Century Russian Piety*. MA diss., Wheaton College, 1991.

Nikol'skaia, Tatiana. "Istoriia Dvizheniia Baptistov-Initsiativnikov." In *Al'manakh po Istorii Russkogo Baptizma*, edited by M. S. Karetnikova, vyp. 3, 63–94. St. Petersburg: Bibliia dlia Vsekh, 2004.

Noll, Mark. "Primitivism in Fundamentalism and American Biblical Scholarship: A Response." In *The American Quest for the Primitive Church,* edited by Richard T. Hughes, 120–30. Urbana: University of Illinois Press, 1988.

———, editor. *The Princeton Theology 1812–1921*. Grand Rapids: Baker, 1983, 2001.

———. *The Rise of Evangelicalism*. Downers Grove, IL: InterVarsity, 2003.

———. *The Scandal of the Evangelical Mind*. Leicester: InterVarsity, 1994.

O'Brien, Peter T. "Principalities and Powers: Opponents of the Church." In *Biblical Interpretation and the Church,* edited by D. A. Carson, 110–50. 1984. Reprint, Eugene, OR: Wipf & Stock, 2002.

Oden, Thomas C. *After Modernity . . . What? Agenda for Theology*. Grand Rapids: Zondervan, 1990.

———. *The Rebirth Of Orthodoxy: Signs of New Life in Christianity*. San Francisco: HarperSanFrancisco, 2003.

———. *Two Worlds: Notes on the Death of Modernity in America and Russia*. Downers Grove, IL: InterVarsity, 1992.

Olema, Albert W. *History of Evangelical Christianity in Russia*. Dallas: published by the author, 1983.

Oliver, W. H. *Prophets and Millennialists: The Uses of Biblical Prophecy in England from the 1790s to the 1840s*. Auckland: Auckland University Press, 1978.

Olson, Roger E. *The Story of Christian Theology: Twenty Centuries of Tradition and Reform*. Downers Grove, IL: InterVarsity, 1999.

Orr, James. "Science and Christian Faith." In *The Fundamentals*, edited by R. A. Torrey et al., vol. 1, 334–47. Grand Rapids: Baker, 2003.

Panarin, A. S. *Pravoslavnaia Tsivilizatsiia v Global'nom Mire*. Moskva: Algoritm-Kniga, 2002.

Patterson, Sue. *Realist Christian Theology in a Postmodern Age*. Cambridge: Cambridge University Press, 1999.

Pecknold, C. C. *Transforming Postliberal Theology: George Lindbeck, Pragmatism and Scripture*. New York: T. & T. Clark, 2005.

Pelikan, Jaroslav. *From Luther to Kierkegaard*. St. Louis: Concordia, 1950.

Penner, Peter. "Contextual Theological Education among Post-Soviet Protestants." *Transformation* 18 (2001) 114–24.

———. "Critical Evaluation of Recent Developments in the Commonwealth of Independent States." *Transformation* 20 (2003) 13–29.

———. *Nauchite Vse Narody. Missiia Bogoslovskogo Obrazovaniia*. St. Petersburg: Bibliia dlia Vsekh, 1999.

———. "Scripture, Community, and Context in God's Mission in the FSU." In *Mission in the Former Soviet Union*, edited by Walter W. Sawatsky and Peter F. Penner, 10–37. Schwarzenfeld, Germany: Neufeld, 2005.

Peris, Daniel. *Storming the Heavens: The Soviet League of the Militant Godless*. Ithaca, NY: Cornell University Press, 1998.

Phillips, D. Z. *Faith after Foundationalism*. London: Routledge, 1988.

Phillips, Timothy R., and Dennis L. Okholm, editors. *The Nature of Confession: Evangelicals and Postliberals in Conversation*. Downers Grove, IL: InterVarsity, 1996.

Pierson, Arthur T. *George Müller of Bristol*. London: James Nisbet, 1899.

Placher, William C., editor. *Callings: Twenty Centuries of Christian Wisdom on Vocation*. Grand Rapids: Eerdmans, 2005.

———. *The Domestication of Transcendence: How Modern Thinking about God Went Wrong*. Louisville: Westminster John Knox, 1996.

———. "Paul Recoeur and Postliberal Theology: A Conflict of Interpretations." *Modern Theology* 4 (1987) 35–52.

Plett, I. P. *Istoriia Evangel'skikh Khristian Baptistov s 1905 po 1944 God*. Moscow: Izdatel'stvo Soveta Tserkvei, 2001.

Pobedonostsev, K. P. *Pis'ma Pobedonostseva k Aleksandru III*. 2 vols., edited by M. N. Pokrovskii. Moscow, 1925.

Pokrovskii, M. N., editor. *Pobedonostsev i ego Korrespondenty. Pis'ma i Zapiski.* 2 vols. Petrograd, 1923.

Polanyi, Michael. *Personal Knowledge*. London: Routledge, 1958.

———. *The Tacit Dimension*. London: Routledge, 1966.

Pollock, J. C. *The Keswick Story*. London: Hodder & Stoughton, 1964.

———. *Moody*. Chicago: Moody, 1983.

———. *Moody without Sankey*. London: Hodder & Stoughton, 1963.

Popov, V. A. "Evangel'skie Khristiane-Pashkovtsy." Online: http://odessasem.com/publishing/bogomyslie_07_04.html.

———. *Issleduite Pisaniia*. St. Petersburg: Bibliia dlia Vsekh, 1999.

———. *I. S. Prokhanov: Stranitsy Zhizni*. St. Petersburg: Bibliia dlia Vsekh, 1996.

Popov, V. "Voskresnyia besedy g. Pashkova." In *Tserkovnyii Vestnik* 10 (March 8, 1880) 12–13.

Pospelovskii, Dimitrii. *Pravoslavnaia Tserkov' v Istorii Rusi, Rossii i SSSR*. Moscow: Bibleisko-Bogoslovskii Institut Sv. Apostola Andreia, 1996.

Pospielovsky, Dimitry. *Soviet Anti-Religious Campaigns and Persecutions*. New York: St. Martin's, 1988.

Postrel, Steven R., and Edward Feser. "Reality Principles: An Interview with John R. Searle." Online: http://www.reason.com/news/show/27599.html.

Price, Charles W., and Ian M. Randall. *Transforming Keswick*. Carlisle, UK: OM, 2000.

Prokhanoff, I.S. *In the Cauldron of Russia: 1869–1933*. New York: All-Russian Evangelical Christian Union, 1933.

Prokhanoff, Slava. *Experiences with Atheism in Russia*. Enid, OK: Phillips University Press, 1928.

Prokhanov, I. S. *Awakening Russia Now Seeking God*. New York: Russia Evangelization Society, 1925.

———. "Dukh Sviatoi, Ego Dary i Deistviia." Online: http://rus-baptist.narod.ru/pozicia/02b.htm.

———. *Evangel'skii Klich*. St. Petersburg, 1922.

———. *Kratkoe Uchenie o Propovedi*. Korntal, Germany: Licht im Osten, 1989.

———. *A New Religious Reformation in Russia: A Russian Evangelical Reformer Visits America*. New York: Russia Evangelization Society, 1925.

———. *Verouchenie Evangel'skikh Khristian*. Cherkassy, Ukraine: Smirna, 2002.

Prokhorov, Konstantin. "The 'Golden Age' of the Soviet Baptists in the 1920s." In *Eastern European Baptist History: New Perspectives*, edited by Sharyl Corrado and Toivo Pilli, 88–101. Prague: International Baptist Theological Seminary, 2007.

Putnam, Hilary. *The Many Faces of Realism*. LaSalle, IL: Open Court, 1987.

———. *Philosophical Papers*. Vol. 2, *Mind, Language and Reality*. Cambridge: Cambridge University Press, 1975.

———. *Reason, Truth and History*. Cambridge: Cambridge University Press, 1981.

———. *Representation and Reality*. Cambridge: MIT Press, 1992.

Rabow-Edling, Susanna. *Slavophile Thought and the Politics of Cultural Nationalism*. New York: State University of New York Press, 2006.

Radstock, Granville. *Notes of Addresses*. London: J. F. Shaw, 1870.

———. *Propovedi Lorda Radstoka*. St. Petersburg: Vsekh, 2004.

———. *Separated unto God and a Living Sacrifice: Two Addresses by Lord Radstock*. Glasgow: Publishing House, 1884.

Radstock, Granville, and D. L. Moody. *A Gospel Dialogue between Mr. D.L. Moody and Lord Radstock*. London: Morgan & Scott, 1884.

Ramet, Sabrina P. *Nihil Obstat: Religion, Politics, and Social Change in East-Central Europe and Russia*. Durham, NC: Duke University Press, 1998.

———, editor. *Protestantism and Politics in Eastern Europe and Russia*. Durham, NC: Duke University Press, 1992.

Randall, Ian M. "Eastern European Baptists and the Evangelical Alliance, 1846–1896." In *Eastern European Baptist History: New Perspectives*, edited by Sharyl Corrado and Toivo Pilli, 14–33. Prague: International Baptist Theological Seminary, 2007.

———. *Evangelical Experiences*. Carlisle, UK: Paternoster, 1999.

Raschke, Carl. *The Next Reformation: Why Evangelicals Must Embrace Post-Modernity*. Grand Rapids: Baker, 2004.

Regel'son, Lev. *Tragediia Russkoi Tserkvi*. Moscow: Krutitskoe Podvor'e, 1996.

Reid, D. G. "Principalities and Powers." In *Dictionary of Paul and His Letters*, edited by Gerald F. Hawthorne et al., 746–52. Downers Grove, IL: InterVarsity, 1993.

Reshetnikov, Iu. "K Voprosu o Phenomene Evraziiskogo Protestantizma." In *Fenomen Evraziiskogo Protestantizma: Materialy Konferentsii Bogoslovskogo Obshchestva Evrazii*, edited by M. Cherenkov, 97–98. Odessa: Bogoslovskoe Obshchestvo Evrazii, 2003.

———. "Nagal'ni Problemni Pytannia Evangel'sko-Baptistskoi Ekleziologii: Ednist' Soiŭzu chi Nezalezhnist' Gromady." In *Bogoslovie i Bogoslovskoe Obrazovanie v Sovremennom Obshchestve*, edited by M. Cherenkov, 225–39. Odessa: Euro-Asian Accrediting Association and Bogoslovskoe Obshchestvo Evrazii, 2002.

Reshetnikov, Iu., and S. Sannikov. *Obzor Istorii Evangel'sko-Baptistskogo Bratstva na Ukraine*. Odessa: Bogomyslie, 2000.

Riasanovsky, Nicholas V. "Khomiakov on Sobornost'." In *Continuity and Change in Russian and Soviet Thought*, edited by Ernest J. Simmons, 183–96. Cambridge: Harvard University Press, 1955.

———. *Russia and the West in the Teaching of the Slavophiles*. Cambridge: Harvard University Press, 1952.

Ricouer, Paul. *Memory, History, Forgetting*. Chicago: Chicago University Press, 2006.

———. *Time and Narrative*. 3 vols. Chicago: Chicago University Press, 1984–88.

Rogozin, P. I. *Otkuda vse eto Poiavilos'*. N/A

Saloff-Astakhoff, N. I. *Christianity in Russia*. New York: Loizeaux, 1941.

Sandeen, Ernest R. *The Roots of Fundamentalism: British and American Millenarianism 1800–1930*. Chicago: University of Chicago Press, 1970.

Sannikov, S. V. *Dvadtsat' Vekov Khristianstva*. 2 vols. Odessa: Bogomyslie, 2001.

Savinskii, S. N. *Istoriia Evangel'skikh Khristian-Baptistov Ukrainy, Rossii, Belorussii: 1867–1917*. St. Petersburg: Bibliia dlia Vsekh, 1999.

———. *Istoriia Evangel'skikh Khristian-Baptistov Ukrainy, Rossii, Belorussii: 1917–1967*. St. Petersburg: Bibliia dlia Vsekh, 2001.

Savinskii, S. N., P. D. Savchenko, and I. P. Dik, editors. *Istoriia Evangel'skikh Khristian-Baptistov v SSSR*. Moscow: Izdanie Vsesoiuznogo Soveta Evangelskikh Khristian-Baptistov, 1989.

Sawatsky, Walter. "The Re-Positioning of Evangelical Christians-Baptists and Sister Church Unions between 1980 and 2005." In *Eastern European Baptist History:*

New Perspectives, edited by Sharyl Corrado and Toivo Pilli, 187–209. Prague: International Baptist Theological Seminary, 2007.

———. Review of *Russian Baptists and Spiritual Revolution 1905–1929*, by Heather J. Coleman. In *Religion in Eastern Europe* 26 (2006) 58–63.

———. "Slavic Evangelicals in Mission within the Commonwealth of Independent States." *Transformation* 21 (2003) 195–204.

———. *Soviet Evangelicals Since World War II*. Kitchener, Ontario: Herald, 1981.

Sawatsky, Walter W., and Peter F. Penner, editors. *Mission in the Former Soviet Union*. Schwarzenfeld, Germany: Neufeld, 2005.

Schreiter, Robert J. *Constructing Local Theologies*. Maryknoll, NY: Orbis, 1986.

Segovia, Fernando F., and Mary Ann Tobert, editors. *Reading from This Place: Social Location and Biblical Interpretation in Global Perspective*. Minneapolis: Fortress, 1995.

Seitz, Christopher, editor. *Nicene Christianity: The Future for a New Ecumenism*. Grand Rapids: Brazos, 2001.

Shchapov, Y. N., editor. *Russkaia Pravoslavnaia Tserkov' i Kommunisticheskoe Gosudarstvo: 1917–1941. Dokumenty i Fotomaterialy*. Moscow: Bibleisko-Bogoslovskii Institut Sviatogo Apostola Andreia, 1996.

Shevzov, Vera. *Russian Orthodoxy on the Eve of Revolution*. Oxford: Oxford University Press, 2004.

Sinichkin, A. "O Dinamike Rosta Bratstva EKhB s 1945 po 1965 god." In *Fenomen Evraziiskogo Protestantizma: Materialy Konferentsii Bogoslovskogo Obshchestva Evrazii*, edited by M. Cherenkov, 89–96. Odessa: Bogoslovskoe Obshchestvo Evrazii, 2003.

Skopina, I. N. "Iz Biographii I. V. Kargelia i ego Docherei." In I. V. Kargel, *Sobranie Sochinenii*, 689–701. St. Petersburg: Vsekh, 2002.

Smirnov, P. A. *Zhizn' i Uchenie Feofana Zatvornika*. Moscow: Sintagama, 2004.

Smolich, I. K. *Russkoe Monashestvo 988–1917*. Moscow: Pravoslavnaia Enciclopedia, 1997.

Soussi, M. "Evangel'skaia Protestantskaia Traditsiia i Uchenie Pravoslavnoi Tserkvi." In *Bogoslovie i Bogoslovskoe Obrazovanie v Sovremennom Obshchestve*, edited by M. Cherenkov, 110–18. Odessa: Euro-Asian Accrediting Association and Bogoslovskoe Obshchestvo Evrazii, 2002.

Sperrle, Irmhild Christina. *The Organic Worldview of Nikolai Leskov*. Evanston, IL: Northwestern University Press, 2002.

Spurgeon, C. H. "Mr. Grant on 'The Darby Brethren.'" Online: http://www.spurgeon.org/s_and_t/dbreth.htm#note1.

———. "Plymouth Brethren." Online: http://www.spurgeon.org/s_and_t/pb.htm.

Stackhouse, John G., Jr., editor. *Evangelical Futures: A Conversation on Theological Method*. Grand Rapids: Baker, 2000.

Stackhouse, Max. "Alasdair MacIntyre: An Overview and Evaluation." *Religious Studies Review* 18 (1992) 203–8.

Starogorodskii, Sergii. *Pravoslavnoe Uchenie o Spasenii*. Kazan': Imperatorskii Universitet, 1898.

Steele, Daniel. *A Substitute for Holiness, or, Antinomianism Revived*. New York: Garland, 1984.

Steeves, Paul D. "The Russian Baptist Union, 1917–1935: Evangelical Awakening in Russia." PhD diss., University of Kansas, 1976.

Steinmetz, David. "The Superiority of Pre-Critical Exegesis." In *The Theological Interpretation of Scripture: Classic and Contemporary Readings*, edited by Stephen Fowl, 26–38. Oxford: Blackwell, 1997.

Stern, J. P. *On Realism*. London: Routledge & Kegan Paul, 1973.

Storkey, Alan. *Jesus and Politics: Confronting the Powers*. Grand Rapids: Baker, 2005.

Stott, John. *The Cross of Christ*. London: InterVarsity, 1986.

Struve, Nikita. *Christians in Contemporary Russia*. London: Harvill, 1967.

Stunt, Timothy C. F. *From Awakening to Secession: Radical Evangelicals in Switzerland and Britain 1815–35*. Edinburgh: T. & T. Clark, 2000.

Subtelny, Orest. *Ukraine: A History*. 3rd ed. Toronto: University of Toronto Press, 2005.

Sugirtharajah, R. S. *Vernacular Hermeneutics*. Sheffield, UK: Sheffield Academic Press, 1999.

Surin, Kenneth. *The Turnings of Darkness and Light: Essays in Philosophical and Systematic Theology*. Cambridge: Cambridge University Press, 1989.

Tanner, Kathryn. *Theories of Culture: A New Agenda for Theology*. Minneapolis: Fortress, 1997.

Tanner, Kenneth, and Christopher A. Hall, editors. *Ancient and Postmodern Christianity: Paleo-Orthodoxy in the 21st Century*. Downers Grove, IL: InterVarsity, 2002.

Terletskii, G. *Sekta Pashkovtsev*. St. Petersburg: Tuzov, 1891.

Thiel, John E. *Nonfoundationalism*. Minneapolis: Fortress, 1994.

Thiselton, Anthony C. *New Horizons in Hermeneutics*. Grand Rapids: Zondervan, 1992.

Thomson, John B. *The Ecclesiology of Stanley Hauerwas: A Christian Theology of Liberation*. Aldershot, UK: Ashgate, 2003.

Tkachuk, Vitalii. *Metody i Principy Tolkovania Sviashchennogo Pisania*. Lutsk, Ukraine: Centr Kristianskoi Zhizni Ukrainy, 2000.

Torrey, R. A. *The Baptism with the Holy Spirit*. New York: Revell, 1895.

———. *How to Pray. How to Study the Bible*. Peabody, MA: Hendrickson, 2001

———. *How to Study the Bible for the Greatest Profit*. New York: Revell, 1896.

Tracy, David. *The Analogical Imagination: Christian Theology and the Culture of Pluralism*. New York: Crossroad, 1981.

Troeltsch, Ernst. *Social Teaching of the Christian Churches*. New York: MacMillan, 1931.

Trond, Enger. "Pietism." In *The Oxford Companion to Christian Thought*, edited by Adrian Hastings, Alistair Mason, and Hugh Pyper, 539–41. Oxford: Oxford University Press, 2000.

Trotter, Edward. *Lord Radstock: An Interpretation and a Record*. London, New York: Hodder & Stoughton, 1914.

———. *Undertones of the Nineteenth Century and After*. London: Elliot Stock, 1916.

Trotter, William. "Events at Plymouth and Bethesda." Online: http://www.mybrethren.org/history/framwt.htm.

Turlac, Oleg P. "The Crisis in Evangelical Christian-Baptist Theological Education in the Former Soviet Union." *East-West Church and Ministry Report* 15 (2007) 19.

Turner, George Allen. *Churches of the Restoration: A Study in Origins*. Lewiston, NY: Mellen, 1994.

Turner, Max. "Historical Criticism and Theological Hermeneutics of the New Testament." In *Between Two Horizons: Spanning New Testament Studies and*

Systematic Theology, edited by Joel B. Green and Max Turner, 44–70. Grand Rapids: Eerdmans, 2000.

Valliere, Paul. *Modern Russian Theology*. Grand Rapids: Eerdamans, 2000.

Vandevelde, Pol. *The Task of the Interpreter: Text, Meaning, and Negotiation*. Pittsburgh: University of Pittsburgh Press, 2005.

Vanhoozer, Kevin J., editor. *The Cambridge Companion to Postmodern Theology*. Cambridge: Cambridge University Press, 2003.

———. *The Drama of Doctrine*. Louisville: Westminster John Knox, 2005.

———. *First Theology*. Downers Grove, IL: InterVarsity, 2002.

———. *Is There a Meaning in This Text?* Leicester, UK: Apollos, 1998.

———. "Once More into the Borderlands: The Way of Wisdom in Philosophy and Theology after the 'Turn to Drama.'" In *Transcending Boundaries in Philosophy and Theology: Reason, Meaning and Experience*, edited by Kevin J. Vanhoozer and Martin Warner, 31–54. Burlington, VT: Ashgate, 2007.

Vanhoozer, Kevin J., James K. A. Smith, and Bruce Ellis Benson, editors. *Hermeneutics at the Crossroads*. Bloomington: Indiana University Press, 2006.

Vasil'eva O. A. *Sovremennyi Russkii Protestantizm: v Poiskakh Sebia*. Symposium. St. Petersburg: Sanktpeterburgskoe Filosofskoe Obshchestvo, 2004.

Vidu, Adonis. *Postliberal Theological Method: A Critical Study*. Carlisle, UK: Paternoster, 2005.

Volf, Miroslav. *After Our Likeness: The Church as the Image of the Trinity*. Grand Rapids: Eerdmans, 1998.

———. *The End of Memory: Remembering Rightly in a Violent World*. Grand Rapids: Eerdmans, 2006.

———. "Theology, Meaning, & Power: A Conversation with George Lindbeck on Theology & the Nature of Christian Difference." In *The Nature of Confession: Evangelicals and Postliberals in Conversation*, edited by Timothy R. Phillips and Dennis L. Okholm, 45–66. Downers Grove, IL: InterVarsity, 1996.

Volf, Miroslav, and Michael Welker, editors. *God's Life in the Trinity*. Minneapolis: Fortress, 2006.

Wall, Robert W. "Reading the Bible from within Our Traditions: 'The Rule of Faith' in Theological Hermeneutics." In *Between Two Horizons: Spanning New Testament Studies and Systematic Theology*, edited by Joel B. Green and Max Turner, 88–107. Grand Rapids: Eerdmans, 2000.

Wardin, Albert W. *Evangelical Sectarianism in the Russian Empire and the USSR*. Lanham, MD: Scarecrow, 1995.

Ware, Steven L. *Restorationism in the Holiness Movement in the Late Nineteenth and Early Twentieth Centuries*. Lewiston, NY: Edwin Mellen, 2004.

Warfield, Benjamin Breckinridge. *Perfectionism*. Philadelphia: Presbyterian and Reformed, 1980.

Watson, Francis, editor. *The Open Text: New Directions for Biblical Studies?* London: SCM, 1993.

———. *Paul and the Hermeneutics of Faith*. New York: T. & T. Clark, 2004.

———. *Text, Church and World*. Grand Rapids: Eerdmans, 1994.

———. *Text and Truth*. Grand Rapids: Eerdmans, 1997.

Watts, Michael R. *Dissenters*. Vol. 1, *From the Reformation to the French Revolution*. Oxford: Clarendon, 1978.

———. *Dissenters*. Vol. 2, *The Expansion of Evangelical Nonconformity*. Oxford: Clarendon, 1995.

Wayne, Kenney R. *A Great Conspiracy: Evangelical Ministry and Education in Russia before 1987*. Mount Joy, MA: Published by the author, 1997.

Weber, Timothy P. "The Two-Edged Sword: The Fundamentalist Use of the Bible." In *The Bible in America: Essays in Cultural History*, edited by N. Hatch and M. Noll, 101–17. New York: Oxford University Press, 1982.

Webster, John. *Holy Scripture: A Dogmatic Sketch*. Cambridge: Cambridge University Press, 2003.

Wertsch, James V. *Voices of Collective Remembering*. Cambridge: Cambridge University Press, 2002.

Whewell, Tim. "The Kremlin and the World." Online: http://www.bbc.co.uk/worldservice/specials/1123_wagrussia.

Wiles, Maurice. "Scriptural Authority and Theological Construction: The Limitations of Narrative Interpretation." In *Scriptural Authority and Narrative Interpretation*, edited by Garrett Green, 42–58. Philadelphia: Fortress, 1987.

Williams, C. Peter. "Healing and Evangelism: The Place of Medicine in Later Victorian Protestant Missionary Thinking." In *The Church and Healing*, edited by W. J. Sheils, 271–85. Oxford: Blackwell, 1982.

Williams, Daniel H. *The Free Church and the Early Church*. Grand Rapids: Eerdmans, 2002.

———. *Evangelicals and Tradition*. Grand Rapids: Baker, 2005.

———. *Retrieving the Tradition and Renewing Evangelicalism*. Grand Rapids: Eerdmans, 1999.

Williams, Rowan. *Open to Judgement: Sermons and Addresses*. London: Darton, Longman & Todd, 1994.

Wilson, Andrew. *Ukraine's Orange Revolution*. New Haven: Yale University Press, 2005.

Wilson, Jonathan R. "Toward a New Evangelical Paradigm of Biblical Authority." In *The Nature of Confession*, edited by Timothy R. Phillips and Dennis L. Okholm, 151–61. Downers Grove, IL: InterVarsity, 1996.

Wink, Walter. *The Powers*. Vol. 1, *Naming the Powers: The Language of Power in the New Testament*. Philadelphia: Fortress, 1984.

———. *The Powers*. Vol. 2, *Unmasking the Powers: The Invisible Forces that Determine Human Existence*. Philadelphia: Fortress, 1986.

———. *The Powers*. Vol. 3, *Engaging the Powers: Discernment and Resistance in a World of Domination*. Minneapolis: Fortress, 1992.

———. *The Powers That Be*. New York: Doubleday, 1999.

———. *When the Powers Fall*. Minneapolis: Fortress, 1998.

Witte, John, Jr., and Michael Bourdeaux, editors. *Proselytism and Orthodoxy in Russia: The New War for Souls*. Maryknoll, NY: Orbis, 1999.

Wittgenstein, L. *Philosophical Investigations*, translated by G. E. M. Anscombe. New York: MacMillan, 1958.

Wolfe, David L. *Epistemology: Justification of Belief*. Downers Grove, IL: InterVarsity, 1982.

Wolffe, John. "The Evangelical Alliance in the 1840s: An Attempt to Institutionalize Christian Unity." In *Voluntary Religion*, edited by W. J. Sheils and Diana Wood, 333–46. London: Ecclesiastical History Society, 1986.

Wood, W. Jay. *Epistemology*. Downers Grove, IL: InterVarsity, 1998.

Woodcock, George, and Ivan Avakumovic. *The Doukhobors*. New York: Oxford University Press, 1968.

Wright, N. T. *Jesus and the Victory of God*. London: SPCK, 1996.

———. *The New Testament and the People of God*. London: SPCK, 1993.

———. *What Saint Paul Really Said*. Grand Rapids: Eerdmans, 1997.

Yoder, John Howard. *The Original Revolution: Essays on Christian Pacifism*. Scottdale, PA: Herald, 1998.

———. *The Politics of Jesus*. Grand Rapids: Eerdmans, 1972.

———. *The Royal Priesthood: Essays Ecclesiological and Ecumenical*. Grand Rapids: Eerdmans, 1994.

Yong, Amos. *Spirit-Word-Community*. Aldershot: Ashgate, 2002.

Zenkovsky, V. V. *A History of Russian Philosophy*. Translated by G. L. Kline. 2 vols. New York: Routledge & Kegan Paul, 1953.

Zernov, Nicolas. *The Russians and Their Church*. London: SPCK, 1945.

———. *The Russian Religious Renaissance of the Twentieth Century*. London: Darton Longman & Todd, 1963.

———. *Three Russian Prophets: Khomiakov, Dostoevsky, Soloviev*. London: SCM, 1944.

———. *St. Sergius—Builder of Russia*. London: SPCK, 1938.

Zherdev, V. "Nuzhen li Protestantizmu Mistitsizm?" In *Fenomen Evraziiskogo Protestantizma: Materialy Konferentsii Bogoslovskogo Obshchestva Evrazii*, edited by M. Cherenkov, 67–77. Odessa: Bogoslovskoe Obshchestvo Evrazii, 2003.

Zhuk, Sergei. *Russia's Lost Reformation: Peasants, Millennialism, and Radical Sects in Southern Russian and Ukraine, 1830–1917*. Baltimore: The Johns Hopkins University Press, 2004.

Zizioulas, John. *Being as Communion: Studies in Personhood and the Church*. Crestwood, NY: St. Vladimir's Seminary Press, 1993.

INTERNET SITES AND RESOURCES

Asotsiatsiia Missionerskikh Tserkvei Evangel'skikh Khrisitan Ukrainy. Russian. Online: www.amcecu.org.

Euro-Asian Accrediting Association of Evangelical Schools. Russian and English. Online: www.e-aaa.org.

My Brethren. English. Online: www.mybrethren.org.

Religion in Eastern Europe. English. Online: http://www.georgefox.edu/academics/undergrad/departments/soc-swk/ree/index.html.

Svitlo na Skhodi. Russian and Ukrainian. Online: www.sns.org.ua.

The Christian Brethren on the Internet. English. Online: http://rylibweb.man.ac.uk/data2/spcoll/cba/links.html.

The East-West Church and Ministry Report. English. Online: www.eastwestreport.org.

The Spurgeon Archive. English. Online: http://www.spurgeon.org/s_and_t/pb.htm#note2.

The Victorian Web. English. Online: http://www.victorianweb.org.

ARCHIVAL SOURCES

Birmingham:

University of Birmingham Information Services, Special Collections Department
Pashkov Papers (PP)

London:

School of Slavonic and Eastern-European Studies
Bevan Collection

Moscow:

The Archive of the Evangelical Christians-Baptists in Moscow (Archive ECB)
Prokhanov Collection

Nashville:

Southern Baptist Historical Library and Archives
Microfilms of the following newspapers and journals: *Bratskii Listok, Evangel'skaia Vera, Khristianin, Modolodoi Vinogradnik, Russkii Rabochii,* and *Utrenniaia Zvezda*

ELECTRONIC RESOURCES

History of Euro-Asian Evangelical Movement: Primary Sources 1.0. CD ROM. Odessa: Euro-Asian Accrediting Association, n.d.

History of Euro-Asian Evangelical Movement: Primary Sources 2.0. CD ROM. Odessa: Euro-Asian Accrediting Association, n.d.

History of Euro-Asian Evangelical Movement: Primary Sources 3.0. CD ROM. Odessa: Euro-Asian Accrediting Association, n.d.

History of Euro-Asian Evangelical Movement: Primary Sources 4.0. CD ROM. Odessa: Euro-Asian Accrediting Association, n.d.